PUBLIC FINANCE

THE ECONOMICS OF
GOVERNMENT REVENUES
AND EXPENDITURES

*

PUBLIC FINANCE

THE ECONOMICS OF GOVERNMENT REVENUES AND EXPENDITURES

Ansel M. Sharp and Kent W. Olson

Oklahoma State University

West Publishing Company

St. Paul • New York • Los Angeles • San Francisco

Library of Congress Cataloging in Publication Data

Sharp, Ansel Miree, 1924-
    Public finance.
    Includes index.
    1. Finance, Public—United States. 1. Olson,
Kent W., joint author. II. Title.
HJ257.S472   336.73   77-18750
ISBN 0-8299-0172-8

CONTENTS

CONTENTS

CONTENTS

CONTENTS

PART 5 FISCAL FEDERALISM

*

PREFACE

This book has evolved out of the experience of the authors in teaching public finance in several state universities and private colleges. As such, it consists of what we believe to be the essential concepts and issues for students to learn in their first course in the field.

Economists differ, of course, over what topics should be included in an introductory text. This book is not an attempt to provide an exhaustive survey all of the literature in the field. We have deliberately tried to keep this text short enough to allow most of it to be covered in one term. At the same time, we believe that students beginning their study of public finance should be exposed to the broad spectrum of concerns which engage the leading practitioners of the art. Thus, we have attempted to provide a balanced survey of the issues as well as a concise exposition.

More specifically, the book reflects our view that a basic text in public finance should: (1) provide a balanced treatment of the three major functions of government budget policy (allocation, distribution, and stabilization); (2) analyze the effects of both public expenditures and revenues on the economy's goals; (3) develop a broad description and evaluation of the major issues in taxation; (4) consistently apply the principles developed to important current issues; (5) analyze significant trends in government finance and expenditures; and (6) provide a balanced view of economic failure in both the private and public sectors.

Part I lays the foundation for determining the appropriate economic role of government, building heavily on the conceptual framework of modern welfare economics. Part II is a relatively thorough analysis of the expenditure side of the budget, based on the principles of cost-benefit analysis developed during the past two decades. Part III discusses the economics of taxation as organized around the three major tax bases: income, wealth, and consumption. Part IV concerns the principles which underlie the government's role in helping the economy to achieve full employment, stable prices, and economic growth. Finally, Part V analyzes the growing fiscal interdependence among the various levels of government.

The comments and advice of several reviewers during our development of this text have proved invaluable. We would like to acknowledge especially the assistance rendered by Professors Donald Losman, C. David Billings, and John Pisciotta. We accept full responsibility, however, for any errors, omissions, and other deficiencies that remain.

We also appreciate the editorial assistance and encouragement provided by the West Publishing Company staff. In addition, we thank Kathy Deevers and Cherrie Thornton for their splendid work, good humor, and patience in helping to prepare the several versions of the manuscript. June, 1977

ANSEL M. SHARP
KENT W. OLSON

†

PART 1

THE ECONOMIC ROLE OF THE GOVERNMENT

ONE

THE GOVERNMENT'S ROLE IN THE AMERICAN ECONOMY

Economics as a field of study is concerned with the allocation of scarce resources among alternative uses to satisfy relatively unlimited wants. Most allocative decisions are made in markets directed largely by consumer choice. The idea of market allocation is a necessary but insufficient concept on which to base an understanding of our economic system. It is necessary because it is a central organizing principle; it is insufficient because other mechanisms are also used to allocate a significant proportion of our resources.

The most important exception to market allocation takes place in the public sector, where budget decisions determine the size and composition of government expenditures and revenues. This sector is now so large in relation to the rest of the economy that some understanding of the principles by which it operates seems essential for private citizens whose economic welfare will be influenced by the direction of public choice.

This chapter's primary purpose is to introduce the reader to the major themes of the book. Since it is important to get some initial idea of just how large government is in economic terms, we begin with a comparison and evaluation of several measures that have been widely used as indicators of its size. Following that, we discuss the central theme around which the book is organized: namely, that government expenditure and revenue policies should be designed to move the economy closer to its goals. The final section of the chapter briefly discusses how this theme is reflected in the book's organization.

THE SIZE OF THE PUBLIC SECTOR

The economic influence of the public sector is too important to ignore; it is not easy, however, to measure its extent. The reason is quite simple: the influence of the government on the direction of resource allocation is not recorded directly in any data that are generally available. Indeed, the economic influence of government has so many dimensions that it is difficult even to envision the development of a satisfactory comprehensive index.

In the arena of public debate, certain measures of the relative size of the public sector have been widely used as indexes of the volume of economic activity that is affected by government choices. The most frequently cited measures relate either government *purchases,* or *expenditures,* or *revenues* to the level of the gross national product. Each of these provide a different view of the extent of government economic activity.

GOVERNMENT PURCHASES

Of the three measures suggested above, the influence of the government sector appears smallest when government purchases (G) are expressed as a proportion of gross national product (GNP). However, slightly over 20% of all goods and services produced since 1954 have been purchased for use by the various governmental units (see Table 1-1). Thus, the government sector is an important buyer of the economy's output.

Perhaps the most significant feature of this measure (G/GNP) is its relative stability in the last two decades. This stability is not evident in the other two indexes proposed above.

GOVERNMENT EXPENDITURES

When government *expenditures* (E) instead of *purchases* are related to GNP, a somewhat different view of the size of government emerges. As the last column in Table 1-2 clearly shows, the growth in expenditures has been significantly greater than the growth in GNP since World War II. In addition, according to this measure (E/GNP), government economic activity

TABLE 1-1   GOVERNMENT PURCHASES,[a] SELECTED YEARS,
1946-1975

Year	Federal	State and Local	Total(G)	G/GNP
1950	18.7	19.8	38.5	.14
1954	47.9	27.8	75.7	.21
1958	53.9	41.1	95.0	.21
1962	63.7	54.3	118.0	.21
1966	78.8	79.8	158.6	.21
1970	95.6	123.2	218.8	.22
1972	102.1	151.0	253.1	.22
1974	111.7	189.4	301.1	.21
1975p	123.1	207.8	330.9	.22

SOURCE: *Economic Report of the President,* January, 1976.

a. in billions of dollars

p. preliminary

accounts for much larger proportion of total economic activity than that accounted for by G/GNP. These differences in results are due solely, of course, to differences between government expenditures and purchases. Government expenditures are defined simply as purchases plus *transfer payments.* Thus, the key to the apparent growth in the government sector is the growth experienced since World War II in government transfer programs.

Transfers are payments to individuals that are not made for goods and services supplied. They include such things as social security benefits, welfare payments, veterans' benefits, and unemployment compensation. Generally, they reflect a commitment to achieving greater equality in the distribution of income. Most of the recent relative growth in the government sector, then, is accounted for by the growing importance of this objective of public policy.

GOVERNMENT REVENUES

The third measure, government revenues (R) as a proportion of GNP (R/GNP), is developed in Table 1-3. It is evident from this index that the public sector has been growing relative to the total economy, although not

TABLE 1–2   GOVERNMENT EXPENDITURES,[a] SELECTED
YEARS, 1946–1975

Year	Federal	State and Local	Total (E)[b]	E/GNP
1946	35.6	11.1	45.6	.22
1950	40.8	22.5	61.0	.21
1954	69.8	30.2	97.0	.26
1958	88.9	44.3	127.6	.28
1962	110.4	58.0	160.5	.28
1966	143.6	84.3	213.6	.28
1970	204.2	132.2	311.9	.32
1972	244.7	163.7	370.9	.32
1974	300.1	201.3	457.5	.33
1975p	356.9	222.4	525.1	.35

SOURCE: *Economic Report of the President,* January, 1976.

a. in billions of dollars

b. eliminates intergovernmental transfers recorded in expenditures
for state and local governments

p. preliminary

as rapidly as indicated by the ratio E/GNP. Because expenditures in excess
of revenues are usually financed by selling government bonds, the more
rapid growth in E/GNP has been paralleled by an increase in the size of
the public debt.

The average citizen would probably express the greatest concern over the
ratio, R/GNP. Most of R accrues in the form of taxes—perhaps the most
visible and frequent reminder of the power that government authorities
can exercise over the allocation of economic resources.

THE INFLUENCE OF
THE PUBLIC SECTOR

Unfortunately, none of the three measures introduced above—government
expenditures, purchases, and revenues—is an accurate index of the influence of the government budget on the American economy. No single index
is. Because they are so widely employed, however, it is useful to review
the shortcomings of the measures proposed.

We have already indicated that government purchases understate the

TABLE 1-3   GOVERNMENT RECEIPTS AND GNP,[a] SELECTED YEARS,
1946–1975

Year	Federal	State and Local	Total[b] (R)	GNP	R/GNP
1946	39.1	13.0	51.0	209.6	.24
1950	50.0	21.3	69.0	286.2	.24
1954	63.7	29.0	89.9	366.3	.25
1958	78.7	42.0	115.0	448.9	.26
1962	106.2	58.5	156.7	563.8	.28
1966	141.8	84.8	212.3	753.0	.28
1970	192.1	134.9	302.6	982.4	.31
1972	227.5	177.4	367.4	1171.1	.31
1974	288.4	209.4	453.9	1406.9	.32
1975p	283.5	232.4	461.7	1499.0	.31

SOURCE: *Economic Report of the President,* January, 1976.

a. Both R and GNP are in billions of dollars

b. eliminates intergovernmental transfers recorded in receipts for state and local governments

p. preliminary

scope of government activity because they exclude transfer payments. The exclusion of transfer payments also provides a misleading view of the role that government expenditures can play in redistributing income. As indicated later in this book (Chapter 6), governmental expenditure policy has had an important influence on the distribution of income among individuals and families. For this reason alone it is not sufficient to rely on a measure of government activity which excludes transfers.

It follows, of course, that government expenditures are a better indicator of the economic influence of government than are government purchases. However, the use of expenditures as an index is also imperfect; perhaps the most important reason for this is that each dollar of expenditures does not necessarily provide equal benefits to the populace. Expenditure programs vary widely in their abilities to fulfill the preferences of the citizenry for publicly-provided goods and services. Moreover, some programs that are quite small in terms of expenditure outlays, such as government regulatory activities, exert an influence on the private sector that is only superficially related to the level of outlays involved.

Finally, what is true for expenditures is also true for revenues; the total amount of revenues collected is not an accurate indicator of the effect of government activity of this kind. Each dollar of revenues, like each dollar of expenditures, does not necessarily have the same impact on the economy. Taxes, the chief form of revenue, differ widely in terms of their effects on prices, employment, output, and growth. In addition, as we will demonstrate later, tax levies may actually keep the level of production below its potential, thereby adding to the real costs of government finance.

THE METHODOLOGICAL FRAMEWORK

A thorough study of the economic influence of government requires a blend of description and analysis. Description provides information on the institutional structure of the economy and the nature and magnitude of important economic variables; analysis is necessary if one is to gain a broad understanding of why, how, and to what degree government activity affects resource allocation. The essential tool of economic analysis is theory: the logical ordering of elements of reality to provide an explanation of economic events. Our study of the public sector contains both institutional and theoretical approaches.

Our objectives are as follows: (1) to provide an explanation of how and why government budgetary choices are made; (2) to explain how these choices influence the allocation of resources; and (3) to evaluate these choices with respect to certain social goals.

The achievement of the first two objectives requires the use of *positive economics;* the third objective requires the use of *normative economics.* The field of public finance contains many examples of studies employing each method. Some initial understanding of the characteristics of each is helpful in gaining an overview of the organization of our analysis.

POSITIVE ECONOMICS

Most students beginning the study of public finance are already familiar with the methodologies that economists employ. The bulk of their previous exposure, however, has probably been in the realm of positive economics. In positive economics, the primary objective is to explain how the production, exchange, and distribution of goods, services, and resources are determined. The goal is to arrive at testable propositions concerning these activities. It is this orientation which, in a formal sense, makes economic theory a part of scientific theory.

Typically, the beginning student does not complete the final step in the scientific method—the process of empirical verification of testable hypotheses. However, economic logic is widely employed to construct theories of the production and consumption choices of firms and households under different competitive constraints, and of the implications of these theories for the achievement of particular goals.

The beginning student is seldom exposed to the problem of deciding whether the effects predicted by positive theories (and hopefully verified by empirical studies) are good or bad from the point of view of society at large. This is ultimately an ethical and not a scientific question, and economists do not agree about the exact dimensions of the public interest; that is, they disagree about the relative importance of the goals which each believes the economic system should achieve. Such disagreements may never be fully resolved. However, over the past three decades a framework has been developed within which most economists conduct their discussions of ethics. This is the framework of normative, or welfare, economics.

NORMATIVE ECONOMICS

The majority of economists probably view the operation of the public sector within a normative framework. Much work has been done since World War II to develop a set of rules, or prescriptions, for how the government should conduct its economic affairs to promote economic welfare.

The dominant approach is reflected in Richard Musgrave's conceptualization of the proper role of the public sector.[1] According to Musgrave, the performance of an economic system should be judged by the degree to which it provides an equitable distribution of income, an efficient allocation of resources, full employment, a stable price level, and long-run growth in real output. Maximum performance requires the simultaneous attainment of each goal.

Within this context, Musgrave argues that a market economy is likely to malfunction in three important ways. First, even if each of the other goals were achieved, there would be no assurance that the attendant distribution of income would be judged as equitable; i.e., regarded by society

---

1. Richard Musgrave, *The Theory of Public Finance* New York: McGraw-Hill, 1959, Chapter 1.

as the most desirable one. Thus, it is argued, *distribution failures* imply that public activity is necessary in order to attain the desired pattern of income distribution among individuals or family units.

Second, drawing upon the results of modern *macroeconomics,* Musgrave argues that a wholly unregulated market economy would not necessarily generate full employment of resources (a necessary condition for efficient allocation), a stable price level, or adequate long-run real growth. Indeed, such an economy will tend to experience periods of waste caused by idle resources and low growth rates, and periods in which inefficiencies and inequities are generated by inflation. A second task of the public sector, therefore, is the employment of tools of monetary and fiscal policy to maintain low rates of unemployment and inflation and an appropriate rate of real growth.

Third, certain instances of resource misallocation are likely to occur in a market economy. Externalities (including the extreme case of the pure public good), decreasing-cost industries, and market power may result in excessive levels of some activities and deficient levels of others.[2] Consequently, taxes, subsidies, regulation, or public provision of certain goods may be necessary to ensure an efficient pattern of resource use.

In summary, Musgrave perceives the public sector as having three primary functions to perform if it is to assist the economy in achieving its goals: (1) the distribution function (to ensure the attainment of an equitable distribution of income); (2) the stabilization function (to ensure the maintenance of low rates of unemployment and inflation and an adequate rate of real growth); and (3) the allocation function (to ensure the establishment of an efficient allocation of resources).

Of course, it is easier to distinguish between these functions on a purely conceptual level than it is to separate them either in theory or in practice. At a purely formal level, maximum performance requires the simultaneous and mutually consistent operation of all three functions. Moreover, in

---

2. This statement presumes that the reader is familiar with this terminology from previous study of economics. As a reminder, however, externalities are of two types: external costs and benefits. Good examples of the former are air and water pollution; of the latter, greater participation in civic affairs as a result of education. A pure public good is one which provides mainly external benefits, such as national defense. A decreasing cost industry is sometimes called a "natural monopoly." Public utilities fall into this category. Finally, market power is quite often experienced by firms with some degree of control over the output of an industry. All of these cases will be explained in greater detail in subsequent chapters (especially Chapters 2, 4, and 12).

practice, almost every tax or expenditure decision will have some impact on all three. Thus, while Musgrave's framework is useful for conceptualizing the problem, one usually encounters difficulty in implementing this approach in the design and evaluation of actual institutions and programs.

In spite of its widespread use, the Musgrave formulation is not acceptable to all economists. One important reason for this is that universal agreement does not exist as to the nature of the "public interest"; i.e., the general desirability of the objectives enumerated above. This results largely from disagreements over objectives that cannot be resolved even on theoretical grounds. Moreover, many economists have observed that the political decision-making process does not (perhaps cannot) yield a clear resolution of these conflicts. Nor is there any guarantee that the incentive structure relevant to government decision-makers will ensure the effective design or implementation of the policies necessary to achieve the goals of equity, efficiency, and stability.

These reservations about the normative framework have led to a greater interest in the positive economics of public choice; i.e., in the study of how government decisions are actually made. The primary objective of this inquiry is to develop positive, testable hypotheses about how public choices are made, which will presumably enable us to better predict the future course of government actions or decisions. As yet, we do not have a set of propositions as powerful as the theories of business and private decision-making that characterize the microeconomic analysis of the private sector. However, progress is being made in explaining behavior in this essentially political-bureaucratic arena.

Studies in this area, however, represent only a small proportion of the positive analyses of the public sector which the student of public finance can consult. A large number of theories exist regarding the influence of government tax and expenditure decisions on economic choices made in the private sector. Moreover, many of these theories have produced hypotheses that have been the subjects of empirical studies. Through this methodology, for example, we have learned much about how various tax and expenditure policies affect private consumption, saving, and investment decisions—on both individual and aggregate bases.

Economists are working hard to improve our knowledge of how the public sector operates and to achieve a consensus with regard to how it should operate. Much remains to be done, and many issues remain unresolved. It is our conviction, therefore, that the person beginning a study of public finance should be exposed to as wide a range of views as possible, and to a judicious application of the methodologies of both positive and normative economics. A brief preview of the way in which we believe this can be accomplished is outlined in the next section.

THE BOOK'S ORGANIZATION

In Chapter 2, we initially adopt the normative view that economic activity should be organized to achieve maximum economic welfare. This requires the development of some basic criteria of efficiency and equity. Given these criteria, we then outline a number of instances where the private sector "fails" to be either efficient or equitable, thus establishing, as it were, a minimum rationale for government activity.

The presumption of market failure, however, does not imply that society is necessarily better off with, rather than without, government activity. Government budget decisions must themselves score well according to the welfare criteria. In Chapter 3, these criteria are used to develop a set of rules which should guide government expenditure policy.

Once some guidelines for public expenditure policy have been established, they are used in chapters 4–6 as a basis for evaluating expenditures in three areas: national defense, natural resources and transportation, and income redistribution. This set of programs not only constitutes the majority of federal expenditures, but also illustrates the broad and complex range of issues involved in expenditure evaluation.

In Chapter 7, the focus shifts from the expenditure to the revenue side of the budget, beginning with an exposition of the principles of taxation. These principles provide both equity and efficiency criteria for evaluating the current tax structure, analyzing tax issues, and suggesting reforms.

The important issue of *who* ultimately pays taxes is the subject of Chapter 8, which draws upon basic economic principles to demonstrate that the individual upon whom a tax is levied is not necessarily the one who bears the opportunity cost of taxation.

This discussion of taxes continues in chapters 9, 10, and 11 with a broad description, analysis, and evaluation of the major taxes, and an examination of current issues in taxation. The various taxes are categorized according to the three major tax bases (income, wealth, and consumption) to facilitate comparisons.

The final chapter in the section on revenues, Chapter 12, contains an analysis of the issues related to the pricing of public products and a discussion of the use of taxes as a regulatory device. In the latter case, special attention is devoted to an evaluation of taxes to curb pollution.

Chapter 12 completes our discussion (for the national government) of the allocation and distribution functions. In chapters 13 through 16, we turn to the problems associated with performing the stabilization function. Chapters 13 and 14 are devoted to constructing a framework for national income analysis, while chapters 15 and 16 provide a concise yet relatively thorough discussion of the leading issues in fiscal policy and debt management.

In the final section of the book, we shift our attention from the fiscal problems of the national government to the fiscal problems created by a federal system. Failure to do so would constitute a denial of two outstanding modern trends: the growth of intergovernmental fiscal relations, and the rapid increase in the size of the state and local sectors. In Chapter 17, we outline the principles by which a federal fiscal system should operate, and review the problems it creates. Finally, in Chapter 18, we examine the system of conditional and unconditional grants between various levels of government, including the program of federal revenue sharing.

SUMMARY

The most frequently cited measures of the size of the government sector are those which relate government purchases, or expenditures, or revenue to the size of the GNP. The ratio of purchases to GNP has remained remarkably close to 20 percent for the last 20 years. The ratio of expenditures to GNP exhibits a steady upward trend, reaching 35 percent in 1975. The ratio of revenues to GNP—perhaps the greatest source of taxpayer concern—increased from 24 to 31 percent during the post-World War II period.

None of these measures is an accurate index of government's influence on economic activity. Measures of government purchases do not include the rapidly growing outlays for transfer programs. Government expenditures include the latter, but expenditures are not an accurate index of program benefits. Finally, government revenues tend to be an underestimate of the real effect of government finance on the level and composition of economic activity.

In gaining a fuller understanding of the economic influence of government budget activity, economists employ the methodologies of both positive and normative economics. The primary concern of the former is to explain how the economy is, or is likely to be, affected by particular activities. The objective of the latter is to determine how public policies should be structured to help the economy better achieve its primary social goals. Both methodologies are employed in this text in the process of describing and evaluating government tax, expenditure, and grant programs.

SUGGESTIONS FOR FURTHER READING

Schultze, Charles L., "Federal Spending: Past, Present, and Future," in H. Owen and C. L. Schultze, Eds., *Setting National Priorities,* Washington, D.C.: The Brookings Institution, 1976, pp. 323–369.

This chapter presents a broad overview of the growth in federal spending. In addition, it contains data adjusted for changes in the relative price of inputs used by the federal government, which indicate that real federal spending has actually declined as a proportion of real GNP since 1950.

Musgrave, Richard A., *The Theory of Public Finance,* New York: McGraw-Hill, 1959, Chapter 1.

This is the classic reference on the normative view of the public budget presented earlier in this chapter. Although the Musgrave text is rather advanced, the first chapter is readily accessible to readers with a limited background in economics.

EFFICIENCY AND EQUITY IN THE PRIVATE SECTOR

The proper role of government in the American economy is an issue of broad social significance. This fact is confirmed daily by debates in the U. S. Congress, in state legislatures, in city and county governments, and in the nation's news media. Indeed, many economists argue that this is *the* crucial issue of public finance because its resolution determines the basic environment in which all economic decisions are made.

The economic activities of government provide shape and substance to the nation's political institutions. In addition, they have a broad though not always easily discernible influence on the whole fabric of American culture. The economic role of government is, therefore, an important aspect of its social role. Informed social choice requires careful consideration of the questions of whether and in what ways government direction of economic resources can help us to achieve more fully our economic and social goals.

The issue of the *proper* role of government is ultimately an ethical, or normative, one. It is necessary to be clear, therefore, about the premises on which our inquiry is based. The basic proposition is that, in a system where resource allocation in accordance with individual preferences is an important social objective, the direction of resources by public institutions requires some assurance that the welfare of the populace will improve when individual preferences are superceded or influenced by choices made through the public sector. Our task, then, is to determine the circumstances in which economic welfare is increased by public sector activity.

If welfare can be increased by substituting public activity for private, then well-defined situations must exist in which the private sector would fail to achieve maximum economic welfare. It is with these circumstances that we are concerned in this chapter.

Our analysis begins with a brief examination of welfare criteria. Following that, the two dimensions of economic welfare—efficiency and equity—are discussed in separate sections. In each case, we outline the relevant criteria and identify the primary cases in which the market system fails to perform well according to these criteria.

WELFARE CRITERIA

How do we know whether we have achieved maximum economic welfare? According to a test proposed by the Italian economist Vilfredo Pareto, we fail to achieve maximum economic welfare whenever we can change the allocation of resources, and by doing so, increase the welfare of at least one member of the community without reducing that of any other member. Conversely, economic welfare is maximized when it is not possible to improve the welfare of one or more individuals without reducing the welfare of at least one other individual.

Although it is not possible to prove that these propositions are ultimately correct, they are consistent with the premise that the welfare of society is the sum of individual welfares, and they have enjoyed a wide degree of support from economists. It is generally recognized, however, that they are not very practical guides to decision-making.

The chief weakness of the Pareto criterion is that it cannot be applied to a situation in which a reallocation of resources increases the welfare of some individuals while reducing that of others. Unfortunately, changes which produce gains for some and losses for others are encountered much more frequently than situations in which no one loses. Thus, the Pareto criterion cannot be used to determine whether such changes should be made.

As a result, we need to establish a criterion to aid us in determining whether the gain in welfare of some individuals exceeds the loss of welfare to others. Since the presumed end of economic activity is individual satisfaction, this criterion would enable us ideally to measure changes in satisfaction, or *utility,* and to add up the positive and negative utility produced by some economic event. Generations of thought, however, have failed to produce an ideal method of measuring utility.

The economist has turned instead to measures which are based on objective data, principally to the monetary values of particular resource uses. It is assumed that an alternative with a larger monetary value yields a greater level of satisfaction than one with a lesser monetary value. It is presumed that a choice of the former alternative will produce a *net* gain (a gain on the first alternative less the loss on the second) in economic well-being.

The careful economist will refer to a change in which the gains exceed the losses (both measured in money terms) as an *efficient* change, or as a change which produces a *more efficient* allocation of resources. He/she will not claim, on the basis of this test alone, that economic *welfare* has increased.

The reason for this is relatively straightforward. Ideally, aggregate community economic *welfare* is the sum of individual satisfactions or utilities. Monetary valuations reflect the satisfaction derived from resource uses. However, the amount of money individuals are willing to pay for a particular use also depends upon the amount of money they have. Thus, monetary valuations depend upon the prevailing distribution of income as well. It follows, therefore, that monetary measures of economic welfare are a composite of both individual staisfaction and the distribution of income among individuals. Indeed, if preferences were the same at two points in time but income was distributed differently, the market would produce a different mix of goods and services at each point.

The possibility arises, then, that an economic change could produce net gains, as defined above, but have an undesirable effect on the distribution of income. Alternatively, the *existing* allocation of resources may produce the greatest possible net gains, but be consistent with a socially undesirable distribution of income.

Faced with these conflicts, the economist generally suggests that a practical approach is to separate the problem of evaluating an economic change into parts, and then ask whether objective agreement can be reached on some or all parts of the total change. Thus, it is common practice to subdivide the general goal of economic *welfare* into partial goals such as *efficiency* and *equity in the distribution of income.* A given situation can then be studied to determine whether it is more or less efficient than its alternatives and whether, at the same time, it is more or less equitable.

This division of effort will not necessarily solve all the problems of evaluating and comparing alternatives. Changes may occur which have conflicting effects on efficiency and equity, and the decision-maker must then decide how much a gain (loss) in efficiency is worth relative to a loss (gain) in equity. However, the information gained by this method of study should make the trade-offs more clear and result in more rational decisions.

EFFICIENCY

An efficient allocation of resources can be achieved in several ways. A necessary condition, however, is the full employment of factors of production. Without full employment, it would be possible under a wide variety of circumstances to achieve gains in excess of losses merely by employing previously unemployed resources. Indeed, if *no* currently utilized factors are required to work in conjunction with presently unemployed resources, an increase in employment would produce pure gains. If it became necessary, however, to draw resources from other uses to work in conjunction with unemployed factors, then some losses (opportunity costs greater than zero) would occur.

Even if all resources were employed, however, unexploited changes might still exist that would increase efficiency. There is one general circumstance in which this can occur: if inputs are producing a combination of goods and services with a smaller total money value than they *could* be producing (value in current use is less than value in alternative uses). Regardless of the sector responsible for production or purchase—private or public—existing resources are allocated efficiently only when they are producing the highest value combination of goods and services.

EFFICIENCY CRITERIA

Production of this combination is achieved when the level of *each* resource-using activity is such that: (1) the *difference* between total social benefits (TSB) and total social costs (TSC) attributable to this activity is maximized; and (2) total net social benefit (TNSB = TSB − TSC) is not negative. Condition (1) is also fulfilled when marginal social benefits (MSB) are equal to marginal social costs (MSC). These criteria can be applied, for example, to determine the efficient level of production of good A.

Total social benefit is the sum of the monetary values individuals place on each unit of A, while total social cost is the sum of the monetary values individuals place on each unit of the various activities that are sacrificed for the production of A. The efficiency test requires a comparison of the gains from providing A with the opportunities given up as a result of its provision. It is clearly rational to provide A as long as the gains (TSB) exceed the losses, or *opportunity costs* (TSC).

The rule to provide A as long as TSB exceeds TSC does not prescribe the efficient *level* of A, however. This occurs when TSB exceeds TSC by the largest amount possible, or when TNSB is maximized. TNSB is maximized, in turn, when MSB = MSC. MSB is defined as the addition to TSB resulting from the provision of one additional unit of A; MSC is defined as the addition to TSC from the provision of this same unit. As long as MSB exceeds MSC, a greater amount is added to TSB than to TSC, and TNSB grows. Conversely, when MSC exceeds MSB, a greater amount is added to TSC than to TSB, and TNSB declines. It follows, therefore, that TNSB is *maximized* (neither growing nor declining) only when MSB = MSC.

To help the reader understand these ideas more clearly, some hypothetical data, consistent with widely applicable economic principles, are presented in Table 2-1. Columns 1 and 2 depict the notion that a larger amount of A yields a larger amount of satisfaction and, hence, a greater monetary value of A. Similarly, the figures in columns 1 and 3 imply that larger amounts of A require the sacrifice of larger amounts of all other activities; hence, larger amounts of satisfaction, and correspondingly larger monetary values are forgone. We would expect to encounter these ranges of *increasing total social benefit* and *increasing total social cost* for all goods and services.

Columns 5 and 6, however, imply that additional units of A produce successively smaller additions to TSB and successively larger additions to TSC. If we should continue to transfer resources out of alternative uses and into the production of A, we would normally and eventually encounter both diminishing MSB and increasing MSC. MSB must diminish as a consequence of the law of demand; MSC must increase because successively larger amounts of A must eventually be produced with resources that are less suitable to the production of A than they are to the production of other goods and services. When this point is reached, it is necessary to sacrifice successively larger amounts of these alternatives in order to produce additional units of A.

Given these interpretations of the data, the reader can verify that TNSB is maximized at 5 units of A. MSC = MSB between 5 and 6 units, however.

MSB is determined by dividing the change in TSB (ΔTSB) by the change in A (ΔA), while MSC requires the division of ΔTSC by ΔA. Since ΔA

TABLE 2-1   BENEFITS AND COSTS OF GOOD A

(1) A (Units)	(2) TSB ($)	(3) TSC ($)	(4) TNSB ($)	(5) MSB ($)	(6) MSC ($)
0	0	0	0	–	–
1	10	1	9	10	1
2	19	3	16	9	2
3	27	6	21	8	3
4	34	10	24	7	4
5	40	15	25	6	5
6	45	21	24	5	6
7	49	28	21	4	7
8	52	36	16	3	8
9	54	45	9	2	9
10	55	55	0	1	10

equals 1 unit in this illustration, ΔTSB and ΔTSC can be found easily as the difference between successive values for TSB and TSC, respectively.

The apparent conflict between the "total test" (maximize TNSB) and the "marginal test" (equate MSB and MSC) results from using discrete intervals. Ideally, because the marginal test is an application of a theorem in calculus, the two tests give identical results only when all cost and benefit schedules are continuous. In an example using integers, however, the difference between the two rules can be reconciled logically. Under these circumstances, the "producer" of good A must decide between 5 or 6 units, and will probably choose unit 5 because MSB < MSC on unit 6.

EFFICIENCY IN A MARKET ECONOMY

We now turn to the question of whether existing mechanisms for resource allocation are efficient according to the criteria outlined above. At issue are the allocation decisions made in the private, market-directed sector of the economy.

The link between our previous analysis and the allocation of resources through markets is straightforward. The level of production (and sales) in a market is determined by the relationship between the decisions of consumers and producers or, as every beginning student knows, by the forces of demand and supply. The relationship between quantity demanded and the price of a good or service (the demand relationship) provides the basic data for determining TSB. Similarly, the relationships which underlie the supply decision provide the basic data for determining TSC.

The demand schedule is actually an expression of the monetary valuation by individuals of successive units of some good or service. A demand schedule which indicates that individuals (consumers) are willing to pay $10 and $9, respectively, for the first two units also indicates that consumers value the first unit at $10 and the second at $9, in money terms. Thus, the total benefit of the first two units is $19, and the marginal benefit (MB) is $10 on the first and $9 on the second. The demand schedule, as it were, is nothing more than a schedule of MB.

If the demand schedule for some good includes the monetary valuations of *all* individuals who benefit from the provision of successive units of that commodity, then the demand schedule is a schedule of marginal *social* benefit. Thus, the data in columns 1 and 5 of Table 2-1 can be derived directly from the demand schedule for commodity A. These data, when diagrammed, yield the familiar demand curve (D_a) of Figure 2-1. This demand curve illustrates the law of demand; that larger quantities demanded are associated with lower prices of a good, and lower marginal social benefits. Thus, TSB is assumed (correctly) to increase at a decreasing rate.

Turning to the other side of the market, costs of supplying an additional unit of A are equivalent to the marginal cost of A. If *all* the costs of supplying such successive unit are accounted for, then the schedule relating marginal cost to units supplied also relates the latter to marginal *social* costs. Under this assumption, columns 1 and 6 in Table 2-1 depict the data relevant to a social supply decision. These columns are diagrammed as MSC in Figure 2-1.

In terms of social efficiency, the appropriate level of A is the quantity, E_a, where the demand curve (D_a) intersects the marginal social cost (MSC_a) curve. This is not a level that will be achieved automatically by *all* markets in the economy. Some of the reasons for this will be explained later. However, there is a set of circumstances in which the market *will* automatically provide the efficient level of output.

Perfect Competition

The relevant case is that of perfectly competitive markets. These markets consist of buyers and sellers who are too small to influence market prices by virtue of their individual actions. Under these circumstances, if all sellers of goods and services are successful in producing the rate of output

FIGURE 2–1
MARGINAL SOCIAL BENEFITS AND COSTS OF GOOD A

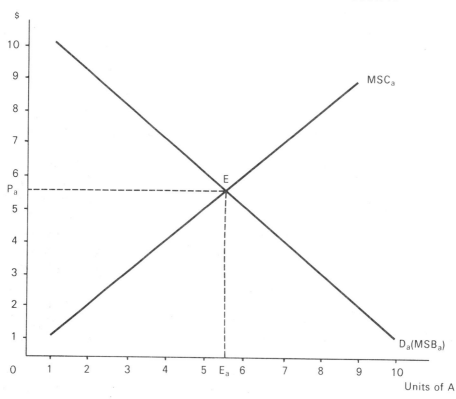

at which their individual profit is maximized, the output of the group as a whole (the so-called "market") will be the efficient level of output.

Total profit (π) is defined as total revenue (TR) minus total cost (TC). Profit is maximized when marginal revenue (MR; equal to the change in TR for a change in A) equals marginal cost (MC; equal to the change in TC for a change in A), and $\pi \geq 0$. The rationale for the first part of this rule is similar to that which we used to explain why maximum TNSB requires an equality between MSB and MSC; namely, if MR exceeds (is less than) MC, additions to total revenue exceed (are less than) additions to total cost and π is increasing (decreasing). It follows that π is maximized (neither increasing nor decreasing) when MR = MC.

Given the characteristics of perfectly competitive product markets, each seller views the demand curve for his/her output as perfectly elastic (parallel to the quantity axis) at the market-determined price, P_a. To each individual seller, P_a represents the marginal revenue from the sale of each successive unit. Each seller then chooses to supply the rate of output where *his/her* marginal cost equals P_a.

The *total* market quantity supplied at each price in a competitive market is merely the sum of the profit maximizing outputs of each individual seller at that price. The distance $P_a E$ in Figure 2-1, therefore, must be equal to the total amount that all sellers supply together at price P_a.

Thus, the forces of competition and the profit motive dictate that a perfectly competitive product market will operate at E_a. This is an efficient level of output, provided that the demand curve is an accurate measure of MSB and that the supply curve is an accurate measure of MSC. This will be the case on the demand side as long as the valuations of all individuals who benefit from the provision of A are accounted for. Whether this is the case is totally unrelated to the degree of competition that prevails in product markets. It can be assumed initially, therefore, that all valuations are expressed in market transactions.

Whether the supply curve is an accurate measure of MSC, however, depends both upon whether all costs are accounted for and on the degree of market competition. We assumed provisionally that the first condition is met. However, it is necessary to assume further that the resources used by competitive producers are themselves supplied competitively. If they are, then resource prices measure the maximum values (at the margin) of these resources in alternative uses. If, for example, industry A must pay $5 an hour to hire labor, it is because labor could earn $5 elsewhere. Other industries are willing to pay $5 because labor would add that much to the value of *their* output. Thus, the price of labor is a measure of its value in alternative uses. It follows, therefore, that the marginal cost of producing an additional unit of A measures the value of output forgone by virtue of shifting labor from other uses to A.

INEFFICIENCY IN A MARKET ECONOMY

Because the conditions which are necessary for perfect competition are not generally fulfilled in actual markets, inefficiency occurs in a private market economy.

The following conditions were assumed to hold in the efficiency analysis above:

1. all sellers maximize profits;
2. all sellers in a market supply a homogeneous product;
3. all market participants have perfect knowledge of alternative sources of supply and demand;
4. all resources are perfectly mobile (and, as a corollary, there is relatively low-cost market entry and exit by sellers); and
5. all buyers and sellers are price-takers.

We now relax these conditions to develop commonly-encountered market situations which are less than "perfect" and, therefore, less than efficient. We continue to assume, as above, that MC = MSC and MB = MSB.

Real markets are characterized frequently by sellers who do not succeed in maximizing profits, by sellers who are not price-takers, by sellers who do not market homogeneous products, by market participants who lack perfect knowledge, by relatively immobile resources, and by relatively high costs of entry and exit. Consequently, there are many instances in which markets provide relatively inefficient quantities of goods and services.

It is impossible to develop many of these cases in a textbook on public finance; nor is it necessary to do so, since their existence has induced the expenditure of only a small proportion of the government budget. It is instructive, however, to illustrate how market imperfections create inefficiency. For this purpose, it is easiest to develop the classic case of the pure monopolist.

Monopoly

As the sole supplier of a particular commodity, the pure monopolist perceives the entire market demand curve as the one which defines his/her selling possibilities. To facilitate a comparison with our earlier analysis, assume that he/she faces the demand curve (MSB_a) in Figure 2-1. Also assume that the cost of each additional unit is defined by the MSC curve in this same figure.

The monopolist who wishes to maximize profits will produce at the rate where MC = MR. MC is assumed equivalent to MSC, the data for which is reproduced below in Table 2-2. MR, however, is *not* equivalent to MSB, or to the price at each quantity demanded.

Marginal revenue (MR) is the change in total revenue (ΔTR) resulting from a change in units sold (ΔA). Total revenue (TR) is the product of price per unit and the number of units sold. In this example, TR is the product of the numbers in columns 1 and 5 of Table 2-1, because MSB = price per unit.

The monopolist maximizes profit at 4 units (MC = MR). This is less than the efficient output level, and it implies a higher price ($7) than the one consistent with the efficient output level, E_a ($5.50).

Other Imperfect Markets

This example of the inefficiency of less than perfect markets is indicative of a wide variety of circumstances which result in an output less than the efficient output, and a price higher than the efficient price. Similar results occur, for example, where: (1) sellers are successful in differentiating their products from those of their rivals, even though the products share greatly similar technical characteristics; (2) financial and non-financial barriers to entry are quite high; (3) several sellers act in concert to maximize industry profits, and/or to maintain price above the level that would be achieved in perfect competition; and (4) buyers act similarly to maximize their well-being by maintaining resource prices below those consistent with perfect competition.

Corrective Action

It is generally acknowledged that these instances of "market failure" may require corrective action initiated through the public sector. Indeed, laws forbidding or regulating monopolization and various price-fixing practices have been passed and enforced through activities of government agencies; principally, the Anti-Trust Division of the Justice Department, the Federal Trade Commission, the Interstate Commerce Commission, the Federal Power Commission, the State Public Utilities Commissions, and others. It is not always clear, however, that the actions taken by these agencies have succeeded in correcting market failures. Indeed, the soundness of regulatory practices is a subject of vigorous debate.

Externalities

The preceeding cases can be viewed as situations in which the public interest is not served well by individuals pursuing their own interests through market exchange. The market itself, however, faithfully records all the valuations attributable to various resource uses. Unfortunately, a large

TABLE 2-2   COSTS AND REVENUES FOR A MONOPOLIST

A (Units)	MC ($)	TR ($)	MR ($)
0	–	0	–
1	1	10	10
2	2	18	8
3	3	24	6
4	4	28	4
5	5	30	2
6	6	30	0
7	7	28	−2
8	8	24	−4
9	9	18	−6
10	10	10	−8

number of instances occur in which the market system does not work well in this latter regard either.

Those situations in which some valuations do not influence exchange values are characterized by the existence of (efficiency-relevant) *externalities*. Externalities are individual valuations of the gains or losses of some resource-using activity that do not influence the level of the activity. They are divided into two categories: *external benefits* and *external costs*. External benefits are individual valuations of gains which do not influence the demand for a particular resource use; external costs are individual valuations of losses (or alternatives forgone) which do not influence supply. Externalities are also often called *spillovers* (positive or negative).

Examples of externalities are easy to construct. On the cost side, we have the classic cases of air and water pollution. They occur frequently because various individuals or institutions use both airsheds and water resources without full consideration of the value of the alternatives that must be sacrificed. The overuse of these environmental resources occurs as a consequence.

On the benefit side, we encounter instances like the following: education (especially at the elementary and secondary level) provides benefits to others and not only to students; a dam built to provide hydroelectric power also provides positive values to water-using recreationists; a well-trimmed lawn provides positive values to neighbors; immunization of a subgroup of society provides protection to many who are not immunized. In these cases, we often get too little of the activity in question because the valuations of individuals who do not directly receive the good or service in question are not considered by the supplier.

The effect of externalities on economic efficiency can be illustrated with the aid of elementary supply-demand analysis. We will begin with the case of external costs.

External Costs

When external costs are present, there is a difference between the costs *producers* must pay and the costs paid by *society* as a whole. To illustrate this difference, we distinguish between three separate marginal costs: marginal social costs (MSC), marginal private costs (MPC), and marginal external costs (MEC). MSC was defined previously as the value of *all* the alternatives sacrificed by virtue of producing an additional unit of some commodity. MPC is a narrower measure, referring only to the costs of an additional unit that the producer (and, where appropriate, the consumer) *must* pay. MEC, then, is simply a measure of the value of the sacrificed alternatives that are *not* paid for by the producer (or consumer) of the additional unit, but rather by some individual or individuals not involved in the production or consumption of the commodity in question. Given these definitions, MSC = MPC + MEC.

The relevant cases now are those in which MEC > 0 and, therefore, MSC > MPC. This may occur, for example, in the production of paper made from wood pulp, where paper producers pay for labor, logs, chemicals, and other materials but fail to pay for the use of a stream into which various residuals resulting from the production of pulp are dumped. If this stream would have value as a household water supply or for waterbased recreation, however, these values may be sacrificed by virtue of the disposal of residuals. Consequently, the paper producers pay only part of the social costs of each additional unit of paper produced. Therefore, from the point of view of social efficiency, too much paper is provided.

This last proposition can be demonstrated with the aid of a conventional supply-demand diagram. We assume that the paper industry is highly competitive. Each seller, moreover, desires to maximize profits. To do so, each will equate the market price to the *private* cost of producing an additional unit, MPC. The market as a whole, then, is in equilibrium at Q_m units of paper (see Figure 2-2).

As explained previously, however, economic efficiency requires the rate of output where MSC = MSB. Since this occurs at Q_e, it is easy to see that

27

FIGURE 2-2
EXTERNAL COSTS OF PAPER PRODUCTION

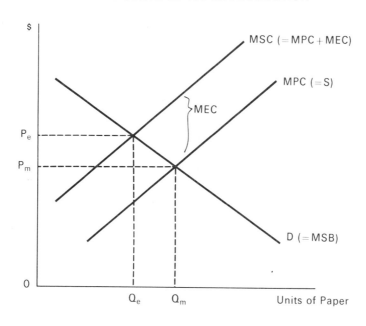

the industry is producing more than the efficient amount. From the point of view of efficiency, we have too much paper. Resources need to be transferred out of paper production and into the production of other goods and services. This process would include both the transfer of *some* of the stream into the production of more household water and recreation, and the transfer of the other resources that would have been used in producing units Q_e to Q_m into the production of a variety of alternatives.

External Benefits

The case of external benefits works in a way opposite from that of external costs. Here, the key is that some relevant valuations are not perceived by the producer as part of the demand for a product. There is an excess, then, of marginal social benefit (MSB) over marginal private benefit (MPB).

As indicated previously, MSB is derived by summing the valuations of *all* individuals who benefit by virtue of the provision of a unit of a good or service. MPB, on the other hand, includes only the valuations of those individuals who are potential buyers; i.e., those who *directly* benefit from

FIGURE 2–3
EXTERNAL BENEFITS FROM EDUCATION

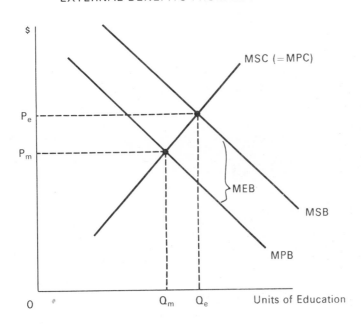

the purchase of a good or service. The sum of the marginal valuations of those individuals who benefit *indirectly* is equal to the marginal external benefit (MEB) of the item in question. It follows, therefore, that MSB = MPB + MEB.

The effects that external benefits have on efficiency can also be illustrated with the aid of a simple supply-demand diagram. We will use elementary education as an example.

Elementary education is produced and sold in the market sector, although public education is more common. Moreover, given that relatively small producing units are technically efficient, there is reason to believe that this service is supplied under highly competitive conditions. The combined actions of all suppliers, therefore, would result in the provision of quantity Q_m at a price of P_m, as in Figure 2-3, where MPB = MPC (=MSC).

This is a perfectly rational solution for private producers because they can charge prices equivalent only to MPB for various levels of output. If they were to produce beyond Q_m, they would not be maximizing profits. However, Q_m is a rate of output less than the socially efficient level, Q_e,

29

where MSB = MSC. The difference between the privately-determined rate and the efficient rate is due to the existence of positive external benefits, or MEB.

The fact that MEB > 0 implies that private elementary education yields benefits to individuals other than those who directly receive it. The general population benefits, for example, if an educated individual is less likely to engage in antisocial pursuits or to be unemployed. As relevant as these values are from the point of view of the group as a whole, however, they are not relevant from the point of view of the individual. The individual places a value on a unit of elementary education which reflects the returns the individual expects to reap as a result. The seller, therefore, could charge prices only as great as MPB. It follows that private sellers will not produce in accordance with social demand (MSB), but only in accordance with private demand (MPB).

Corrective Action

The existence of externalities, then, implies an inefficient combination of goods and services if the allocation is determined solely by market exchange. In the case of external costs, sellers acting solely on the basis of the costs they must pay supply an output which would be greater than the efficient output. In the case of external benefits, sellers acting solely on the basis of the prices that direct beneficiaries are willing to pay supply an output which would be less than the efficient output.

When externalities of the type outlined above are or would be encountered in the private sector, government action may be necessary if efficiency is to be achieved. This action may take many forms: public production or subsidies to correct for external benefits; taxes or special charges to force private industry to consider external costs; administrative regulation to prohibit the generation of external costs; or publicly financed expenditure programs to correct adverse consequences of private sector activities. These alternatives are the subject of intense debate within the economics profession. They may differ greatly with respect to their administrative feasibility, their effectiveness, and their cost, depending upon the circumstances in which they would be applied.

Unanimous agreement, moreover, does not exist on the degree of importance of externalities in any particular instance. The reason is fairly simple: the value of both external benefits and costs is extremely difficult to determine. So, even if their existence is non-controversial, their size remains a matter of dispute.

PURE PUBLIC GOODS

So far, we have examined external benefits that are only "partial," i.e., MEB accounts for only *part* of MSB. There is a class of goods, however, for which MEB accounts for virtually all of MSB, or for which, in other words, MPB is virtually zero. These goods are commonly referred to as *pure public goods.*

A pure public good is available for consumption by all members of a social group once it is provided. If one individual purchases a unit of this good, there is no feasible way to exclude non-purchasers from enjoying the services provided by this unit. While this type of good is not encountered as frequently as are goods with partial external benefits, it is nevertheless quite important. If the relevant social group is defined as the national population, then the court system and national defense fall into this category. Similarly, if the relevant group is defined as the local population, then the local law enforcement agency and the street system may be so categorized.

Because any individual who does not pay for the provision of a pure public good cannot be excluded from consuming its services, there is little incentive for any potential consumer to reveal his/her true valuation of a unit of this product. It would be logical for any single individual *not* to reveal his/her valuation on the chance that others would, and thereby ensure the provision of the good at no cost to the individual. However, if each potential buyer reacts in this way, the good will not be paid for or the valuations revealed will be for a lesser amount than the true total. Under these circumstances, the private supplier, by catering only to the valuations actually revealed, would supply less than the efficient amount. Indeed, the tendency for individuals to understate their true willingness to pay could be so pronounced that the good might not be provided at all in a pure market economy.

The preceding discussion provided a brief review of the instances of market (efficiency) "failure" mentioned most prominently in the literature of public finance. It was not intended to be exhaustive in terms of its coverage of the cases analyzed, nor was it intended to provide a discussion of all conceivable failures. As brief as it has been, however, it does develop a set of concepts that are useful in providing a rationale for a wide range of public sector economic activities. The exact dimensions of this activity are the subject matter of the next chapter. First, however, we must evaluate the market economy in terms of how well it achieves equity rather than efficiency.

EQUITY IN THE
DISTRIBUTION OF INCOME

In an economy where resources are allocated according to the expenditure decisions of individuals, the prevailing distribution of income is a primary determinant of who consumes the output of goods and services. Since the level of economic welfare is determined inclusive of the total utility derived from consumption, economic welfare is also dependent upon the prevailing distribution of income. Therefore, it is not possible to determine whether economic welfare is maximized by determining if economic efficiency alone is achieved. It is necessary at the same time to evaluate the distribution of income.

Ideally, we would like to determine which distribution yields the greatest aggregate, or community, satisfaction. It is not possible to do this because we cannot measure individual satisfaction.

The primary consequence of our inability to measure satisfaction is the (necessary) treatment of the distribution question as an ethical issue. The ultimate question becomes: what is the *proper* distribution of income? This is clearly a normative question, and one for which we would not expect to find a single, unanimous answer. Indeed, the opinions of American society widely differ on this issue.

Generally, people disagree about two basic aspects of distribution. First, disagreement exists over the manner in which the distribution of income *should be* determined. Not surprisingly, one of the most prominent bases for disagreement among economists is the presumed effect of alternative distributions on efficiency in resource allocation. Second, even if there is agreement on the first matter, there is some question whether the distribution of income *could be* (or is) determined in the manner prescribed. These issues are featured prominently in the following discussion.

MARKET-DETERMINED
INCOME DISTRIBUTION

In a purely competitive market economy, the amount of income any individual earns would be determined by the amount of resources to which the individual had a property right and the market prices of these resources. The distribution of income among individuals, therefore, would be a result of the pattern of resource ownerships and resource prices. Such prices, in turn, would be set at market-clearing levels; i.e., at levels where quantity supplied equaled quantity demanded.

The demand for resources is a schedule of the valuations buyers place on successive resource units. The maximum valuation is equal to the amount that each additional unit adds to total revenues. Economists call this the *value of the marginal product* (VMP). It is determined by multiplying the marginal physical product (MPP) of the resource times the price (P_o) the output fetches when sold to consumers. MPP, in turn, is the physical addition to output made by an additional unit of an input. Thus, if the input is labor and the hiring of an additional unit increases output by 5 units, and this output sells for $10 a unit, MPP of labor equals 5, and VMP $= 5 \times \$10 = \$50$. If forced to by competition, the firm hiring labor in this instance would pay up to $50 for this unit of labor.

A consequence of a *competitive* resource market being cleared at a price where quantities supplied and demanded are equal is that the last resource unit purchased *is* paid an amount equivalent to its VMP. Thus, economists often say that the distribution of income is determined by the marginal productivity of resources.

The preceding is a brief explanation of how a perfectly competitive economy *would* determine the distribution of income. As such, it is a part of positive economics. Many individuals argue, however, that this is how the distribution of income *should* be determined. When arguments like this are encountered, the discussion has shifted to the realm of normative economics.

Those who propose that we accept a distribution determined by marginal productivity generally argue from four major premises:

1. that is a "fair" method of income determination;
2. that it promotes an efficient allocation of resources;
3. that it enhances personal freedom; and
4. that an efficiently operating economy would provide for some private redistribution in any case.

It Is a Fair Method of Income Determination

The notion that market exchange of resources is a fair method of determining the distribution of income is based on the *premise* that people *should* be rewarded according to the contributions they make to national output, and on the *belief* that market-determined prices generally do just that. The premise, of course, is a value judgment and cannot be evaluated on the

33

basis of economic criteria. The belief, however, is grist for the mill of both economic theory and observation.

Resource incomes are of four basic types: wages, rent, interest, and profit. Wages, it is argued, are merely rewards for the productive effort of labor. Rent is paid to the owners of land and natural resources. It is more difficult to establish a link between rent payments and productive effort than it is for labor; however, rent does perform the socially necessary function of directing land and natural resources to their highest-value uses, both at a point in time and over long periods of time. Interest payments, on the other hand, lie somewhere between wages and rent. Surely they at least partially serve as a reward for thrift and a willingness to forgo current consumption, although this may be less true for certain interest-earning assets (especially those to which a property right is gained via inheritance). Finally, profits can be viewed as a reward for risk-taking and organizational effort.

Generally, then, there is a link between resource payments and socially productive effort. It is widely acknowledged, however, that the correspondence is not perfect, for reasons additional to those already mentioned.

First, resource markets are marred by imperfections in competition, some of which ensure that resources are not paid an amount equal to VMP. Market power exercised by resource buyers (e.g., *monopsony,* discrimination) produces resource prices less than VMP. Since the latter is often cited as a measure of productive contribution, this creates a situation where rewards at the margin are less than contributions. Market power exercised by sellers (e.g., monopoly in labor markets), naturally results in rewards exceeding productive contribution at the margin.

The criticisms just mentioned relate to the failures of resource markets to achieve the ideal situation; namely, one in which resource prices equal VMP. A more fundamental criticism is that the market exchange mechanism is not capable of accurately determining VMP even under ideally competitive conditions. The reason for this is fairly straightforward: most productive processes require the cooperation of several resources, and it is frequently not possible to determine how much of the final output is attributable to each.

Little doubt exists that resource markets do not function as perfectly as advocates of the marginal productivity theory of income distribution wish they would. The harder issue remains: is this an ethically unobjectionable method? Many would argue that it is not.

Some would surely object to it on the grounds that not everyone has an equal opportunity to earn income. They would stress that the system rewards more richly those who are the products of more favorable environments, as well as those who are simply more talented. Or they would point out that the thrift and foresight of one's parents or grandparents are often the bases for rewards accruing to the present generation.

Finally, one could add to all these objections the rather obvious point that the marginal productivity theory of income distribution implicitly assumes that the prevailing distribution of human resources potential is acceptable. Some would surely propose, on the grounds of fairness, that we undertake various compensatory measures to improve the lower end of this distribution.

It Promotes Efficient Resource Allocation

The second defense for the marginal productivity theory of income distribution is that rewards in line with productive effort promote economic efficiency. In this view, resource prices are conceived to perform several socially important functions. Wages serve as an incentive to labor, in general, to exert maximum feasible productive effort. Differentials in wages promote the specialization of labor and economizing on this resource. Interest payments induce individuals to forgo present consumption, and allow the economy to build a more productive capital stock. Rents induce the owners of land and natural resources to economize on the use of these assets, and to allocate them to their highest value uses. Profits induce experimentation, innovation, invention, and the search for more efficient methods of organization.

A reading of American economic history indicates that these are powerful engines for economic progress, even though they have not always functioned perfectly. Still, it is fair to ask whether the resulting differentials in the distribution of income need be as large as they are in order to generate an acceptable level of performance. Evidence from the literature on taxation and government transfer programs (to be reviewed later in this book) indicates that we have *re*distributed a significant proportion of income via tax and expenditure programs without seriously impairing our ability to produce. There is and has been a trade-off between greater efficiency and a more equal distribution of income, but it has not been as severe as some might imagine it to have been.

Indeed, theory and evidence indicate that there may be additional ways to redistribute income without promoting large increases in inefficiency. We will refer to some of these programs in subsequent parts of this book when we discuss existing and proposed tax and expenditure programs designed to redistribute income. For now, however, our point is simply that the goals of a more equal distribution of income and economic efficiency may not always conflict.

Still, in a wide number of instances, efforts to promote a more equal distribution of income may impair incentives to work, save, take risks, or to economize on the use of scarce resources. If efficiency in resource allocation is a desirable social goal, then we need to consider seriously the efficiency cost of income redistribution.

It Enhances Personal Freedom

The third defense for a market-determined distribution of income is that it enhances personal freedom. In its purest form, private property rights are bestowed by the state on the widest possible range of productive assets. Individual owners are then free to exercise their own preferences regarding the disposition of these assets, and this phenomenon widens the scope of individual choice.

In earlier times, when producing units were quite small and enterprises were owned by a handful of individuals, a close link probably existed between the freedom to use productive assets and personal freedom. The enterprise was actually an extension of the individual. However, this is certainly much less true today when so many of our productive assets are directed by corporations, wherein owners often exercise very little choice.

The development of the modern corporation has also helped to weaken the link between economic freedom and political freedom. It is easier to argue that political favors cannot be purchased in a world of small producing units than it is in an economy where relatively large concentrations of incomes are prevalent. Once again, the vision does not quite match the reality.

Even if it did, however, there would undoubtedly be instances in which society would choose to place limitations on the free use of resources. Historically, we have made certain resource uses illegal; e.g., prostitution and clandestine production and distribution of habit-forming drugs and hard-core pornography. Moreover, we have regulated the production of certain services, such as medicine and law. More recently, we have recognized more fully that the freedom to use resources is also the freedom to discriminate, and we have passed laws to regulate this activity. Of course, not all of the restrictions which have been placed on the free use of resources are justified. Many of them have been based on an ethical rationale with which we may take exception. But that, of course, is the point: the proper degree of economic freedom is ultimately an ethical matter.

It is extremely difficult to draw the line on the extent of government intervention at any particular point in time. Most of us could probably agree that government command of a substantial proportion of resources would effectively suppress dissent, induce conformity, and extinguish political democracy. The evidence provided by social experiments of this variety in other countries is too clear to ignore. However, this does not constitute evidence that government command of *some* resources would require an unacceptable reduction in personal freedom.

It Provides for Private Redistribution

The final argument in defense of market-determined income distribution is that a certain amount of redistribution would take place naturally as a result of individual choice. The evidence, of course, is consistent with this view. A considerable amount of private charity has always existed. The relevant question is whether it would be large enough from a social point of view should market-determined income distribution prevail.

Recent arguments indicate that the amount of privately-determined redistribution would be less than that which is consistent with an *efficient* allocation of resources. This is an important result because it implies that equity arguments are not necessary to demonstrate that a market-determined distribution of income is socially unacceptable.

The basic idea is the one which underlies private charity; namely, that the welfare of other individuals is important to many people, and that they would enhance their own satisfaction by contributing to the satisfaction of others. Many people, therefore, would be willing to contribute to a program which redistributes income. It is unlikely, however, that the program would be of efficient size.

The problem is similar to the one encountered for the pure public good; namely, that people will not reveal their true preferences. The reason in this case, however, is not extreme externality in consumption. Rather, each individual believes that his/her contribution is such a small part of the total amount necessary to finance the program that it is possible to understate a willingness to pay without undermining the program. Of course, if each potential contributor reasons in this way, the program will be either nonexistent or, at best, be too small from an efficiency point of view.

The immediately preceding discussion has been a consideration solely of the case for a market-determined distribution of income. We have chosen for now to limit our analysis to this issue, partially because it is familiar ground for economists, but primarily because it is the prevailing distributive ethic in a market-directed economy, the adequacy of which is the subject of this chapter. Our objective, then has not been to review competing distributive ethics, but rather to provide the reader with an evaluation of the dominant view. Some alternative views are considered later in chapters 3 and 6.

SUMMARY

One of the primary concerns of economics is whether resource allocation results in the attainment of maximum economic welfare. The modern view is that practical measures of a change in welfare require the monetary valuation of benefits and costs, plus an evaluation of changes in the distribution of income. If a change in allocation produces monetary gains exceeding monetary losses, there is an increase in economic efficiency. An efficient change will not necessarily increase economic welfare, however.

To achieve efficiency, it is necessary to arrange production so that total social net benefits are maximized, or so that $MSB = MSC$. This occurs automatically in a perfectly competitive market system free of externalities. Inefficiency occurs, however, in the presence of monopoly, other types of imperfect competition, and externalities.

Externalities are a particularly important cause of market failure. Where products are accompanied by this provision of external benefits, output tends to be inefficiently small. This is especially true in the extreme case of a pure public good, such as national defense. Where external costs are present, output tends to be inefficiently large. Government tax and expenditures programs should, and can be designed to correct many of these efficiency failures of the private market system.

Although the efficiency critique of a private market economy is widely accepted, there is considerable controversy over whether the private sector produces an equitable distribution of income. Some economists argue that the market-determined distribution of income is ethically justified on the grounds that it is fair, that it promotes efficiency, that it enhances personal freedom, and that it provides resources for private redistribution activities. Other economists argue that there are important weaknesses in the arguments which underlie this position. At the present time there appears to be no firm consensus as to which side is ultimately correct. Even in the absence of such a mandate, government officials have not hesitated to undertake many programs designed to correct the market-determined distribution of income.

SUGGESTIONS FOR
FURTHER READING

Bator, Francis M., *The Question of Government Spending,* New York: Collier Books, 1960.

Although the data in this volume is out of date, this is still one of the best elementary developments of the rationale for public economic activity.

Haveman, Robert Henry, *The Economics of the Public Sector,* New York: John Wiley and Sons, 1970.

Chapters 1–3 in this reference, although fairly elementary, provide a sound discussion of the range of issues involved in defining the limits of private sector activity.

Kohler, Heinz, *Welfare and Planning,* New York: John Wiley and Sons, 1966.

Chapters 1–5 provide a fairly rigorous demonstration of the conditions for economic efficiency, and a critique of the performance of the American economy in terms of efficiency, equity, and aggregate stability.

*

PART2

GOVERNMENT EXPENDITURES

THREE

EFFICIENCY AND EQUITY IN THE PUBLIC SECTOR

In the previous chapter we demonstrated several instances in which the private sector fails to achieve certain desirable economic goals. This type of analysis is sufficient to establish a public interest in the provision of various goods and services. By itself, however, interest is not a sufficient basis for public action. The latter is justified only if we are better off as a consequence.

The premise on which this chapter is based is that we cannot merely assume that the government will succeed where the private sector has failed. Government activities should be required to pass the same tests as private ones; namely, whether they move us closer to the goals of efficiency, equity, and stability. If they do not, then it may be better to rely on the private sector, for even though it is imperfect it may be less imperfect than the governmental alternative.

Governments may engage in a wide variety of activities to correct the failures of the private sector. However, the study of public finance traditionally focuses on only two of these: the provision of goods and services through expenditure programs, and the financing of these programs through the collection of revenues—chiefly in the form of taxes. Thus, the primary concern of the discipline is the effect of the size and composition of the government budget on our economic goals.

We begin this chapter by developing the economic criteria by which the budget should be evaluated. Following this, we outline the contours of the ideal budget—i.e., one which fulfills these criteria. Next, we examine the more important ways in which the actual budget diverges from the ideal, and some of the consequences this has for the more detailed appraisal of expenditure programs which occurs in chapters 4–6. The perspective assumed throughout is that of government officials charged with promoting the national interest. Our primary focus, therefore, is on the federal budget.

ECONOMIC WELFARE FOUNDATIONS OF BUDGET EVALUATION

The reader will recall that our evaluation of the private sector was based on criteria developed in the subject of welfare economics. To facilitate the analysis at that stage, however, we paid little attention to the analytical foundations of these criteria, preferring to work instead with operational versions. Because we rely so heavily on these criteria in the analysis which follows, however, it is now necessary to develop them more carefully.

Ideally, the government should allocate expenditures among programs, and finance each program so that its choices effect an improvement in economic welfare. Originally, "economic welfare" was used as a synonym for satisfaction or utility. The goal of expenditure allocation and finance, then, is simply to increase the level of aggregate satisfaction or utility.

If we could measure utility, it would be relatively easy to determine whether a proposed public activity would increase economic welfare. The activity itself would affect both the expenditure and revenue sides of the budget. The expenditure effect would be a source of utility gains to the recipients of the goods or services provided; the revenue effect would produce utility losses attributable to the private goods and services that taxpayers must forgo. If the total gains exceeded the total losses, there would be a net gain in aggregate utility, and provision of the proposed activity would produce an improvement in economic welfare.

Unfortunately, we have no way of measuring changes in utility. This forces us to rely upon tests which assume that people are able to determine only whether one situation affords *more* or *less* utility than another, but that the *amount* of the difference (in terms of utility) cannot be discovered. Two tests built upon this foundation have been proposed: the Pareto Improvement Criterion and the Potential Pareto Improvement Criterion.

EFFICIENCY CRITERIA

According to the Pareto Improvement Criterion, a change in some public budget activity produces an increase in economic welfare if no one loses (is placed in a less preferred position) by virtue of the change, and at least one individual gains (is placed in a more preferred position). In situations where no one loses and some persons gain, it makes no difference whether utility is measurable or not because there is no need to compare the effects on individuals.

This criterion would probably not command unanimous consent because changes in accordance with it could produce wide disparities in the distribution of total utility and the underlying distribution of income and commodities. However, there is little need to explore this shortcoming further because the criterion is largely non-operational. Few, if any, potential changes in resource allocation would not make some people worse off. Surely, all changes in the public budget produce both gains (to recipients of program outputs) and losses (to taxpayers), and the gainers are rarely synonymous with the losers.

In recognition of the limited applicability of the Pareto Improvement Criterion, some economists have suggested the employment of a less restrictive version: the *Potential* Pareto Improvement Criterion. According to this test, an increase in welfare pursuant to a change in allocation exists if the losers could be fully compensated by a transfer to them of *some,* but not all, of the gains. The criterion is a "potential" test because the transfer from gainers to losers need not occur; it is sufficient that it *could* occur. However, if the transfer was effected, no one would lose and the change would constitute a Pareto Improvement.

It is easy to see that this criterion, if operational, could serve as a test in those situations where the Pareto Improvement Criterion cannot. The potential compensation test is operational, however, only if a way can be found to measure gains and losses. Obviously, utility measures cannot be considered. Programs produce physical units of output, but measures of losses or gains in terms of such units would be relatively useless for comparing programs with outputs of different kinds—the usual situation.

The measuring rod that is most commonly used is money. Dollar values of gains and losses can at least be estimated, unlike utility measures. Moreover, the valuation of program outputs in money terms makes comparisons between programs with different outputs possible. However, a money measure of gains and losses is not a sufficient basis for evaluating the effects of budget changes on economic welfare.

Ideally, gain measured in dollars is equivalent to the amount of money people are willing to pay rather than going without the output of some program. Similarly, the dollar value of losses equals the amount people are willing to pay for the alternatives sacrificed to provide this output. The former serves as an index of utility gains; the latter, of utility losses. If the index of gains exceeds the index of losses, the program is considered *efficient.*

EQUITY CONSIDERATIONS

This efficiency test has some weaknesses, however. First, it implicitly assumes a one-to-one relationship between increases in money gains or losses and corresponding gains or losses in utility. Thus, if a program increases the value of aggregate net money gains (gains minus losses) by 10%, it is assumed to increase aggregate utility by 10%. This implies that the marginal utility of income (change in total utility/change in income) is constant, or that a dollar yields the same utility regardless of an individual's income. It follows, then, that a program which provided gains solely to the very rich, and was financed solely by the very poor, would be adopted as long as the money value of the gains exceeded the money value of the losses.

Surely, a large number of individuals would object to this choice; some on the grounds that it widens existing disparities in the distribution of income, others because they believe that an extra dollar yields more satisfaction to a poor individual than it does to a rich individual (thus, they assume implicitly that the marginal utility of income declines as income increases). The example chosen is extreme, but the point it makes should be clear: there is a great deal of social concern about *who gets* the gains of public programs and *who pays* the costs or suffers the losses. In the more general case, some assurance must be provided that the distribution of gains and losses does not worsen the distribution of income. The efficiency test is not sufficient; programs must also be evaluated according to their effect on income distribution.

Another way to view the issue is to recognize that if compensation is not paid by redistributing part of efficiency gains, acceptance of a project solely because it is efficient also implies acceptance of the existing distribution of income. This is due to the fact that the amount that individuals are willing to pay depends, in part, upon their ability to pay; this depends, in turn, on the underlying distribution of income. The discussion in Chapter 2, however, indicates that the existing distribution of income is not necessarily optimal. Thus, there may actually be a public interest in promoting projects which distribute their gains and losses so as to *correct* the existing distribution. Again, the efficiency test constitutes an insufficient basis for program choice.

Given that we must, for all practical purposes, rely on money measures of gains and losses, the effect of a program on economic welfare can be determined only by a consideration of its effect on both economic efficiency and the distribution of income. Having settled the issue of which criteria are appropriate, however, merely evokes additional questions: what constitutes a gain or loss in terms of income distribution, and how can efficiency and distribution effects be combined to formulate a judgment about the desirability of government programs?

THE EFFICIENCY CRITERION

The operational version of the efficiency criterion has already been introduced in chapter 2. It is necessary to measure gains as the monetary value of social benefits, regardless of who receives them, and to measure losses as the monetary value of social costs, regardless of who pays them. Any government program which produces total social benefits (TSB) in excess of total social costs (TSC) passes the efficiency test. If the marginal social benefits (MSB) just equal the marginal social costs (MSC) of the program, it is of optimally efficient size.

The efficiency criterion which applies to public programs is identical, then, to the one which applies to private goods. It is somewhat easier to apply the criterion to private goods, however, because product and resource prices established in private markets provide considerable information about the benefits and costs attributable to these goods. Government programs, on the other hand, commonly provide outputs that are not sold, or that are sold at a nominal price (below marginal costs of provision), making it difficult to estimate gains, or benefits. Moreover, government programs are financed by taxes, which in turn are not necessarily a good estimate of the value of losses, or costs.

SOCIAL BENEFITS

For private goods, the relevant measure of efficiency benefits is the appropriate area under the marginal social benefit or demand curve. This area includes MSB for all units of output where MSB $\geq$ MSC.

The same measure is valid for publicly-provided goods as well. We are not accustomed to thinking in terms of demand curves for such goods, however, because they are often distributed free of direct charge; even where charges are collected, the goods are not sold in a free-exchange context. Without the prices and quantities that normally would be determined by the exchange mechanism, MSB is harder to estimate and the efficient level of output is more difficult to establish.

One reason why the social benefits of public goods are difficult to estimate is that a high incidence of spillover or external benefits exists as a result of their provision. That such externalities are present is hardly surprising, in view of the fact that this is a primary economic rationale for public provision. However, spillover benefits are difficult to measure, precisely because they are not marketable, and public provision does not alter this characteristic. Difficulties in measurement vary, of course, depending on the good or service involved. At the easy end of the spectrum, for example, are recreation benefits provided by reservoirs designed for flood control, water supply, or electric power generation. At the opposite end is national defense, where all benefits are external. In between lie cases like public health and education, both of which provide some benefits enjoyed by persons other than the direct recipients of the public service.

We will have more to say in subsequent chapters about the problems of estimating spillover benefits. The national defense case is examined in Chapter 4, while Chapter 5 develops some examples from natural resource and transportation programs.

Even the benefits to direct recipients of publicly-provided goods are difficult to estimate. In many cases, because outputs are not sold, considerable ingenuity must be used to define and evaluate some proxy variable or variables. Some examples should clarify what is required.

Education is a good that is often provided publicly at zero or nominal prices. To estimate the benefits of education, economists cannot rely on market data. Instead, they measure the value of increased lifetime earnings attributable to additional schooling, and use this value as one index of benefits.

Irrigation water from public reservoirs is often sold at nominal prices. Again, economists cannot rely on market data for benefit estimation. Instead, they view irrigation water as an input in the production of agricultural crops, and estimate the increase in the value of crops produced with the aid of irrigation, as a proxy for benefits of public irrigation projects.

Highway services are often provided free of direct charge. In this instance, benefits of a new or improved highway are estimated as the sum of: (1) transportation cost-savings to individual, commercial, and government users; (2) the value of travel time saved; (3) the value of lives saved; and (4) the value of the reduced incidence of injuries.

In each of the above cases the economist is trying to measure the amount people are willing to pay to avoid having to go without something. Thus, increased lifetime earnings serve as benefits for education because it seems reasonable to infer that people would be willing to pay these earnings rather than go without the education. Similarly, the increased value of agricultural crops can be inferred to be the upper limit of the amount that would be paid for irrigation water. Such is also the case for the benefits of a new or improved highway. It follows, then, that these are really estimates of areas under demand curves, because the upper limit of any such curve is established by the maximum amounts that people are willing to pay.

We will return to this notion of demand for publicly-provided goods later in the context of examining particular expenditure programs. For now, we merely wanted to emphasize that the link established earlier between demand and marginal social benefits also holds for public sector goods.

SOCIAL COSTS

The task of measuring social costs appears to be much easier. In order to provide public sector goods, it is necessary to purchase resources and produced outputs, largely from the private sector. Government expenditures, then, serve as the counterpart of cost outlays for business firms. They are like the latter in the sense that objective data is available for their estimation. However, they also share some of the faults of cost outlays as indexes of benefits forgone.

Like private sector costs, government expenditures are true indicators of social costs only if prices of purchased inputs are determined in reasonably competitive markets. Ideally, outlays in both sectors should be adjusted by anyone seeking measures of social costs at any time during which the price of an input differs from the value of its marginal product. However, assuming that both sectors draw from the same pool of inputs, failure to make this adjustment may not seriously bias the choice between public and private programs. A similar conclusion follows for the choice between government programs, if the same premise holds for the public sector alone.

Another imperfection shared by the two sectors is the generation of external costs. Publicly-owned utilities pollute watercourses and airsheds; public expressways generate congestion and air pollution; public timber harvesting has adverse effects on downstream communities or on other users of the national forests. If the government is going to redress the social losses created by private spillovers, then surely it must take its own external costs into account and add them to money outlays when estimating social costs. Failure to do this may result in inefficiently large public expenditures for programs which produce these spillovers.

A further important problem remains which is *not* common to both sectors. The manner in which programs are financed in the public sector may produce a difference between expenditures and social costs. Expenditures are financed largely by taxes, so tax revenues serve as a first approximation of social costs. However, taxes themselves may produce extra social costs by altering consumption, work, and investment choices. If an excise tax induces people to choose less preferred combinations of goods, there is a utility loss over and above the one represented by receipts from this tax. If an income tax induces people to work less, there is a loss in output which exceeds the value of taxes collected. If a tax on corporate profits changes the size and/or composition of investment expenditures, social losses also exceed tax revenues. Care must be exercised, then, in using taxes as a proxy for social costs. Often, taxes used to finance a program underestimate the program's social costs. We will explore this theme more fully in Chapter 7.

THE DISTRIBUTION CRITERION

The nature of the efficiency objective is clear; namely, to allocate resources among various activities, public or private, such that the difference between total social benefits and total social costs (for all activities combined) is maximized. It is not easy to achieve this, nor to estimate the relevant benefits and costs. However, we do know the target at which we are aiming.

This is not the case for the distribution objective. There is no widespread agreement on the nature of the most preferred distribution. Without a clearly defined distribution target, it is difficult to determine whether various programs produce a better distribution. With such a target it would be possible to weight benefits and costs according to who received or paid them. Suppose, for example, that the appropriate target was equality in the distribution of family income (with some adjustment for differences in family size). In this case, benefits received by families with incomes above the average would have smaller weights than those received by families whose incomes were below average. Similarly, costs paid by families with below average incomes would be given larger weights in program evaluation than the ones given to costs paid by above average income families.

The fact that we do not have a clearly defined distribution objective is not a very good excuse for ignoring the distribution effects of public programs. Such a position merely serves to perpetuate the existing distribution, and it ignores the nature of political reality: programs will be adopted that will affect distribution in any case. Some of the resources of economics should be devoted, then, to the search for the socially preferred distribution.

Nineteenth and early twentieth century economists believed that the best distribution was the one which maximized total social utility. Given this criterion, redistribution of income was appropriate as long as the increase in utility of the "recipients" exceeded the loss in utility of the "donors." By the 1940s, however, there was widespread agreement among economists that this approach was non-operational, and it was abandoned.

Distribution issues did not command much attention in economics from 1940 until well into the 1960s. This was a time during which the major concerns were those of unemployment and economic growth. However, the question of distribution emerged late in this period as a political issue and, somewhat belatedly, sparked renewed interest in the question of what constitutes the best distribution.

In recent years, two approaches to determining the best distribution have been widely discussed. One suggests that this distribution could be discovered by studying past decisions on taxes and expenditures made by the federal government; i.e., the appropriate distribution could be inferred from the results of the political process. The other suggests that the best distribution would be defined in the process of establishing a social contract. All we would have to do in this case would be to determine the conditions under which the contract would be made, and deduce from those the distribution criterion.

POLITICALLY-DETERMINED WEIGHTS

The basis for the first approach is the undeniable fact that governments have made many tax and expenditure decisions in the past for the purpose of providing differential support to various segments of the population. According to this view, the existence of non-proportional tax rate schedules may imply a social judgment that the marginal utility of income is not the same at all income levels. In addition, many expenditure programs have been tailored to provide benefits to various income, age, and racial groups, and to certain geographic areas. Even public regulatory and subsidy programs have been designed to aid particular groups. The hope is that careful study of a meaningful sample of tax, expenditure, and regulatory programs will reveal the relative importance implicitly attached by government decision-makers to the welfare of various groups, and that indicators of relative importance can be constructed and used as weights in evaluating new programs.

That a weighting system was implicit in past decisions cannot be denied. It will not be discovered easily; more is involved than determining only, for example, the marginal utility schedule implicit in the individual income tax. If we can ever obtain reliable results, they may be useful as predictive tools; provided, of course, that the underlying decision model is stable. Many economists do not believe, however, that the results would have very compelling normative significance.

If we accept the individualistic theory of the social interest, then the implicit weights of the political process must faithfully reflect individual distributional preferences. We probably cannot determine the exact degree to which this requirement is met, but there is reasonable doubt that the fit would be close. One reason for this is the fact that abundant evidence exists that political choices are often influenced strongly by narrow, special interests whose support is more important to success at the polls than the support of the electorate at large. If this is true, then using the set of weights implicit in past decisions to evaluate future programs would merely perpetuate the power of these special interests.

Moreover, even if we could be sure that individual preferences were faithfully represented, government could still make mistakes. Indeed, there is growing evidence that many programs designed to achieve some distribution objectives actually have failed to do so. Charles L. Schultze has documented such a failure for the farm price-support program; Burton A. Weisbrood and W. Lee Hansen have done so for higher education; as have M. Mason Gaffney for navigation projects, A. Myrick Freeman for reclamation programs, R. W. Bahl and J. J. Warford for federal aid, and Bruce Stuart for Medicare and family assistance programs.[1] We would certainly

---

1. Charles L. Schultze, *The Distribution of Farm Subsidies* (Washington: Brookings), 1971; W. L. Hansen and B. A. Weisbrod, "The Distribution of Costs and Direct Benefits of Public

not want to repeat these errors by incorporating them into program evaluation techniques.

Finally, the important objection has been raised that political decisions are highly unlikely to be stable over time. Indeed, they reflect to a great extent the philosophy of the party in power. These philosophies may perfectly reflect the electorate's preferences at the time, though this too is doubtful, but they are hardly the stuff from which an enduring approach to the distribution question can be built. It is hard to escape the conclusion that the distributional weights inferred from past decisions are unlikely to constitute the elements of the best distribution. On the other hand, research along these lines may reveal that the implicit weighting system is not one that "society" would approve, and that is surely worth knowing.

SOCIAL CONTRACT WEIGHTS

In recent years, considerable excitement has been generated by an approach to determining the appropriate distribution objective which uses the social contract paradigm usually associated with the political philosopher Jean-Jacques Rousseau. The approach is due to John Rawls, whose work suggests that the proper distribution is the one individuals would agree upon in a hypothetical situation, called the "original position," in which they choose the shape of the future society into which they will agree to enter.[2] Each individual is assumed to make his/her choices rationally, with the understanding that he/she must live with the chosen institutions. However, the individual chooses behind a "veil of ignorance" which prevents him/her from knowing his/her future position in life; i.e., rich or poor, ruler or subject.

Higher Education: The Case of California," *Journal of Human Resources* Vol. IV, Spring, 1969; M. Mason Gaffney, "The Water Giveaway," in R. Haveman and R. Hamrin, eds. *The Political Economy of Federal Policy* (New York: Harper and Row), 1973; A. M. Freeman III, "Six Federal Reclamation Projects and the Distribution of Income," *Water Resources Research,* Vol. 3, No. 2, 1967, pp. 319–332; R. W. Bahl and J. J. Warford, "Real and Monetary Dimensions of Federal Aid to States," in K. Boulding and M. Pfaff, eds. *Redistribution to the Rich and the Poor* (Belmont, CA: Wadsworth), 1972, pp. 116–130; B. C. Stuart, "The Impact of Medicaid on Interstate Income Differentials," *ibid.,* pp. 149–168.

2. John Rawls. *A Theory of Justice* (Cambridge, Mass.: The Belknap Press of the Harvard University Press), 1971.

In this position, Rawls argues that individuals would choose certain principles of justice. One of these would govern the shape of the income distribution; namely, that economic inequality is permissible only if it is to the "greatest expected benefit of the least advantaged member" of society. Rawls argues that this principle will be adopted because individuals are very adverse to risk; hence, they will chose to maximize the minimum, or worst possible, outcome. Thus, if one does achieve the worst outcome, he/she avoids the worse possible disaster. In game theory, this is known as the maximin rule for choice under uncertainty.

Although it is possible for some degree of inequality to exist in this situation—if, for example, inequality produces a larger amount for the least advantaged—the maximin equity criterion probably requires a relatively equal distribution of income. Certainly, it would seem to require greater equality than we currently have. It needs to be emphasized, however, that the Rawls approach cannot specify an exact ideal distribution without more information on the degree of risk aversion or the distribution of probable outcomes.

Many economists have been attracted to the Rawls approach by its procedures if not by its results. It appears to be a fair game. However, it is not altogether clear, some argue, that people would be as eager to adopt the maximin criterion as Rawls' results require. Empirical evidence indicates that lotteries which do not maximize the minimum prize are quite viable; people are willing to risk a little for a small chance at a large prize. Moreover, critics point out that it will not be easy to verify increases or decreases in the position of the least advantaged groups, especially where possible arrangements of social output are numerous and opinions conflict, short of measuring the utility of each affected group. It is conceivable that many of the objections raised to economists' procedures for defining the distribution objective will be answered by subsequent research. At this time, we have not succeeded in our quest for a distribution criterion that can help us to resolve all issues that may arise. Until we achieve such a lofty goal, however, it is necessary to develop some type of strategy that will help us to avoid serious mistakes in program choice.

INTEGRATING EFFICIENCY AND DISTRIBUTION

Given their inability to specify the contours of the ideal distribution function, economists have assumed several different positions on the appropriate treatment of distribution effects. Some believe that estimates of benefits and costs should merely be supplemented with information on how these totals are divided among relevant population groups, leaving it up to government decision-makers to weight the effects on each group. This procedure has been criticized by others, however, on the grounds that the political process does not necessarily produce a weighting system consistent with individual preferences.

A second approach is one we have alluded to earlier: design one set of tax and expenditure programs to achieve efficiency, and another set to achieve the ideal distribution. This is the approach championed by Richard Musgrave, who suggests that the budget be divided into separate branches to facilitate such a solution.[3] The allocation branch would be responsible for providing efficient programs, financed by benefit taxes. The distribution branch could secure the appropriate degree of income redistribution by levying allocatively neutral taxes on some groups and transferring the proceeds to others in the form of money payments.

This scheme does appear to provide a way to handle efficiency and distribution effects without integrating them both in some process of program selection. However, it is difficult to design taxes that are truly allocatively—or distributionally—neutral. Moreover, to implement this approach it would still be necessary to trace the incidence of all allocation branch expenditures, to compare the resulting distribution with the ideal distribution, and to offset any undesirable results with taxes or transfers. On close examination, then, the Musgrave scheme is seen to be a device for *integrating* efficiency and distribution effects, rather than for treating them separately.

A third approach is to integrate efficiency and distribution effects on a program-by-program basis, rather than as part of the process of making two separate "budgets" mutually consistent. In this scheme, the government would have to place different weights on dollars of benefits and costs, depending on who receives or bears them. Ideally, these weights would be those prescribed by the optimal distribution objective.

As an example of how this weighting procedure would operate, consider a program for which the value of benefits is $3 million and the value of costs is $1 million, yielding net benefits of $2 million, or a benefit-cost ratio of 3. The distribution of benefits and costs is shown in Table 3-1, in

---

3. Richard Musgrave. *The Theory of Public Finance* (New York: McGraw-Hill, 1959). The Musgrave scheme was introduced in Chapter 1 of this text.

TABLE 3-1   PROGRAM EVALUATION WITH DISTRIBUTION WEIGHTS

(1) Income Class ($)	(2) Weights	(3) Social Benefits	(4) Weighted Social Benefits	(5) Social Costs	(6) Weighted Social Costs
0–9,999	2.0	300,000	600,000	800,000	1,600,000
10,000–19,999	1.0	900,000	900,000	100,000	100,000
20,000 or more	.5	1,800,000	900,000	100,000	50,000
Totals		3,000,000	2,400,000	1,000,000	1,750,000

columns (3) and (5) respectively. Note that benefits tend to be distributed to relatively high income classes, while costs are paid predominantly by lower income families.

Assume that the ideal distribution requires redistribution from rich to poor. The set of weights in column (2) reflects this goal, assigning a value to a dollar of the lowest income class four times that of a dollar of the highest class. When these weights are applied to social benefits and costs, generating the weighted benefits and costs in columns (4) and (6), the net benefits of the project fall from $2 million to $650,000, and the benefit-cost ratio falls from 3 to 1.37. What originally appeared to be an attractive project judged solely by the efficiency criterion appears to be much less attractive when the regressive distribution of costs and benefits is account-ed for. If this kind of calculation were performed for all expenditure alter-natives, those favoring lower income classes would tend to have an advantage.

Although we do not know the ideal set of weights to use for all programs at present, some economists have suggested hat we employ weights that reflect strong social concern about the least advantaged members of soci-ety. One way to do this would be to assign a weight of 1 to the poverty-line income, and larger and smaller weights to incomes below and above this line, respectively. Use of such a scheme would tend to favor those programs which made the largest contribution to reducing poverty, after considering both the benefits and the costs. Unfortunately, it is not easy to agree on the income which should be assigned a value of 1, and it is even more difficult to agree on the weights which should be attached to other in-comes.

However, if weights can be prescribed it is clear that we have a different set of rules for determining the optimal budget than when efficiency is the sole criterion. Under these circumstances, each potential program must be evaluated in terms of both weighted social benefits (WSB) and weighted social costs (WSC). Each program would be of optimal size when marginal WSB (MWSB) equals marginal WSC (MWSC), and be eligible for funding if TWSB > TWSC at that size.

If there is no effective budget constraint, all programs for which total weighted social net benefits (TWSNB, or TWSB-TWSC) equal or exceed zero should be undertaken. If the tax system is relatively fixed, as it commonly is for a given year, and potential tax revenues set the upper limit on available funds, then programs should be ranked according to TWSNB per tax dollar. Programs would then be ranked on the basis of this measure, and chosen for funding by starting with the program that has the largest value and descending through the ranking until available funds are used. In either case, the valuation procedure determines both the total expenditure budget and its composition—i.e., which programs will be undertaken.

In the long run, of course, the tax structure becomes much more malleable, and it is necessary to design an optimal tax structure. This would be difficult to do, undoubtedly, but it is easy to specify the objective of this enterprise; namely, to *minimize* TWSNC.

INTEGRATING EFFICIENCY, DISTRIBUTION, AND STABILIZATION

The budget procedure just described is good, however, only in an economy characterized by full employment, a stable aggregate price level, and an optimal rate of economic growth. If there is inadequate performance in terms of employment, prices, and growth, the budget can be used to improve performance. How can this be done without interfering with the allocative and distribution functions of the budget?

If the problem can be solved merely by increasing or decreasing the full employment surplus (see Chapter 15), the change should be effected solely through changes in tax collections. Ideally, the members of each income group would have their tax bills increased or reduced by the same percentage of their incomes. Changes in expenditures are not usually appropriate under these circumstances, unless they have also passed the appropriate efficiency/equity test. Presumably, if they met this criterion, they would be included in the budget already. If they did not meet this criterion, they should not be included because the losses elsewhere would exceed the expected gains. It should be noted, however, that social costs of public sector expenditures will be somewhat smaller when widespread unemployment prevails; i.e., as long as public programs can tap resources that would otherwise remain idle. Under such circumstances, or course, some expenditure increases are appropriate both on efficiency and stabilization grounds. Such was undoubtedly the case for many increases which occurred during the period between 1930 and 1945.

There are cases, of course, in which stabilization goals cannot be achieved solely by manipulations in the size of the full employment surplus. One such instance is when high unemployment and inflation occur simultaneously. Under these circumstances, a decrease in the surplus could lower unemployment but could also increase the rate of inflation. This is a case in which expenditure changes may be necessary if we are to achieve both lower unemployment and lower prices; for example, personnel training programs may help, as may increased expenditures on antitrust activities. Rational choice in this instance, however, may not require a more sophisticated choice procedure as long as we have a distribution criterion with a weight assigned to an income level of zero.

BUDGET PROCEDURES IN PRACTICE

Our primary goal in this chapter has been to develop the basic principles of rational budgeting. We have established four that seem to be necessary components of the process: (1) to evaluate expenditures, and means of financing expenditures (largely taxes) simultaneously; (2) to choose among expenditures on the basis of total weighted social net benefits; (3) to minimize the total weighted social costs of the revenue system in the long run; and (4) to depend upon tax changes to achieve aggregate stability, unless expenditure changes also pass the total weighted social net benefit test. However, close examination of the federal budget process indicates that it falls far short of fulfilling these requirements.

Although some evaluation takes place in the various agencies and institutions involved in budget determination, the amount falls far short of that which would be necessary to rationalize the choice process in the manner outlined in this chapter. Moreover, certain practices have been developed for coping with the budget process over the years which place effective constraints on the extent to which the principles in this chapter can be implemented. To some degree, of course, these practices may simply reflect rational rules of thumb in the face of uncertainty about budgetary consequences, and the high cost of acquiring the information necessary for successful application of our so-called "rational" procedures.

One practice of long standing is the separate consideration of taxes and expenditures, except when the effect of the total size of the budget on aggregate stability is being examined. This may produce a good budget for stabilization purposes, but it does not aid the cause of efficiency and equity in distribution. It is difficult to determine in which direction this practice biases expenditures; i.e., whether the budget is supra- or sub-optimal in size. However, there is evidence that Congress designs many expenditure programs to serve a smaller clientele than the one which pays for the program. If so, there is a presumption of excessive spending because this practice tends to diffuse the costs, and the opposition to expenditure programs, while concentrating the benefits and solidifying support.

Deviations from an optimal budget should be expected for many additional reasons, not the least of which is that federal budget-makers appear to have different objectives in mind than do welfare economists. Instead of economic welfare and stability, Congress and the executive branch appear to think primarily in terms of the budget's effect on national defense, stability, and distribution, and only secondarily of its effect on efficiency. Moreover, they appear to establish priorities among these objectives.

The establishment of priorities among objectives tends to promote the use of various tax and expenditure policies which achieve the top priority objective, or objectives, but which conflict with the achievement of lower-ranked objectives. In the ideal budgetary process there is no ranking of objectives, and policies are chosen which reduce conflicts among objectives. In periods when stability is the major concern, however, Congress often uses expenditure variations as a stabilization tool. Similarly, when distribution becomes most important, programs are adopted which may conflict seriously with efficiency; or when national defense is preeminent, cuts are often made in the non-defense budget without consideration of the effect on economic welfare.

The practice of establishing priorities among goals, coupled with shifts induced in these priorities by conditions external to government, has led to the development of de facto separate budgets within the overall budget. Discussion does not revolve about "the" budget, but about its most important components. Two of these can be easily identified by the objectives they are intended to serve; the defense and distribution "sub-budgets." Much of what remains is accounted for by transportation, natural resources, and agricultural programs. We call this the "social overhead capital" sub-budget because of its emphasis on the provision of items which promote the everyday operation and long-run growth of the private sector.

The most important result of this development of sub-budgets from the point of view established in this chapter is that programs within each budget tend to be insulated from direct comparisons with programs in the other sub-budgets. Indeed, separate criteria seem to have been developed for each division, so that the common metric required for rational comparisons across agencies and programs is missing. Moreover, the criteria used are often non-economic ones; the size of the defense budget, for example, is determined largely by military-political considerations.

The actual budgetary process is quite different, then, from the one envisioned for implementing the principles of rational budget determination. There is good reason to believe, also, that the actual process is a relatively stable one. For the purpose of doing further analysis, we accept, then, the basic facts of budget reality; namely, that expenditure program decisions will be determined exclusive of tax considerations; that the total size of the budget is determined largely independently of its composition; and that expenditure decisions are not based solely on the weighted net benefit criterion.

In the next three chapters we divide the federal budget into the three sub-budgets suggested above: defense, social overhead capital, and distribution. In each chapter we analyze the way in which expenditure decisions are made, and evaluate some of the contributions that economics has made and can make to produce better decisions.

SUMMARY

To achieve maximum economic welfare, government programs, as well as private, should promote greater efficiency and equity. As with private goods, this requires the adoption of programs only if TWSB> TWSC, and their expansion to the level at which MWSB = MWSC.

It is more difficult, however, to estimate the social benefits and costs of government programs than it is to estimate the revenues or costs of privately-supplied products. Few government programs produce outputs that are sold at market clearing prices, thus complicating the task of benefit estimation. Moreover, most government programs are financed by taxes, which may produce social costs greater than the amount collected. This factor, alone, makes it more difficult to estimate the true social costs of government programs than it is to estimate the social costs of private goods.

A task of even greater difficulty, however, is that of determining the contours of the ideal distribution. Two approaches to the problem have been suggested in recent years. The first method is to discover the distribution implicit in government expenditure and tax decisions. The second approach is to deduce the ideal distribution from certain principles governing the social contract among individuals. Neither approach is free of conceptual problems, and neither has succeeded in providing an operational version of the proper distribution.

As mentioned several times, the distribution and efficiency effects of government programs must be combined to determine the over-all effect of government activity on economic welfare. Ideally, this could be achieved by weighting benefits and costs according to who receives or pays them. This can be done, however, only *after* we reach agreement on the dimensions of the proper distribution.

Because the budget *is* used to achieve not only efficiency and equity, but also full employment, a stable price level, and optimal economic growth, it is necessary in reality to plan simultaneously for the effects of the budget on all of these social goals. Although it is theoretically possible to design a budget that is mutually consistent in this regard, it is almost impossible to do so in practice. In fact, various institutional features of the budgetary process virtually assure that such a lofty goal will not be achieved.

SUGGESTIONS FOR FURTHER READING

Dasgupta, A. K. and Pearce, D. W., *Cost-Benefit Analysis: Theory and Practice,* London: Macmillan, 1972.

The first half of this chapter is based on propositions developed in the field of applied welfare economics. The serious reader could learn more about them by reading the first three chapters in Dasgupta and Pearce.

Dorfman, Robert and Dorfman, Nancy, Eds., *Economics of the Environment,* 2nd Ed., New York: W. W. Norton, 1977, pp. 1–37.

Although designed to provide a framework for evaluating environmental policy, the introductory essay by the editors of this volume is an excellent discussion of the rules which should guide public authorities seeking to achieve an increase in economic welfare.

Thurow, Lester C., "Toward a Definition of Economic Justice," *The Public Interest,* No. 31 (Spring, 1973), pp. 56–80.

This essay is one of the few modern attempts to specify the dimensions of economic equity. The interested reader will also want to consult the comments on this essay in the Fall, 1973 edition of the same journal by Richard Posner and the reply by Thurow.

FOUR

EXPENDITURES FOR NATIONAL DEFENSE

Traditionally, economics has recognized the provision of national defense as a legitimate and necessary function of government in a market economy. Economic analysis of the military budget is a relatively recent phenomenon, however. This is more than mildly surprising, given the large amount of resources devoted to this component of federal expenditures.

This neglect is undoubtedly due, in large measure, to our inability to do in practice what we can do in theory; namely, specify the optimal level of expenditures for a pure public good. Because of this, economists have tended to accept the prevailing budget as one consistent with, and justified by, national security objectives. Events of recent years, however, have made it clear that these objectives are important matters for debate, and that changes in them may have significant budgetary and economic consequences. Moreover, there is growing recognition among economists that given objectives can be achieved in a variety of ways, many of which differ in terms of their consequences for efficiency and equity.

The new view of the military budget, therefore, is that it is a document with profound implications for the economy, and that it can conceivably be altered to fulfill more substantially both our military and economic objectives. It is this view which guides our analysis in this chapter. We begin by establishing the basic contours of the defense budget—its overall size in relation to the total budget and to the national output. Following that, we demonstrate why it is not possible to specify the economically optimal budget for national defense. We turn next to the issue of how the budget *is* determined, and specify some of the inefficiencies that appear to be created by this decision process. The chapter concludes with an analysis of alternatives for achieving greater efficiency in military expenditures.

THE COST OF NATIONAL SECURITY

Total federal outlays for military and non-military purposes were $361.3 billion in fiscal year 1976. How much of this is attributable to national security? How important are these expenditures relative to other government expenditures? Are expenditures for military purposes an accurate index of the social opportunity costs of national defense? The answers to these questions are not as easy to determine as one might think. However, it is useful to begin by examining the information contained in the budget of the federal government.

THE SIZE OF THE DEFENSE BUDGET

The major component of expenditures for national defense is the budget of the Department of Defense (DOD). The total *obligational authority* (the amount authorized by Congress) and *outlays* (the amount actually spent) by this department for selected fiscal years are shown in Table 4-1. Given the estimate of total federal outlays mentioned above, the DOD budget accounted for 25.7% of this total in 1976.

Whether measured in terms of outlays or obligational authority, the size of the DOD budget indicates a significant commitment of resources to national security. However, this amount alone is undoubtedly an *understatement* of defense expenditures. The primary reason for this is that many expenditure programs not administered by DOD should be credited to the defense account and are not. This fact is partially recognized in the federal budget where some items are listed with the DOD budget in the defense category; namely, atomic energy, the stockpiling of strategic and critical materials, the expansion of defense production, and emergency preparedness activities. However, a number of programs which are not so identified also make a direct contribution, in whole or in part, to national security, or probably would not be undertaken if not required for this purpose. In

TABLE 4–1   DEPARTMENT OF DEFENSE BUDGET, BY COMPONENT
Selected Fiscal Years, 1965–1976

Component	Actual		Estimated	
Total obligational authority (in billions of 1976 dollars)	1965	1968	1975	1976
General Purpose Forces	67.9	69.8	66.0	72.3
Strategic Nuclear Forces	30.6	28.4	18.5	18.0
Mobility Forces	4.5	4.7	2.8	3.8
Retired Pay	2.9	3.9	6.6	6.9
Incremental Cost of Vietnam War	1.6	38.4	1.5	1.4
Support of Other Nations	2.3	1.5	1.6	1.9
Allowance for Petroleum Reserves				.2
Total Authority	109.8	146.7	96.9	104.7
Total Outlays (1976 dollars)	100.0	148.8	93.2	92.8

SOURCE: Table 4–1 in B. Blechman, E. Gramlich and R. Hartman, *Setting National Priorities: the 1976 Budget* (Washington: Brookings, 1975), p. 91.

this category are outlays for the Coast Guard, veterans' programs, the Department of State, the U.S. Information Agency, the Arms Control and Disarmament Agency, the National Aeronautics and Space Administration, the National Security Council, and interest on the national debt. In addition, portions of other programs have also been justified in the past as "essential to national security": among these are included the oil import program, maritime subsidies, impacted areas school aid, the national defense highway system, and airport subsidies.

Experts differ on the question of whether all of the above should be considered as expenditures primarily for defense, but there appears to be considerable support for including the bulk of outlays for international affairs, space and technology, veterans' benefits and services, and interest on the national debt in this category. Each of these, it can be argued, is due primarily to current or future military requirements, or has been incurred as an obligation of past wars.

In our judgment, expenditures which fulfill any of the following criteria should be considered a part of the costs of national defense:

1. total outlays of the DOD for military purposes;
2. outlays which directly support defense programs, regardless of which agency administers them;

3. outlays of all other programs justified on the grounds of national security; and

4. all payments for past wars or military programs.

Only when all expenditures which fulfill these criteria are accounted for will we know the full costs of national security, as reflected in federal budgetary outlays, and will we be able to exercise effective control over the defense "budget."

As a very rough indication of the difference such an accounting could make, we have developed a national security budget for fiscal year 1976 from data readily available in secondary sources. This budget, outlined in Table 4-2, is approximately 48% larger than the budget of the DOD alone (measured in terms of outlays). Surely this is a large enough difference to warrant the development of improved methods of accounting for national security expenditures.

To a large extent, of course, the proper content of the defense budget is determined by the choices facing decision-makers. Since payments for veterans' programs are determined largely by past legislation, the comprehensive version of the budget is an overstatement of the outlays subject to choice in the shortrun. However, the comprehensive budget provides a better indication of what we need to pay for in terms of future expendi-

TABLE 4–2   NATIONAL SECURITY BUDGET
BY MAJOR CATEGORY, FISCAL YEAR 1976
(Amounts in billions of 1976 dollars)

Department of Defense	92.8
International Affairs[a]	4.1
Space and Technology[b]	3.1
Veterans Benefits and Services	15.6
Interest on Nation Debt[c]	19.6
Total	135.2

SOURCE: Derived from data in B. Blechman, E. Gram-lich and R. Hartman, *Setting National Priorities: the 1976 Budget* (Washington: Brookings, 1975), p. 691.

a. equals two-thirds of expenditures for international affairs

b. equals two-thirds of general science, space and technology expenditures

c. equals three-fourths of total interest payments.

tures. This is especially important, in view of the fact that a large portion of the financial cost of war is incurred after the conflict ceases, in the form of veterans' programs and interest on war-related government borrowing.[1]

Suppose that we adopt the narrow measure of defense expenditures used in the federal budget (largely, outlays for the DOD and international affairs). How important are defense expenditures in a relative sense? The answer, again, is not straightforward, for it depends on the benchmarks used for making comparisons.

Over the period 1965–1976, DOD obligational authority grew from $50.7 to $105.7 billion, measured in current dollars. However, when these figures are converted to constant 1976 dollars, as in Table 4-1, it is clear that defense actually had a smaller absolute claim on resources in 1976 than it did eleven years earlier. Real spending for defense activities actually declined over this period by $5.1 billion ($109.8 − $104.7 billion).

Because the economy continued to grow during this period, the real share of GNP devoted to defense also diminished. The extent to which this occurred can be clearly seen in Table 4-3, where line 5b indicates that the real share of nonrecession (or potential) GNP going to defense and foreign affairs has fallen since 1955 from 11.2% to 4.5%. The data in this table indicates that this decline has been offset to some extent by an increase in federal expenditures for domestic programs. However, the increase in real outlays (adjusted for the increase in the price of federal purchases relative to the increase in the price of private sector purchases) for these programs was not large enough to keep the federal government's share of GNP from falling (line 5).

THE SOCIAL OPPORTUNITY
COST OF DEFENSE

On the basis of the data just presented, it appears that the real opportunity cost of defense has been falling over time; slightly when measured in absolute terms, and significantly when measured in relative terms. What-

---

1. James L. Clayton estimates, in fact, that the ultimate cost of the Vietnam conflict will be at least twice as large as the outlay made during the period 1965–1970. For this estimate, and estimates of the ultimate cost of other wars, see: James L. Clayton, "The Ultimate Cost of the Vietnam Conflict," in R. Haveman and R. Hamrin, eds., *The Political Economy of Federal Policy* (New York: Harper and Row, 1973) pp. 107–111.

TABLE 4-3 FEDERAL EXPENDITURES IN RELATION TO
NONRECESSION GNP, SELECTED FISCAL YEARS, 1955–1977
(Billions of dollars and percent)

	1955	1960	1965	1970	1975	1977*
1. Total Federal Outlays	68.5	92.0	118.4	196.6	324.6	413.7
2. Baseline Budget**	68.5	92.0	118.4	196.6	316.8	399.2
3. Nonrecession GNP	377	507	652	954	1588	1990
4. (2) as Percent of (3)	18.2	18.1	18.1	20.8	19.1	20.1
5. (4) Adjusted for Relative Increase in Price of Federal Purchases	18.2	17.0	16.4	17.5	15.9	15.8
a. Domestic Programs	7.0	7.8	8.7	10.5	11.1	11.3
b. Defense and Foreign Affairs	11.2	9.2	7.7	7.0	4.8	4.5

SOURCES: From Tables 8–2, 8–3, and 8–4 in H. Owen and C.L. Schultz, eds., *Setting National Priorities: the Next Ten Years,* (Washington: Brookings, 1976), pp. 328–332.

* Estimate

**Total Federal outlays less recession-related outlays. (Assumes full employment equals 5 percent. In 1970, full employment was less than 5 percent; hence, recession-related outlays were less than baseline level)

ever the cause, a real change seems to have taken place in national priorities relative to what they were twenty years ago. Arguments over the nation's commitment to national defense often fail to recognize this fact.

Of course, it is not necessarily true that real expenditures are an accurate measure of the real social opportunity costs of national defense. First, there may be costs unaccounted for, in addition to goods and services sacrificed for the defense effort, such as the national *in*security that may have been induced by the escalating race in nuclear weapons. However, even if we restrict the measure to that of real economic costs, expenditure totals may still not be a very accurate index of alternatives forgone. One reason, as noted above, is that other components of the national security budget are not conventionally used in effecting comparisons. Additionally, comparisons are usually made between expenditures and potential GNP, while implicitly assuming that the latter is not affected by the diversion of resources for military purposes.

Some economists challenge this assumption, however, by arguing that military expenditures are not "productive"; that is, they do not create additions to our capacity to produce, as do private expenditures for human and physical capital, or other public expenditures for human and physical capital. Thus, to the extent that resources for defense come from potential private and public capital formation, the rate of growth in potential GNP is lower than it would be otherwise. The loss in GNP attributable to this diminished rate of growth must be added to the defense budget to get an accurate total of the social opportunity costs of national security.

The logic of this position seems sound. However, it is also conceivable that military programs provide social spillover benefits that may offset these costs, in whole or in part. The armed services provide a significant amount of education, both in the classroom and on-the-job, for example, that is later used in civilian occupations by former military personnel. Moreover, new technologies are developed in both the military and space programs that are later transferred to civilian uses. Examples are jet transport aircraft, inexpensive nuclear power technology, miniaturized computer components, and many other electronic developments. Whether in the final analysis the external benefits of defense expenditures are greater than the external costs is a matter at present of pure conjecture. However, it is a subject worthy of a major research effort.

NATIONAL DEFENSE AS A PUBLIC GOOD

Having established some of the absolute and relative dimensions of the defense effort, we turn now to the question of how large it ought to be. This is an extremely easy question for an economist to answer on a purely theoretical basis: the appropriate national defense budget is the one which makes the greatest contribution to economic welfare among all conceivable budgets. It is not easy, however, to develop an actual list of programs to fulfill this criterion. Indeed, for reasons outlined above, it appears to be impossible to define the optimal defense budget in operational terms, using the criteria of welfare economics.

National defense is an example of what economists call a "public good." Such a good confers external benefits impartially on all members of a social unit. If one unit of the good is made available, each individual receives one unit's worth of utility from it without reducing the utility received by any other individual. A good with this characteristic is said to be "non-exclusive," as opposed to private goods whose benefits can be enjoyed exclusively by the owners of the rights prescribed or implied by the titles to the properties in question. If a good is non-exclusive in consumption, as is national defense, the cost of serving an additional individual is zero once the good is provided because no resources have to be used to do so.

A public good is "public," then, because it confers benefits publicly—upon society at large, rather than exclusively upon specific individuals. It is public also because the demand for it must be expressed through the public decision-making process. This point is easy to appreciate where national defense is concerned. The benefits typically accruing to any individual are much smaller than the costs of providing a unit of defense. To provide this unit, then, individual demands must be aggregated. However, this aggregation cannot be achieved by a private market because each individual will understate his/her willingness to pay for benefits received, on the assumption that the good, if provided by others, will be available to him/her. If each person reasons this way (as a "free rider"), effective private demand will be virtually zero. The government must step in, then, and aggregate these preferences to achieve some sort of expression of aggregate demand for national defense, or too little defense will be provided—even though aggregate marginal benefits exceed marginal costs of provision.

Although national defense is available equally to all individuals, it does not follow that individual valuations of this good are also equal. Citizens differ in their preferences between defense and other goods, just as they differ in their preferences between purely private goods. Moreover, there are differences among individuals in terms of the income they have to devote to the purchase of available goods, including defense. Consequently, there is bound to be a wide variety of individual demand curves for this good. It is this variability in individual demands which ultimately makes it impossible for government to define the optimal quantities of defense activities.

To illustrate why this is so, we have constructed a relatively simple example. Suppose, to begin with, that the social unit contains only three individuals, A, B, and C, each of whom understands the public good aspects of national defense; namely, that if it is provided no one can be excluded from "consuming" its benefits. The individuals differ, however, in terms of their willingness to pay for successive units of defense, as indicated by their demand, or marginal benefit, curves in Figure 4-1 (where MB_a, MB_b, and MB_c refer to demand curves for individuals A, B, and C, respectively).

It is assumed further that additional units of national defense can be

FIGURE 4–1
THE EFFICIENT LEVEL OF DEFENSE

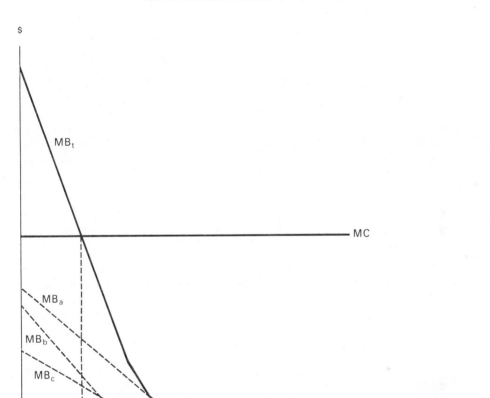

produced at a constant cost per unit; hence, the horizontal marginal cost (MC) curve in Figure 4-1. The diagram indicates, however, that MC exceeds MB for any single individual. Thus, if each individual acts as a "free rider," and marginal benefits are not aggregated into an expression of effective demand, the equilibrium level of national defense will be zero.

Since each unit of protection is available to all three individuals, if it is provided, benefits are aggregated properly by adding the MB received by all three on each unit. In the diagram, this aggregation process yields MB_t, which is the *vertical* addition of the MB curves for each unit of protection. Thus, $MB_t = MB_a + MB_b + MB_c$.

Given the MB_t curve, the efficient quantity of defense is D_e, where MB_t

71

just equals MC. Any level smaller or larger yields smaller total social net benefits from the provision of the good. Expansion from smaller levels provides additional social net benefits because $MB_t > MC$. Contraction from larger levels has the same effect because the saving in costs exceeds the reduction in benefits.

Because the good is being provided publicly, it is necessary to levy taxes in order to pay for its provision. To assure provision at the efficient level, each individual must be charged a tax-price that would just induce him/her to purchase D_e units. Only then is there a coincidence between aggregate efficiency and the level of defense preferred by each individual. However, because each individual's MB is different at D_e, each must be charged a different price; more specifically, a price equal to his/her MB at D_e. Such a pricing scheme would also provide for aggregate collections sufficient to pay for costs of provision in our particular example.

This necessity to levy variable tax payments goes a long way in rendering the model non-operational. Public officials simply do not have, nor could they be expected to acquire (at reasonable cost, at least), the information required to implement such a plan. We already know that individuals have an incentive not to reveal this information voluntarily.

Moreover, even if this information was available at low cost and the model could be implemented, the result would not necessarily be an optimal one. The reason, of course, is that the MB schedule of each individual reflects the prevailing distribution of income, and this distribution may not be the one which is considered socially optimal. Thus, it would be necessary to assign weights to both the marginal benefits and tax-prices of each individual, according to his/her place in the optimal distribution. Not only can this not be done with any precision, but even if it could be it would be due only to sheer coincidence that D_e would be the level yielding maximum total weighted social net benefits.

Where public goods such as national defense are concerned, then, economists are in a peculiar position of knowing the criteria to which the optimal budget should conform, but of being unable to determine the contours of the budget which would accord with these criteria. Decisions do get made without guidance from welfare economics. However, these decisions can often be improved by using other tools of economics. Costs of information are too high to determine the optimum allocation of resources to national defense, but we may be able to determine such matters at relatively reasonable costs if we are moving in the right direction. Such is the spirit which guides the inquiry that follows.

DETERMINANTS OF DEFENSE EXPENDITURES

Before examining the alternatives that have been proposed as means of achieving greater efficiency in defense spending, we need to explore the manner in which these expenditures are formulated. Surely they are not made using the public goods model. How, then, are they made? And in what directions, if any, does this decision process bias expenditures? The fact that a section follows on the means of achieving greater efficiency reveals the conclusion prematurely; namely, that there appears to be an upward bias in total defense expenditures. The reasons for this bias deserve an extended discussion.

Although it strains the analogy a little, it is useful to think of the various determinants of spending as arguments in demand and supply functions, with the final budget representing a rough balance between these two sets of forces. The chief elements on the demand side are the nature of the perceived threat from foreign aggressors, and the basic attitude toward risk held by the key actors in the decision process (the military, Congress, the President, and presidential advisors). The primary element on the supply side is the degree of efficiency attained in using resources to reduce the effect of the expected threat. To a greater extent than is true for private goods, however, there is a possibility that demand and supply are not determined independently.

DEMAND FACTORS

The demand for defense expenditures is based ultimately upon a number of key propositions, some of which are more important than others in terms of their budgetary consequences. Students of international and military affairs perceive two threats to our national security: one is a direct nuclear attack on the U.S., and the other is an attack upon our interests abroad via conventional or nuclear war against our allies. The first threat creates a "need" ("demand") for strategic nuclear forces (SNF), whose combat mission is both to protect against nuclear attack and to deliver a devastating retaliatory blow to any enemy initiating a nuclear attack on the U.S. The second threat creates "demand" for general purpose forces (GPF), whose missions are somewhat broader than those of the SNF. The GPF missions create a "demand," in turn, for various mobility forces (MF).

The demand for GPF is derived from the assumption that protection of our interest requires a "forward defense" strategy of active involvement in the affairs of Europe, the Middle East, and Asia, including the deployment of combat units in these areas and the maintenance of large backup forces at home ticketed for these areas. This strategy is designed to: (1) prevent the expansion of Soviet influence in Europe and the Middle East, and Chinese influence in Asia; (2) deter the use of Soviet or Chinese force in these areas; (3) obviate the necessity of large armed forces in West Germany and Japan; and (4) advance our foreign economic interests. Mobility forces are required simply to transport troops and equipment to these areas in the event of covert or overt hostilities.

The demand for defense spending by the military depends not only upon these general contingencies, but also upon some estimate of the severity of the perceived threat; that is, upon the enemy's degree of hostility, military strength, and expenditures for defense. An additional element of some importance is the probability of the enemy developing new weapon systems. In general, the demand for funds is growing: the larger the number of simultaneous contingencies for which we plan to prepare, the more we view our enemies as implacably hostile, the greater the military expenditures of our enemies, the less we view our adversaries as acting in ways which compensate for our actions, and the less disposed we are to assume risks.

Given these basic parameters, military strategy is then devised to diminish the perceived threat, and this strategy is translated into specific requests for personnel and materials for each of the major combat missions. These missions were identified earlier as general purpose forces (GPF), strategic nuclear forces (SNF), and mobility forces (MF). GPF consist, in turn, of the ground combat forces (GCF), tactical air forces (TAF), and naval general purpose forces (NGPF). Within this latter division are five major combat missions. Their budgets for fiscal year 1975 are outlined in Table 4-4.

Ground combat forces are composed of army and marine battalions whose primary mission is the defense of Europe. Out of 411 active or reserve battalions, 298 were committed to the European theater in fiscal year 1976. The remainder were earmarked largely for Asian contingencies.

The tactical air forces are the air support complements to the ground combat forces. Given their inherently greater mobility, however, their allocation to particular contingencies is not defined as clearly as it is for GCF. About 80% of air force tactical squadrons are justified primarily to cover

European contingencies. Many of these are based in the U.S., however, and they could be deployed elsewhere on short notice. The navy air wing is split evenly between Europe and Asia; two-thirds of the marine squadron is earmarked for Asia.

Naval general purpose forces are split fairly evenly to meet the European and Asian contingencies. Strategic nuclear forces, consisting largely of land and submarine-based missiles, manned bombers, air and missile defense systems, and warning and surveillance systems, are governed almost solely by estimates of the U.S.-Soviet strategic military balance. Finally, mobility forces, consisting largely of long- and medium-range cargo aircraft, are justified primarily to supply the European theater.

The figures in Table 4-4 represent much more, of course, than simply the military's estimates of what it would take to protect the U.S. against the major contingencies that they perceive. Somehow Congress must be persuaded that the threat estimates on which the contingencies are based are genuine, and that existing contingency plans are the most sensible among the available alternatives. Then, too, Congress must be convinced that the programs for which funds are requested are worth the opportunity costs they impose in terms of other public programs or private goods sacrificed. Finally, the figures also reflect supply, or cost, conditions for requested personnel, equipment, and major weapons systems.

TABLE 4–4   ESTIMATED COSTS OF DEFENSE COMBAT MISSIONS, BY CATEGORY, FISCAL YEAR 1976
(Total obligational authority in billions of 1976 dollars)

	GCF[a]	TAF[a]	NGPF[a]	SNF[a]	MF[a]	Totals
1. Major Weapon Systems acquisition	1.7	5.6	5.4	4.4	0.1	17.2
2. Other Investment	5.7	6.5	4.1	4.3	0.8	21.4
3. Direct Operating Costs	10.7	6.2	5.6	4.4	1.5	28.4
4. Indirect Operating Costs	10.6	5.5	4.7	4.9	1.3	27.0
Totals	28.7	23.8	19.8	18.0	3.7	94.0

SOURCE: Calculated from data in Chapter 4 in B. Blechman, E. Gramlich and R. Hartman, *Setting National Priorities: the 1976 Budget* (Washington: Brookings, 1975), pp. 98–121.

a. GCF: Ground Combat Forces; TAF: Tactical Air Forces; NGPF: Naval General Purpose Forces; SNF: Strategic Nuclear Forces; MF: Mobility Forces.

SUPPLY FACTORS AND THE
MILITARY-INDUSTRIAL COMPLEX

In recent years there has been much controversy over whether we are actually spending more than is necessary for these missions. In the next section, we will examine some of the ways which have been proposed to effect savings in the defense budget. In the remainder of this section, however, we examine the possibility that this budget is biased upward.

The factor cited most often as a cause of upward bias is the influence of the so-called Military-Industrial Complex (MIC)—that "conjunction of an immense military establishment and a large arms industry" against which President Eisenhower warned in his farewell address to the nation in 1961. At the core of this "conjunction" presumably lies a unique buyer-seller relationship that generates a mutual interest in a large military establishment among the various parties involved.

The defense scenario developed above generates a demand not only for the traditional items of war, but also for the development and production of sophisticated weapons systems. Lacking a manufacturing and development capability of its own, the military is forced to buy these systems from private producers. This requires the purchase of a large number of products which have not yet been designed and for which production experience is nil. Because of this, the military buys at prices for which there are few precedents and guidelines. It deals with a relatively small number of prime contractors to whom defense business is very important, either to the corporation as a whole or to particular corporate divisions. It confronts powerful sellers in a market where technical capability rather than price is the controlling variable. All of this takes place, moreover, in an atmosphere where uncertainty breeds fear that the enemy will somehow develop their systems first in the absence of an extraordinary American effort. In the process of all this, it is argued, government becomes dependent upon the very institutions it has created.

The other side of the coin is the fact that various powerful groups also become dependent upon the military for sustenance. This dependency, moreover, is spread widely throughout the economy, touching many major industries, labor groups, and Congressional districts. The alleged "complex" is not a conspiracy, then, between merchants of destruction and power-hungry generals, but a natural coalition of interest groups, including the armed forces, industrial contractors, labor unions representing workers in the defense industries, universities which do contract research, and legislators whose constituents depend on military expenditures for their livelihood.

In the face of this powerful coalition, it is argued, the guardians of the public purse are few in number and relatively powerless. The Office of Management and Budget can do little to thwart the designs of this group, and university-based critics can provide little more than interesting intellectual commentary.

Considerable "evidence" has been amassed, largely by journalists, to illustrate the kernel of truth in this characterization. It must be shown, however, that the Military-Industrial Complex (MIC) promotes one or more of the following: (1) exaggeration of the potential threat estimates; (2) inefficiency in the production of defense capabilities; and (3) underestimates of the social opportunity costs of national defense.

Several characterizations of the MIC have been mentioned that presumably produce these effects. First, there is the use of fear. Anything which relates to war, especially wars of annihilation, touches a sensitive public nerve. This sensitivity is played upon easily to generate public support and to gain acceptance of exaggerated budget requests.

Second is the veil of secrecy which shrouds weapons development and intelligence information. The need for defense, it is argued, is exaggerated by those who have access to secret or classified information. Moreover, classification protects inefficiency in arms production by making it more difficult to acquire information on producer performance.

Third, the complexity of weapons systems makes it difficult for outside observers to judge the degree of efficiency attained in production. Indeed, it becomes difficult for the military itself to do this. Obviously, this phenomenon also protects the less efficient manufacturers.

Fourth, there is an absence of countervailing power to oppose or control the MIC. As a result, estimates of costs and threats are not challenged sufficiently. Traditionally, Congress has not been organized to perform this function very well. Moreover, most of the major weapons contracts are not awarded under very competitive bidding. In fact, most development and production is under the primary control of single suppliers, who merely subcontract the development and production of various components of the total system. Such an arrangement is probably inevitable in an environment of complex and uncertain technology.

Fifth, conflicts of interest exist within the MIC which escalate both costs and demand. Those who determine demand (military officials, armed services committees in Congress, defense intellectuals) are in a position, or will be in a position, to benefit from supplying products at high cost. The primary example is afforded by the many (2000 in 1972) one-time high ranking military officers later employed in key executive positions in the defense industry.

Sixth, there is the purported absence of institutional change within the military, which stifles innovation and adaptation. This factor works especially to maintain inefficient utilization of personnel and elevate related costs.

AN UPWARD BIAS IN DEFENSE SPENDING?

This list could probably be lengthened, but the items which appear above are the characteristics of the MIC mentioned most often by critics. To what extent are they descriptively accurate? And, if they are, do they produce an upward bias in defense outlays?

In terms of descriptive accuracy, the most questionable purported characteristics are the fourth and sixth. Regarding the former, it can be argued that there is a considerable amount of public and congressional debate on the development of new major weapons systems. Because it is in the development and production of such systems that the MIC probably has its greatest effect, discussion in the public forum may play an effective countervailing role. In addition, although defense has few countervailing groups with which it must contend directly, it faces stiff competition for federal revenues from other powerful claimants within the executive branch of government.

Some observers would also argue that the characterization of the military as an organization devoid of change is an exaggeration. New methods of planning, budgeting, and procurement have been introduced in the past decade. In addition, accounting procedures have been adopted which promote greater efficiency in internal allocation. The armed services continue to operate "by the book," but the established constraints permit some meaningful variation.

However, even if all the characteristics mentioned above turn out on close examination to be relatively accurate, it is not certain that they would have the *effects* claimed by critics. It is easier, for example, to believe that the MIC has an important effect on supply conditions than it is to believe that it has a significant effect on basic threat estimates. The latter would appear to be subject to military and Congressional influence, but not to the influence of the industrial community. Nor is there any compelling assurance that the MIC will have a significant effect on congressional estimates of the social opportunity costs of national defense.

The reason for this last conclusion is that the characteristics attributed to the MIC are present to some extent in the decision-making processes for all government programs. This is true even for fear and secrecy. We often hear of "crises" in the provision of health care, education, energy, or other goods and services. Appeals based on this emotive terminology should be just as suspect as those based on induced fear of the enemy. A counterpart to fear, or a "scare tactic," is present in the persuasion kits of proponents for many kinds of public programs.

There is also a counterpart to secrecy. For most social programs, information is not classified. However, secrecy per se is not the problem. The problem is that citizens and public decision-makers are not able to acquire all relevant information. Information need not be secret to be difficult to obtain, and very few individuals have relatively complete information on most public programs.

One reason very few people have complete information is that most significant public programs are complex. Military weapons systems have no corner on the market in this regard. We are a long way from using simple delivery systems with simple consequences in the areas of health, education, welfare, and transportation, for example. Similarly, most major public programs lack effective countervailing power to some extent, and conflicts of interest are not rare outside the defense decision process. Finally, when compared to other public agencies, such as those in the areas of health and education, the rate of innovation in the military may compare quite favorably.

The point of all this, of course, is that biases also operate on other government expenditures to increase demand and costs. Because the military must compete with these programs for scarce funds, there is little guarantee, *a priori,* that the MIC is successful in reducing the social opportunity cost of national defense. However, it does not follow automatically that these biases will serve as an effective countervailing force to hold defense expenditures down. It is altogether possible that government spending, in general, is biased upward because special interests can influence the legislative process in a large number of areas.

ALTERNATIVE DEFENSE BUDGETS

In spite of the fact that real defense expenditures have been declining steadily since 1955, many individuals still argue that we are devoting too large a proportion of our national resources to this program. This is the view, of course, of those who subscribe to the belief that we are under the influence of the MIC. One needn't conform with this view to argue that military spending is too high. However, one can also champion an increase in expenditures without serving as a willing or unwilling spokesperson for the MIC. In the first instance, one need only establish cost-savings that could result from changing the basic threat estimate, force structures, personnel utilization, and weapons procurement practices. Only the last of these is related very closely to the MIC issue. In the second instance, individuals totally free of the influence of the MIC can subscribe to the belief that we are not fulfilling minimum security needs, or that we are following improper military strategy, and argue therefore for larger defense budgets.

As mentioned previously, the percentage of real GNP devoted to national defense has declined significantly. In terms of the DOD budget, most of this decline can be explained by a reduction in outlays for strategic nuclear forces. This reduction was based on the belief adopted in the 1960s that total prevention against a nuclear attack is not possible. Consequently, the mission of the SNF switched from that of defense-retaliation to one which emphasized retaliation to a much greater degree—a far less expensive contingency.

PROGRAM BUDGETING IN THE DEPARTMENT OF DEFENSE

At the same time that we were adopting the policy of "mutual assured destruction," a new budget process was introduced in the DOD by then Secretary of Defense Robert McNamara. This process, known as program or performance budgeting, had been employed successfully in private business for years, and prior to McNamara's appointment had been applied to military decisions by analysts at the RAND Corporation.

The intent of program budgeting is to aggregate outlays according to the programs on which they are expended; not, as was the prevailing practice, on the basis of items purchased. Armed with such information, the decision-maker could better compare the costs of alternative programs for achieving the same or similar objectives.

If program budgeting works as intended, it does rationalize decision procedures by facilitating a comparison among alternative courses of action. Moreover, where the military is concerned, it promises to promote the analysis of similar programs offered by different branches of the armed forces. Such programs had always escaped direct quantitative comparison under the old budgeting procedures.

The heart of the program was a Five Year Defense Program, divided into major missions, which cut across the traditional boundaries of the established armed services. Such a division is reflected in Table 4-4. This program projected costs over a five-year period; a considerable improvement over the annual plan it replaced. Within each mission, decisions about force levels were justified in Program Memoranda. Underlying these statements were special studies of alternatives, usually designed to ascertain the least costly ways of achieving given military objectives.

Although viewed with general approval by outside observers, especially by economists, the McNamara experiment was not an unqualified success. However, the Planning-Programming-Budgeting System (PPBS) was well integrated with the decision and budget procedures of the various branches of the military by the time McNamara left the DOD. Has its development reduced the total size of the military budget? Most observers are doubtful that it has. Requests for funds still originate with the various services, based on their estimates of military contingencies. However, the PPBS did make budget constraints more explicit than they previously were, and it probably resulted in the choice of less costly alternatives in many instances.

One additional explanation remains of the decline in defense expenditures over the time period in question. The number of military personnel was reduced significantly, largely as a consequence of changes in commitments to the defense of Asia. However, military pay per individual also increased significantly as the result of the switch from conscription to recruiting on the open market. In fact, the increase in rate of pay due to this factor was great enough to offset most of the reduction in personnel, and the budget for this purpose declined only a small amount.

MORE ECONOMICAL
DEFENSE ALTERNATIVES

Are there further adjustments in the defense budget that can be justified? Currently, only about 30% of the budget appears fixed, with the bulk of this accounted for largely by retired pay and benefits, research and development expenditures, and general support costs. Thus, a relatively high proportion of the defense budget is potentially controllable in the short run. Whether the amount represented by this proportion should be increased or reduced is a matter of intense debate, however.

Those who believe that savings can be affected point to several possible sources. First is the view that we can reduce our expenditures on the SNF without sacrificing our essential security interests. Critics argue that we need not match the Soviet Union in terms of specific weapons systems in order to assure mutual deterrence, and that attempts to do so merely result in excessive force levels, an unjustified pace of weapons modernization, and the development of unproductive military capabilities. They suggest instead that we strive to maintain rough overall parity which, it is argued, is sufficient in its destructive potential to dissuade anyone from ever using nuclear weapons. This can be achieved, according to this group, along with a reduction in existing force levels, slower modernization programs, and a reduction in expenditures for research and development.

Second, some observers believe that significant savings could be made in weapons procurement. The nature of the problem is well-known; major weapons systems frequently end up costing several times the initial estimated cost. Indeed, according to some individuals, this is *the* major consequence of the MIC.

It is generally believed that competition cannot be counted on to force down the costs of major weapons systems. Development and production costs are so high and uncertain that the government must depend on a few contractors who can assemble the necessary technical and production expertise. However, ways to control costs more effectively may exist within these enterprises.

Some experts think that better initial cost estimates could be made. A technique of some promise is the use of independent evaluations of the degree of engineering difficulty likely to be encountered in the tasks assigned, although this device may have to be restricted to cases where the tasks are similar to those performed in non-defense work. However, this would probably effect savings relative to the prevailing practice, which is to base estimates on information submitted by contractors. The latter is bound to be biased to present programs in a favorable light when seeking contracts.

Another view is that the military strives to incorporate technical capabilities in weapons that will rarely be used. Such "gold-plating," it is argued, could also be reduced in design stages, resulting in cost-savings.

Savings could also be achieved through better enforcement of contract provisions combined with a reduction in the willingness of the government to reimburse producers for cost increases not contracted for originally. To accomplish this, it would probably be necessary to change incentives facing military contract officers, who are generally rewarded for system completion and not for saving costs.

Finally, savings are possible by relying on independent analyses from "think-tanks" such as the Institute for Defense Analyses and the Rand Corporation. This source has been tapped extensively by the military, with generally good results. A truly important countervailing force could be created, however, if Congress engaged such aid on a regular basis.

In spite of these possibilities, most observers are more hopeful about achieving savings in personnel costs than they are about reducing the costs of weapons procurement. In fact, given the increasing relative importance of this component of the defense budget, and a high probability that it will continue to grow in importance, there is a great incentive for both military officials and Congress to look carefully for ways to achieve economies in personnel utilization.

One suggestion encountered frequently is the reduction of the ratio of support troops to combat troops, especially in those forces earmarked for Europe. Here, it is argued, we should be prepared for a short war, as the Soviets appear to be, and not for one which would require sustained, long-range staying power. Another suggestion involves the reduction of the number of personnel in the "pipeline"; i.e., those in transit or in training. Both of these changes would increase the number of combat-ready troops and could conceivably permit an overall reduction in force sizes.

Some observers also believe that considerable savings could be effected in the area of military personnel training. The ratio of students to teachers in the military, for example, is far lower than it is in the civilian sector. This suggestion makes good economic sense, of course, only if an increase in this ratio would not result in learning losses with greater value than personnel costs saved.

It has also been argued that savings in the personnel budget could be achieved by reducing the size of domestic support functions; for example, by closing some military bases located in the U.S. Events of the past few years, however, make it clear that it is not easy to persuade Congress that such closures are in the public interest.

Finally, there are those who believe that we can reduce the personnel budget further by changing our Asian strategies. Such a belief is based on the view that our potential influence in this region is relatively slight, and that the Communist Chinese and North Koreans constitute a much smaller threat to our security than we previously imagined. If we subscribe to this new belief, reductions could be made in active and reserve forces ticketed for the Asian contingency.

Of course, not all observers believe that the defense budget should be reduced. The greatest opposition to the proposals outlined above is directed against reducing the capabilities of the strategic nuclear forces. Proponents of more spending in this area argue that we must develop and deploy better nuclear defense systems, which they believe will become necessary as the U.S.S.R. catches up to us in offensive weaponry under the pause afforded by the doctrine of mutual assured destruction ("MAD," to the critics). They argue that it is particularly important to: (1) construct an antiballistic missile system that serves all land-based offensive missile sites; (2) rebuild U.S. air defenses against bomber attacks; and (3) make greater preparation for defense of populated areas.

Almost as much concern is expressed, however, about the adequacy of the on-line strength of our European forces. Although we potentially out-number the Soviets and their allies in both personnel and equipment, a much larger proportion of our force is not combat ready, nor could it be on short notice. Thus, it is argued that greater expenditures are necessary to acquire a force structure that more closely fulfills the required strategy.

Opponents of reduced spending are concerned not only about our prepa-rations in Europe but also about our policies in Asia. Of particular concern is the probable adverse effect of further troop withdrawals from our major allies in this region: Japan, South Korea, and Taiwan. Many observers doubt that we can continue to convince these countries of our commitment to their defense if U.S. presence diminishes.

These, of course, are matters that are far removed from the economist's area of expertise. In fact, given the nature of the debate over the defense budget, it is clear that much of it cannot be influenced directly by econo-mists, even though its resolution has significant implications for the size and composition of the federal budget. Given these circumstances, the economic analyst should perhaps restrict his/her advice to matters that can be resolved by using the traditional tools of program budgeting and sys-tems analysis. As appropriate as this might be for the analyst, however, it is surely not enough for the citizen whose fortunes are tied so closely to the resolution of the larger issues. In the broader arena of allocative deci-sions, these issues prove to be the most significant ones.

SUMMARY

Real expenditures for defense constitute a large but declining portion of both total government expenditures and GNP. Conventionally used measures, however, typically provide an underestimate of the size of our total commitment to national security. Unfortunately, it is not possible at present to provide an accurate estimate of the total social cost of this use of our resources.

It is easy to specify on economic grounds how large our commitment to national defense ought to be. However, it is virtually impossible to estimate the size of this commitment in operational terms, because of the peculiar characteristics of a pure public good, and differences among individual preferences.

Expenditures for defense are not determined, however, by the implementation of economic criteria. Rather, they are the result of a complex political process in which the nature of the perceived threat from foreign aggressors and basic attitudes toward risk play a much larger role than do considerations of efficiency and equity. Basic demands for resources reflect military strategies designed to diminish perceived threats in the possible theatres of future armed conflicts.

Critics have argued that because these demands reflect the preferences of military planners, they are bound to produce inefficiently large defense budgets. Others argue that this tendency is reinforced by factors which produce inefficiency in the provision of goods to the defense establishment, most notably, the influence of the Military-Industrial Complex. However, not all of the arguments and evidence on behalf of this thesis pass close inspection.

Finally, the possibility remains that resources could be saved for other purposes by achieving greater economy in the use of defense expenditures. The Department of Defense first attempted to formalize this process by adopting program budgeting, an experiment of limited success. In recent years, attention has been focused on the possibilities of cutting our Strategic Nuclear Forces, on exercising stricter controls over weapons procurement, on achieving more efficient use of manpower, and on changing our Asian strategies as means of effecting a reduction in the defense budget. However, these alternatives have not been adopted readily by the military, nor pursued vigorously by Congress.

SUGGESTIONS FOR
FURTHER READING

_____, *Setting National Priorities* (author varies), Washington, D.C., The Brookings Institution, 1970–1977 (annual volumes).

Each volume in this annual financed by the Brookings Institution contains one or more chapters on defense expenditure issues. The reader desiring a more informed view of defense alternatives is strongly advised to consult these sources, especially the 1971, 1973, 1976, and 1977 editions.

Melman, Seymour, *Pentagon Capitalism,* New York: McGraw-Hill, 1970.

Melman is one of the leading students of the so-called Military-Industrial Complex. This book is a good review of his thesis that the MIC is an important force in the American economy.

FIVE

EXPENDITURES FOR NATIONAL RESOURCES AND TRANSPORTATION

It is widely known that sustained growth requires the accumulation of a stock of productive capital. Throughout our history, we have relied upon private initiative to provide most of this resource. However, we have been unwilling to rely heavily on the private sector for the provision of some types of capital; most notably, transportation networks and water resource facilities.

In the first part of this chapter, we examine how large our public commitment is to these types of investment. Then we review the reasons why this commitment is considered to be one of the responsibilities of the public rather than the private sector. Following that, we outline procedures that economists favor for evaluating these investments; namely, those which have been developed in the literature of cost-benefit analysis. The chapter concludes with a comparison of actual evaluation procedures to the cost-benefit benchmarks.

EXPENDITURES AND COSTS

Federal, state, and local governments spent approximately $40 billion in fiscal year 1975 for natural resources and transportation.[1] Approximately

---

1. The figures in this paragraph were developed from data in *Survey of Current Business*

$29.5 billion of this total was for transportation, with nearly $15 billion accounted for by state and local units. The remaining $10.5 billion for natural resources was split almost equally between the federal and state-local sectors.

Not all of these expenditures were for investments in physical facilities, nor were all of the natural resource expenditures devoted solely to water resource projects. However, the bulk of highway expenditures was related directly or indirectly to road construction or maintenance, while nearly 60% of natural resource expenditures were for the construction of water resource facilities—including $3 billion for waste treatment plants designed to reduce the level of pollution in the nation's watercourses.

Altogether, then, total government investment in water resource and transportation facilities approached $35 billion in fiscal year 1975. Although this constitutes less than 7% of the combined government budgets, it was equal to nearly 25% of gross private domestic investment. In the broader picture, moreover, the opportunity costs of these expenditures are far from negligible. We could have financed the entire military weapons procurement program with these funds, significantly reduced (perhaps eliminated) the incidence of poverty, or greatly increased the level of private capital formation. In addition, the outlays which did occur were of great importance to particular industries and regions. How these funds are spent is thus a matter of significant social concern.

As was true for national defense, however, expenditures for natural resources and transportation reported in government budgets are not necessarily an accurate index of the social costs of government involvement in these areas. One omission of growing importance concerns the various tax subsidies received by natural resource firms in the private sector, chief among which is the percentage depletion allowance for oil and gas exploration and development. This subsidy exceeded $2 billion in 1974, according to the federal Office of Management and Budget.

The various budgets also fail to record the social opportunity costs of government regulations which affect the extraction, processing, transportation, and consumption of natural resources. Among the more important of these devices are oil pro-rationing, price controls on natural gas, sustained yield-even flow timber harvesting, protective tariffs and import

---

(U.S. Department of Commerce, Office of Business Economics, July, 1976). The total of $40 billion was derived by crediting the federal government only with expenditures in the form of grants to state and local governments.

quotas on various minerals and energy resources, controls on timber exports, and the growing number of regulations to achieve environmental quality. Because we are concerned with investment expenditures in this chapter, an extended discussion of these costs is not appropriate at this time.

A RATIONALE FOR GOVERNMENT ACTIVITY

The private sector invests a large amount in both natural resource development and transportation. However, certain types of projects in these areas are financed largely by governments; namely, highways, airports, water transportation routes, irrigation and reclamation projects, hydroelectric dams, and flood control facilities. Surely this practice reflects the operation of political forces to some degree; it can be justified, however, on the basis of the potential for inefficiency and inequity created by leaving production, distribution, and investment decisions solely to the discretion of private decision-makers.

MARKET FAILURE: EFFICIENCY ASPECTS

The general argument for public activity is that private provision would not be optimal because of the existence of various types of market failures. These failures may require public activities such as regulation, taxation, pricing, subsidies, and public expenditures. In this chapter we are interested only in the last of these, so that the particular examples we will use have been chosen to illustrate cases where public investment in resource and transportation facilities appears especially desirable. We begin with the assumption that economic efficiency is the appropriate objective.

It is well known that private markets may produce inefficient output levels in the face of externalities. This type of failure would frequently accompany the development of natural resources and the provision of transportation facilities.

On the positive side, many water resource projects produce external benefits. The provision of a dam for hydroelectric power generation may provide flood control to downstream communities and business enterprises, opportunities for water-based recreation activities, or more dependable streamflow for waste disposal. Deepening a channel to facilitate water transportation may provide new areas for recreational boating. Even irrigation projects produce external benefits, as any resident of the green metropolitan oases of the arid American west is well aware.

Water resources and transportation projects also exhibit some of the characteristics of a public good. Once the facilities are in place, their services can be provided to additional customers at nearly zero cost, provided that the facilities remain uncongested.

It is doubtful, however, that externalities of these types explain much of the historical involvement of government in providing these facilities. That phenomenon is explained better by the presumed generation of dynamic external economies: certain growth-inducing spillovers of large-scale capital investments.

Transportation and water resource facilities have long been viewed as necessary ingredients in the recipe for economic growth. However, they have often been ascribed a uniquely important role, stemming from their ability to generate widespread cost-savings—some of which can be counted as external economies.

Initially, investments in social overhead capital facilitate the development of basic industries by lowering costs of production. These savings are not external economies. However, lower costs in basic industries may facilitate the development of complementary industries that can reap economies of scale, and offer their outputs at lower prices. The cost-savings in these complementary industries are true external economies of the investments in social overhead capital.

Additionally, general industry expansion may be successful in attracting new residents to the developing area. This produces an expanded market for consumer goods and, along with this market, expanded economies from increased specialization in the production of these commodities. At the same time, the clientele also expands for existing public services, many of which can be provided at decreasing average cost. In both cases, residents are able to acquire goods and services at lower real cost per unit as time passes. These cost-savings are attributable also to the social investment decision.

As real as these economies appear to be, they cannot be appropriated by any private investor. The large-scale investment necessary for their creation, then, must be made by government. Without provision by the latter, the pace of economic growth will be less than it could be. Even if it were possible for the private sector to provide these facilities, it would probably do so at a slower pace, thus deterring the realization of external benefits and reducing their present value.

The logic of these arguments seems sound. It is doubtful, however, that much of the current public investment in natural resources and transportation could be justified on the basis of these arguments alone. Surely, though, they had some applicability when the U.S. was underdeveloped, and much of our earlier large-scale investment in roads, canals, railroads, hydroelectric dams, and massive irrigation projects probably yielded significant external benefits.

Not all of the externalities associated with social investments in resources and transportation are positive, however. Communities and business firms generate waste products that are often dumped into water courses. To reduce this flow of residuals, government may finance new sewage treatment facilities or new techniques for cleaning industrial emissions.

It is also not unusual for transportation routes to become congested. Such congestion is simply a special type of externality, whereby the marginal vehicle entering a transportation facility imposes additional costs (in terms of increased travel time or operating costs) on other motorists. Often, public authorities view congestion as evidence that additional investment is needed in highways or mass transit facilities.[2]

Congestion is not limited to highways, however. Many airports exhibit a similar phenomenon, as do government-owned recreation areas. Here, too, one possible solution is government provision of additional facilities.

One final source of concern is the size of the facility that is necessary to reap economies of scale in the provision of water resource and transportation services. Often, a very large enterprise would be required, thus raising the specter of monopoly. Government provision of these services could avoid the undesirable consequences of this market phenomenon.

MARKET FAILURE: EQUITY ASPECTS

If project outputs were produced by private enterprises, they would be sold at prices reflecting the prevailing distribution of individual or family in-

---

2. The reader should not assume that we are advocating this solution. In many instances, there are other solutions with greater merit. One of the most promising is greater reliance on congestion charges (see Chapter 12).

come. If this distribution did not conform to the social ideal, projects could be financed and outputs could be distributed through the public sector to effect a favorable redistribution of income. Although it would be difficult to measure the incidence of costs and benefits by income group, no theoretical reason exists why finance and distribution could not be arranged to achieve a favorable result.

Some economists argue against this particular use of the budget, however. Basically, their point is that *all* sales in a market system have the same shortcoming; that is, they reflect the prevailing distribution of income. Given this, it seems to them more reasonable to effect a redistribution of general purchasing power rather than a transfer based solely on the fruits of public projects. A policy of general money transfer allows each individual to maximize satisfaction to a greater degree than does a policy which, in effect, transfers particular goods and services. In addition, such a policy is likely to be much less costly to administer because knowledge of individual preferences is not required.

These are strong arguments against the use of public projects as a tool of redistribution policy. However, they are not necessarily decisive. First, there are some goods whose purchase we are unwilling to leave to private choice because they are viewed as essential to individual welfare. It is doubtful, however, that water and transportation project outputs fit into this category of "merit" goods.

A more important reason for using public projects as a redistribution tool is the probability that a sufficiently large and effective general transfer of money income will not be made. Under this circumstance there is greater need to be aware of the distribution effect of particular projects.

Finally, government agencies have not hesitated to allocate project funds and outputs on the basis of distribution criteria. Given the existence of this practice, it is appropriate to evaluate this practice on the basis of widely accepted equity criteria.

PRINCIPLES OF INVESTMENT EVALUATION

The preceding remarks established the possibility of market failure in water and transportation. However, as we have argued previously, this is an insufficient basis for proceeding with public activity. It is also necessary to establish that net social gains result from these activities.

Investments in public projects should be made, then, only if they make a positive contribution to economic welfare. In the next section we will illustrate what must be done to determine whether the project promotes economic efficiency. Following that, we consider the relationship between project choice and equity in the distribution of income.

EFFECTS ON ECONOMIC EFFICIENCY

If public projects yield outputs which can be assigned a dollar value, the proper tool for investment evaluation is cost-benefit analysis (CBA). This type of analysis is restricted neither to investment evaluation nor to water resource and transportation projects. However, these uses illustrate its principles and pitfalls very well. In addition, government-conducted CBA first appeared in federal water resource agencies, and it was largely the study of these practices by economists that induced the development of the existing set of principles.

Every CBA requires the following steps: (1) the specification of an objective function; (2) the identification and measurement of benefits and costs; (3) the specification of an investment criterion; and (4) the adjustment of benefits and costs for time of occurrence. We will briefly develop each of these steps.

The Objective Function

An objective function is a shorthand (often mathematical) expression which specifies the desired objectives of public expenditure and the appropriate relationships between them. It is sufficient to assume at present that a single objective exists—economic efficiency—and that authorities wish to invest in a project only if it yields an increase in efficiency. All consequences of project construction, maintenance, operation, and finance which affect efficiency are relevant components of the evaluation. Those consequences which make positive contributions to this objective are, strictly speaking, efficiency benefits, while all negative consequences are efficiency costs.

It is normally assumed that the economic welfare of society is the sum of the various welfares of the several individuals of which it is comprised. Such is the case here; we want to add up the efficiency benefits and costs that affect any individual in the relevant social unit. The most widely-used measures of benefits and costs have been developed under the assumption that the proper unit is the nation. Because we will follow this tradition, our results are not necessarily applicable to an evaluation of state and local expenditures for water resources and transportation.

Project Benefits

Ideally, national efficiency benefits (simply "benefits" hereafter) attributable to a public project are equal to the maximum amount individuals are willing to pay for project outputs. However, it is sometimes impossible to estimate all positive consequences in this fashion. Those effects for which this is true are called *intangibles*. Effects which can be estimated in money terms are called *tangibles*. Benefits also accrue as a result of outputs distributed directly to project users, or indirectly in the form of externalities or spillovers. There are four general types of benefits, then: (1) tangible direct; (2) intangible direct; (3) tangible spillovers; and (4) intangible spillovers.

Tangible benefits of each type of project output are roughly equivalent to the area beneath the demand curve for each that is accounted for by the project in question.[3] It is not easy to estimate the value of this area in many instances, however, because some outputs are either not marketable (tangible spillovers) or are not sold at prices which accurately reflect willingness to pay. Considerable effort, ingenuity, and expense is often required, then, to recreate demand functions for relevant outputs, or even demand prices for small increments of these outputs.

The notion of demand curves for intangible outputs is not very useful. Nevertheless, fully-informed investment decisions require recognition of these outputs and, wherever possible, some estimate of their physical magnitudes.

To demonstrate what is involved in benefit estimation, we will develop a few examples.

Many water resource and transportation projects produce tangible direct outputs which can be appropriated only by individuals willing to give up their time or money for complementary inputs. The transportation services of highways, airports, and water routes will be enjoyed only by those both willing to spend the necessary travel time (which has a positive monetary value) and to buy the resources necessary to make the trip (extra gas, oil, maintenance, repairs, and others). The direct benefits of irrigation projects

---

3. It may be helpful at this point to review the discussion of benefit measures introduced in Chapter 2. Also, for the professional reader, the authors acknowledge again that this area is only an approximation of what we would like to measure.

are derived from the value of additional crops grown with the aid of project water. To grow these crops, farmers must invest large amounts of time and money in other resources. Similar "investments" are also required for the use of recreation areas and hydroelectric power.

This fact has two primary implications. First, in order to get an accurate measure of efficiency benefits it is necessary to subtract the costs of complementary inputs (including the value of time) from benefits measured as the relevant area under a demand curve. Second, where new projects reduce complementary costs, these cost-savings can be counted as benefits.

Suppose that two cities are connected by a highway that facilitates trade and travel. We can be confident that this highway yields benefits; that is, that users would pay a sum of money rather than forgo the services provided. In fact, if we use a trip between the cities as the unit of service, we can be sure that different values will be placed on trips of different individuals. If these values are arranged from high to low they will trace a demand, or marginal benefit, curve for trips, as in Figure 5-1. The area under this curve is an estimate of the gross efficiency benefits of the highway.

Each trip requires the expenditure of time and money, however. Suppose that this amount is the same for each trip, and equal to OM_1. This vertical distance thus measures the benefits forgone in order to make a trip.

With marginal costs equal to OM_1, the equilibrium number of trips is T_1. Gross benefits at equilibrium are equal to the area $OABT_1$. The total value of benefits sacrificed is equal to M_1BT_1O. The difference between these two areas, the area M_1AB, is an estimate of the efficiency benefits afforded by the existing highway.

Now suppose that a shorter route between the two cities is proposed. If it is built, users would save both time and money on each trip. The effect of adopting this route is shown in Figure 5-1 by a reduction in MC from MC_1 to MC_2. Because of this reduction in complementary costs, total trips will increase from T_1 to T_2.

The efficiency benefits of the new route are equal to the area, M_1BCM_2, which is the aggregate difference between $MB - MC_1$ and $MB - MC_2$. The proportion equivalent to area M_1BEM_2 represents cost-savings relative to the existing route. The remainder, BCE, represents the net benefits from traffic generated by the new route.

Although simple in design, similar models apply to a wide variety of transportation investment choices. The alternatives need not be restricted to competing *routes,* however. Competing *modes*—for example, water and rail—can also be evaluated in this way as the proposed project is expected to change the existing differential in complementary costs.

FIGURE 5-1
BENEFITS OF HIGHWAY SERVICES

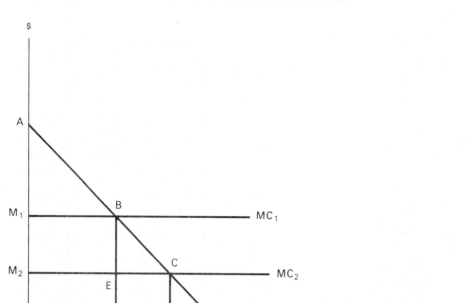

Of course, the estimation of benefits is not as simple as our example makes it appear. A great deal of work is necessary to determine how much time, gasoline, oil, and other factors will be saved per trip. Then, too, each resource unit saved must be given a dollar value. This is relatively easy to do for physical resources, but not for time.

An effort must be made to estimate the induced volume of traffic. Any analysis which fails to do this will produce an underestimate of benefits. At the same time, accurate estimation requires an estimate of the shape of the demand curve over the range from B to C. This will be relatively expensive to obtain in most instances.

The analysis should be extended in some obvious ways. First, we have ignored the fact that the new route may avert loss of life, personal injuries, and property damage by reducing the expected frequency and severity of vehicle accidents. A dollar value for these should be estimated whenever possible. Second, analysts must deal with the other benefit categories ignored to this point.

Transportation projects frequently create both tangible and intangible spillover benefits. An attempt should be made to determine the dollar value of the former and to estimate at least the physical dimensions of the latter.

One positive tangible spillover is the relief of congestion on alternative routes. Here, the reduction in congestion costs on these routes is counted as a project benefit. Alternatively, a new route may reduce noise levels for residents living near the existing route. The value these residents attach to the noise reduction is a benefit of the new route.

Water transportation routes can also create tangible spillover benefits. A deeper channel may improve recreation; a river may be tamed for navigation and provide flood control and recreation as joint products of better navigation. These spillovers may be totally unintended consequences, but they are nonetheless relevant to the efficiency calculation.

Finally, water resource and highway projects can provide intangible benefits as well. A new transport route may provide visual pleasure to motorists (intangible direct benefits) or non-motorists (intangible spillover benefits). As real as these effects may be, it would be extremely difficult to estimate their value.

Project Costs

In allocative economics, costs are equal to the maximum value of benefits sacrificed as a consequence of project construction, maintenance, and operation. It follows, therefore, that there are four types of costs: (1) tangible direct; (2) intangible direct; (3) tangible spillover; and (4) intangible spillover.

If resource markets are reasonably competitive, and full employment prevails, the prices of inputs used directly in construction, maintenance, and operation are close estimates of tangible direct benefits sacrificed and, therefore, of tangible direct costs. However, when inputs are drawn from non-competitive markets, prices are not reliable indexes of efficiency costs. Instead, the analyst must estimate the value of the marginal product of each input and use this as proxy for price. In addition, market prices are not an accurate index of benefits forgone if inputs are drawn from a pool of otherwise unemployed resources. In this case, the relevant price is not what these resources would earn if employed, but rather the cost of inducing them to work.

The big problems on the cost side, however, are not usually associated with tangible direct costs but rather with the estimation of tangible and intangible spillover costs. In the former category are the air pollution, noise, and congestion costs associated with transportation projects. The latter category includes effects such as the visual disamenities which often accompany project construction and operation.

Perhaps the greatest difficulty involved in a decision involving a public project is the determination of the value of the natural environment. Water resource projects which include major physical structures, such as a hydro-electric dam, effect a drastic change in the natural state of the environment; wilderness areas are invaded, free-flowing streams are tamed, historical sites are flooded, and natural wonders are destroyed. In these cases, a value should be placed on the alternatives provided by the undeveloped environment.

Few market prices exist which can be consulted in determining these values. However, people would probably be willing to pay something for the preservation of natural sites. Indeed, some economists argue that people would be willing to pay for preservation even if they were not certain of visiting the sites. In other words, they would pay *some* amount for the option of visiting at a later date, or for an option that their descendants could exercise.

Many additional difficulties exist in estimating the efficiency costs of public investment. Our objective has not been to treat them exhaustively, but merely to point out the need for a broad and imaginative approach. Usually, much more is involved than equating costs to tax funds spent for the project.

Investment Criteria

Most of the benefits of public projects—and often a significant proportion of their costs occur in the future. Thus, choices among alternatives involves a comparison of the timestreams of benefits and costs associated with these projects. The investment criterion is designed to facilitate this comparison.

The issue of the correct investment criterion has been one of the more controversial topics in the theory of capital budgeting. Although a variety of criteria have been evaluated in the theoretical literature, the most important arguments have concerned the respective merits of the present value criterion and the internal rate of return criterion.

To facilitate a comparison between the two, we assume an investment which yields a stream of benefits (B_t), and which occasions costs (C_t), for each of t years $(t = 0 \ldots n)$. The present value of the investment is determined by subtracting the present value of costs from the present value of benefits, as follows:

$$(1) \; PV = \left[B_0 + \frac{B_1}{1+r} + \frac{B_2}{(1+r)^2} + \cdots + \frac{B_n}{(1+r)^n} \right] - \left[C_0 + \frac{C_1}{1+r} + \frac{C_2}{(1+r)^2} + \cdots + \frac{C_n}{(1+r)^n} \right],$$

where r is the appropriate rate of interest (to be discussed in the next section). If PV equals or exceeds zero, the investment is efficient.

To illustrate the internal rate of return, we use the same stream of B_t and C_t. However, instead of assuming a value for r, the objective is to solve for an implicit average discount rate, i, which makes the present value of the investment equal to zero. Thus, equation (1) is transformed into:

$$(2) \; 0 = \left[B_0 + \frac{B_1}{1+i} + \frac{B_2}{(1+i)^2} + \cdots + \frac{B_n}{(1-i)^n} \right] - \left[C_0 + \frac{C_1}{1+i} + \frac{C_2}{(1+i)^2} + \cdots + \frac{C_n}{(1+i)^n} \right].$$

In this equation, the values of B_t and C_t are known, and it is necessary to determine i, which is the internal rate of return. If the solution value for i equals or exceeds the required rate of return, the investment is efficient.

It is easy to see from comparing (1) and (2) that a given project will be judged efficient by either criterion, provided that i ≥ r, and that i ≥ the required rate. This implies clearly that PV ≥ 0.

In situations where more than one project is being evaluated, however, and a budget constraint precludes the choice of all projects, or some projects are mutually exclusive (if one is undertaken the other cannot be—such as two projects on the same physical site), the present value and internal rate of return criteria can yield conflicting rankings of projects. Consider the example in Table 5-1. Assume that there is a budget constraint of $100, so that either A or B can be built, but not both. The internal rate of return criterion ranks A over B; the present value criterion ranks B over A.

The correct choice in this case depends upon the rate of return that can be earned on profits of the project. The internal rate of return test assumes that profits can be reinvested and earn 10% and 7.2% for A and B, respectively. The present value criterion assumes that profits can be reinvested and earn 3% for both projects. Ideally, r *is* equivalent to the rate of return on the next best opportunity. In this example, then, as is often the case in

TABLE 5–1

Project/Variable	C_0	B_1	B_2	i	PV (r=.03)
A	110	100	0	.10	6.8
B	100	0	115	.072	8.3

SOURCE: Adapted from E.J. Mishan, *Cost-Benefit Analysis,* (New York: Praeger 1976).

reality, the internal rate of return criterion implicitly assumes opportunities for reinvestment that are not generally available. The correct choice is B, because the present value criterion uses a more general measure of the value of alternatives.

The internal rate of return criterion has another shortcoming as well; more than one solution value may exist for equation (2). Because of these two problems, economists tend to favor the general use of the present value criterion. However, if the present value criterion is employed, an appropriate value of r must be determined.

The Rate of Discount

It used to be fashionable for government water resource agencies to discount benefits and costs at a rate equal to that which the government paid on long-term loans. Because these securities are relatively risk-free, they often sell at rates far below those at which private investors can borrow. Thus, public investments were commonly discounted at rates below those that were used for private investments.

When economists began to study cost-benefit analysis in these agencies, they severely criticized the use of discount rates this low, largely on the grounds that the practice would divert resources from private sector uses that yielded a higher rate of return than did public investment in water resources. Such investments, they argued, should not be made unless they showed positive present values when discounted at the same rates used in the private sector.

This argument is merely an extension of the basic principle of allocative economics: namely, that resources should be allocated to their highest value uses. Most economists now accept this view. However, several issues required clarification before the present degree of approval was achieved.

One of the strongest objections to using private sector rates is that they reflect various institutional or market imperfections that render them inappropriate for public sector discounting. Presumably, the appropriate rate is one which would prevail in a perfectly competitive capital market, and if actual rates diverge from this ideal we should not rely on actual rates.

The competitive market solution appeals to economists because it automatically produces the most efficient quantity of investment. It is easy to show why with the aid of Figure 5-2.

In this figure, the demand curve for investment funds (D_b : ignore D_a for now) indicates the maximum rate of interest borrowers would pay per dollar of funds borrowed. This amount is equal to the value of the marginal product of investment, expressed as a rate of return per dollar invested. The height of D_b is equal, therefore, to the marginal rate of return on investment

FIGURE 5-2
THE RATE OF INTEREST

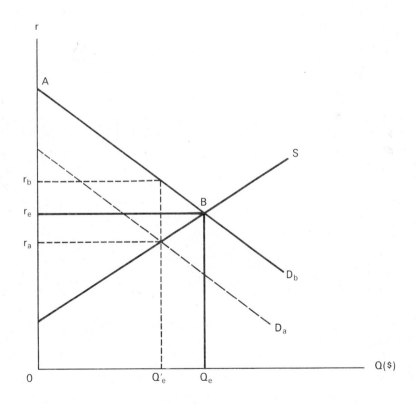

or, assuming the absence of externalities, to the marginal social rate of return.

The supply curve, on the other hand, indicates the maximum amount society sacrifices for each dollar invested, again expressed as a rate or percentage per dollar. This rate indicates what suppliers (savers) require in order to forgo spending each dollar for current consumption. This *rate of time preference* is normally positive. In this example, it is assumed to rise as the level of savings grows, primarily because some individuals have a higher rate of time preference. In the absence of externalities, the height of S at each level of investment is equal to the marginal social rate of time preference.

A competitive market for investment funds is in equilibrium at Q_e, of course. At smaller levels of investment, the marginal social rate of return exceeds the marginal social rate of time preference. Thus, each dollar invested yields positive net benefits, and it pays to expand the level of investment. The opposite is true for levels of investment exceeding Q_e. At Q_e there are no net advantages to society from investing either more or less, and maximum potential efficiency is achieved.

Economists writing on this topic commonly refer to the equilibrium rate, r_e, as the *social rate of time preference.* It should be obvious why this label is appropriate. Now, to the imperfections.

First, some economists claim that the appropriate social rate of time preference is below r_e. The great English economist, A. C. Pigou, based his claim to this effect on "a defective telescopic faculty" in individuals which induces them to systematically undervalue the welfare of future generations.[4] Given this bias toward the present, people tend to discount future values at too high a rate. The Pigovian argument, therefore, implies a socially rational supply curve to the right of S, and a lower social rate of time preference.

Stephen Marglin has also argued for a similar shift to the right in S in order to accurately depict the social rate of time preference.[5] In his view, many individuals would be willing to sacrifice more for future generations (or save more at each r) than is indicated by their private rate of time preference. However, without some assurance that others will make a

---

4. A. C. Pigou, *The Economics of Welfare,* 1st ed., (London: Macmillan & Co., Ltd., 1920), pp. 24–25.

5. Stephen Marglin, "The Social Rate of Discount and the Optimal Rate of Investment," *Quarterly Journal of Economics,* Vol. 77, No. 1 (Feb., 1963), pp. 95–111.

similar sacrifice, it appears to each individual that his or her effort will make little difference in the amount available to future generations. Private markets provide no mechanism for securing this assurance. Thus, market supply is governed by private rather than social rates of time preference.

It is now generally conceded that the true social rate of time preference may be less than r_e for the reasons just indicated. However, many economists are unwilling to accept the notion that such a rate could or should be used to discount public investments. First, a rate below r_e would tend to transfer more wealth to future generations. Given the continuation of economic growth, though, these generations are likely to be wealthier than the present one even without such a transfer. Use of the lower rate, then, smacks of redistribution from poor to rich, and many economists find this objectionable.

Second, it would be extremely difficult to calculate the true social rate of time preference. We have almost no clues concerning the size of the sacrifice individuals are willing to make, nor can we rely on the political process to determine this, as has been argued by some observers.

Most importantly, however, even if we could determine the true rate, it would not be appropriate to use it for discounting public projects alone. Such a practice would induce us to use our resources in the public sector for projects which earn a lower social rate of return than could be earned if the funds were left in the private sector. The only way to avoid this type of inefficiency is to use public policy to lower the market rate to the level of the true social rate so that both sectors would discount on the same basis. In this way, we would give adequate scope to concern for future generations and also use our resources efficiently.

Another group of economists has argued that actual rates are likely to be higher, instead of lower, than r_e. The three sources of difference most frequently mentioned are taxes, monopolistic imperfections, and provisions (premiums) for risk. Although differences exist between the three sources, the nature of the argument can be established by analyzing the effect of taxes.

Assume, as before, that D_b in Figure 5-2 depicts the marginal social rate of return on investment. The private rate of return is less, with the difference between the two due to the effect of taxes on investment income. There is, in other words, an after-tax demand curve (D_a) which lies below D_b, with the vertical distance between the two directly related to the rate of taxation.

Private investors will base their decisions on D_a, not on D_b. As a consequence, the equilibrium level of investment (Qe) is less than Q_e, and the before-tax rate of return (r_b) exceeds the after-tax rate (r_a). Some people argue that the before-tax rate should not be used for discounting public investment, and that the after-tax rate, or r_e, should be used instead.

The argument that taxes drive before-tax rates to a level exceeding r_e cannot be disputed. However, it does not follow that this provides a rationale for using a lower rate than the actual rate. Indeed, as in the previous case, public investment should be discounted at the marginal social rate of return in the private sector to avoid using funds in the public sector that earn less than they could in private endeavors.

It is true, of course, that taxes create efficiency losses by encouraging investment at a level below Q_e. However, to solve this problem, taxes should be reduced. Discounting public investments at less than actual before-tax rates will not improve this situation.

It appears, then, that it is appropriate to use the before-tax rate of return earned on private investment as the social rate of discount. How can this rate be calculated?

The problem, of course, is that public investment funds are drawn from a wide variety of sources, including private consumption and a myriad of private investment opportunities. It is necessary, therefore, to determine both the proportion of funds derived from each source, and the before-tax rate of return associated with each. Armed with this information, the analyst can calculate a weighted average rate of return that will be appropriate for discounting public projects.

To illustrate this concept, suppose that funds come from three sources: private consumption (50%) and two private investments, A (25%) and B (25%). Assume that the marginal rate of time preference for consumers can be approximated by the rate paid on savings accounts (5%): that investment A earns 15% before taxes; and that B earns 20%. Under these conditions, the social rate of discount is:

$$(5 \times .5) + (15 \times .25) + (20 \times .25) = 13.25\%.$$

Of course, this is an oversimplification of the actual process that would be necessary to calculate r. It is not as easy to determine the sources or the rate of return on each source as we have assumed it to be. The reader should have a fair idea by now, however, of what the economist means when he/she says that public investment should be discounted by a rate which represents the opportunity cost of investment funds.

EFFECTS ON INCOME
DISTRIBUTION

We have concentrated our attention up to now on some of the major features of cost-benefit analysis for an assumed objective of economic efficiency. Normally, however, the objective function would also include a goal relating to income distribution.

We argued earlier that projects may be designed to effect a redistribution of income, provided that there is little assurance of a general income transfer that will achieve the desired distribution. Under ideal circumstances, we would know the social importance of a dollar to each individual, or at least to individuals categorized, for example, according to income level. We could then use this information to weight the benefits and costs of a project according to who would receive or pay them.

In terms of the present value criterion, each B_t and C_t would be determined by calculating the sum of the weighted benefits received and weighted costs paid by all income groups. A simplified example of such a procedure was presented earlier in Chapter 3, without all the trappings of the investment criterion, and the reader may refer to it for an idea of the objective of the weighting procedure.

The major task of the analyst in this instance is to trace the incidence of each benefit and cost. This would not be easy to do under even the best of circumstances.

The major drawback to this procedure, of course, is that no ready-made set of social weights exists. In the face of this dilemma, some economists have attempted to infer them from decisions made in the past by government agencies or Congress. Robert Haveman studied water resource appropriations, for example, to determine if any implicit redistribution objective would be found in terms of either income groups or regions of the country.[6] Burton Weisbrod performed a similar task for a smaller sample of projects, and strongly advocated expanded research of this type.[7] In related work, some economists have studied the tax structure to determine the

---

6. Robert H. Haveman, *Water Resource Investment and the Public Interest* (Nashville: Vanderbilt University Press, 1965).

7. Burton A. Weisbrod, "Collective Action and the Distribution of Income: a Conceptual Approach," in Joint Economic Committee, *The Analysis of Public Expenditures,* 91st Congress, 1969.

redistribution objectives implied by the pattern of statutory and effective rates.[8]

In spite of the flurry of activity in this area, most of the information obtained so far falls short of what is needed to define the ideal distribution of income. Still, improvements in expenditure policy need not wait until we know the exact contours of this distribution. It seems clear from the events of the past decade that there is a social commitment to increase the standard of living of families whose incomes place them in the lowest quartile. Any project which worsens the income position of this group could probably be ranked very low without a detailed distribution criterion. Similarly, any project which significantly redistributes income to the families in the upper quartile of the income distribution would also be a cause for social concern. The point, of course, is that a successful determination of the incidence of benefits and costs may provide very useful information to policy-makers.

GOVERNMENT INVESTMENT
EVALUATION PRACTICES

Armed with the principles developed above, we now turn to an appraisal of the procedures used by government agencies. Cost-benefit analyses have been submitted in the past as part of the "justification statements" of agencies requesting funds from Congress. Critics argue that this label accurately reflects agency intentions: namely, to develop a set of figures to justify what the agency intended to do anyway. Surely there is some truth in this view. It is in an agency's interests to define and measure benefits and costs so as to produce upward and downward biases, respectively, and to choose a rate of discount as low as Congress allows.

It is extremely difficult for someone untrained in cost-benefit analysis to detect errors. The errant practices can be very subtle and often appear correct to the untutored observer. Most of the examples which follow, however, have been widely trumpeted by economists, and decision-makers should continue to be informed of them.

---

8. As an example of this work, see Koichi Mera, "Experimental Determination of Relative Marginal Utilities," *Quarterly Journal of Economics,* Aug., 1969, pp. 464–477.

EFFICIENCY EFFECTS

Most analytical errors that can be traced more or less directly to policy evaluations represent failures to conform to the requirements of the efficiency criteria established earlier.

Benefits

One argument used frequently to justify public projects is that they provide benefits to individuals other than those who directly receive project outputs. These presumably widespread benefits are called *secondary* or *indirect benefits.* Water resource agencies, in particular, have long advocated their inclusion as part of project evaluations. Economists have long argued that they are inappropriate for this purpose. The practice persists, however.

Although different meanings are ascribed to this type of benefit by different agencies, what is meant most often is the expected increase in income in secondary activities. For example, suppose the project is an irrigation system used to grow wheat. Secondary benefits would be income earned in transporting, storing, processing, and marketing at all stages between the primary farming stage and the production of the final products, such as breads and cereals. Economists reject this measure because, in a fully-employed, competitive economy, these incomes are offset by the opportunity cost of the resources employed in all of these stages.

A practice of equally dubious merit concerns the treatment of increases in property values occasioned by a public project. It is not unusual for government studies to include estimates of primary benefits of projects, and then to add the estimated increase in property values in the project area. Economists have long argued that this practice constitutes "double-counting," but to little avail.

An example is helpful at this point. Suppose that the government plans to finance a new highway project. One of the primary benefits will be costs saved in the form of lower fuel, reduced maintenance costs, and shorter trip time. Because of these savings, the demand for land and properties close to the highway will increase, driving up their prices. Government analysts often include these price increases as benefits in project evaluations. However, it is clear that they increase only because the highway affords cost-savings. Indeed, in a competitive market, land and structure prices will rise eventually by as much as costs fall. Thus, property value increases are merely an indirect reflection of cost-savings. To add them to benefits would be equivalent to counting these savings twice.

Experience indicates, however, that even when cost-savings are counted only once estimates must be examined carefully to determine whether or not the correct cost figures are being used. One situation in which they are not is encountered frequently in water transportation project evaluations.

Theoretically, the bulk of the primary benefits of these projects are equivalent to the difference in costs of water transportation and some alternative mode of transportation—usually rail. Government analysts equate primary benefits, however, to the difference between railroad and waterway *rates,* instead of costs. This creates an estimate exceeding cost-savings because rail rates exceed rail costs by more than waterway rates exceed waterway costs.

Given the political history of this case there is little doubt that agency analysts are aware of the bias created by this practice.[9] Sometimes, however, it *is* appropriate to use prices as measures of benefits. Care must simply be exercised to choose the right price. Irrigation projects have typically been justified, in part, on the basis of the value of crops produced with project water. However, a price supported above the equilibrium level by government farm policy is inappropriately high. Such prices have been commonly used, nevertheless.

The benefit estimates of water resource and transportation projects do not deal exclusively with cost-savings and prices, however. Sometimes benefits are derived from losses averted; e.g., the loss of life and property averted by flood control and highway projects. Here, too, there are biases in government estimates. One of the more important sources is the understatement of the level of development induced in the flood plain by flood control projects. Robert Havemen argues that "with the higher level of development, even the reduced stream flows cause damages in excess of what they would have been without flood protection."[10]

Given the ingenuity government agencies have shown in defining and measuring benefits to make projects appear more efficient, it is surprising that greater efforts to measure spillover benefits have not been made. However, project evaluations have been devoted traditionally to tangible direct consequences. The primary effect of this practice was the long ne-

---

9. A good review of this history appears in: R. Haveman and P. Stephan, "White Elephants, Waterways, and the Transportation Act of 1966," in R. Haveman and R. Hamrin, eds. *The Political Economy of Federal Policy* (New York: Harper and Row, 1973), pp. 220–226.

10. Robert R. Haveman, "Efficiency and Equity in Natural Resource and Environmental Policy," in A. Harberger, *et al.,* eds., *Benefit-Cost and Policy Analysis—1974* (Chicago: Aldine, 1975) p. 232.

glect of the benefits of recreation services provided as a joint product of hydroelectric power and improved navigation systems. Even though the value of these services has recently been estimated with greater frequency, the estimates often bear little resemblance to efficiency benefits.

Costs

Abundant errors can be found on the cost side of the balance sheet as well. We will emphasize these to the exclusion of the estimates that are done correctly.

Earlier, we argued against including secondary benefits in efficiency evaluations because their generation produces no net increase in the value of real output. There is a similar resolution for an issue that appears frequently in discussions of project costs. Here one encounters the claim that projects will reduce the volume of unemployment, and that costs will be lowered to reflect the reduction in unemployment compensation payments. It is conceivable, of course, that project construction, maintenance, and operation will reduce unemployment. However, the decrease in unemployment compensation is not a saving in efficiency costs: it is a reduction in a transfer payment, and it does not change the value of real output.

Although the accuracy of estimates of other tangible direct costs is a concern, the biggest source of error on the cost side has been the failure of public agencies to estimate spillover costs—tangible or intangible. Little attention has been devoted in highway project evaluation to the air pollution or noise which accompanies highway construction or use. Water project evaluations have traditionally ignored spillover costs—especially the intangible but nevertheless real effects on the natural environment.

This is especially disturbing because a primary rationale for public activity is the correction of spillovers. However, the public decision-maker, like his/her private counterpart, will not take these costs into account unless there is an incentive to do so. The private decision-maker has an incentive *not* to do so; namely, his/her profits are higher if he/she doesn't. The public servant also has an incentive not to consider these costs: he/she secures the support of a powerful constituency—the primary beneficiaries of the project.

Recently, however, the pendulum appears to have begun the swing in the opposite direction. The constituency for the natural environment has grown in numbers and political influence, and project decisions have begun to reflect this drift in the locus of power and influence. Whether or not the degree of drift is excessive is one of the hotly debated topics of the present.

There is abundant evidence, though, that project evaluations do not generally include measures of the effects of spillovers that would meet the standards of allocative economics.

One final source of error is the tendency to underestimate the opportunity cost of resources used. This, too, occurs frequently for resources that are not sold in markets. A good example is the practice by the Bureau of Reclamation of not charging to irrigation projects the opportunity cost of water diverted from streams. This makes it much easier, of course, to justify huge transfers to water-intensive crops in regions where water is seemingly so scarce.

The Discount Rate

In spite of the large number of errors made in benefit and cost estimates, their effects on efficiency are probably no greater than those resulting from the employment of the wrong discount rate. In fact, careful choice of a value for this parameter can easily turn around an otherwise unfavorable evaluation. Because of this possibility, economists have focused a great deal of attention on discount rates employed by government agencies.

Historically, there is little doubt that discount rates used for water resource and transportation projects have been below the social opportunity cost rate of return. In fact, the generally prevailing practice until recently was to use the interest rate on long-term government bonds—a rate unrelated to and surely below the correct rate. As a result, projects have been built which were too large, too durable, and premature. The general public fails to perceive the costs of these biases, but this hardly justifies the practice.

Discount rates have increased for many agencies in recent years. However, water resource projects are still dear to Congress, and sponsoring agencies still employ rates that are too low. This practice tends to bias allocation in the direction of water resource investments, in general, and also to divert resources from alternative modes of transportation. It is possible that the demise of rail transport, at least partially, has occurred as a consequence.

Non-uniformity of discount rates is consistent with economic efficiency, of course, if funds for different agencies displace private alternatives which yield different rates of return. It is doubtful, however, that water resource projects have a claim on sources that are consistently less profitable than those which supply the funds for other public projects.

DISTRIBUTION EFFECTS

Evaluation practices can also be criticized on equity grounds. Such a critique is rather short, however, for government project evaluations do not typically include a formal analysis of distribution effects. What passes for distribution analyses are usually nothing more than displays of a project's impact on regional employment or income.

This kind of information is largely irrelevant to the assessment of projects according to the strictures of economic welfare, which require (presumably) that benefits and costs be distributed on an individual basis. A project which distributes all of its benefits to high-income families and all of its costs to low-income units within the same region could be assessed favorably in terms of its effect on regional income. This is regrettable because it appears that regional income and employment effects are important criteria in the congressional budgetary process. Indeed, the support for inclusion of secondary benefits probably comes from this source.

It is probably safe to say that project evaluations have not been designed deliberately to make the distribution of personal income more unequal. However, the neglect of income distribution effects, combined with the distribution of project outputs at nominal or zero price, have produced many instances in which this result has occurred. We will review several of these cases in Chapter 12.

A REFORM PROPOSAL

Although cost-benefit analysis has been highly developed and widely used in academic studies, it has not had a great impact on public investment decisions. In many cases, this type of evaluation is not performed at all; in others, the operation of agency self-interest has stifled objective analysis or biased results, and inappropriate efficiency and equity concepts continue to be used in spite of the criticism leveled by economists.

The persistence of these practices is evidence of strong incentives to produce evaluations that may conflict with those based on economic criteria. Agencies respond to pressures exerted by a constituency that is much narrower than the general interest served by the economist. Congress relies heavily on agency evaluations, and projects are often championed as well by a coalition of legislators for whom regional interests are more important than those of the nation.

It would be extremely difficult to change this institutional structure.

However, some of its influence could probably be reduced by the establishment and operation of an independent policy evaluation agency responsible to Congress, which would conduct objective evaluations of existing and proposed programs.[11] Perhaps as time goes by the recently created budget committees in the House and the Senate will even be able to add this important capability to their growing ability to analyze the macroeconomic impact of the budget.

SUMMARY

Government expenditures for water resources and transportation represent a large and important commitment to investment in social overhead capital. These projects have been financed historically largely through the public sector. Moreover, it is likely that purely private finance would produce inefficiency or inequity as a result of the provision of these goods. Water resource and transportation projects often provide significant external benefits in the traditional sense. A more important reason for financing them publicly, however, is that they may produce long-run growth-inducing spillovers that are not appropriable by private firms, nor a consequence of small-scale investment.

Public expenditures in this area can also be justified on equity grounds. The clearest case is where general money transfers will not be made, and investment projects can be designed to redistribute income to individuals or groups disadvantaged by the normal operation of the market economy.

To determine if a project would improve efficiency if adopted, it is necessary to conduct a cost benefit analysis (CBA). Each CBA should include five steps: (1) specification of an objective function, (2) identification and measurement of benefits and costs, (3) specification and employment of an investment criterion, and (4) adjustment of benefit and costs for time of occurrence.

Most CBA is based on the assumption that the sole objective is economic efficiency. Ideally, efficiency benefits are equal to the maximum amount individuals are willing to pay for project outputs, and efficiency costs are equal to the maximum value of benefits sacrificed. It is not easy to estimate benefits or costs, but values can be imputed to each by estimating the value of appropriate proxy variables.

Some of the benefits of transportation routes and water projects can

---

11. This suggestion is outlined more fully in *Harberger,* pp. 235–256.

often be determined by estimating expenditures for complementary inputs, and supplemented with estimates of the value of lives saved, congestion relieved, noise reduced, and visual amenities provided. Project costs can be approximated initially by money outlays for resources, but these estimates must often be adjusted for the extent and duration of unemployment. In addition, external costs must be estimated; these should include all effects on the natural environment.

To compare benefits and costs, economists favor use of the present value investment criterion, in which the data are discounted by a rate equal to the opportunity cost of investment funds. In a world of perfect competition and perfect foresight, this rate would be equal to the social rate of time preference. In reality, actual market rates must be adjusted for various capital market imperfections, investor myopia, and sources of funds, before they can serve as an accurate index of opportunity cost.

Projects should also be evaluated for their effect on income distribution. Here again, progress in this direction requires the prior determination of the ideal distribution. Given this, both benefits and costs can be weighted accordingly.

Many government agencies conduct CBA's of water resource and transportation projects. Unfortunately, many errors are committed in these analyses. Some of the more common errors on the benefit side are: the inclusion of secondary benefits, double-counting, the use of incorrect shadow prices, and failure to estimate externalities. On the cost side, analyses often fail to produce true opportunity costs, especially where externalities are involved.

Agencies have also been guilty of using inappropriately low discount rates, and of ignoring distribution effects. These errors, and those enumerated above, could probably be reduced, however, if projects were evaluated by an independent agency responsible to Congress, rather than by the agencies requesting funds.

SUGGESTIONS FOR FURTHER READING

Mishan, E. J., *Cost-Benefit Analysis,* New and Expanded Edition, New York: Praeger Publishers, 1976.

Each of the theoretical issues raised in this chapter is treated more exhaustively in this reference.

Mohring, Herbert, "Urban Highway Investments," in Robert Dorfman, ed., *Measuring Benefits of Government Investments,* Washington, D.C.: The Brookings Institution, 1965, pp. 231–291.

A good review, at a more advanced level than that of this text, is here presented of the problems encountered in estimating the benefits and costs of transportation projects.

Eckstein, Otto, *Water Resource Development,* Cambridge, Mass.: Harvard Univ. Press, 1958.

This source develops a critique of both theory and practice in the area of water resource investment; it is still very much up to date in spite of its publication date.

EXPENDITURES FOR INCOME REDISTRIBUTION

During the period since World War II, total government expenditures have increased as a proportion of total expenditures or GNP.[1] Much of this growth in the relative size of the public sector is attributable to the rapid increase in social welfare expenditures; i.e., outlays for social insurance, public aid, health, pension, education, and housing programs.[2] The existence of these programs is largely a reflection of collective dissatisfaction with a purely market-determined distribution of real income. Our primary concern in this chapter, therefore, is to examine whether these programs have moved us closer to a more satisfactory distribution.

Although we have not yet reached agreement on what constitutes a

---

1. The increase has been from 22% in 1946 to 35% in 1975. See Chapter 1.

2. The term "social welfare expenditures" is used by the Social Security Administration to describe the government expenditure programs which redistribute real income. The public aid component of social welfare expenditures (about 13% of the total in 1973) corresponds most closely to the lay notion of "welfare." We employ the SSA terminology only because it is widely used in the literature. We would prefer the use of a term with more positive connotations, such as "expenditures for human resource development."

satisfactory distribution of income, there appears to be a social consensus that the elimination of poverty would move us closer to such a distribution. In the following analysis we assume that this is the case, and we evaluate social welfare expenditures primarily in terms of their effect on the incidence of poverty. We begin, however, by reviewing data which relate these expenditures to the overall distribution of income. Following that, we review existing evidence to determine how successful these expenditures have been in reducing poverty. Next, we examine these programs more closely to discover where reforms are needed. Finally, we evaluate the most popular reform proposal: the adoption of a negative income tax.

THE EFFECTS OF GOVERNMENT EXPENDITURES ON INCOME DISTRIBUTION

Total social welfare expenditures exceeded $215 billion in fiscal year 1973, or slightly over $1,000 for each person in the United States.[3] Nearly 40% ($85.9 billion) of the total was for social insurance programs at all levels of government, with the federal social security program accounting for 84% of this component. The next largest program was education, constituting 32% of the total ($65.2 million), financed largely by state and local governments (90%). The remainder was accounted for by expenditures for public aid ($28.3 billion), health and medical care ($14.6 billion), veterans' programs ($13 billion), housing ($4 billion) and miscellaneous ($4 billion).

These expenditures constituted over 55% of total government spending, as compared with only 36% in 1959. The most dramatic increase occurred in the federal budget, with a virtual doubling of federal social welfare expenditures as a percentage of federal expenditures over the period 1959–1973. These trends clearly reflect the reordering of social priorities which has taken place in the last two decades.

As a consequence of this shift, total social welfare expenditures grew from 11.3% of Net National Product in 1959 to over 19% in 1973. To what extent has this growth been reflected in the distribution of income?

---

3. Edgar K. Browning, *Redistribution and the Welfare System* (Washington: American Enterprise Institute for Public Policy Research, 1975), p. 19.

THE DISTRIBUTION
OF MONEY INCOME

The most widely used estimate of the distribution of income is the distribution of money income published annually by the Bureau of the Census. Table 6-1 displays this distribution by quintiles (fifths) for three selected years.[4] It appears from these figures that money income is distributed quite unequally, and that there has been little change in the degree of inequality over the twenty–year period represented. However, the Bureau's data exclude various components of income and taxes that are not distributed in equal proportions among income classes. When adjustments are made for these exclusions, income appears to be much more equally distributed, and social welfare expenditures appear to be a major force in this trend toward greater equality.)

It is essential to recognize that the distribution of money income as shown in Table 6-1 already includes governmental money transfers. Thus, the effect of this component of social welfare expenditures is hidden in the official figures. To determine how equalizing cash transfers have been, they must be distributed by families and then subtracted from the total money income of families. Richard and Peggy Musgrave have done this for 1968, and have also studied the distribution of money income minus cash transfers by quartiles; their results are found in Table 6-2. It is clear from this exhibit that cash transfers have played an important role in redistributing money income.

TABLE 6-1 PERCENT OF MONEY INCOME BY FAMILY

Quintile	Lowest	2nd	3rd	4th	Highest
1952	4.9	12.2	17.1	23.5	42.2
1962	5.0	12.1	17.6	24.0	41.3
1972	5.4	11.9	17.5	23.9	41.4

SOURCE: U.S. Bureau of the Census, "Money Income in 1972 of Families and Persons in the United States", *Current Population Reports,* Series P-60, No. 90. Washington: U.S.G.P.O., 1973, Table 16.

---

4. Although this data is now available for later years, we have not incorporated it in Table 6-1 because we want to show later how certain adjustments affect the distribution displayed in this table, and data on these adjustments are not available for other years.

TABLE 6–2   PERCENT OF MONEY INCOME BY FAMILY (1968)

Quartile	Lowest	2nd	3rd	Highest
Income including transfers	6.4	14.9	26.2	52.5
Income minus transfers	1.9	15.1	28.0	55.0

SOURCE: Richard A. and Peggy B. Musgrave, *Public Finance in Theory and Practice.* New York: McGraw-Hill, 1976, p. 400.

The major fault with the Bureau's distribution figures lies not with what they include, however, but with certain components of real income that they exclude. To get a more accurate picture of relative economic welfare, we must make certain additional adjustments.[5] First, we must correct for the different impact among income brackets of various taxes ignored by the Bureau. Second, we must include the value of in-kind transfers and education. Third, we must adjust for differences in the average size of families in different income brackets.

ADJUSTMENTS IN THE DISTRIBUTION OF MONEY INCOME

The Bureau's "money income" is a measure of income after taxes, but does not take into consideration all taxes. The most prominent omissions are personal income taxes, employees' contributions to the social security or payroll tax, and state and local property taxes. There is good reason to believe, however, that a distribution of money income after these taxes are subtracted may be more equal than the one indicated by the figures in Table 6-1. This follows from the widely accepted view that personal income taxes are distributed progressively, especially at the low end of the scale of distribution, and the fact that their size is greater than the admittedly regressive payroll tax and the possibly regressive property tax. Indeed, figures in a recent study by Edgar Browning indicate that income taxes alone are large enough to make the combination of income and

---

5. These adjustments are based on suggestions in: Edgar K. Browning, "How Much More Equality Can We Afford?" in *The Public Interest,* Spring, 1976.

payroll taxes progressive.[6] When Browning combines the two, he finds that the money income of the lowest quintile is reduced by only 3.5%, but that the reduction for the highest quintile is nearly 24%.

The second and most significant omission is that of government expenditures for in-kind transfers and education. Both of these are important components of real income to recipients, and they have been growing rapidly in the past two decades. This is especially true for in-kind transfers, as indicated by the expansion which has occurred in Medicare and Medicaid, and the public housing and food stamp programs. Moreover, Browning's estimates indicate that lower income families gain relative to higher income families when these expenditures are added to money income. In 1972, for example, in-kind expenditures constituted nearly 60% of money income for the lowest quintile and less than 1% for the highest, while the percentage contributions of education expenditures were approximately 25% and 6%, respectively.

Both of the preceding adjustments provide a better measure of the ability of family units to achieve economic welfare than the Bureau's unadjusted figures. Families with equal adjusted real incomes and of unequal sizes are not in the same relative position, however. Thus, a distribution of *per capita* adjusted real income is more meaningful than one based on family units alone. Moreover, contrary to popular opinion, family size falls as income falls, indicating that conversion to a per capita distribution would have the effect of equalizing further.

EFFECTS OF THE ADJUSTMENTS

The total effect of these three adjustments can be seen in the figures displayed in Table 6-3. A comparison of these figures with those reported in Table 6-1 indicates, first, that adjusted per capita real income is distributed more equally than the Census Bureau's "money income" and, second, that there has been a much larger redistribution of the former than the latter during the period 1952–1972.

The effect of redistribution on the distribution of income can be determined roughly by comparing the change over time in the proportions going to the lowest and highest quintiles. Distributions based on both definitions of income indicate some redistribution from the latter to the former. Clear-

---

6. Edgar K. Browning, "The Trend Toward Equality in the Distribution of Net Income," *Southern Economic Journal,* 1976, pp. 912–923.

TABLE 6-3   PERCENT OF ADJUSTED REAL INCOME PER CAPITA
BY FAMILY

Quintile:	Lowest	2nd	3rd	4th	Highest
1952	8.1	14.2	17.8	23.2	36.7
1962	8.8	14.4	18.2	23.1	35.4
1972	11.7	15.0	18.2	22.3	32.8

SOURCE: Edgar K. Browning, "How Much More Equality Can We Afford?", *The Public Interest,* Spring, 1976, p. 93.

ly, however, the volume of redistribution is greater when measured in terms of adjusted per capita real income.

Of the 3.6% relative gain (or 44% increase) registered for the lowest quintile in Table 6-3, over one-half is attributable to the inclusion of in-kind transfers and education.[7] When these results are combined with the findings reported in Table 6-2, it is clear that social welfare expenditures have played a major role in equalizing per capita real incomes. Without them, the relative share of the lowest quintile would have been only approximately 6% rather than the 11.7% recorded in Table 6-3. Social welfare expenditures, then, have nearly doubled the relative share of the lowest quintile.

THE INCIDENCE OF POVERTY

The data provided in the preceding section should give the reader a broader and essentially more correct view of the role of government in redistributing income than the one which is afforded by uncritical acceptance of widely-used measures of income distribution. These results have important implications for determining the effect of social welfare expenditures on the incidence of poverty. In fact, conventional measures probably understate the effectiveness of government expenditure policy.

The dominant view in economics is that poverty is symptomatic of an uneven distribution of command over economic resources; that is, that enough material goods are available to provide everyone a standard of living comfortably above subsistence, but a significant proportion of the

---

7. Calculated from Browning, "The Trend Toward Equality . . . ," p. 914.

American populace lacks the means, chiefly in the form of income, to purchase an adequate amount of these goods. Thus, it is implied that we can reduce poverty simply by increasing either the flow of goods or money income to the poor.

THE OFFICIAL POVERTY INDEX

Below what level of income is an individual or a family considered poor? The most widely used poverty index is a measure of money income first championed by the President's Council of Economic Advisors (CEA) in the 1964 *Economic Report of the President.* According to this measure, a family is poor if it has a yearly income less than three times the cost of the U.S. Department of Agriculture's "Economy Diet Plan." In 1973, this amounted to a little over $4,500 for an urban family of four.

The economy diet plan is one described as applicable for "temporary or emergency use when funds are low." It is not a diet intended for the long-run maintenance of vigorous health. Despite this shortcoming, the CEA combined this estimate with budget data from Social Security Administration (SSA) studies which indicated that low-income households spent about one third of their income on food; hence, the poverty income is three times the cost of the economy diet plan.

This level of income has been widely criticized for its inadequacy. If it is inadequate, of course, evidence should exist to show that the poor either cannot or do not choose to live on the food outlay assumed in the CEA-SSA poverty index. That this is the case is substantiated by government budget studies subsequent to the 1964 *Report* which indicate that even the richest of the poor (i.e., families right at the poverty line) spend nearly 43% of their income for food, and consequently have an even smaller amount of income left over for other essentials than the level deemed adequate according to the CEA-SSA index.[8]

Another criticism of this index is that it assumes a constant level of *real,* but not *relative,* income. Each year's index is adjusted for the increase that has occurred in the general price level, so that the real purchasing power of the poverty line income remains constant. However, the growth of money income reflects increases in productivity as well as in prices. Because the poverty index does not incorporate a correction for the former,

---

8. President's Commission on Income Maintenance Programs, Report, *Poverty and Plenty* (Washington: U.S.G.P.O., 1969).

the poverty line income constitutes a smaller proportion of average income as time passes, reflecting a deteriorating relative position for the poor.

THE FUCHS CRITERION

It is partly because of this effect that some economists have argued for a relative, rather than an absolute, measure of poverty income. The most widely-known of the relative income measures is the one championed by Victor Fuchs, which defines poverty as an income less than one-half the median income.[9] The poverty line prescribed by this criterion increases as median income grows, either as a result of increases in prices or productivity. Thus, it is a superior indicator of the relative progress of the poor.

Which of the two indexes is used to measure progress in alleviating poverty is an important choice. According to the official index, the percent of families in the poverty category fell from 32.7 to 9.7 between 1950 and 1973. According to Fuchs' criterion, however, the percent of families in this category remained at approximately 20% over the same period.

Perhaps our lack of success according to the Fuchs criterion provides a partial explanation of why, in spite of the large government effort to eliminate poverty, the level of social criticism remains high. Some observers have argued that we seem to have made little progress against poverty primarily because the aspirations of the poor have changed; i.e., people continue to feel poor because of their *relative* position in society. The Fuchs criterion indicates little change in relative positions over time.

The data referred to above indicate, then, that the number of "officially" poor families has declined, but that relative positions have changed very little. How can this be, in view of the results of the preceding section which indicated that social welfare expenditures have redistributed a significant proportion of real income from rich to poor? The key to this question is that both poverty measures rely on the same definition of money income used by the Census Bureau to estimate the distribution of income. Thus, when the money incomes of poverty families are adjusted as described in the preceding section of this chapter, the incidence of poverty is reduced significantly. Indeed, as we shall see, enough total real income has been transferred to the poor to raise all families above the official poverty line,

---

9. Victor R. Fuchs, "Redefining Poverty and Redistributing Income", *The Public Interest,* Summer, 1967, pp. 88–95.

assuming that the total is distributed more or less equally on a per capita basis among the poor.

THE BROWNING CRITERION

This last point is developed most fully in the 1975 study by Browning.[10] The most relevant results of this study for our purposes are reproduced in Table 6-4, which records estimates of the distribution of social welfare expenditures, taxes, and pre-transfer income. The crucial figures are those appearing in the last row of each column. According to these, adjusted average real income for a family of four grew from $2412 to $7248 between 1960 and 1973. In 1960, this amount was still insufficient to bring every family above the poverty line income of $3025. However, by 1973 the amount received was sufficient to bring each family more than $2700 above the poverty line. Browning concludes, therefore, that we are transferring enough real income to the poor to wipe out the problem completely, at least in terms of the official poverty index. Indeed, the adjusted income in 1973 exceeded even the more stringent Fuchs poverty index, so that we would have recorded some progress in terms of this statistic if we had only been using the correct measure of real income.

The biggest omission in the officially used measure of income, according to Browning, consists of the outlays for in-kind transfers (except education) that subsidize the consumption of particular goods and services, such as food stamps, public housing, Medicare, and Medicaid. These items make no apparent contribution to alleviating poverty because the government does not count them as part of money income. Nevertheless, they are a very important component of real income, constituting about 40% of government transfers to the poor.

Once again, it appears that social welfare expenditures have been more successful in moving us toward our distribution goals than official data indicate. This does not mean, however, that social welfare expenditures have been successful in completely eliminating poverty, nor does it mean that there is no room for improvement in the existing expenditure system. In the first place, there are still many gaps in coverage; for example, few programs benefit the 40% of the poverty households headed by working individuals. In the second instance, the existing structure has potentially

---

10. *Redistribution and the Welfare System.*

TABLE 6–4   SOCIAL WELFARE BENEFITS TO LOWEST QUARTILE

	1960	1966	1973
1. Total social welfare expend. ($ billions)	51.4	87.6	214.6
2. Percent of (1) to lowest quartile	44	43	47
3. Gross transfer to lowest quartile ($ billions)	22.8	37.6	100.7
4. Tax paid by lowest quartile ($ billions)	8.4	12.5	22.5
5. Net transfer: (3)–(4)	14.4	25.1	78.2
6. Education expend. to lowest quartile ($ billions)	3.2	5.9	11.8
7. Net transfer less educ. expend. ($ billions)*	11.2	19.2	66.4
8. Net transfer (less educ.) per capita (dollars)	247	387	1248
9. Pre-transfer income (dollars)	356	458	564
10. Adjusted real income per capita: (8)+(9)	603	845	1812

SOURCE: Edgar K. Browning, *Redistribution and the Welfare System,* Washington: American Enterprise Institute for Public Policy Research, 1975, p. 19

*Browning excludes education expenditures to highlight the growing importance of other in-kind transfers, and to make his data comparable over the 1960–1973 time period.

serious effects on efficiency. Both of these shortcomings will be developed further in the next section.

CRITICISMS OF EXISTING PROGRAMS

Although the total effort to eliminate poverty appears to be large enough, most observers are unwilling to label it an unqualified success. Among economists alone there appear to be four major sources of concern. First, as mentioned above, some of the poor are inadequately covered by existing programs, in spite of the large amount of money spent on such programs. Second, the design of many programs appears to reduce efforts to earn income. Third, the manner in which aid is given often distorts individual choices among goods and services. Fourth, some programs are quite costly to administer. Because these criticisms provide much of the rationale for proposed changes in the anti-poverty program, it is necessary to review each of them carefully before considering possible alternatives.

Each of these criticisms is based on the efficiency criterion that was introduced in Chapter 4 for evaluating alternative defense programs, in which we argued that the social net benefit test could not be employed because it was not possible to measure the efficiency benefits of government expenditures for defense. Alternatives were compared, however, by using cost-effectiveness criteria.

In this case, it is possible to measure efficiency benefits for many of the programs, but it is not appropriate to do so because the primary objective is redistribution rather than efficiency. However, given the fact of resource scarcity, it is legitimate and socially useful to evaluate redistribution programs according to the cost of achieving the redistribution objective. Those programs which are more effective in redistributing income should be chosen over those which have the same degree of effectiveness but higher opportunity costs. Alternatively, if the programs to be compared are equal in terms of costs, expenditures should be allocated according to their degree of effectiveness.

For each of the above criticisms, there is an implied failure in terms of the cost-effectiveness criteria. First, the belief that the poor are not adequately covered reflects a judgment that the level of effectiveness (measured in terms of the percentage of total program expenditures transferred to the poor) is lower than that which is achievable for a given level of costs. Second, the effect of the redistribution program which results in a lessening of income-earning effort is a reminder that costs can exceed money outlays, and that the social cost of achieving a given level of effectiveness will vary according to this effect. Third, we make the point below that in-kind transfers do not yield as high a level of satisfaction among recipients as would money transfers. In cost-effectiveness terms, this implies a lower level of effectiveness per dollar for the in-kind transfer program. Finally, if the existing programs are more costly to administer than an alternative would be, the cost per unit of effectiveness would probably be less for the alternative.

GAPS IN PROGRAM COVERAGE

Nearly $215 billion was spent for social welfare purposes in fiscal year 1973 by the various units of government. According to Browning, only 47% of this total was transferred to the lowest (income) quartile.[11] The remaining 53% was either transferred to units in the upper three quartiles or spent for program administration and operation. Among the various expenditure categories, only public aid programs (principally, Aid to Families with

---

11. See Table 6-4, Row 2.

Dependent Children) transferred to the poor a proportion significantly exceeding 50%.

This situation is not surprising in view of the fact that many social welfare programs were not established for the sole purpose of alleviating poverty. Still, with the exception of education, the proportion of program benefits going to the poor exceeds the proportion of the poor within the total population.

Some of the poor have not fared as well as others, however. Existing programs afford the least amount of relief to poor families headed by a male of prime age (21–65 years) working either part-time or full-time. Although the growing volume of in-kind transfers has lowered the incidence of poverty in this group, existing program eligibility requirements still reflect the philosophy that redistributive transfers ought to be reserved for those who are least able to support themselves. This philosophy, combined with relatively generous levels of support for the non-working poor, produces not only some inequality in the distribution of benefits but also an incentive for the poor not to be gainfully employed.

The amount of support provided to the poor also varies considerably from state to state. In general, higher levels of support are associated positively with per capita incomes. Thus, the poor who live in the wealthier states receive greater levels of support than do their counterparts in the poorer states, while those who live in the South are especially disfavored by virtue of their place of residence.

Observers have long been aware of the disparities in support created by inequalities in the geographic distribution of income, and some attempts have been made to offset this factor by using federal categorical grants (for Medicare and public aid) that have formulas with federal matching ratios inversely related to state per capita income. Obviously, these grant programs have been designed to equalize the distribution of social welfare expenditures. Unfortunately, the available evidence indicates that they have not had this effect; in some instances, the disparities in support actually increased after the equalizing formulas were adopted.[12] Apparently, welfare expenditures are highly income-elastic, and matching formulas simply make it relatively easier for wealthier states to increase their level of support.

---

12. For a fuller discussion of these results see: Bruce C. Stuart, "The Impact of Medicaid on Interstate Income Differentials," in K. E. Boulding and M. Pfaff (eds.), *Redistribution to the Rich and the Poor,* (Belmont, Ca.: Wadsworth, 1972), pp. 149–168.

EFFECTS ON WORK EFFORT

A second problem with the existing program structure is its potential deleterious effect on work effort. The chief source of difficulty is that benefits from many of the programs are reduced significantly as earned income increases. Where this is the case, program design prescribes a high marginal tax rate (MTR) on earned income. A few programs have an MTR equal to 100%. Perhaps the most notable is the program of unemployment compensation, wherein any income earned from employment results in a 100% loss of unemployment benefits. Other programs prescribe lower but significant MTRs; for example, Aid to Families with Dependent Children (67%), social security (50%), and food stamps and low-rent housing (25 to 30%).

Any of the above, coupled with the 12% payroll tax, would yield an MTR that may be high enough to discourage individuals from working. However, it is misleading to view transfer program effects in this way. Many families receive benefits from more than one program simultaneously, and their effective MTR is the sum of the separate MTRs. It is entirely conceivable, then, that some individuals are faced with an effective MTR that exceeds 100%, and that they are better off not working, provided only that their subsistence needs are being met via in-kind or cash transfers—an extremely likely situation in several states.

To date no reliable data exist which indicates the effects of combined, or effective, MTRs on work effort. We strongly suspect, however, that at least some of the substitution of leisure for work predicted by economic theory is occurring. This suspicion is reinforced by an example of the cumulative impact on the MTR of just two of the many in-kind transfer programs for which a poor family may be eligible.

In Table 6-5, we show the income possibilities facing an average family of four, headed by a female, which is eligible for both Aid to Families with Dependent Children (AFDC) assistance and the food stamp program. If the female works, she must pay both social security and income taxes.

Columns (1) and (2) illustrate a positive relationship between income from earnings and taxes. Columns (3) and (4) indicate clearly that both AFDC and food stamps benefits decline as earnings increase. A similar relationship would be evident for other in-kind transfer programs, such as housing and health care.

Column (5) depicts net real income—earnings *plus* AFDC and food stamp payments and *minus* social security and income taxes. The numbers in column (6) are equal to the differences between adjacent numbers in

TABLE 6–5 EFFECT OF POVERTY PROGRAMS ON INCOME

Earnings	Soc. Sec. & Income Taxes	AFDC	Food Stamps	Net Real Income	Change in Net Real Income	"Tax"	Marginal Tax Rate
$ 0	$ 0	$2400	$1992	$4392	–	–	–
1000	59	2213	1992	5146	$754	$ 246	24.6%
2000	117	1547	1752	5182	36	964	96.4
3000	176	880	1452	5156	−26	1026	102.6
4000	234	213	1152	5131	−25	1025	102.5
5000	293	–	852	5559	428	572	57.2
6000	351	–	552	6201	642	358	35.8
7000	667	–	252	6685	484	516	51.6

SOURCE: Adapted from Sar A. Levitan, *Programs in Aid of the Poor,* 3rd. ed., (Baltimore: The Johns Hopkins Press, 1976), Table 5.

column (5). The "tax" in column (7) is the difference between change in earnings ($1000) and change in net real income. It represents the reduction in income attributable to the combined effects of the social security and income taxes and the induced decrease in AFDC payments and food stamps. Finally, in column (8), the "tax" is expressed as a percentage of each $1000 increase in earnings.

Although this particular exampl would not fit all of the poor, it should clarify the point we have been mking. When existing programs are designed to reduce transfers as earnings increase, and families are eligible for more than one program, the cumulative effect may be to create high "tax" rates on earned income. Sometimes the rate can be high enough to discourage any work effort at all, as would probably be the case for the family exemplified in Table 6-5 which falls within the $2000–4000 earnings range.

EFFECTS ON CONSUMPTION CHOICES

As mentioned earlier, the fastest growing components of the social welfare program are those which subsidize the consumption of particular goods and services—i.e., the in-kind transfer programs. In spite of the fact that they have elevated many families above the poverty line in terms of real income, many economists are critical of the way these programs distort family consumption choices.

It is a well-known proposition in microeconomics that, of two equal-size transfers, one in cash and one in goods, the former will allow the recipient to achieve a higher level of satisfaction. This follows from the fact that a cash transfer allows the recipient to choose any combination of goods that corresponds most closely to his/her preferences. Conversely, the in-kind transfer interferes with this choice process by substituting the preferences of elected officials and government employees for those of the individual, confining his/her choices to less-preferred combinations.

The chief predictable consequence of an in-kind transfer is that recipients will end up spending a different (normally a larger) proportion of their real income on the good transferred than they would have done otherwise. Thus, for example, low-income recipients of subsidies for food and medical care will spend larger amounts on these items than they would if their money incomes were increased by the amount of the subsidy. If follows that a cash transfer could make recipients better off at no additional cost to taxpayers, or at least as well off as the in-kind transfer, at reduced taxpayer cost.

Perhaps the most widely-used rationale for in-kind transfers is that they accord with the preferences of taxpayers better than cash transfers do. According to this view, the taxpayer is concerned about raising the level of consumption of certain "essential" goods, such as food, housing, and medical care. However, taxpayers fear that low-income families would not spend enough of a cash transfer for these items, but would squander it instead on "non-essentials."

The preferences of both taxpayers and recipients are relevant when choosing among alternative types of redistribution. If cash transfers are an inferior alternative to taxpayers, then their use creates welfare losses exceeding those attributable solely to the taxes collected. However, there is no guarantee that the basic premise is correct; i.e., that the poor will "squander" their money, or that the extra loss to taxpayers is greater than the extra gain to those who receive the cash rather than the in-kind transfer.

Probably the most compelling economic rationale for in-kind transfers is the argument that certain goods—e.g., education, housing, and medical care—generate significant external benefits, and that individuals would tend to underspend on these items from a social point of view because they would ignore these externalities. If this is true, however, it provides a rational for social support at all income levels, and not just among low-income households.

THE HIGH COSTS OF ADMINISTRATION AND PARTICIPATION

The final source of concern is the presumably high cost of administering the governmental effort to alleviate poverty. Besides alleged cheating on the welfare rolls, no other criticism of social welfare programs appears to be more widely acknowledged in the popular news media. Here, too, public assistance programs are singled out for special attention; in order to minimize the incidence of payments to ineligible participants, it has been necessary to create relatively large staffs of welfare workers. This imposes a high cost on both taxpayers and program participants.

Another feature of the poverty effort which increases administrative costs is the multiplicity of available programs. This increases the number of governmental employees per poor family, and also increases the costs of participation by requiring the poor to establish eligibility several times. The former of these evokes little controversy; the latter is sometimes alleged to be trivial, but can be considered so only if the leisure time of the poor is of very little value.

Careful study and analysis may indicate that administration and compliance costs are not as great as critics believe them to be. In the final analysis, however, what really counts is how great these costs are relative to what they would be for an alternative program structure. We will develop this point further in the next section.

THE NEGATIVE INCOME TAX

Many alternatives have been suggested as substitute for or complements to the existing anti-poverty programs. Among these are various broad-based cash transfers (such as negative income tax, demogrants, and family assistance plans), wage subsidies, increased educational expenditures, stricter enforcement of anti-discrimination laws, and public employment. Economists have devoted the bulk of their attention, however, to the first of these: the negative income tax.[13]

---

13. Our concern in this section is primarily with the basic principles of a negative income tax. Such a scheme is more than a theoretical possibility, however. In fact, the Nixon administration proposed a limited version of the negative income tax in the form of its Family Assistance Plan in 1969. The FAP was actually approved by the House of Representatives, but not by the Senate.

The negative income tax (NIT) is a cash transfer program which normally imposes a single criterion for eligibility: current income below some prescribed level. It is typically conceived of as being national in scope and presumably directed by federal tax authorities. Benefits, of course, would be financed by general federal tax revenues. Lower-level governments would be involved only in program administration, if at all; no intergovernmental grant mechanism would exist.

The NIT (or a similarly-constructed broad-based cash transfer program) enjoys wide support among economists. Presumably, then, it offers certain advantages relative to the existing set of anti-poverty programs. These advantages can be viewed as correctives for the criticisms developed in the preceding section.

ADVANTAGES

An NIT's first advantage would be the nature of its coverage. With income as the sole criterion for eligibility, all of the poor could participate in the program. Levels of support would not vary according to the personal characteristics of participants or their places of residence. Relative to the existing program structure, some redistribution of income from richer to poorer states would probably occur, as would efficiency gains from a reduced rate of migration induced by differentials in public support payments.

Because it is a pure cash transfer, an NIT would also be free of the consumption-distorting effects of in-kind transfer programs. Substitution of the NIT for in-kind transfers would surely create welfare gains to participants. Whether total social welfare would increase is less certain for reasons reviewed above.

We can be relatively certain, however, that substitution of an NIT for existing programs would result in lower costs of administration and compliance. Presumably, the NIT would be administered by using the existing federal income tax structure; i.e., cash transfers would be determined from federal income tax returns. Although this would require that a number of families file returns who do not do so at present because their income is too low, the marginal cost attributable to the added burden on these individuals and on the tax collecting apparatus is likely to be quite low. It is almost certain to be lower than the cost of the existing social welfare bureaucracy.

Whether the NIT would have a lower adverse effect on work effort than the existing program structure is a matter of great dispute, however. Surely it is difficult, for reasons explained below, to design an NIT that has *no* adverse effects. It seems possible, though, to design one that has a smaller adverse effect than present programs especially for families which currently receive transfers from more than one program, provided that the NIT is a substitute for rather than a supplement to existing programs.

STRUCTURE

To explain the reasoning which lies behind these statements, it is necessary first to acquaint the reader with the mechanics of the negative income tax. Although a wide degree of variation in NIT plans is possible, there are three common elements: the minimum guaranteed income, the breakeven income, and the negative tax rate. Each NIT plan specifies a guaranteed annual income (G), which a family with no earned income (E) would receive. At all levels of E greater than zero, the cash transfer (Tr) declines. The decline in the cash transfer (ΔTr) per additional increment of E (ΔE) is the marginal negative tax rate MTR. The break-even income (B) is that level of earned income where a family neither receives cash transfers nor pays taxes.

Policy-makers must establish a value for G and the schedule of MTR. While G may be set at any level, those levels advocated by policy-makers are commonly less than or equal to the official poverty income. The schedule of MTR could be regressive, proportional, or progressive, but it is common practice to prescribe a proportional schedule. Hence, MTR has the same value at all levels of E—at least up to a level of E where Tr equals zero.

The simple arithmetic of an NIT plan is illustrated in Table 6-6. The example assumes a guaranteed income of $5000 (close to the official poverty line in 1974). The MTR schedule is proportional and has a value of .50. Although Tr declines as E rises, Tr is positive for all E up to $10,000, the break-even income (B). Above B, presumably the regular tax-rate schedule would apply, with marginal rates starting at 22% and gradually increasing to 50% at E of $44,000.

PROBLEMS

A value for B of $10,000 implies that a cash transfer will be given to many non-poor families, with the proportion of the total going to this group

TABLE 6-6   NEGATIVE INCOME TAX PLAN

G	E	Tr	E+Tr
$5000	$ 0	$5000	$5000
5000	2000	4000	6000
5000	4000	3000	7000
5000	6000	2000	8000
5000	8000	1000	9000
5000	10000	0	10000

dependent upon the number of families in the income range between zero and $10,000. Some people may object to this feature of the NIT, but it must be remembered that over one-half of current social welfare expenditures are also distributed to the non-poor. Moreover, it is entirely possible that redesigning the plan to materially reduce or eliminate this transfer will significantly increase the real cost of the program. One way to eliminate the transfer to the non-poor would be to raise the MTR to 100% for all E of $5000 and below. However, this would provide a strong incentive for poor families not to work at all, inasmuch as their income would be $5000 regardless of their employment status. Moreover, it would discourage some recipients with E above $5000 from working because they would sacrifice little by not working. If, for example, the positive MTR is 22% on E from $5000 to $6000, then families with a potential E of $6000 would give up only $780 by not working at all. This works out to only $15 per week—a relatively small price to pay for 40 hours of leisure. Of course, to the extent that the labor supply is reduced by such a plan, the value of GNP would be lower and the opportunity cost of the program elevated by that amount.[14]

There are other ways in which to reduce transfers to the non-poor. If G is set low enough (in this example, at $2500), then B can occur at a level below or equal to the poverty line income. However, this level of G is not sufficient to provide adequate support to the poorest of the poor. Conversely, MTR could be raised to a level between 50 and 100% (for a given

---

14. The NIT also exempts families from taxes they would have paid on earnings up to $10,000. This will create a reduction in government revenues which must be made up by imposing higher tax rates on income above the break-even level. According to Browning ("How Much More Equality Can We Afford?"), *marginal* tax rates on incomes above the break-even level may have to be increased so much because of this that the NIT is almost certain to have a noticeable effect on work incentives.

G) and B reduced below $10,000; again, the adverse effect on work effort would probably be pronounced.

The example is sufficient to illustrate the basic dilemma of an NIT plan: if G is high enough to eliminate poverty for the poorest of the poor, and the MTR is low enough so as not to discourage people from working, then B is high enough to ensure transfers to many non-poor families. Conversely, a low B implies either low levels of support or adverse work effects. Before rejecting the NIT because of this conflict, however, the reader should remember that existing programs also have this feature; and, indeed, that the value of the MTR is likely to be as high as or higher than the 50% used in the example above. Thus, substitution of an NIT may have no greater effect on work effort than does the current anti-poverty program.

THE NEW JERSEY EXPERIMENT

Concern about the probable effect of an NIT on work effort, has prompted the development of several experiments. The best known of these is the so-called New Jersey Negative Income Tax Experiment, conducted with the cooperation of some 1300 low-income families between 1968 and 1972 in four eastern cities. In this program, families were guaranteed various levels of G, ranging from 50 to 100% of the poverty line income, with their earned income E subject to MTRs ranging from 30 to 70%.

The objective of this experiment was to determine if higher values for G and MTR had significantly greater effects on hours worked than did lower values. The results of studies of the experiment indicate that the adverse labor supply effects of these variables was very small.[15] Indeed, the effect of variations in MTR was so small that it was determined to be statistically insignificant. Moreover, the bulk of the response which did occur was primarily in the form of fewer hours worked or second jobs given up. Very few subjects actually quit the labor force entirely.

Although the results of the New Jersey experiment are not necessarily indicative of what we could expect from a nationwide NIT plan, many observers have been encouraged by these results, which have stimulated further investigations of the NIT as a practical policy alternative. In order for it to be adopted, however, considerable political resistance would have

---

15. See the thorough discussion of the New Jersey experiment in: *Journal of Human Resources,* Vol. 9, Spring, 1974.

to be overcome, as indicated by the opposition to the Nixon administration's Family Assistance Plan—an NIT-type plan with an extremely low G which was proposed as a supplement to existing programs. The political resistance to change would be even more formidable if the NIT were proposed as a replacement for a large part of the current government effort against poverty. Yet, to minimize the real cost of the poverty program, the latter alternative is probably the appropriate choice. To simply add the NIT without simultaneously reducing other programs would require a further increase in tax rates, perhaps to levels which would have an adverse effect on work and investment decisions of non-poor taxpayers.

SUMMARY

There has been a remarkable growth in social welfare expenditures during the last two decades. Contrary to common opinion based on the distribution of money income figures published annually by the Bureau of the Census, these expenditure programs have effected a significant change in the fortunes of the lower-income classes. To reach such a conclusion we have made what we think are reasonable adjustments to the Bureau's data: (1) the separation of government cash transfers from earned income, (2) the inclusion of in-kind transfers and education expenditures as components of real income, and (3) adjustments for differences among income classes in family size.

Similar adjustments give us what we refer to as the Browning poverty criterion or index, which indicates that we are transferring enough income to the poor to virtually eliminate poverty in the United States. This is a different conclusion from the ones based on the official poverty index or the Fuchs criterion.

Although the total effort to eliminate poverty appears to be large enough, the existing program structure fares poorly on a cost-effective basis. There are four major reasons why it does: (1) some of the poor are inadequately covered, (2) many programs reduce efforts to earn income, (3) the type of aid given distorts individual choice among goods and services, and (4) administrative costs are relatively high.

Existing programs offer the least amount of help to families headed by prime-age working males, and the amount of support varies greatly by state and region. Families are often eligible for several programs simultaneously. However, in many instances, the combination results in a high marginal tax rate on earned income, producing a significant disincentive to work. Moreover, much of the governmental redistribution to the poor is made in the form of goods and services, rather than cash. Economic theory indicates that the poor could be made better off for a smaller outlay of tax dollars if the redistribution were in the form of money instead.

Several economists have suggested that many of the failures of the existing poverty program could be corrected by adoption of a negative income tax. This is a cash transfer program wherein the amount transferred is related inversely to earned income and directly to family size. Such a program could be universal in coverage, free of the distorting effects of in-kind transfers, and less costly to administer than the existing program structure.

The negative income tax will also have some negative effect on work effort. However, it appears possible to design a tax scheme that has less effect in this regard than that of the existing poverty program. Encouraging results have been achieved in an experiment conducted with the aid of low-income families in New Jersey.

SUGGESTIONS FOR
FURTHER READING

Browning, Edgar K., *Redistribution and the Welfare System,* Washington, D.C.: American Enterprise Institute for Public Policy Research, 1975.

This book presents a critical analysis of the ways in which we measure poverty, of the current poverty program, and of proposed alternatives.

Green, Christopher, *Negative Taxes and the Poverty Problem,* Washington, D.C.: Brookings Institution, 1967.

This document is a good review of the mechanics of a negative income tax and its probable economic effects.

Perlman, Richard, *The Economics of Poverty,* New York: McGraw-Hill, 1976.

The text provides a relatively thorough summary of the issues at an elementary level.

PART 3

GOVERNMENT REVENUES

SEVEN

PRINCIPLES OF TAXATION

Taxes provoke concern and controversy because they take a large amount of income from almost every American family. Indeed, most taxpayers pay more than one dollar of every four dollars they earn to governments. (In 1974, the ratio of federal, state, and local taxes to the GNP was approximately 28%). Of course, taxpayers get something in return for their payments: external and internal protection, streets and highways, education, health care, welfare, recreation, and so on.

This chapter develops a framework that will foster a rational discussion of taxes. The primary component in this framework is a "set of principles" that can be used in selecting and evaluating alternative taxes. These principles are a necessary part of any economic theory of taxation. However, there are some tax questions that cannot be answered by theory no matter how logical the theory may be. For example, the answer to the question "What is a fair tax?" depends in the final analysis on individual values and beliefs as to what is fair. The fact that much emotion may enter tax discussions underlines the need to develop a framework for discussion and analysis.

In the next section, the major functions of taxes and two philosophical views concerning taxes are presented. Following that, we develop the basic principles of taxation, and then use them to evaluate major types of revenue sources.

MAJOR TAX FUNCTIONS

Taxes have four major functions: (1) to finance goods and services provided by the government; (2) to change the allocation of resources; (3) to redistribute income; and (4) to stabilize aggregate demand in the economy.

THE FINANCING
FUNCTION OF TAXES

Traditionally, the primary purpose of a tax was to pay for goods and services provided by the government. The financing function of taxes remains important although taxes have other purposes today. Taxes are the main source of revenue or income for governments and provide the chief means of covering current costs or expenditures.

The major issue involving the financing function of taxes is their effect on the efficient use of scarce resources. Taxes divert resources away from alternative uses. These uses may be a source of lesser benefits than the uses to which these resources are put in the public sector. However, if taxes divert resources away from their best alternative use, they are a source of allocative inefficiency. As indicated in previous chapters, then, the efficient distribution of resources to the public sector via taxes requires that benefits derived from government spending have a value equal to or greater than the alternative uses these resources would have in the private sector of the economy.

THE ALLOCATION
FUNCTION OF TAXES

In the financing function, the diversion of resources by taxes from the private sector is done under the presumption that resources are used efficiently in the private sector. Thus, the primary concern is to divert resources in a manner that does not interfere, or interferes the least, with the allocation of resources in the private sector. If resources are not efficiently allocated in the private sector, taxes can be purposely used to have non-neutral effects; that is, taxes can be used to change the allocation of resources. More is said about the allocation function of taxes later in this chapter and in Chapter 12. It suffices now to merely point out that taxes can be and are used to encourage or to discourage specific patterns of behavior in the private economy.

THE REDISTRIBUTION FUNCTION OF TAXES

The redistribution function of taxes raises the question of the appropriate way of distributing taxes among taxpayers. Taxes and tax rates can be selected in a manner that alters the pattern of income among taxpayers. Taxes can shift the pattern of income away from certain income groups and towards others. For example, progressive income tax rates take a higher percent of income for higher incomes than for lower; thus, they tend to reduce the after tax income of higher income groups more than they reduce the after tax income of lower income groups. Progressive income tax rates, then, would be expected to shift the after tax income pattern away from higher income groups to lower income groups. This effect, however, can be offset in part or in whole by tax deductions, credits, and the like which higher income groups can take advantage of in order to minimize their tax payments. Tax incidence studies try to find out who really pays taxes—that is, to find out who bears the real burden of taxation. Such studies will be examined in the next chapter.

THE STABILIZATION FUNCTION OF TAXES

The stabilization function of taxes views taxes as a variable that can be altered to direct the economy toward economic stability; that is, full employment and a stable price level. An increase in taxes normally reduces private consumption and saving, therefore reducing private spending. A decrease in taxes increases private consumption and saving, and therefore has the opposite effect on private spending. Thus, taxes can play an important role in changing the level of private demand. When the economy is near or at full employment and is experiencing inflation, tax rates can be increased to reduce inflationary pressures. When the economy is experiencing declining real output and rising unemployment, tax rates can be cut in order to increase private spending.

Taxes, then, can be viewed as a fiscal policy variable to be changed depending upon overall economic conditions. This role places taxes in quite a different perspective than the role in which they are traditionally seen—simply as a method of finance. The 1964 income tax cut, the 1968 surtax, and the 1975 and 1976 income tax cuts are illustrations of taxes being used to stabilize the economy. Tax credits, such as the investment tax credit, have also been used for this purpose.

The American tax system also has properties which provide the economy with some economic stability. During periods of economic expansion, tax collections tend to automatically rise because of the growth in tax bases such as sales and income. This automatic growth in taxes tends to slow down the expansion. During periods of economic contraction, tax collections automatically decline because of the decline in sales and income in the economy. This automatic fall in taxes tends to slow down the decline in economic activity. Therefore, even if tax rates are not changed during the ups and downs in the economy, tax collections automatically change in a way that tends to stabilize the economy. This automatic countercyclical behavior in tax collections has made an important contribution to economic stability in the past.

PHILOSOPHICAL VIEWS CONCERNING TAXES

Two philosophical views exist concerning the relationship between the government and the taxpayer. The first view considers the relationship to be voluntary, and the second view considers it to be involuntary or coercive.

TAXES AS VOLUNTARY PAYMENTS

Taxes may be viewed as voluntary payments; that is, as amounts paid voluntarily by taxpayers for goods and services demanded by them. In this "voluntary exchange" relationship, taxes are prices that reflect, on the demand side, the marginal valuation that taxpayers have for public goods and services; on the supply side, they reflect the economic cost of producing goods and services.

The voluntary payment view of taxes stresses a quid pro quo relationship between the government and the taxpayer; namely, taxpayers give up something in the form of taxes in order to get in return what they are willing to pay for—government goods and services. The voluntary payment view of taxes presupposes that taxpayers' preferences are transmitted through the ballot box to the representatives of taxpayers, just as consumers' preferences are transmitted through prices to producers. Thus, this view of taxes perceive the objectives of taxpayers as identical to those of government.

TAXES AS INVOLUNTARY PAYMENTS

A contrasting view perceives taxes as involuntary payments. This view stresses the point that taxpayers have no choice but to pay their taxes. Thus, it is argued that the relationship between the government and taxpayers is not analogous to the voluntary relationship between sellers and buyers in the private economy.

Both of these views can be beneficial in helping to understand taxes and the relationship between taxpayer and government, although neither fully describes the relationship. Buyers in the economy, as compared to taxpayers, are generally freer to "buy" or not to buy. Once decisions are made concerning government expenditures, individual taxpayers do not have the choice to pay or not to pay taxes. However, the relationship between the government and taxpayers in a democratic society is not totally coercive. If the democratic decision-making process is working correctly, taxpayers are in general getting what they are demanding. In the event that taxpayers as a group are not getting what they want, they can choose to elect new representatives. It should be acknowledged, however, that individual wants are better fulfilled in the private economy than they are in the public sector. The efficiency of both depends upon how well they provide the goods and services demanded by the public.

TAX CRITERIA

Two criteria will be used to evaluate taxes: *equity* and *efficiency.* Equity is concerned with the way in which taxes are distributed among the taxpayers, and efficiency is concerned with the effects of taxes on the efficient operation of the economy.

HORIZONTAL EQUITY

Equity in taxation simply means that a tax should be "just." Certainly, most people agree that taxes should be just, but a real problem arises in trying to determine exactly what this means. One idea of tax justice or tax fairness that may be traced through western thought is that of equal tax treatment for people in equal economic circumstances. The *equal tax treatment doctrine* clearly suggests that taxes should not be arbitrary and discriminatory. Taxpayers in identical economic circumstances—that is, taxpayers who have the same capacity to pay taxes—should pay the same amount of taxes. Assuming that income is the accepted measure of ability to pay, the equal tax treatment doctrine is violated if taxpayers having the same incomes pay different amounts of taxes. If spending is the tax base, equal rates of spending should result in equal tax payments. A tax distribution that adheres to the equal tax treatment doctrine provides a horizontally equitable distribution of taxes.

The controversial aspect of horizontal equity does not concern the underlying concept; the principle is widely accepted. The controversial issue involves what is meant by equal economic circumstances and how such circumstances should be measured. Should family size make a difference? Should wealth be considered along with income as an indicator of the amount of taxes which should be paid? These questions and others along similar lines are difficult to answer. The American tax system is full of inconsistencies concerning tax treatment of equals. Strict adherence to the principle of horizontal equity should preclude preferential tax treatment of any sort by type of income. Many well-known tax inequities, such as unequal effective property tax rates on property with the same market value, would be eliminated if the principle of horizontal equity was better understood and applied in practice. In England, and recently in the U.S., a form of income called "unearned income" (income from property) is taxed more heavily than income from labor. This tax treatment of different forms of income would be at odds with the equity principle enumerated above.

VERTICAL EQUITY

A corollary to the principle of equal tax payments for equals is the principle of *relative tax treatment for individuals in relative economic circumstances*—the principle of vertical equity. Two tax principles have evolved that are consistent with vertical equity: the ability to pay principle and the benefits received principle. These principles of taxation have a long history and many scholars have contributed to their development.

The Ability to Pay Principle

The ability to pay principle states that taxes should be distributed among taxpayers in accordance with their ability to pay taxes. Using income as the measure of ability, this would mean that taxpayers with more income would pay more taxes. But how much more? Should the tax rate be *regressive, proportional,* or *progressive?*

In a *regressive* rate structure the ratio of tax payments to income declines as income rises. In a *proportional* structure, this ratio stays the same; in a *progressive* structure, this ratio rises as income rises. Using only three income groups, Table 7-1 shows progressive, proportional, and regressive tax rates, and Figure 7-1 illustrates these rates graphically. Although the ability to pay principle of taxation is generally interpreted to suggest progressive rates, Table 7-1 shows that proportional rates are consistent with this principle. Moreover, even a regressive structure may be consistent with the ability to pay principle. For example, a millionaire paying at a tax rate of only 10% would be paying a greater amount than a $25,000-a-year worker paying a 50% rate. The regressive rates column in Table 7-1 illustrates that, the $20,000 income earner, although paying at a lower tax rate (15%), is paying more than the lower income earner paying at a higher rate. The use of progressive income tax rates means that the ratio of taxes paid to income rises as income rises. In other words, an individual's average tax rates have to rise when he/she moves from one income bracket to a higher bracket. For this to occur, the *marginal* tax rate has to rise; that is, the rate that applies to the incremental part of a person's income. Suppose, for example, that on the first $5000 of income the tax rate is 10%, that on the second $5000 the rate is 15%, and so on. Now, a taxpayer with $10,000

TABLE 7-1 REGRESSIVE, PROPORTIONAL, AND PROGRESSIVE INCOME TAX RATES

| Income | Regressive | | Proportional | | Progressive | |
	Rate	Taxes Paid	Rate	Taxes Paid	Rate	Taxes Paid
$10,000	20%	$2,000	20%	$2,000	20%	$2,000
$20,000	15%	$3,000	20%	$4,000	25%	$5,000
$30,000	10%	$3,000	20%	$6,000	30%	$9,000

FIGURE 7–1
PROGRESSIVE, PROPORTIONAL, AND REGRESSIVE RATES

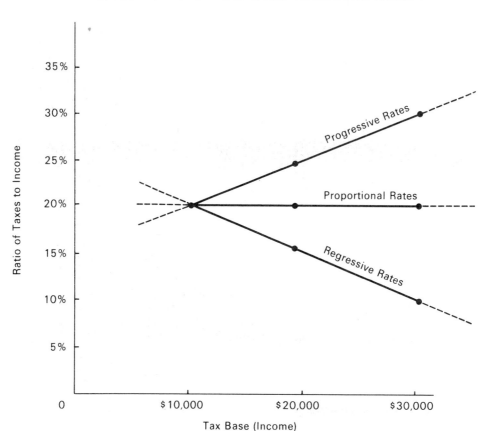

would pay $1250 in taxes ($500 + $750). The average rate on the taxpayer's entire income is 12½% with the average rate increasing from 10 to 12½% between the two brackets. The marginal rate is 15%—the rate levied on the second $5000 and increasing from 10%. The marginal tax rate is the one which has the greatest impact on incentives to work and save. This matter and other aspects of tax rates, such as the difference between normal and effective rates, are examined later in this chapter and in chapters to come.

Can a theoretical case be made in support of progressive rates? The case for progressive rates is an uneasy and inconclusive one. It is uneasy because progressive rates can be rationalized only on the basis of dubious assumptions: (1) that interpersonal comparisons can be made; (2) that people have equal capacities to enjoy income; and (3) that marginal utility of income declines as income rises. The case is inconclusive because even if we accept these assumptions, it is clear that progressive rates are not always logically suggested in regard to the ability to pay principle. Let us briefly explain why.

Three alternative rules or doctrines have been developed to interpret the meaning of tax equity in terms of "equality of sacrifice." These rules are the *equal absolute,* the *equal proportional,* and the *equal marginal sacrifice* rules. Given the assumptions enumerated above, progressive rates are the logical outcome only under the *equal marginal sacrifice* rule. Under this rule, taxes are distributed in such a manner as to equalize tax sacrifices at the margin. Assuming identical and declining marginal utility schedules, this rule suggests not only progressive rates, but maximum progression: that is, taxes levied first on those with the highest incomes, and then on successively lower incomes until the required amount of tax revenue is raised. The effect of this would be the leveling of income after taxes through successive income classes until enough revenue is raised.

Under the equal absolute and equal proportional sacrifice rules, progressive rates are not always implied. For example, under the equal absolute sacrifice rule, which attempts to equate the total loss of utility of each taxpayer, progressive rates are called for only if the slope of the declining marginal utility schedule has an elasticity greater than unity.[1] It may not be so unreasonable to accept the assumption that the marginal utility schedule is a negative sloping curve, but to have to assume the precise slope of the schedule in order to justify progressive rates significantly weakens the case.

If the theoretical case for progressive rates is inconclusive, how can progressive rates be defended? In the final analysis, the case for progressive rates relies essentially on the social desirability of redistributing income via the tax process. Interestingly, the next chapter will show that in fact most American families pay approximately proportional rates.

---

1. This would mean that the negative slope of the marginal utility schedule falls more rapidly than the percent increase in income. If the negative slope of the marginal utility schedule falls at the same percentage rate as the percent increase in income, the absolute sacrifice rule would call for proportional rates. For a full discussion, see Richard A. Musgrave, *The Theory of Public Finance* (New York: McGraw-Hill Book Co., Inc., 1959), Chapter 5.

The Benefits Received Principle

The benefits received principle of taxation is an attempt to apply the rule of the market to tax distributions. In the market, the equilibrium price reflects the marginal benefit, or the valuation that consumers place on the last unit sold, as well as the economic cost of producing that unit. Under certain circumstances, this is both an equitable and an efficient allocative mechanism. The benefits received principle of taxation applies the same reasoning to the distribution of taxes; namely, that taxes should be distributed in accordance with the individual marginal benefits received by taxpayers from government goods and services. An illustration of the benefits received principle in practice is the use of excise taxes on gasoline to pay for highways. People that benefit and use highways pay for them when they buy gasoline. Generally, people that use highways the most both benefit the most and pay the most.

In contrast to the ability to pay principle, which considers only the tax side of the tax-expenditure process, the benefits received principle integrates both sides of this process. Thus, this principle provides not only a criterion for tax justice, but also a guide to efficient resource allocation. The benefits received principle and the ability to pay principle are similar in instances where the best index of benefits is the ability to pay, measured in terms of income.

The benefits received principle of taxation has some well-known limitations. Individual benefits from government goods and services may be difficult to measure (fire and police protection), and the cost of collection from the user may be high in some instances (city streets). Individual preferences for some government services may not be revealed, and the purpose of the government service may be incompatible with the benefits received principle (public assistance). However, whenever it is possible to measure individual benefits and when the purpose of the government service is not to redistribute income, taxes may be selected that could be defended by this principle.

TAX EFFICIENCY

Tax efficiency has three aspects. The first involves the *administration and compliance* costs of taxes. Tax efficiency is concerned with the convenience and certainty of a tax to the taxpayer, and with the cost of collection and compliance to the taxing unit. An efficient tax would not impose excess cost to the taxpayer in the payment of the tax and would be collected and enforced at the lowest possible costs. Administrative costs vary, of course, among individual taxes. Some taxes are more costly to administer than others. The cost of collecting and enforcing the federal income tax is large; yet these costs do not appear high, as a percent of revenue collected, although there is no real basis for making an objective determination. In regard to the compliance costs of taxes, they could be rather high for certain taxes while appearing to be low enough to require little emphasis. The second and third aspects of tax efficiency will be stressed instead, primarily because they involve a most important aspect of tax efficiency; namely the effect of taxes on the efficient operation of the economy.

The second aspect of tax efficiency involves an understanding of *tax neutrality*. Traditionally, economists view the economy as operating under a purely competitive framework. Given this framework, the allocation of resources in the private economy would be optimal or at least efficient. As we have learned, the opportunity cost of increasing the size of the public sector is equal to the value of the private goods and services sacrificed. But if, in addition to opportunity cost, private decision-making in the market is interfered with and relative prices and individual behavior patterns are altered, taxes may cause an additional cost and have *non-neutral* effects and move the economy away from the most efficient use of its resources.

Taxes are usually never completely neutral in their impact on individual choice. They generally have an income effect, a substitution effect, or both. Taxes reduce the amount of private disposable income and may change the relative income positions of taxpayers. These income effects reduce the amount of private spending and saving, and may alter the distribution of expenditures. The substitution effects of taxes are recorded in terms of their effects on relative prices of goods and services, among other things. Taxes may increase the price of a good, and thereby cause a shift in spending toward nontaxed goods. Similarly, some taxes may cause the substitution of leisure for work by decreasing the price of leisure relative to work. Taxes differ in terms of neutrality, however, thus requiring that they be evaluated in terms of their relative neutrality.

The final aspect of tax efficiency again relates to the efficient operation of the economy. Although as a general rule taxes should be neutral so as to interfere as little as possible with the operation of the market, in the case of market failures we wish taxes to be non-neutral in order to correct for market imperfections and possibly induce more efficient behavior in the market. Market failures were discussed in Chapter 2 and will not be reiterated here; it is important to remember that in the evaluation of individual

149

taxes, which follows in this text the primary emphasis will be on the *relative* non-neutral effects of taxes. Also, it should be pointed out that the use of tax receipts is largely ignored in the subsequent discussion. It should be clear that if we want to determine whether a tax reduces efficiency in resource allocation, we must also consider the uses of tax revenues. Only if these uses in the public sector yield benefits smaller than uses to which resources would have been put in the private sector can we say for certain that the tax created inefficiency in resource allocation.

TAX EQUITY AND EFFICIENCY ANALYSIS

Major tax sources will now be analyzed in terms of equity and efficiency. Based on the analysis, each source is ranked high or low depending upon how well it meets the criteria of equity and efficiency. The relative ranking of taxes presented in the text is not meant to be absolute or final. Instead, it could serve for as a basis for further discussion. The search for taxes that meet or best meet the criteria of equity and efficiency is the intent of the rankings.

PERSONAL INCOME TAXES

Income taxes are a direct and broadly-based source of revenue. Taxes levied on income are considered to be direct taxes because they have to be paid out of income regardless of how they are levied. They are considered a broad-based tax because they are levied on a large subgroup of the populace.

Tax collections from a given source depend upon the tax *base* and the tax *rate.* In the case of income taxes, collections vary directly with changes in both the base and in the rate. Three income tax rate structures are possible: *proportional, progressive,* and *regressive.* Each structure ranks somewhat differently with regard to the aforementioned tax criteria.

Proportional Income Taxes

As has been previously stated, a proportional income tax is levied at the same rate at all levels of income. Thus, every taxpayer pays the same

TABLE 7–2 SELECTED REVENUE SOURCES RELATIVELY RANKED BY EFFICIENCY AND EQUITY

Revenue Source	Efficiency		Equity	
	High	Low	High	Low
Personal Income Tax				
Proportional Rate	X		X	
Progressive Rate		X	X	
Regressive Rate		X		X
Sales Tax				
General Sales Tax (in practice)	X			X
Selected Sales Tax		X		X
Property Tax		X		X
Licenses				
Fixed Dollar Amount	X			X
Variable Dollar Amount	X		X	
Charges				
Fixed Dollar Amount	X			X
Variable Dollar Amount	X		X	

NOTE: See the discussion in the text for the bases for the relative ranking of these revenue sources.

percent of taxable income. For example, if the tax rate is 20%, every taxpayer will pay twenty cents of every dollar of taxable income.

Many economists, but not all, would rank a proportional income tax relatively high in terms of equity because it adheres to the ability to pay principle of taxation; namely, the amount collected varies directly with the capacity of people to pay taxes. With this tax, people with the same taxable income would make equal tax payments, thus adhering to the principle of horizontal equity. Also, people with unequal taxable incomes would make unequal tax payments in accordance with relative differences in their incomes, thus adhering to the principle of vertical equity.

A proportional income tax rate structure meets the criterion of efficiency better than do alternative income tax rate structures and many others. Proportional income taxes do reduce income but do not change the relative income position of taxpayers. Thus, although the amount of spending may be reduced, the pattern of spending should not be affected by proportional income taxes. The fact that incomes are reduced may encourage people to work harder. On the other hand, proportional income taxes may encourage people to substitute leisure for work, thus reducing the amount of work.

The net effect of proportional income taxes on the amount of work depends upon the relative dominance of the income and substitution effects.

Progressive Income Taxes

Many economists also rank a progressive rate structure high in terms of equity because it too adheres to the ability to pay principle. Progressive income tax rates are an alternative to proportional rates. The personal choice between progressive and proportional rates is a matter of judgment as to which of the two rates best meets the principle of tax equity. We shall rank both high in terms of tax equity.

Progressive income tax rates can be strongly criticized because of the way in which they affect the operation of the economy. First, a progressive tax changes the pattern of income distribution. It tends to redistribute income away from certain income groups (high-income groups) to other income groups (low-income groups). Second, since the pattern of income distribution is different after taxes than it is before, a progressive tax alters spending patterns and consequently changes relative commodity prices and the pattern of resource allocation. Third, a progressive tax tends to fall more heavily on saving than on consumption, and therefore it tends to reduce the rate of investment. Fourth, a progressive tax will tend to reduce investment and production in another way; it may reduce *incentives* to work, for it tends to increase the price of work and decrease the price of leisure. Finally, progressive tax rates have the adverse feature of increasing the difficulty in moving from low- to high-income status. In summary, a progressive tax warrants a relatively high ranking in terms of equity, but ranks low in terms of the efficiency criterion.

Regressive Income Taxes

A regressive income tax structure can be in violation of the ability to pay principle of taxation, depending upon the pattern of regression. Regressive tax rates usually result in tax distributions where the burden of taxes falls most heavily on those in the worst economic circumstances. Such rates take a higher percent of income from low-income groups than they do from higher income groups. Furthermore, they can result in tax payments falling as income rises. There is general agreement that regressive tax rates are the worst choice on the basis of tax equity.

Similar to a progressive tax with respect to tax efficiency, a regressive tax does not have a neutral impact on the economy. It alters the pattern of income distribution and as a result, spending and resource allocation. It tends to fall more heavily on consumption than on saving, and it increases the price of leisure relative to the price of work.

SALES TAXES

Sales taxes are levied either as a percentage of the sales value per unit or as a fixed amount per unit sold. Two types of sales taxes can be distinguished: general sales taxes, and selective sales taxes or "excises." The general sales tax is a proportional levy on the value of retail sales. It is a broad-based tax, since sales of many commodities are included in the tax base. A truly general sales tax would include in the tax base all final goods and services sold. On the other hand, selective sales or excise taxes are levied on specific commodities, whether on the sales value itself or on a per unit basis. Excise taxes are sometimes levied on goods at the time of production, whether or not they are taxed again at the wholesale or retail sales level.

General Sales Taxes

A truly general sales tax would be somewhat similar to a proportional income tax, and would meet the criteria of tax equity and efficiency relatively well. The major difference is that a general sales tax can be avoided by saving, since under a general sales tax only spending is taxed. Citizens will be encouraged by the general sales tax to spend less; the proportional income tax contains no such encouragement. However, general sales taxes vary among states as to final goods and services included in the tax base, and are usually levied on consumption goods. In practice, then, general sales taxes tend to have "regressive effects" and, to the extent that this is correct, general sales taxes do not score well in terms of the ability to pay principle.

The regressiveness of the general sales tax is a result of the commodities which are usually included in the tax base and of the spending patterns of different income groups. For example, P and R are two taxpayers. P has an income of $10,000 a year, and R has income of $20,000 a year. Each spends $10,000 annually on the commodities subject to the general sales tax. A general sales tax rate of 4% would mean that each would pay $400 in the form of taxes. In terms of income, however, taxpayer P would be paying at a rate of 4% ($400/$10,000), while taxpayer R, with twice the income,

153

would be paying at a rate of 2% ($400/$20,000). Thus, proportional levies on sales may not result in proportional rates on income. States that include food in the general sales tax base, for example, are very likely to have a sales tax system that is regressive, as in the above example. In general, general sales taxes, as they are designed in practice, are ranked low in regard to tax equity because the consumption of goods generally subject to such a tax is not a good indication of the ability to pay taxes.

To the extent that general sales taxes are regressive, they fall more heavily on consumption, and shift the patterns of income distribution, spending, and resource allocation. Ideally, the broad base of the tax, however, promises to minimize the non-neutral effects of the tax. Relative commodity prices may not be altered very much by the general sales tax. Again, this will depend on how broad the tax base is in any given state. In comparison to selective sales taxes, the ideal general sales tax meets the criterion of tax efficiency very well. Thus, the general sales tax can be ranked high from the point of view of efficiency, subject to the qualifications noted above.

Selective Sales Taxes

In general, selective sales taxes are ranked low in terms of our tax criteria. Some selective sales or excise taxes, however, may be considered "fair," and some can be defended on the ability to pay or the benefits received principles of taxation.

Selective sales taxes can be placed into three groups—sumptuary excises, such as tobacco and liquor taxes; luxury excises, such as those on jewelry, electrical appliances, and firearms; and benefit-base levies, such as the gasoline tax. Sumptuary excises are difficult to justify on either the ability to pay or the benefits received principle. The argument usually used to defend sumptuary taxes is based on the social undesirability of consuming these products. Normally, one would think that luxury excises could be defended on the ability to pay principle; however, many so-called luxuries are consumed by low-income groups, and excises levied on certain commodities called luxuries may have regressive effects. Some benefit-base levies such as the gasoline tax can be defended on the benefits received principle of taxation. This tax is levied on a per gallon basis, and allocated to finance streets and highways for the benefit of automobile users.

Selective sales taxes do not meet the tax criterion of efficiency because they tend to change relative commodity prices. Thus, the allocation of resources after a selective sales tax has been levied will be different than the allocation prior to the tax. Whether this allocation is less efficient depends upon the use to which the tax funds are put in the public sector, as well as upon the prevailing state of efficiency before the tax.

PROPERTY TAXES

Property taxes are levied on the assessed values of personal and real property. The assessed value of property is the value that the assessor places on property for tax purposes; it is usually some fraction of a property's full market value. In contrast to income and sales taxes which are levied on *flows,* property taxes are levied on *stocks* such as land and buildings. Thus, property taxes are a wealth type of tax.

Property taxes have been defended on both the ability to pay and the benefits received principles of taxation; however, many tax experts believe that property taxes in practice are the worst taxes in existence. Part of the low evaluation of this tax is due to the administration and the operation of the property tax system.

First, the administration of the property tax involves the listing of taxable property on the tax rolls. A great deal of personal property and some real property may not be listed on the tax rolls and therefore not be taxed at all. Second, different types of property are usually classified differently for tax purposes. Both tax rates and the assessment ratio (the ratio of assessed value to market value) may vary by classification. Third, within each property classification the equal and relative tax treatment doctrines are usually violated because assessment ratios are not equal. Two pieces of property of the same market value should be assessed at the same value regardless of the age of the property, its location, or its type in order for the criterion of horizontal equity to be met. Also, pieces of property of unequal value should be assessed unequally to meet the tax criterion of vertical equity. If the assessment ratio varies depending upon the property's value, age, type, and so on, the criterion of vertical equity is not met.

Assessment ratio studies reveal that the assessment ratio varies significantly, resulting in unfair property tax burdens. In general, the assessment ratio tends to fall as the value of property rises. This results in property taxes having a regressive effect. Commercial and industrial properties are generally assessed relative to market value much more highly than are residential properties. New property is usually assessed at a higher percent of market value than is old property; urban property usually has a higher assessment ratio than rural property; and so on.

In order for property taxes to be distributed fairly among property owners, the property assessment ratio should be equalized among all pieces of property. Given this criterion, property taxes would be the same for pieces of property of equal value and different for properties of unequal value. These differences in property taxes would, then, be in proportion to the differences in the value of property and could be defended on the ability to pay principle. This assumes, of course that the value of property is an acceptable measure of peoples' abilities to pay taxes.

Property taxes are ranked low in terms of efficiency as well as equity. Property taxes tend to distort the pattern of land use. Since property taxes are levied on improvements as well as on land, a lower property tax burden usually falls on unimproved land than on improved land. To the extent that this is true, property taxes will encourage the landowner to hold land for speculative purposes and will tend to discourage improvements. If old property of the same value as new property is subject to lower property taxes, property taxes will tend to discourage new property development. Similarly, higher property taxes on commercial and industrial properties will tend to discourage the development of these properties. Sometimes, the exemption of property taxes is used as a way to attract industries to locate in a given area; although this may benefit one area, it will do so at the expense of another. Further, such use of taxes tends to result in competition for industry on the basis of low tax rates and lax tax enforcement, which can be largely self-defeating.

LICENSES AND CHARGES

Two other revenue sources will be analyzed briefly: licenses and charges. Licenses are imposed to regulate an activity or to raise revenue. The important question about licenses from the viewpoint of tax efficiency and equity is whether the license is a fixed dollar amount or a variable amount, depending upon the use of some index of ability to pay taxes. Dog licenses, as well as hunting and fishing licenses, are usually fixed dollar amounts. In this instance, they are equivalent to a "lump sum" tax and rank high in terms of tax efficiency (they are neutral). They may, however, rank low in terms of tax equity if they are regressive in their incidence. On the other hand, the amounts paid for vehicle tag licenses and some business licenses may vary with some measure of ability to pay. In these cases, licenses will not be nearly as neutral on the allocation of resources, although they may score relatively better in terms of equity.

A direct charge to individual users of government services is an illustration of the pricing or fee principle used in raising revenues. In order for charges to be completely consistent with the pricing principle, the charge per unit of service must be the same for all buyers and the total charge to each buyer must vary in accordance with individual demands. If charges for services are a fixed amount (such as monthly fee for garbage collection) or are graduated in a decreasing marginal rate schedule (such as utilities services), the principle of vertical equity may be violated and charges will be distributed in a regressive way. Nevertheless, charges are an efficient way to distribute costs of government services and may also be an equitable way if the distribution of income is not seriously disturbed.

SUMMARY

In this chapter, a framework was developed by which to evaluate our tax system. This framework consisted of two criteria: equity and efficiency. Equity is concerned with "fairness" and "justice" in taxation, and efficiency is primarily concerned with the impact of taxes on the efficient operation of the economy.

Equity is not easy to precisely define. Two doctrines and two principles elucidate its meaning. The two doctrines are the doctrines of equal tax treatment and relative tax treatment. The first doctrine concerns horizontal equity, or the equal treatment of people in equal economic circumstances. For example, people with the same income should pay equal taxes. The second doctrine concerns vertical equity, or the different treatment of people in different econmic circumstances. People should be treated unequally according to the relative tax treatment doctrine—but how unequally?

In order to probe more deeply into the meanings of horizontal and vertical equity, especially the latter, two principles of taxation were developed: the ability to pay and the benefits received principles. The ability to pay principle makes clear that people with larger incomes should pay more taxes, but the principle does not tell us which alternative rate structure (progressive, proportional, or regressive) is the most just. Thus, the precise rate structure is dependent upon the individual beliefs and values. Regardless of its inconclusiveness, the ability to pay principle is an important guide in reference to tax equity.

The benefits received principle of taxation, although it has numerous limitations, can also be an important guide to our thinking in regard to a rational tax system. This principle applies the rule of the market to tax distribution; that is, it states that taxes should be allocated in accordance with the individual demand for government goods and services.

The efficiency criterion has three aspects: first, economy in collection and payment of taxes; second, the non-neutral effects of taxes—namely, the way taxes may move the private economy from an efficient use to a less efficient use of resources; and third, the way in which taxes may shift an inefficient operating economy to one that is more efficient. This chapter stressed the non-neutral effects of taxes.

In the final section of the chapter, some important revenue sources were ranked on a *relative* basis in terms of equity and efficiency. This ranking should not be construed to mean that there is complete agreement among economists or any sort of an exactness concerning the evaluation of taxes. It is believed, however, that most economists would not find much fault with this evaluation of taxes. Personal income taxes with proportional or progressive rate structures were ranked high in terms of equity. Whereas proportional rates scored well in terms of efficiency, progressive rates were ranked low. Sales taxes found little support based on equity; however, general sales taxes may not interfere very much with individual choices, and were ranked high relative to selective sales taxes and excises. Property taxes, although defended sometimes on both the ability to pay and the benefits received principles, were considered to be low in terms of equity and efficiency essentially because of the administration of the tax. Licenses that are levied as a "lump sum" or a fixed dollar amount were ranked high on efficiency grounds and low in terms of equity because of their probable regressive effects. Licenses levied in such a way as to vary the payment in accordance with some index of ability to pay would improve the license from the viewpoint of equity. Government charges for goods and services provided received a high ranking in terms of our tax criteria, assuming that they do not seriously disturb the distribution of income.

The next chapter is concerned with another important aspect of taxation —the shifting and incidence of individual taxes. The equity and efficiency effects of taxes are dependent, in the final analysis, on incidence.

SUGGESTIONS FOR FURTHER READING

Musgrave, Richard A., *The Theory of Public Finance.* New York: McGraw-Hill Book Company, Inc., 1959.

This is an excellent reference for the reader who wishes to probe more deeply into the ability to pay principle of taxation, the benefits received principle of taxation, and the tax sacrifice rules. Chapters four and five are suggested for further study.

*

EIGHT

THE SHIFTING AND INCIDENCE OF TAXATION

Federal, state, and local taxes in 1974 were $1,826.86 per capita. This statistic does not, however, answer such questions as: who really pays taxes, the poor or the rich? Is the American tax system progressive, proportional, or regressive? What are the effective rate structures of different types of taxes?

Tax incidence studies provide statistics to answer questions like these and show the distribution of taxes among people by income classes. Such studies are based on tax shifting and incidence theory. This chapter first examines the essentials of tax shifting, after which follows a discussion of the assumptions on which tax incidence is based. The final section presents the findings of a recent and thorough study of tax incidence.

THE ESSENTIALS OF TAX SHIFTING

An understanding of tax shifting entails the comprehension of two concepts, *impact* and *incidence.* Taxes may be levied on and paid by one taxpayer but in fact, shifted in part or in whole to another taxpayer. The impact of a tax is at the point of levy, or on the person who initially pays the tax; the final resting place, or the person who really pays the tax, is the burden or incidence of a tax.

Taxes may be shifted forward and backward. Forward shifting of a tax is evidenced by an increase in prices of goods and services, and backward shifting takes the form of a reduction in the demand for resources and the incomes of resource owners. When forward shifting occurs, consumers pay higher prices and the incidence or burden of the tax is said to be on consumers. When backward shifting occurs, owners of resources (such as land, labor, and capital) receive less income, essentially bearing the burden or incidence of the tax. A tax is not shifted forward or backward when the incidence falls on the person or the owners of the enterprise on which it is levied; for example, a tax levied on personal income or the profits of an enterprise may not be shifted. In this case, the incidence of the tax may be said to be on the individual or on the owners of the enterprise.

The shifting of a tax depends primarily on the type of tax and on the elasticity of demand and supply. Two types of taxes are considered: first, a tax levied on each unit produced, called an *output tax* (most of our selective sales taxes and excises fall into this category); and second, a tax levied independently of output (for example, a tax levied on income, such as the personal or corporate income tax).

THE SHIFTING OF AN OUTPUT TAX

A tax of $10 levied on each unit of output will increase the cost of producing each additional unit by $10. The effect of this will be to decrease supply (move the supply curve to the left). As Figure 8-1 shows, the vertical distance (KM) between the pretax supply curve and the posttax supply curve is equal to the amount of the tax. As a consequence of the tax, the new equilibrium price is higher (p_1) and the quantity demanded and supplied is lower (q_1). Given the normal elasticities of demand and supply implied in Figure 8-1, an output tax is shifted in part both forward and backward. This is the most general case, and the one most likely to occur.

In Figure 8-1, it can be observed that a $10 tax on each unit of output increases price by less than $10. Some backward shifting has occurred. This can be seen as a reduction in output from q to q_1 resulting in lower income payments to resource owners.

The part of an output tax that is shifted forward and the part that is shifted backward depends on the relative elasticities of demand and supply. An output tax will be shifted in the direction of the greatest inelastici-

FIGURE 8-1
AN OUTPUT TAX: GENERAL CASE–FORWARD AND BACKWARD SHIFTING

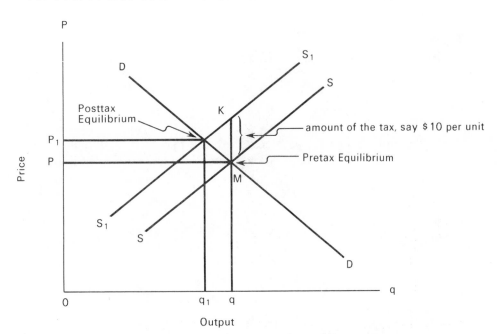

Explanation: Pretax Equilibrium is at a price of *P* and at an output of *q*.
A tax of, say, $10 per unit of output is levied. Supply
decreases from SS to S_1S_1. The vertical distance between
the supply curves is equal to the amount of the tax—$10
in this case. Posttax Equilibrium is at a price of P_1 and at
an output of q_1. Forward shifting is in the form of a rise in
prices and backward shifting is in the form of a decrease
in output. Note that the increase in price is not equal to the
full amount of the tax.

ty. For example, if a demand curve is more inelastic than a supply curve,
a larger part of the tax will be shifted forward. If a supply curve is more
inelastic than a demand curve, a greater part of an output tax will be shifted
backward. Both backward and forward shifting will occur with an output
tax, except in four special cases where: (1) demand is perfectly inelastic;
(2) demand is perfectly elastic; (3) supply is perfectly inelastic; or (4)
supply is perfectly elastic. In these four extreme cases, an output tax will
be shifted either *completely* forward or *completely* backward. We will now
illustrate these cases in order to demonstrate the extreme limits to forward

and backward shifting of an output tax. Keep in mind, however, that the more general case falls within these extreme limits.

Perfectly Inelastic Demand

Given a perfectly inelastic demand curve as shown in Figure 8-2, an output tax would be completely shifted forward to consumers in the form of higher prices. If a $10 tax were levied on each unit of output, as in the previous example, the posttax equilibrium price would be $10 higher than the pretax equilibrium price. The reason for this is due to the fact that although supply decreases as a result of the tax, output demanded and supplied do not change when demand is perfectly inelastic (See Figure 8-2). In this special case, an output tax will be completely shifted forward to consumers. During the 1973 oil crisis, some people argued that an increase in gasoline taxes would only increase prices and would not decrease consumption. This would be the effect only if demand was perfectly inelastic —a most unlikely case. Estimates of demand elasticity for gasoline indicate a high degree of inelasticity, but not perfect inelasticity. Consequently, a gasoline tax would decrease consumption, and the price of gasoline would increase by less than the full amount of the tax.

Perfectly Elastic Demand

A tax levied on output will be shifted backward completely if demand is perfectly elastic. Figure 8-3 shows the pretax and posttax equilibrium under this assumption. Although supply decreases to S_1 because of the tax, price does not change. A perfectly elastic demand means that demand is infinite at the pretax equilibrium price. Forward shifting cannot take place because consumers will not purchase anything at a higher price. Thus, the entire tax is shifted backward in the form of reduced incomes to owners of resources.

Perfectly Inelastic Supply

Figure 8-4 shows a perfectly inelastic supply curve. Under these supply conditions, output supplied is fixed at q. Forward shifting is not possible because output is independent of price. Complete backward shifting occurs in this instance. Owners of resources may be viewed as being so specialized that they have no alternatives but to accept a lower price for their services. In Figure 8-4, P is both the pretax and posttax equilibrium price; P_O is the amount realized per unit by the seller after the tax is paid.

FIGURE 8–2

AN OUTPUT TAX: SPECIAL CASE–DEMAND PERFECTLY INELASTIC–
COMPLETE FORWARD SHIFTING

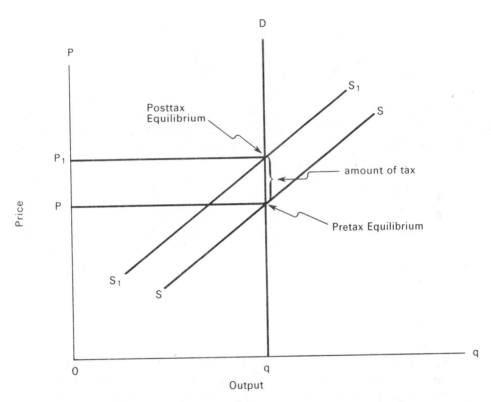

Explanation: Pretax Equilibrium is at a price of P and at an output of q.
An output tax is levied on each unit produced. Supply
decreases to S_1S_1. Posttax Equilibrium is at a price of P_1
and at an output of q. Output demanded and supplied
does not change because demand has a zero elasticity
(perfectly inelastic). The increase in price from P to P_1
equals the amount of the output tax.

Perfectly Elastic Supply

The last of the four special cases assumes that supply is perfectly elastic.
In these circumstances, complete forward shifting of an output tax would
occur. Again, an output tax would shift up the supply curve by the amount
of the tax. As long as the elasticity of demand is less than infinite, the
output tax will increase prices by the full amount of the tax. This can be

FIGURE 8–3
OUTPUT TAX: SPECIAL CASE–DEMAND PERFECTLY ELASTIC–
COMPLETE BACKWARD SHIFTING

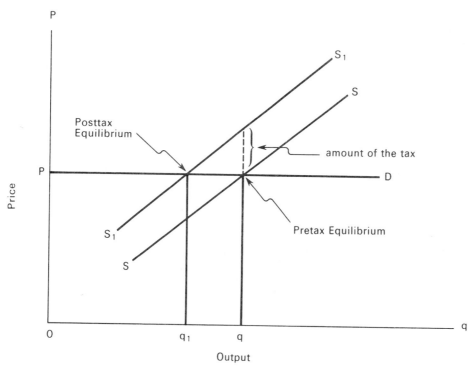

Explanation: Pretax Equilibrium is at a price of P and at an output of q.
Posttax Equilibrium is at the same price of P and at a
reduced output of q_1. There is no forward shifting of the
tax. Complete backward shifting of the tax takes place
because demand is perfectly elastic.

observed in Figure 8-5, where P is the pretax equilibrium price. Supply
decreases from S to S_1. The posttax equilibrium price is P_1. The difference
between P_1 and P, therefore, is equal to the vertical distance between the
two supply curves, or to the full amount of the tax.

A TAX LEVIED INDEPENDENTLY
OF OUTPUT

The incidence or burden of a tax levied independently of output—for
example, a tax levied on net income or profits of a business firm—is not

FIGURE 8–4
OUTPUT TAX: SPECIAL CASE–SUPPLY PERFECTLY INELASTIC–
COMPLETE BACKWARD SHIFTING

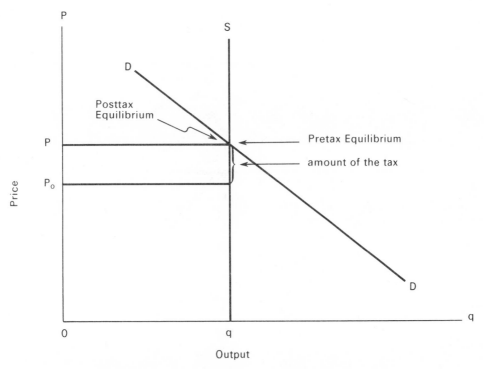

Explanation: Pretax and Posttax Equilibrium is at the price of *P* and at
an output of *q*. Since supply is perfectly inelastic, output
is fixed at an amount of *q*. P_0 is the price the producer
receives after paying the tax.

likely to fall on consumers in the form of higher prices. An important
difference between this type of tax and a tax levied on output is that a tax
levied on net income will not change the marginal cost of producing goods
and services, and hence will not affect short-run output and supply.

If a firm has selected the most profitable output—the output where
marginal cost and marginal revenue are equal before the tax—and has a
profit or net ncome of $100,000, and a 25% tax rate is levied on the income,
the firm will have an after tax net income of $75,000 ($100,000–$25,000).

This type of tax affects only the size of net income and is borne by the
owners of the firm. No output and price changes will result from the tax.

167

FIGURE 8-5
OUTPUT TAX: SPECIAL CASE–SUPPLY PERFECTLY ELASTIC–
COMPLETE FORWARD SHIFTING

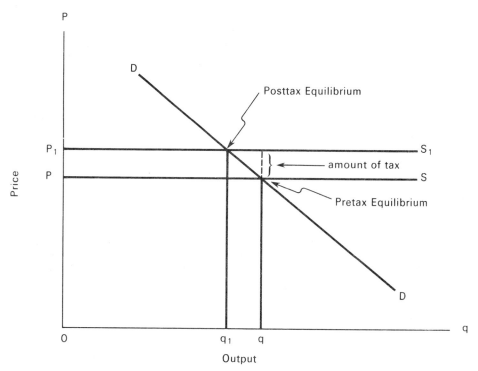

Explanation: Pretax Equilibrium is at P. Output tax causes the output
curve to shift to S_1. The Posttax Equilibrium price is at P_1.
The full amount of the tax is shifted to consumers in the
form of a higher price.

In the long run, there is a possibility of forward shifting of a tax levied on
net income. If the net income after taxes is below the rate of return on
alternative investments, firms may move out of the industry, causing a
decrease in supply and a forward shifting of the tax.

The above analysis of the incidence of a tax on net income assumed that
the most profitable output was selected before the tax. Dropping this
assumption, it may be reasoned that a tax on net income will be shifted
forward in part. For example, managers of corporations may select an
output that is greater than the profit maximization output because they are

168

concerned about the size as well as the profits of the corporation. A tax on net income in this case may reduce after tax profits below a minimum level acceptable to management. A decision may now be made to reduce output in order to restore an acceptable rate of return on investment. This reduction in output would result in a higher price and some forward shifting of the tax. The extent of the forward shifting would depend, as always, upon the elasticity of demand and supply.

In summary, a tax levied independently of output is not likely to be shifted forward in the short run if firms maximize profits. The main reason for this is that this type of tax does not increase cost and reduce output. However, some forward shifting is possible if profits are not maximized before the tax, and if output is reduced as a consequence of the tax.

TAX INCIDENCE ASSUMPTIONS

In order to determine the incidence of individual taxes, the amount of the tax shifted forward and backward has to be determined. The determination of the incidence of individual taxes is based primarily on the incidence and shifting theory previously discussed and on certain practical considerations. Because it is not possible to discover the exact degree of shifting for all taxes, the following presentation concerning the incidence of individual taxes is based on two sets of tax incidence assumptions. The first set of assumptions is the most progressive; assumptions are made that tend to favor progressive tax incidence. The second set of assumptions is the least progressive; assumptions are made that tend to favor the least progressive tax incidence. The results of these two sets of tax incidence assumptions can be looked upon as identifying the upper and lower limits of tax progressivity in the United States. The actual incidence of the American tax system is not likely to be more progressive than the incidence resulting under the assumptions of set one, and it is not likely to be less progressive than the incidence resulting under the assumptions of set two.

INCOME TAXES

It is widely agreed that individual income taxes fall on the income receiver and generally cannot be shifted forward. Thus, in Table 8-1, this tax is shown to fall on the taxpayer under both sets of tax incidence assumptions.

Tax incidence theory reveals that the corporation net income tax may or may not be shifted forward, depending upon certain assumptions about profit maximization. In the incidence assumptions of set one, the most progressive set, the corporation net income tax is shifted backward to the owners of resources. On the other hand, in the incidence assumptions of set two, the corporation net income tax is shifted forward to consumers in the form of higher prices and shifted backward to the owners of resources in the form of reduced incomes.

Another type of income tax, the payroll tax on employees, is not shifted and is therefore placed on wage earners in the incidence assumptions of both sets one and two. The payroll tax on employers is shifted completely backward to wage earners in the form of lower wages in the incidence assumptions of set one; the payroll tax on employers, on the other hand, is assumed to fall on employees and on consumers under the incidence assumptions of set two.

SALES AND EXCISE TAXES

Sales and excise taxes are assumed to be shifted completely forward to consumers in both sets of tax incidence assumptions (Table 8-1). As discussed in the previous sections, this would be true only if demand was perfectly inelastic or if supply was perfectly elastic. Although it is doubtful that either demand or supply of the commodities taxed will have either extreme elasticity, the demand for some products subject to sales taxes is probably highly inelastic. In tax incidence studies, these taxes are usually assumed to be shifted completely forward.

PROPERTY TAXES

Tax incidence theory reveals that property taxes on land will be shifted backward to the landowners, and property taxes on improvements on land may be shifted forward partly to consumers. Taxes on land cannot be shifted forward because the supply of land is fixed; that is, the supply is perfectly inelastic. The supply of improvements on land can be changed, however; the supply can be either increased or decreased by letting the improvements depreciate and not replacing them. Thus, there is a possibil-

TABLE 8–1   TAX INCIDENCE ASSUMPTIONS

Tax Source	Set One (Most Progressive Incidence Assumptions)	Set Two (Least Progressive Incidence Assumptions)
Income Taxes:		
Individual Income Tax	On Taxpayer or Income Receiver	On Taxpayer or Income Receiver
Corporation Income Tax	Shifted Backward to Resource Owners	Shifted Backward to Resource Owners and Forward to Consumers
Payroll Tax on Employees	On Wage Earners	On Wage Earners
Payroll Tax on Employers	On Wage Earners	On Wage Earners and Consumers
Sales and Excise Taxes	Shifted Forward to Consumers	Shifted Forward to Consumers
Property Taxes:		
On Land	On Owner of Property	On Owners of Property
On Improvements	On Owners of Property	Shifted Forward to Consumers

REFERENCE: J.A. Pechman and B.A. Okner, *Who Bears the Tax Burden?*, Brookings Institution (Washington, D.C.), 1974, p. 38.

ity that property taxes on improvements can be shifted forward. Property taxes on land are shifted backward to the landowners in both sets of tax incidence assumptions. Property taxes on improvements are shifted backward to the owners of property in the assumptions of set one, and shifted forward to consumers in the assumptions of set two.

AN EMPIRICAL STUDY OF TAX INCIDENCE

The most exhaustive study of tax incidence study to date was published in 1974 by the Brookings Institution under the co-authorship of J. A. Pechman and B. A. Okner. The discussion of the shifting and incidence of individual taxes in the previous section under the most and least progressive sets of tax incidence assumptions was drawn from their study. This approach will also be used in this section.

The findings of the Pechman-Okner study provide the most accurate information regarding the following questions: What is the distribution of tax burdens by income classes? What are the effective rates of federal, state, and local taxes by types of taxes? What are the effective tax rate structures of federal, state, and local tax systems? What is the impact of taxes on income distribution?

THE DISTRIBUTION OF TAX BURDENS BY INCOME CLASS

Table 8-2 shows a 1966 distribution of all taxes in the United States by income groups. Under the tax incidence assumptions of set one, the effective tax rates are 18.7% for family incomes in the lowest income class and rise progressively to 49.3% for the highest income group. On the other hand, under the tax incidence assumptions of set two, the effective tax rate is much higher—28.1% for the lowest income group—and is regressive between the first two income groups. Also, under the assumptions of set two, tax rates are much less progressive, increasing only to 29% for the highest income group. The effects of shifting part of the corporate income tax to consumers (one-half in the Pechman-Okner study,) and of shifting the property tax on improvements to "shelter and consumption" in the assumptions of set two clearly reduces the incidence of taxes on high income groups and increases the incidence on the lowest income groups. Which set of tax rates is correct?

The two sets of tax rates are based on two sets of incidence assumptions. Thus, both sets are correct in the sense that they were logically derived from certain assumptions. A reasonable position to take is to view the two sets of rates as establishing the upper and lower limits of the actual rate structure. The actual structure, then, can be considered to fall somewhere in between these limits.

A common feature of both sets of distributions of tax burdens is that for most income groups the incidence of taxes is largely proportional at rates between 20% and 25%. Over four-fifths of all families fall within the income classes between $3,000 and $30,000. Within this broad classification, effective tax rates vary little. In set one, the variation in rates is from 20% to 25% over the income ranges; in set two, the variation is from 24% to 25% (Table 8-2).

TABLE 8–2 EFFECTIVE RATES OF FEDERAL, STATE AND LOCAL TAXES UNDER TWO SETS OF TAX INCIDENCE ASSUMPTIONS, 1966

Family Income Class (in thousands of Dollars)	Set One (Most Progressive Assumptions) (in percent)	Set Two (Least Progressive Assumptions) (in percent)
0–3	18.7	28.1
3–5	20.4	25.3
5–10	22.6	25.9
10–15	22.8	25.5
15–20	23.2	25.3
20–25	24.0	25.1
25–30	25.1	24.3
30–50	26.4	24.4
50–100	31.5	26.4
100–500	41.8	30.3
500–1000	48.0	30.3
1000 and over	49.3	29.0
All Classes	25.2	25.9

REFERENCE: J.A. Pechman and B.A. Okner, *Who Bears the Burden?,* The Brookings Institution, (Washington, D.C.), 1974, p. 49.

EFFECTIVE TAX RATES BY TYPE OF TAX

Individual Income Taxes

Individual income taxes—especially at the federal level and, to a less extent, at the state level—are noted for their seemingly progressive rates. Apparently, the progressiveness of individual income taxes is highly exaggerated. Under both sets of tax incidence assumptions, individual income taxes are mildly progressive except at the very high income ranges (Table 8-3). In income classes over $500,000, individual income tax rates are slightly regressive. Under the most progressive tax incidence assumptions (set one), individual income taxes start at a rate of 1.4% at the lowest income class and are progressive up to the $100,000 to $500,000 income class. Under the least progressive set of assumptions, tax rates start at 1.2% and are progressive up to the $100,000 to $500,000 income class.

TABLE 8–3   EFFECTIVE RATES OF FEDERAL, STATE AND LOCAL TAXES
UNDER TWO SETS OF INCIDENCE ASSUMPTIONS BY TYPE OF TAX, 1966

Family Income Classes ($ thousands)	Individual Income Tax		Corporation Income Tax		Property Tax		Sales and Excise Taxes		Payroll Taxes	
	Set One (%)	Set Two (%)	Set One (%)	Set Two (%)	Set One (%)	Set Two (%)	Set One (%)	Set Two (%)	Set One (%)	Set Two (%)
0–3	1.4	1.2	2.1	6.1	2.5	6.5	9.4	9.2	2.9	4.6
3–5	3.1	2.8	2.2	5.3	2.7	4.8	7.4	7.1	4.6	4.9
5–10	5.8	5.5	1.8	4.3	2.0	3.6	6.5	6.4	6.1	5.7
10–15	7.6	7.2	1.6	3.8	1.7	3.2	5.8	5.6	5.8	5.3
15–20	8.7	8.2	2.0	3.8	2.0	3.2	5.2	5.1	5.0	4.7
20–25	9.2	9.1	3.0	4.0	2.6	3.1	4.6	4.6	4.3	4.1
25–30	9.3	9.1	4.6	4.3	3.7	3.1	4.0	4.0	3.3	3.6
30–50	10.4	10.5	5.8	4.7	4.5	3.0	3.4	3.5	2.2	2.6
50–100	13.4	14.1	5.8	5.6	6.2	2.8	2.4	2.4	0.7	1.3
100–500	15.3	18.0	16.5	7.4	8.2	2.4	1.5	1.7	0.3	0.7
500–1000	14.1	17.7	23.0	9.0	9.6	1.7	1.1	1.4	0.1	0.4
1000 and over	12.4	16.6	25.7	9.8	10.1	0.8	1.1	1.3	–	0.3
All Classes	8.5	8.4	3.9	4.4	3.0	3.4	5.1	5.0	4.4	4.4

REFERENCE: J.A. Pechman and B.A. Okner, *Who Bears the Tax Burden?,* The Brookings Institution, (Washington, D.C.), 1974, p. 59.

Corporate Income Tax

The effective tax rates of corporate income taxes are mildly regressive in the low income ranges and become mildly progressive after the $10,000 to $15,000 income range (Table 8-3). Under the assumptions of set one, corporate income tax rates start at 2.1%, fall to 1.6% in the $10,000 to $15,000 income class, and then rise to 26% in the highest income class. Under the assumptions of set two, rates start at 6.1%, decrease to 3.8% in the $10,000 to $15,000 income class, and then increase to only 9.8% in the highest income class. The assumptions of set two show lower effective rates in higher income classes because one-half of the tax is presumed to shift forward to consumers.

Property Taxes

The effects of different tax incidence assumptions on tax rates are revealed clearly in regard to property taxes. Under the assumptions of set one, property taxes are mildly regressive in the lower income class and then become mildly progressive. Under the assumptions of set two, property taxes are regressive throughout the income classes. This latter pattern reflects the assumption that property taxes on improvements are shifted forward to the consumers.

Sales and Excise Taxes

Sales and excise taxes are regressive under both sets of assumptions. They start at about 9% and decline to about 1% in the highest income class.

Payroll Taxes

Over the first three lower income classes, payroll taxes are progressive and then become regressive over the remaining income classes. They are progressive up to the $5,000 to $10,000 income class. For this family income class, the effective payroll tax rate is approximately 6%. After reaching this tax rate of 6%, the payroll tax rate declines rapidly to less than 1% on very high income groups.

    It should be emphasized that the two different rate structures which have been discussed are based on the different assumptions made in regard to the shifting and incidence of certain taxes. The two critical incidence assumptions are in regard to the incidence of the corporate income tax and the property tax. The whole progressivity of the tax system virtually disappears if one half of the corporate income tax is shifted to consumers and if the property tax is also shifted to consumers. On the other hand, if these taxes are said to be borne by stockholders and owners of property (according to the assumptions of set two), a degree of progressivity is evident in the tax system.

THE INCIDENCE OF FEDERAL TAXES AND STATE AND LOCAL TAXES

The federal tax system has always been considered much more progressive than state and local tax systems because the federal tax system relies more heavily on income taxes, while state and local tax systems rely more heavily on sales and property taxes. Table 8-4 shows this to be, in general, a correct evaluation. Under the most progressive tax incidence assumptions,

TABLE 8–4 EFFECTIVE RATES OF FEDERAL, AND STATE AND LOCAL
TAXES UNDER TWO SETS OF INCIDENCE ASSUMPTIONS, 1966

Family Income Class (in thousands of $)	Set One (Most Progressive Assumptions) (in percent		Set Two (Least Progressive Assumptions) (in percent)	
	Federal	State-Local	Federal	State-Local
0–3	8.8	9.8	14.1	14.0
3–5	11.9	8.5	14.6	10.6
5–10	15.4	7.2	17.0	8.9
10–15	16.3	6.5	17.5	8.0
15–20	16.7	5.5	17.7	7.6
20–25	17.1	6.9	17.8	7.4
25–30	17.4	7.7	17.2	7.1
30–50	18.2	8.2	17.7	6.7
50–100	21.8	9.7	20.1	6.3
100–500	30.0	11.9	24.4	6.0
500–1000	34.6	13.3	25.2	5.1
1000 and over	35.5	13.8	24.8	4.2
All Classes	17.6	7.6	17.9	8.0

REFERENCE: J.A. Pechman and B.A. Okner, *Who Bears the Tax Burden?*, The Brookings Institution, (Washington, D.C.), 1974, p. 62.

federal taxes are progressive, starting at 8.8% and increasing to 35.5% for incomes over $1 million. Under this same set of assumptions, state and local taxes are regressive, starting at 9.8% and declining to 5.5% for family incomes between $15,000 and $20,000. After the $20,000 to $25,000 income group, however, state and local taxes appear to be progressive, increasing to 13.8% in the highest income group. Under the least progressive assumptions, the federal tax system is mildly progressive with rates that increase from 14% to 25%. State and local tax systems are regressive throughout the income classes under these assumptions, starting at 14% and decreasing to 4.2%.

To summarize, the federal tax system is progressive but not as progressive as it is probably believed to be, while state and local tax systems are regressive but not as regressive as many believe. At the federal level, the rising importance of payroll taxes has reduced the progressiveness of the federal tax system. Also, because of the many tax advantages that high income groups have, the effective federal tax rates are significantly below the nominal or legislative rates. The increasing importance of income taxes, mainly at the state level, has probably shifted this system in the direction of a less regressive tax system.

THE EFFECTS OF TAXES ON INCOME DISTRIBUTION

One important question remains to be answered: Have taxes shifted the pattern of income distribution? Progressive tax rates would tend to shift the pattern of income after taxes to a more equal distribution; regressive rates would tend to do the opposite—that is, to shift the after tax pattern toward more inequality. Lorenz curves shown in Figure 8-6 indicate the effects of the most progressive tax rates on the distribution of income based on the Pechman-Okner study.

In Figure 8-6, the line of equal distribution means that 10%, 20%, 30%, and so on of families receive 10%, 20%, 30%, and so on of the income. Lorenz curve A shows the distribution of income before taxes, while Lorenz curve B shows the distribution after taxes under the most progressive set of incidence assumptions. A comparison of the two Lorenz curves reveals a slight shift toward income equality. The after tax distribution is 5% closer to an equal distribution pattern. This small impact of taxes on the distribution of income reflects a major conclusion of the Pechman-Okner study; namely, that the difference in effective tax rates over most income classes is small. Since most families pay effective rates between a narrow range of, for example, 20% to 25%, the tax system has only a minor impact on the relative distribution of income.

SUMMARY

This chapter has dealt with the essentials of tax shifting, the assumptions made in tax incidence studies, and the results of a recent tax incidence study. Two broad types of taxes—a tax levied on output and a tax levied independently of output—were considered in the discussion of the shifting and incidence of taxes. A tax levied on output, such as an excise tax, will usually be shifted forward to consumers in the form of higher prices and backward to resource owners in the form of reduced incomes. The extent of the forward and backward shifting of this type of tax depends on the relative elasticity of demand and supply. An output tax would be shifted in the direction of the greatest inelasticity.

FIGURE 8–6
LORENZ CURVES OF THE DISTRIBUTION OF
INCOME BEFORE AND AFTER TAXES

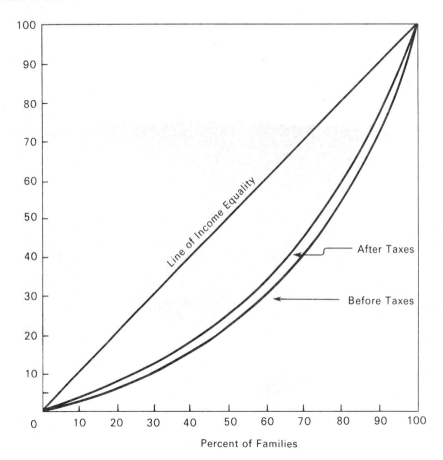

Source: J.A. Pechman and B.A. Okner, *Who Bears the Tax Burden?*, The
Brookings Institution, (Washington, D.C.), 1974, p.7.

The main reason for the backward and forward shifting of an output tax is because this type of tax increases the cost of producing additional goods and services, therefore decreasing supply. In contrast, a tax levied independently of output—for example, a tax levied on net income—may not be shifted in the short run, since this type of tax does not affect marginal cost. Some forward shifting of a tax levied independently of output may be possible in the long run if rates of return after taxes are reduced below competitive rates. A case was presented involving the corporation income tax, where shifting may occur even in the short run if profits are not maximized before the tax and if output is reduced as a consequence of the tax.

Certain assumptions have to be made concerning the incidence of individual taxes. These assumptions are primarily based on shifting and incidence theory. Two sets of incidence assumptions were used in this discussion; set one was the most progressive set, and set two was the least progressive set. The results of the recent Pechman-Okner study were shown concerning the incidence of federal, state, and local taxes under both sets of assumptions. The Pechman-Okner study provided answers to important questions such as: Who really pays taxes, and what is the impact of taxes on the distribution of income? The study reveals that most American families pay almost proportional tax rates, ranging between 20% and 25% of their incomes, and that the relative distribution of income has not been much affected by taxes.

The previous chapter on the principles of taxation established a framework for evaluating taxes. This chapter has probed into the incidence or burden of taxes. These two chapters provide the essential background for the next three chapters; namely, the issues and problems related to taxes on income (Chapter 9), wealth (Chapter 10), and consumption (Chapter 11).

SUGGESTIONS FOR FURTHER READING

Aaron, Henry J., *Who Pays the Property Tax?* Washington, D.C.: The Brookings Institution, 1975.

Professor Aaron challenges the traditional view that property taxes are shifted to consumers in the form of higher prices. Instead, he argues that property taxes are borne by the owners of capital. If Aaron is correct, property taxes are progressive in regard to incidence. Chapter 3 is recommended for further study.

Pechman, Joseph A. and Okner, Benjamin A., *Who Bears the Tax Burden?* Washington, D.C.: The Brookings Institution, 1974.
This is the most exhaustive study to date on tax shifting and incidence. Chapter 8 of this text relies heavily on this reference. It is suggested in its entirety for further reading.

*

NINE

TAX LEVIES ON INCOME:
ISSUES AND REFORMS

Tax levies on income are a major source of tax revenues. They dominate the federal tax picture; they are becoming very important in state tax systems; and, even though they are still a minor revenue source at the local level, they have increased relative to other types of local levies. Income taxes (the individual income tax, the corporate income tax, and the payroll tax) represented 89.3% of total federal tax revenues in 1974 (Table 9-1). They have been the main source of federal revenues for many years. In 1950, for example, they constituted over three of every four dollars collected in federal taxes. In comparison, state income taxes (individual and corporate income taxes only) were relatively unimportant in 1950, accounting for only 14.7% of state revenues; by 1974, however, this figure had risen to 31.1%. At the local level, the income tax is essentially a tax on wages and salaries and on the net profits of professions and unincorporated businesses. Local income taxes accounted for 4.3% of local tax revenues in 1974.

This chapter is organized around the major types of income taxes—the individual or personal income tax, the corporate income tax, and the payroll tax. A new type of income tax, the value added tax, is introduced in the final section of the chapter. The general approach in each section is first to present some of the institutional features, and second to discuss some of the issues and reforms regarding the tax under consideration.

TABLE 9-1 THE PERCENT DISTRIBUTION OF TAX LEVIES ON INCOME BY TYPE OF TAX AND BY LEVEL OF GOVERNMENT IN 1950, 1960, and 1974

Type of Income Tax	Federal Level			State Level			Local Level		
	1950	1960	1974	1950	1960	1974	1950	1960	1974
Individual Income Tax	41.6	45.9	46.6	8.1	12.2	23.0	0.8	1.4	4.3
Corporation Income Tax	27.7	24.0	15.1	6.6	6.5	8.1	–	–	–
Payroll Tax	7.7	14.2	27.6	–	–	–	–	–	–
Total	77.0	84.1	89.3	14.7	18.7	31.1	0.8	1.4	4.3

SOURCE: U.S.Bureau of the Census, *Government Finances*, 1950, 1960, and 1973-74.

THE FEDERAL PERSONAL INCOME TAX

INSTITUTIONAL BACKGROUND

The first moderately successful use of the personal income tax in the United States was made at the federal level in 1861 when Congress passed an income tax—3% on incomes above $800—to help finance Civil War expenditures.[1] Although by today's standards the rates of the first tax and its subsequent revisions were rather low, the tax was successful in raising a substantial share of the revenues needed for war. The 1861 tax law passed through several revisions, reached its rate peak in 1865 (10% on incomes above $5,000) and its revenue peak in 1866 ($73 million), and finally met its demise in 1872. It is interesting to note, in the light of later court decisions, that this first personal income tax was not declared unconstitutional. The court found that this first tax was not a direct tax and, therefore, did not have to be apportioned among the states in proportion to a census or enumeration.[2]

Though the eleven year old tax had served its country well, especially during the war years, it was with considerable relief that it was abandoned in 1872. In fact, the tax had left such a bad impression with politicians that there was no rush to reimpose the tax during the 1870s and 1880s.

---

1. The tax was made slightly progressive in 1862 and remained progressive until 1867. The 1862 tax stipulated a minimum 3% rate rising to 5% on incomes over $10,000.

2. *Springer v. United States,* 102 U.S. 586 (1880). See Erwin N. Griswold, *Cases and Mat* on Federal Taxation (Chicago: The Foundation Press, Inc., 1940), pp. 31–34.

In 1893, however, with the assistance of President Grover Cleveland, Congress started the political wheels rolling for the passage of a personal income tax. The tax was part of a two-part proposal of a personal income tax and a reduction of the tariffs. The tax was to be used to supply the revenue lost as a result of tariff reduction. In its final form, the 1894 act—which temporarily legalized the personal income tax after a lapse of over twenty-four years—was termed the Wilson Tariff Bill. The version of the personal income tax as it finally passed was a watered-down facsimile of what Cleveland and his congressional leaders had in mind. In fact, it was so weakened when it finally emerged from the Senate that Cleveland did not even sign it.

Although the 1894 tax was to the average citizen considerably less obnoxious from a rate and exemption point of view than its Civil War and post-Civil War counterparts, it was less than enthusiastically received. The act as finally passed imposed a 2% rate on personal income over $4,000. Nonetheless, in spite of its relative mildness, it was branded as a class tax and was quickly contested. In the case of *Pollock v. Farmers' Loan and Trust Company,* the Supreme Court ruled that the tax as spelled out in the 1894 act was for all intents and purposes a direct tax and, therefore, could be levied legally only by apportioning the tax among the states in accordance with their populations. Naturally, the Congress and President Cleveland had not levied the tax on this basis and had no thought of doing so in the future. Thus, the 1894 tax was declared unconstitutional. It should be pointed out, however, that the Supreme Court, has never ruled that the income tax per se is unconstitutional, as many people seem to believe. What was declared unconstitutional in 1894 was not the right of the federal government to levy a personal income tax, but the way in which the tax was levied.

The Supreme Court's ruling in *Pollock v. Farmers' Loan and Trust Company* made it mandatory that a constitutional change be made if the federal government was to impose a tax on personal income from whatever source derived without apportioning the tax among the states according to population. In May, 1913, the Constitution was revised via the adoption of the Sixteenth Amendment. The pertinent section of the Amendment reads as follows:

> The Congress shall have power to lay and collect taxes on incomes, from whatever source derived, without apportionment among the several States, and without regard to any census or enumeration.

Before the end of the year 1913, Congress with the approval of President Wilson had enacted a personal income tax. The first post-Amendment personal income tax rates were low as compared to rates today. They ranged from a minimum rate of 1% to a maximum rate of 7%. After a $3000 personal exemption, the minimum tax rate was imposed on personal income up to $20,000. After $20,000, an additional surtax was imposed ranging from 1% to 6%. The maximum tax rate was imposed on personal income over $500,000.

The personal income tax has undergone numerous changes, since 1913, especially with regard to tax rates and exemption provisions. In its formative period between 1913 and 1945, rates were significantly increased and exemptions decreased. The exception was the decade of the 1920s, when the burden of income taxes was somewhat eased. Since 1945, the trend has been in the direction of lowering rates and allowing larger exemptions. This trend reflects the opposition to the high progressive rates which were established primarily during World War II. For example, rates were cut in 1964 from the 1944 range of 14 to 91% to a range of from 14 to 70%, which is the range in effect to date. The Reform Act of 1976 affected the income tax, and more tax legislation is expected in years to come, for many unsettled income tax issues remain. With this brief history as background, we will now examine some of the current features of the personal income tax structure.

THE DERIVATION OF
THE TAX LIABILITY

The federal personal income tax is levied on the income received by individuals; mainly in the form of wages and salaries, dividends, royalties, interest, rent, and profits from unincorporated business enterprises. An individual taxpayer can determine his or her tax liability on this income by solving five simple equations in the order listed:

1. Total Income − Exclusions = *Gross Income*
2. Gross Income − Business Expenses = *Adjusted Gross Income*
3. Adjusted Gross Income − Deductions = *Net Income*
4. Net Income − Exemptions = *Taxable Income*
5. Taxable Income × Tax Rates = *Tax Liability.*

Gross Income

Gross income includes the total taxable receipts of a taxpayer after *exclusions,* or receipts that are not considered taxable income. Some of the more important exclusions are public assistance payments, social security benefits, relief payments, gifts, interest on state and local government securities, fellowship and scholarship grants, and death benefits up to a certain maximum.

Adjusted Gross Income

The adjusted gross income (AGI) is derived by subtracting expenses incurred in earning income. The AGI aggregated over all taxpayers is the potential personal income tax base—over $717 billion in 1972. This tax base is reduced by means of deductions, as follows.

Net Income

Personal deductions such as state and local taxes paid, medical expenses, contributions to charity, and interest payments can be subtracted from the AGI. These personal itemized deductions totalled $92 billion in 1972.

Instead of itemizing personal deductions, a taxpayer may use a *maximum* or a *minimum standard deduction.* For a single person, the standard deduction is 16% of income up to a maximum of $2400; for married couples, it is 16% of income up to a maximum of $2800.[3] The minimum deduction, or low income allowance, is $1700 for a single person and $2100 for married couples. These standard deductions totalled $50.8 billion in 1972. Thus, the sum of all personal deductions in 1972 was $142.8 billion, or 20% of the AGI on taxable returns (See Table 9—2).

Taxable Income

In addition to personal deductions, every person is allowed a $750 *personal exemption* (persons 65 and over and blind persons are allowed $1500). Such an exemption is a relatively permanent feature of the federal personal

---

3. The Carter Administration proposed changes in the standard deduction in 1977. The House-Senate conferees agreed to make the standard deduction a flat $2200 for single taxpayers and a flat $3200 for married couples who file joint returns.

TABLE 9–2   DERIVATION OF TAXABLE INDIVIDUAL INCOME, 1972

Item	Amount ($ billions)
Adjusted Gross Income Estimated from Personal Income	798.4
Deduct: AGI not reported on tax returns	51.8
AGI reported on nontaxable returns	28.9
Equals: AGI on taxable returns	717.7
Deduct: Personal deductions	142.8
Deduct: Personal exemptions	128.3
Equals: Taxable Income	446.6

SOURCE: *Survey of Current Business* (February, 1975), p. 34.

income tax. From time to time, however, temporary tax credits are allowed. In 1975, for example, Congress enacted antirecession tax cuts in the form of a general *tax credit* and an *earned income credit* for low income families with children. The 1976 Tax Reform Bill extended these credits through 1977.[4] The general tax credit is equal to the greater of either 2% of the first $9000 of taxable income, or $35 for each dependency exemption. The earned income credit is equal to 10% of the first $4000 of earnings, and is phased out between $4000 and $8000.

In computing taxes, personal exemptions are first subtracted from net income to derive taxable income. After determining taxable income, the taxpayer computes his or her tax liability by using the appropriate tax rate schedule. All tax credits are then deducted from this tax liability in order to determine the final payment. Tax credits, then, differ from deductions and exemptions in that the latter are subtracted from income to arrive at taxable income whereas tax credits are deducted from the tax liability. A $100 tax credit reduces the amount that must be paid by $100, regardless of the size of the liability or tax bracket. A $100 deduction, on the other hand, saves taxpayers differing amounts depending upon their tax brackets.

Income Tax Structure

Table 9-3 shows the federal personal income tax rate schedule for married persons filing joint returns. Currently, the marginal rate increases from

---

4. These credits are likely to be extended again in 1977; the House-Senate conferees agreed upon their extension through 1978.

TABLE 9-3   FEDERAL PERSONAL INCOME TAX SCHEDULE FOR MARRIED
COUPLES FILING JOINT RETURNS, 1976

Taxable Income Bracket	Bracket or Marginal Tax Rate (Percent)
0– 1,000	14
1,000– 2,000	15
2,000– 3,000	16
3,000– 4,000	17
4,000– 8,000	19
8,000– 12,000	22
12,000– 16,000	25
16,000– 20,000	28
20,000– 24,000	32
24,000– 28,000	36
28,000– 32,000	39
32,000– 36,000	42
36,000– 40,000	45
40,000– 44,000	48
44,000– 52,000	50
52,000– 64,000	53
64,000– 76,000	55
76,000– 88,000	58
88,000–100,000	60
100,000–120,000	62
120,000–140,000	64
140,000–160,000	66
160,000–180,000	68
180,000–200,000	69
200,000 and over	70

14% to 70%. A married couple with a taxable income of $4000 would have
a tax liability of $620, which would be determined as follows:

on the first $1000 .... 14% $\times$ 1000 = $140
on the second $1000 .... 15% $\times$ 1000 = $150
on the third $1000 .... 16% $\times$ 1000 = $160
on the fourth $1000 .... 17% $\times$ 1000 = $170
            Tax Liability   = $620

In this instance, the top marginal rate on the last $1,000 of income is
17%. The couple's average rate on taxable income is 15.5% ($620/$4000).
Of course, the average rate on actual total income could be much less than
this because of exclusions, deductions, and exemptions.

The Tax Reform Act of 1969 introduced a *maximum rate* on earned income and a *minimum income tax* rule. The maximum tax rate is 50% on earned income—namely, income received from wages and salaries and self-employment. The Reform Act of 1976 expanded the 50% marginal tax rate on earned income to cover pensions and deferred compensation. In recognition of this broader coverage, the maximum tax rate applies now to what is called *personal service income.* The minimum income tax rule attempts to prevent a taxpayer from circumventing through tax shelters the payment of some income taxes. Originally, the rule was applied as follows. All "tax preferred income"—that is, income in the form of interest, rent, dividends, etc.—was summed, and $30,000 plus the taxpayer's regular taxes were subtracted from that income. Then, a 10% minimum tax rate was levied on the remainder of the preference income. The 1976 Tax Reform Bill revised the minimum rule and increased the minimum tax rate from 10% to 15%. It also reduced the exemption to $10,000 or half the taxpayer's regular taxes, whichever is greater.

THE MEANING OF INCOME

There are many diverse "issues" surrounding the federal personal income tax. Most of the issues are related to the following topics: (1) the meaning and measurement of income; (2) the erosion of the tax base; and (3) the progressivity of the tax rate schedule.

Ideally, the economist would like to define gross income as consumption plus changes in net worth. This definition considers income to be the total accretion to a person's wealth. It is based on the view that everything that increases the capacity of a person to enjoy goods and services is defined as income. Income from all sources—including regular and fluctuating, expected and unexpected, and realized and unrealized—would be seen as income for tax purposes under this definition.

Exclusions

Most of the exclusions from gross income now allowed would not be permitted if income was defined for tax purposes as the accretion to a person's wealth. For example, government transfers, such as social security payments, would be included in gross income. Interest on state and local government securities would be included in the tax base, as would be capital gains, whether realized or not, and rent from owner-occupied houses.

Although not exactly the same as total accretion, personal income reported in national income statistics can be used to estimate the difference between a more comprehensive concept of adjusted gross income and the adjusted gross income concept used for tax purposes. In 1972, adjusted gross income estimated from personal income was $798.4 billion (Table 9-2). Adjusted gross income reported on taxable returns was $717.7 billion. Most of the difference between these figures ($51.8 billion) represented adjusted gross income not reported on taxable returns.

Many economists believe that tax reforms should include a move toward a comprehensive concept of income for tax purposes. Exclusions from income open the door for preferential tax treatment and violate the principle of horizontal equity. Two taxpayers with the same personal income will not pay the same taxes if one of the taxpayers has income in a form that is excluded from taxes while the other does not.

Capital Gains Taxation

An important instance of preferential treatment involves income in the form of capital gains (gains from an asset's appreciation in value). Capital gains are not taxed at all if they are not realized. If they are realized, long-term capital gains (gains from the sale of assets held nine months or more beginning in 1977, and twelve months or more beginning in 1978) are taxed at one-half their value or, alternately, long-term gains up to $50,000 are taxed at 25%. On the grounds of horizontal equity, there is little or no justification for not taxing unrealized capital gains and, if realized, there is certainly no reason why they should not be taxed like ordinary income. However, the taxation of unrealized capital gains does not enjoy universal support. Some of the arguments against taxing unrealized gains are: (1) capital gains cannot be precisely determined until they are realized; (2) taxing unrealized capital gains would require the owner to sell the asset in some instances in order to get money to pay taxes; and (3) the asset position of taxpayers would be biased toward more liquidity (cash balances) and away from income-yielding assets, if unrealized capital gains were taxed. These arguments are true, in part, but they are not necessarily important enough to justify the loss in tax revenue and the higher rates imposed on taxpayers not eligible for capital gains provisions. The current tax treatment of capital gains provides a major "loophole" for some taxpayers, contravenes the accretion principle, and negates the equal tax treatment doctrine of taxation.

THE EROSION OF THE TAX BASE

Business Expenses

Adjusted gross income is defined as the income remaining after allowances for business expenses. Expenses incurred in earning income are legitimate deductions in principle. Problems do arise, however, because such expenses can be easily overstated and because so-called businesses can be established primarily to take advantage of the deduction. One tennis shoe manufacturer is even reputed to have justified the deduction of the expenses of a cruise to the Caribbean on the grounds that he wanted prospective customers to try out the soles of the shoes on the deck of the yacht! Many such pleasure trips can be, and probably are, made under the guise of being business trips.

Business expenses are scrutinized, probably more so in recent than in past years. When they are discovered, unreasonable or excessive business expenses may be contested and eventually disallowed. The 1976 Tax Reform Bill incorporated tighter restrictions on the deductions that many taxpayers currently take for utilities and other expenses attributable to an office at home.

Tax Shelters

It has become a favorite (and lucrative) pastime for certain taxpayers to invest in activities that enable them to "shelter" a part of their income from taxes. Among these tax-sheltered investments are rental real estate, oil wells, cattle breeding and feeding, and equipment leasing. In these activities, business losses can often be created and/or taxable profits can be drastically reduced by the use of accelerated depreciation or the current expensing of capital costs. If losses can be created, they can be deducted from other sources of income, thereby increasing after tax rates of return from these sources. Opponents of tax shelters have had little success in securing significant changes in the law. However, the 1976 Tax Reform Act represents a major effort on the part of Congress to reduce the tax breaks created by tax shelters. Generally, the tax sheltered provisions in the new act try to limit the amount of deductions that investors can take from income earned from other sources. This is a move in the right direction, but more revisions are needed.

A possible revision would be to disallow the use of losses from one activity as a deduction from income from another *unrelated* activity. For example, losses from an investment in rental property could not be deducted from wage and salary income. Of course, any losses from the former could be used as an offset to net income derived from other investments in rental property. A criticism of this recommended revision is the adverse effect that it may have on investment. Current practice encourages investment by allowing the after tax loss to be less than the before tax loss.

In most sheltered investment schemes, there is a heavy reliance on borrowing. An investor, for example, may use only $20,000 of his or her own wealth in the purchase of a $100,000 asset. Tax advantages could be reduced considerably by restricting the expensing of capital cost and accelerated depreciation privileges to the investor's own outlays and to the reduction of the principle of the loan.

Tax shelters should be eliminated as much as possible, not only because they result in tax inequities but also because they promote an inefficient allocation of investment funds. In the former instance, they are not consistent with the criterion of horizontal equity; in the latter, they direct funds to uses with relatively high after tax but low before tax rates of return. Returns before taxes, however, are the relevent indicators of social value.

Deductions and Exemptions

The elimination of exclusions and preferential tax treatment of capital gains, the removal of advantages from tax-sheltered investments, and the careful scrutiny of business expenses would significantly broaden the personal income tax base. But what about *personal deductions* and *exemptions?* Personal deductions comprise about 20% of the AGI on taxable returns, and personal exemptions about 18% (1972). Together, they reduced the personal income tax base from $717.7 to $446.6 billion in 1972. Would individual taypayers prefer much lower tax rates—for example, a 40% reduction in tax rates—to the continued use of these privileges?

The main purpose of both personal deductions and exemptions is to allow for non-income differences among taxpayers that would affect their capacity to pay taxes. For example, it can be argued that taxpayers in the same income bracket do not have the same capacity to pay taxes if they differ in regard to certain personal expenses, such as those for medical care. Personal exemptions are also often defended on the grounds that the capacity to pay taxes varies inversely with the size of the taxpayer's family.

However, personal deductions and exemptions may also be viewed as tax expenditures; that is, as subsidies to taxpayers in the form of tax reductions. From this point of view, family size may be considered largely a matter of tastes and preferences, making it difficult to justify tax advantages based on this criterion. Indeed, it is entirely conceivable that tax equity may be improved by eliminating all personal deductions and exemptions. Such would be true if the benefits to taxpayers from reduced tax rates exceeded their losses due to elimination of these subsidies. In this event, the elimination of personal deductions and exemptions would be a reform well worth considering.

PROGRESSIVITY

The final issue concerns the progressivity of the tax rate structure. Some people favor a highly progressive schedule and some do not. As discussed in Chapter 7, a progressive structure can be defended on the basis of tax equity, but so can one that is proportional.

It has been observed that the actual income tax rate schedule is much less progressive than the potential allowed by the tax code. This is due to the fact that legal exclusions, deductions, and exemptions remove much of the potential progressiveness. If it can be assumed that Congress, and taxpayers in general, really favor a proportional schedule, then a more direct approach would be to reduce or eliminate the existing gap between personal income and taxable income and levy a single proportional rate on adjusted gross income. Using the AGI on taxable returns shown in Table 9-2, and applying a 15% tax rate, federal personal income tax revenues would be $107 billion—more revenues than were raised using the existing schedule in that year (1972).

Such a change would not significantly reduce the proportion of personal income taxes derived from wealthy taxpayers, such as those with incomes over $50,000, because there are few families in this group. In 1972, this group accounted for only 17% of personal income tax collections. The bulk of the tax is paid by middle income families. Thus, the case for high marginal rates on personal income cannot be made on revenue grounds, but only on the grounds that it is socially desirable to redistribute income through the taxing process.

STATE AND LOCAL PERSONAL INCOME TAXES

STATE PERSONAL INCOME TAXES

A Brief History

Although first used during Colonial times, states had little success with income taxes prior to 1911. The major characteristics of pre-1911 state income taxes were: (1) poor administration by property tax assessors; (2) low flat rates; (3) levies on one's trade or ability to earn income (until the 1870's); (4) an inconsequential source of revenue.

In 1911, Wisconsin passed a model income tax law, which placed the administration of the tax in the hands of the state tax commission. The tax was levied on net income at progressive rates. The tax became a more productive source of revenue than expected, and the success of Wisconsin's income tax encouraged other states to adopt new income tax laws. By 1930, fifteen states had adopted the tax. Still more states (sixteen) adopted income taxes during the 1930s. Between 1937 and 1961, no new states adopted state income taxes. Since then, however, the list of states with income taxes has expanded significantly. By 1975, only six states (Florida, Nevada, South Dakota, Texas, Washington, and Wyoming) did not obtain revenues from personal income taxes.

Structural Features

Many features of existing state income tax systems are similar to those of the federal income tax systems. Many states, but not all, have progressive income tax rates; however, they are not nearly as progressive as federal income tax rates. For example, state income tax rates often vary from about 2 to 6 or 10%. Practically all states grant personal exemptions; for single and married persons, exemptions are usually higher than federal exemptions. State income taxes paid can be deducted in determining the federal income tax liability. Many states permit the deduction of federal income taxes paid wholly or in part. State income tax laws allow many other deductions, and some states grant tax credits to the aged and low-income taxpayers. Finally, state income taxes are usually withheld at the source, as are their federal counterparts.

Variations in Relative Importance

Among individual states, income taxes vary significantly in their relative importance (Table 9-4). A few states receive 40% or more of their total tax revenues from the income tax; these states are Alaska (42.9%), Delaware (40.1%), Massachusetts (44.6%), Minnesota (39.9%), New York (40.1%), Oregon (53.9%), and Wisconsin (40.1%). Some states having income taxes do not rely upon them to any great degree. For example, Connecticut (1.3%), New Jersey (2.2%), Tennessee (1.6%), and New Hampshire (5.0%) obtain 5% or less of their tax revenues from personal income taxes.

Income Elasticity

Overall, state personal income taxes provide an *automatic* expanding source of tax revenues in a growing economy. Although the income elasticities of state income taxes are not as great as the federal personal income tax, empirical studies show that they are nevertheless income elastic; that is, when the economy grows, tax collections from state income taxes grow proportionally greater. This is one reason why state income taxes have become generally more important in state tax systems.

Issues and Reforms

Numerous state income tax issues concern the tax base, rates, exemptions, and deductions. These issues differ only in detail from similar issues already examined in the discussion of the federal personal income tax. Most states have income tax bases that resemble the federal income tax base; a few states have income tax bases that completely conform to the federal income tax base. As noted previously, states allow deductions and exemptions similar to those allowed by the federal government. A few states permit income tax credits in order to reduce the regressiveness and burden of sales and property taxes on low-income groups.

State income tax returns are greatly simplified when state income tax laws conform to the federal law; taxpayers can simply take the adjusted gross income figure shown on their federal tax return, subtract state deductions, exemptions, etc., and apply state tax rates to the calculated state tax base. It would be simpler still were taxpayers allowed to take the taxable income figures shown on their federal returns and apply state tax rates directly to these figures in order to determine their state income tax liabili-

TABLE 9–4   THE RELATIVE IMPORTANCE OF STATE PERSONAL INCOME
TAXES BY STATE, 1975

	Income Taxes as a Percent of Total Tax Revenue		Income Taxes as a Percent of Total Tax Revenue
All States	23.5	Montana	38.1
Alabama	17.1	Nebraska	18.5
Alaska	42.9	Nevada	—
Arizona	16.8	New Hampshire	5.0
Arkansas	19.3	New Jersey	2.2
California	25.7	New Mexico	10.9
Colorado	32.4	New York	40.1
Connecticut	1.3	North Carolina	28.9
Delaware	40.1	North Dakota	24.5
Florida	—	Ohio	15.9
Georgia	24.2	Oklahoma	18.4
Hawaii	29.3	Oregon	53.9
Idaho	30.6	Pennsylvania	21.0
Illinois	25.8	Rhode Island	22.8
Indiana	21.6	South Carolina	22.0
Iowa	33.8	South Dakota	—
Kansas	22.1	Tennessee	1.6
Kentucky	19.4	Texas	—
Louisiana	7.1	Utah	26.3
Maine	12.1	Vermont	29.5
Maryland	38.5	Virginia	32.9
Massachusetts	44.6	Washington	—
Michigan	24.2	West Virginia	16.1
Minnesota	39.9	Wisconsin	40.1
Mississippi	11.6	Wyoming	—
Missouri	23.9		

SOURCE: U.S. Department of Commerce, Bureau of the Census, *State Government Finances In 1975*, p. 7.

ty. Complete conformity of the state income tax with its federal counterpart could also be accomplished in another way. The state income liability could be determined by specifying the state tax rate as a certain percent of the federal income tax liability. For example, if the federal income tax liability were $1500 and the state tax rate were 10%, the state income tax liability would be equal to $500 ($5000 $\times$ .1). A few states levy their income taxes in this manner.

The movement of the state income tax toward conformity with federal practices is encouraging. Complete conformity will probably be gradual, however; many states may be reluctant to have their income tax collections completely dependent upon and subject to changes in the federal law.

LOCAL PERSONAL INCOME TAXES

A Brief History

Charleston, South Carolina was the first city to introduce the local personal income tax in the United States. Similar to the early state income tax, this early nineteenth century local income tax was a failure due to the inability of local authorities to administer the tax. The modern era of local income taxes began in 1938 when Philadelphia developed a successful income tax. Although the State Supreme Court ruled the 1938 tax unconstitutional on the basis that the exemptions allowed under it were in violation of the uniformity clause of the state's Consitution, the Court ruled in favor of a revised version of the tax in 1939.

Over 3500 local units of government have successfully introduced personal income taxes since 1939. Alabama, Delaware, The District of Columbia, Kentucky, Maryland, Michigan, Missouri, New York, Ohio, and Pennsylvania all have local units which levy personal income taxes (1973). Some states have a relatively large number of local units that rely upon income taxes as a source of tax revenues. These states are Indiana, Kentucky, Michigan, Ohio, and Pennsylvania.

Tax Base and Rates

Although practices vary, local income taxes generally are levied on wages and salaries of individuals and net incomes of professionals and unincorporated businesses. Local income taxes levied on wages and salaries are usually withheld at the source, and personal deductions and exemptions are normally not allowed. Rates are usually levied at low, proportional rates ranging from 0.5% to 2%. Most localities imposed a rate of either 0.5% or 1%. Two cities—Washington, D.C. and New York City—have slightly progressive income tax rates; for example, rates vary from 0.7% to 3.5% in New York City (1973).

Issues

Local income taxes are subject to administrative problems. Most of these problems stem from the fact that many persons who earn their incomes in a city—for example, in the central city of a metropolitan area—reside outside of the city and sometimes even in another state. The enforcement of local income taxes can become difficult—and this difficulty increases as people become more mobile.

Another drawback to local income taxes is the narrowness of the tax base. Local income taxes are essentially levies on wages and salaries. Many kinds of income, such as interest, dividends, rent, and capital gains are not taxed. Thus, the local income tax is basically an earning's tax which resembles the payroll tax and tends to be regressive. The local income tax, however, is not as likely to be as regressive as, for example, local sales taxes.

In summary, the trend toward a more generous use of the personal income tax at the local level is likely to continue. Many local units need additional tax revenues to finance essential services. Local personal income taxes are productive sources of revenue, and can also be used to tax nonresidents who use local services. Any other tax used in its place would probably be more regressive.

THE FEDERAL CORPORATE INCOME TAX

Although it has declined in relative importance, the corporate income tax remains an important source for the federal government. It is also a tax source to state governments, although it is relatively less important at this level. Despite increased corporate tax collections, this source of revenue declined from 27.7% to 15.1% of federal tax revenues between 1950 and 1974. During the same time span, the yield of this tax at the state level grew very slowly, increasing from 6.6% to 8.1% of total tax revenues.

INSTITUTIONAL BACKGROUND

The law establishing the federal corporate income tax was enacted in 1909; it was called an excise tax at that time in order to circumvent the issue of its constitutionality. The law was later challenged and upheld by the U.S. Supreme Court. The Court ruled that the tax had been levied as an excise on the privilege of engaging in the corporate form of business enterprise, and that profits of corporations were returns from such privileges.

After its inception, this tax became a vital revenue source and was second only to the individual income tax for a long time. However, in 1968, payroll taxes assumed this position. In some years prior to 1941, before individual income tax rates were sharply increased, the corporate income tax produced more revenue than did the individual income tax. It is not likely to regain its past prominence.

Since the original rate of 1% was levied on corporate income under the 1909 Act, rates have changed appreciably. Progressive rates were introduced in 1936, and were removed in 1950 in favor of a single proportional rate plus a surtax. A levy on excess profits was added to the regular levy during both World War II and the Korean War but was allowed to expire at the end of each. Prior to 1975, the normal rate was 22% of the first $25,000, plus a surtax of 26% on corporate taxable income over this amount, yielding an effective rate for most corporations of nearly 48%. In 1975, this was changed to 20% on the first $25,000, 22% on the second $25,000, and 48% on the remainder.

The main difference between the personal income tax and the corporate income tax is that the latter is a tax on business enterprise rather than on individuals. Yet both are similar in the sense that many deductions from total income are possible in the derivation of taxable income.

Total corporate income includes gross profits from sales, dividends, property, interest, rent, royalties, and other income received by the corporation. The main deduction from this sum consists of "ordinary and necessary expenses" of business. Included among the latter are domestic taxes paid, losses from fire and theft, charitable contributions, advertising expenses, entertainment expenses, depletion of mineral deposits, depreciation on buildings and equipment, and net operation losses carried backward or forward. Also, corporations receive preferential tax treatment on their long-term capital gains, with a rate of only 30% levied on corporations with taxable incomes over $25,000.

ISSUES AND REFORMS

Who Pays the Tax?

The incidence of the corporate income tax is a highly controversial matter among both economists and business people. Some economists argue that the tax is not shifted in the *short run* (a time period too short to adjust

investment). They visualize competitive market conditions and firms selecting their most profitable outputs before the tax, which would remain
their best output after the tax. In the long run, when there is time for
investment to be altered, it is granted that the tax could be shifted depending upon alternative rates of return on investment. Other economists reason that the corporation income tax can be shifted in the short run. They
believe that prices are determined under imperfectly competitive market
conditions and that prices are set to include cost, including taxes, plus a
markup. Alternatively, they argue that firms set an aftertax target rate of
return, and believe that if the corporation income tax reduces the rate of
return below the target rate attempts will be made to shift the tax either
forward to consumers or backward to workers.

In the discussion of the incidence of the corporate income tax in Chapter
8, the tax was shifted to the owners under the most progressive set of
incidence assumptions, and it was shifted in part to the owners and in part
foward to consumers under the least progressive set. The incidence results
are markedly different. When the incidence of the tax is completely on the
owners, the effective rate is lower at the lower end of the scale but becomes
higher and progressive at the upper end of the income scale. On the other
hand, when the incidence of the tax is assumed to be one-half on the
owners and one-half on the consumers, the effective rate is higher at the
lower end of the income scale and becomes slightly higher and mildly
progressive at the upper end.

Economic Effects

The corporate income tax has received more than its share of criticisms on
economic grounds. Among these criticisms are: (1) investment and economic growth are discouraged; and (2) corporate debt financing is encouraged. Corporate income taxes can adversely affect investment in two
ways; investment can be discouraged both by the reduced aftertax rate of
return and by the reduced amount of investible funds.

Unquestionably, corporate income taxes can discourage investment.
However, the main question is one of whether they actually *have*. The
answer to this question can only be suggestive. Corporate investment
depends upon many variables operating in the market, and the corporate
tax is just one of those variables. A more important determinant of investment is likely to be the strength and growth of the overall economy. For
example, even high corporate income taxes imposed during World War II
did not reduce investment. In addition, the impact of corporate income

taxes on investment has been lessened by other tax reductions—such as the investment tax credit, accelerated depreciation, and depletion allowances on income from natural resources—to encourage investment.

Assuming that other things were equal, the corporate income tax would certainly decrease corporate retained earnings, and as a result, tend to reduce investment. However, given the present income tax rate structure, the corporate income tax may encourage the retention of earnings. The more progressive rates on personal income, the "double taxation" of corporate income and dividend income, and the preferential tax treatment given to capital gains would tend to encourage retained earnings and investment financed from such earnings.

Corporate income taxes do tend to encourage debt financing relative to equity financing because interest paid on debts is deductible and dividends paid are not. Although usual corporate management practices tend to discourage debt financing, the ratio of corporate debt to total capital has been rising; reflecting, perhaps, the lower cost of debt financing due to the corporate income tax.

EQUITY CONSIDERATIONS

Perhaps the major controversial equity issue concerns the separate treatment of corporate and personal incomes. Some economists argue for the complete integration of the two income sources, while others believe that they should be treated separately for tax purposes. The integration of the two essentially could be brought about in either of two ways. The first would treat corporations as partnerships for tax purposes. In this event, taxable income would be distributed to each shareholder on a pro rata basis. For example, a shareholder with 10% of the stocks would be distributed 10% of corporate taxable income. Stockholders would include their proportional shares in corporate net income in their personal income tax returns. This approach to integration effectively eliminates the corporation income tax; its biggest disadvantage is that stockholders would have to make tax payments on unrealized dividends—that is, the part of corporate profits not paid out in the form of dividends.

A second approach to integration would allow the corporation a credit for dividends paid or the stockholder a credit for dividends received. In either case, the corporate income tax would be retained. If corporations were allowed a credit for dividends paid to stockholders, the corporate income tax would be a tax on undistributed profits. If stockholders were given a credit for dividends received, the tax would be on total profit income but "double taxation" would be eliminated. Under the current federal statutes, stockholders do receive a $100 dividend exclusion.

Any approach that fails to eliminate the corporate income tax must resolve the issue of different rates on corporate and personal incomes. Tax equity would seem to require corporate income tax rates that are identical to personal income tax rates, or vice versa. Little or no justification can be found for levying different tax rates on income from different sources.

STATE AND LOCAL TAXATION OF CORPORATE INCOME

The vast majority of states and a few cities impose taxes on corporate net income. State corporate income taxes, representing about 8% of state tax revenues, do not fall within the same category of relative importance as do state personal income and sales taxes; however, they do add in a vital way to tax collections of state governments. Among the cities that have entered the corporation income taxation field are Baltimore, Detroit, Kansas City, St. Louis, and New York City.

STATE CORPORATE INCOME TAXATION

Early History

Early state taxation of corporations was in the form of flat fees charged for state charters spelling out the nature of the business and the right to establish a corporate form of business enterprise. During the latter part of the nineteenth century, states began to view the incorporation fees more as sources of revenue. At the beginning of this century, most states (approximately forty) imposed a fee or a capital stock tax. Today, all states levy a fee for the privilege or right to organize and operate as a corporate enterprise.

The year 1911 marked the beginning of the modern era of state taxation of corporate income. The state of Wisconsin, which in 1911 paved the way for the beginning of state taxation of personal income, adopted a corporate income tax at the same time and started the movement toward the taxation of corporate income. The need for additional revenues to finance the expansion of state government goods and services encouraged and resulted in most states adopting the tax. In 1975, all but four states (Florida, Nevada, Texas, and Wyoming) derived revenue from levies on corporate net income. In the aggregate, state corporate income tax revenues amounted to $6.6 billion in 1975.

Administrative Features and Issues

State corporate income tax rates are much lower than rates imposed at the federal level. They range between 1% to 10%. The most frequent rate is about 6%, and it is most often imposed at a single proportional rate. However, some states—Arizona, Arkansas, Iowa, North Dakota, and Wisconsin—do have mildly progressive rates over several income brackets. A number of states also have progressive rates over two income brackets, such as Alaska, Hawaii, Indiana, Kansas, Kentucky, Maine, Massachusetts, Mississippi, New York and Ohio.

States vary as to what is included in the corporate income tax base. For example, some states exempt capital gains while others don't. A few states allow federal corporate income taxes to be deducted. A large number of states have essentially adopted the federal tax base, and the trend had increasingly been in this direction.

The state corporate income tax base is the corporate income produced within the state. Since many corporations do business in more than one state, problems and issues can arise in determining each state's share of the tax base. It is not always practical and possible for a corporation to identify income earned in each state and to keep separate accounts by state. As a consequence, other allocative methods are used.

A formula is used by most states to determine the allocation of the corporate income tax base when the income, or part of the income, produced within the state cannot be specifically identified. State allocation formulas include "indicators" of income, such as gross sales within the state. For example, if only gross sales are used and gross sales within the state are 40% of the total, the state would use 40% of corporate taxable income as the state's tax base. If several indicators are used, the average percent of all of the indicators would be used to allocate the corporate income tax base.

The problem of unfair tax treatment arises with almost any method of allocation because of the lack of uniformity among the states. Even in the formula allocation, indicators can be selected that favor the taxing state. The result can often be multiple taxation of some part of corporate net income. The trend, however, is in the direction of greater uniformity.

About 56% of the states with corporate income taxes in 1973 followed the Uniform Division of Income for Tax Purposes Act. If all states conformed to this act, the equity of state corporation income taxes would be increased.

PAYROLL TAXES

Payroll taxes are levied on only one type of income—wages and salaries. The most significant change in the federal tax system has been the rise in prominence of payroll tax collections which increased from 7.7% of federal tax revenues in 1950 to 27.6% in 1974. They are now second to the personal income tax in relative importance in the federal tax system.

INSTITUTIONAL BACKGROUND

Payroll taxes are "earmarked taxes" used to finance the federal social security system. This system, established in 1935, consists of a social insurance program, old age survivors insurance (OASI), and an unemployment compensation program. The first two programs are financed by a payroll tax on both employees and employers, and the third is financed by a payroll tax on the employer.

The social insurance program, originally a retirement program for the aged, has been extended to include benefits to disabled workers (1956) and health benefits to the aged (1965). It is now referred to as OASDHI (Old Age Survivors Disability Health Insurance).

The social insurance program has been expanded in coverage over the years until it now includes all employees except those covered under other systems, such as federal and railroad retirement. Consequently, payroll tax rates have increased substantially, and they are scheduled to increase even further in the future. In 1976, the rate for the social insurance program was 11.7% on earnings up to $15,300, with both the employer and the employee presumably paying one-half. Beginning in 1977, this rate will be imposed on earnings up to $16,500.

ISSUES AND REFORMS

The major issues concern the credibility of the social insurance principle and the burden that payroll taxes place on low-income groups. It was intended initially that the social insurance program would operate as a trust from which tax contributions would be invested to provide future benefits to the individual contributors. Although this private insurance principle was never strictly adhered to in practice, payroll taxes did exceed current benefit expenditures for many years and surpluses were accumulated. However, in recent years the social insurance program has operated on a pay-as-you-go basis; annual payroll taxes have been just large enough to cover annual benefits. Some people have received benefits exceeding their tax contributions, while others have received benefits less than their tax contributions.

Today (1976), the social insurance trust fund has a balance in the form of assets of about $36 billion. This is not an enormous figure in view of the fact that current cash benefits are greatly in excess of this reserve. Should no income flow into the trust fund, it would be exhausted in less than a year. This situation has caused much concern and popular debate over the financial soundness of the trust fund.

The social insurance trust fund is not financially sound in the same way in which a private insurance trust fund would be, but neither does it have to be wholly or, in fact, actuarially sound; current payroll tax rates do not have to be set high enough to build up a reserve in order to cover the expected value of future benefits. As long as Congress stands behind its commitment and is willing to increase payroll tax rates as required or use other tax sources to finance the program, the financial soundness of the program is not in jeopardy.

A more serious issue concerning the social insurance program involves the burden or incidence of payroll taxes. In the discussion of payroll taxes in Chapter 8, payroll taxes levied on *employers* are shifted wholly or in part to *employees.* The rationale for doing this is based on the reasoning that wage earners would receive higher wages if there was no payroll tax on employers. Thus, wage earners either nearly or fully bear the burden of payroll taxes.

The payroll tax is undoubtedly a heavy burden on wage earners. At the lower end of the income scale, in fact, payroll taxes exceed personal income tax payments. The effective rate is progressive up to about $12,000 and then becomes regressive. The burden of the tax on low-income groups could be reduced by introducing a low-income exemption.[5] Alternatively,

---

5. Congress did enact a temporary earned income credit for low-income groups with children in 1975, and extended this credit in 1976 through 1977.

the rate schedule could be made progressive and the ceiling on taxable earnings could be removed. Either approach would make this tax a more equitable fiscal instrument.[6]

VALUE ADDED TAX (VAT)

The value added tax (VAT) has been seriously considered as a federal revenue source on several occasions, particularly during the past fifteen years. Interest in the VAT, however, is not new; the idea of this tax was first advanced in the U.S. by T. S. Adams in 1921. Although never used in this country, the VAT is commonly found in Europe. It has often been viewed here as an alternative to the federal income tax and, in recent years, it has received much attention as a means of replacing property tax revenues for school finance.

THE NATURE OF A VALUE ADDED TAX

In its most general form, the value added tax is levied on the value added at each stage of production. Because the summation of the value added at each stage of production equals the final value of output, a completely general VAT is a tax on the total output of the economy. However, because total output and total income (wages + rent + profit + interest) are equal, the VAT is also a tax on total income. At the level of the firm, a general VAT would be levied on net sales (the difference between total sales and purchases from other firms).

Three tax bases have been discussed as practical alternatives: gross value, net value, and consumption. A value added tax levied on either gross or net value would be an income tax. The gross value added tax *includes* in the tax base the depreciation of capital assets; hence, it is a tax on gross national income. The net value added tax is a levy on net national product because depreciation of capital assets is *excluded* from the tax base. The consumption variation excludes the purchase of capital goods from the tax base, and therefore is a tax on the added value of consumer goods at each

---

6. The Carter Administration has proposed several changes in the payroll tax. Among them are: (1) the eventual removal (1981) of the annual earnings limit on which employees are required to pay taxes; and (2) the transfer of general revenue funds to the social security trust fund when the unemployment rate exceeds 6%.

stage of production. This type of value added tax is not an income tax, and could be considered as an alternative to other kinds of consumption taxes discussed in Chapter 11.

TAX INCIDENCE

A value added tax will be shifted forward in the form of higher prices or backward in the form of reduced incomes to the factors of production (land, labor, and capital). Its incidence should be similar to that of a proportional personal income tax levied on personal income before personal deductions and exemptions. It should also be similar to a truly general retail sales tax; that is, a tax levied on the value of all final goods and services.

As a substitute for the corporate income tax, a value added tax would probably reduce the progressiveness of the federal tax system and increase the degree of income inequality. This is due to the fact that a value added tax would reduce the income of all factors of production, whereas the corporate income tax probably has its major impact on profit income. On the other hand, as a substitute for property and sales taxes, a value added tax would tend to increase progressivity and reduce inequality. Given these somewhat conflicting effects, a new VAT levied on either gross or net value would probably have little influence on the distribution of income.

TAX EQUITY AND TAX EFFICIENCY

The VAT would probably receive a high ranking in term of both equity and efficiency. It would be levied on a broad base of either gross or net national income. It could be a very productive revenue source with low proportional rates.

In comparison to indirect taxes, such as sales taxes and excises, the VAT is probably more equitable. Even in comparison with the personal income tax, the VAT can be more equitable if the various deductions from the base of the former are a serious source of inequity. This follows from the fact that a value added tax would be levied on a base similar to personal income before personal deductions and exemptions. Still, the argument is often advanced that the VAT is regressive. Usually, however, this is based on an implicit comparison with the corporate income tax, or on a view of the tax base as consumption rather than income. Under these circumstances, the value added tax probably has a differential regressive effect.

The value added tax would probably have largely neutral effects on resource allocation and relative commodity prices. If the tax was completely shifted forward, the prices of all final goods and services would tend to rise, leaving relative prices unchanged. Given this lack of impact on relative prices, the allocation of resources would not be significantly affected.

An income-type VAT has many attractive features. Most economists would probably rank it behind the personal income tax and ahead of other taxes in terms of equity. In terms of efficiency, most economists would probably favor this tax over progressive personal income tax rates and over the corporate income tax. On the basis of both equity and efficiency considerations, a value added tax would be comparable to a proportional personal income tax and a truly general sales tax.

SUMMARY

The discussion of personal income and corporate income taxes at the federal, and state and local levels of government occupies most of the pages in this chapter. In addition, this chapter covers the significance of payroll taxes as well as introducing a new tax source, a value added tax. For each of these taxes, some historical highlights and institutional features are presented first and then followed by an economic analysis centered around the major issues and reforms.

The personal income tax is the mainstay of the federal tax system, representing close to one-half of federal tax collections. Ideally, the federal personal income tax ranks high among taxes, especially in terms of tax equity; however, in practice this tax has many shortcomings. Major tax reform is essential in order for this tax to be in practice what it could be ideally.

The issues surrounding the federal personal income tax are related to the following topics: (1) the meaning of income, (2) the erosion of the tax base, and (3) the progressivity of the tax rate schedule. Adherence to the tax principle of equity suggests that income from all sources should be included as income for tax purposes. Almost any exception opens the door for unfair tax treatment. A comprehensive approach to the meaning of income for tax purposes would be based on the view that income is anything that increases the capacity of a person to enjoy goods and services. More specifically, personal income is the total accretion to a person's wealth—consumption plus changes in net wealth. Under this definition, the current practice of permitting exclusions such as interest on state and local government securities, and unrealized capital gains to go tax free would not be allowed.

In current practice, the personal income tax base is significantly eroded resulting in much higher tax rates on non-favored taxpayers. This erosion in the tax base takes place essentially because of the over-statement of business expenses, the establishment of tax sheltered investment plans, personal deductions, and personal exemptions. Tax reform could include a close scrutiny of business expenses and the elimination of investment plans aimed at reducing income for tax purposes. The 1976 Tax Reform Act tightened up restrictions in regard to tax shelters.

The purpose of personal deductions and exemptions is to make allowances for non-income differences among taxpayers. In general, however, deductions and exemptions rather than improving tax equity, may be reducing it. Many deductions and exemptions may be viewed as tax expenditures, that is, subsidies to taxpayers in the form of tax deductions.

Concerning the progressivity of the federal personal income tax structure, we have observed that the actual income tax rate schedule is much less progressive than the potential allowed by the tax code. This is the result of the legal ways that certain taxpayers have available to them to reduce their taxable income. On grounds of equity, progressive rates can be defended; however, highly progressive rates can have adverse effects on the efficient operation of the economy. If it can be assumed that taxpayers and Congress really prefer a proportional or mildly progressive rate schedule, instead of reaching this kind of schedule through setting up a highly progressive rate schedule and then permitting exclusions, deductions, exemptions, etc., it would probably be more equitable and straight forward to establish the preferred rate schedule in the first place.

Since the State of Wisconsin established the first successful personal income tax in 1911, many states have adopted the tax. Today it is a major tax source to most states, contributing, in the aggregate, almost one-fourth of state tax revenues. On an individual state basis, the relative importance of personal income taxes varies, with a few states not having the tax at all and some states relying upon the tax for over 40% of their tax revenues.

Most of the issues and needed reforms discussed in regard to the federal personal income tax also pertain to state personal income taxes. Most states have income tax bases that resemble the federal income tax base. A few states have income tax bases that completely conform to the federal counterpart. State income tax returns are greatly simplified when state income tax laws conform with the federal law.

Many local units of government, primarily cities, have introduced personal income taxes (taxes on wages and salaries) since 1939. Although not important in the aggregate, personal income taxes to the local unit levying the tax can be a very important source of tax revenue. There are often administrative problems with local income taxes stemming from the fact that many persons who earn their income in a city may reside outside of the city—even in another state. The trend is in the direction of a more generous use of income taxes at local levels.

The corporate income tax is a controversial tax. The incidence of the tax is in dispute, and there are different views concerning the economic effects of the tax. Some argue that the tax represents double taxation since dividend income is already taxed as personal income. The complete integration of corporate and personal income taxes could be accomplished by treating corporations as partnerships for tax purposes. Under this arrangement, the corporate income tax would be eliminated but taxable corporate income would be distributed to each shareholder on a prorata basis and taxed as personal income. At the present time, corporate income taxes are important sources of tax revenue to federal and state governments.

Payroll taxes have risen to great importance since 1950, and represent close to 30% of federal tax collections. This places payroll taxes second only to personal income taxes in relative importance in the federal tax system. Many taxpayers pay more taxes in the form of payroll taxes than they do in personal income taxes.

Payroll taxes finance the federal social security system, a system established in 1935 consisting of two programs: a social insurance program and an unemployment compensation program. The social insurance program provides retirement and health benefits to the aged, and disability benefits to persons covered under social security. The unemployment compensation program provides benefit payments to workers that are temporarily unemployed.

The major issue concerning payroll taxes is the heavy burden of these taxes on wage earners, especially wage earners at the low end of the scale. This burden could be reduced by introducing a low income exemption. Alternatively, payroll taxes could be more progressive. At the present time, they are mildly progressive up to about $12,000, and then become regressive.

The value added tax has been considered as a possible new source of federal revenue on several occasions. It is a tax that is levied on the income created or the value added at each stage of production. In general, a value added tax would receive a high ranking in terms of both equity and efficiency. It would be levied on a broad base—the nation's income. Thus, it could be a very productive revenue source with low proportional rates.

SUGGESTIONS FOR FURTHER READING

Pechman, Joseph A., *Federal Tax Policy,* Third Edition, Washington, D.C.: The Brookings Institution, 1977.

Chapters 4 and 5 provide a thorough coverage of the federal personal income tax and the corporation income tax, respectively. More structural problems are covered in Chapters 4 and 5 than are covered in this chapter. One problem that may be of special interest is that of indexing for inflation (p. 116). In addition to Chapters 4 and 5, Chapter 7 on the payroll tax is suggested to supplement what is covered in this chapter.

Goode, Richard, *The Individual Income Tax,* Revised Edition. Washington, D.C.: The Brookings Institution, 1976.

An exhaustive treatment of the individual income tax is offered by this reference. Chapter 12, entitled "The Future of the Income Tax," contains interesting ideas for discussion.

TEN

TAX LEVIES ON WEALTH:
ISSUES AND REFORMS

The previous chapter considered tax levies on the *flow* of income; this chapter examines taxes on the stock of assets, or wealth. Most of the revenue from wealth taxes comes from levies on existing property rights; however, some is also derived from property right transfers. The property tax exemplifies the first type, while examples of the second are inheritance and estate taxes.

Among the various levies on wealth, only the property tax has been an important source of revenue and will be examined in more detail than the others discussed in this chapter. However, we will also evaluate inheritance, estate, and gift taxes, and briefly consider the possibility of raising revenue from a new source—a tax on net worth.

AN OVERVIEW

Wealth taxation is as old as taxation itself. Almost all articles of wealth have been taxed at some time or place, including land, fences, buildings, stocks, bonds, furniture, appliances, glass windows, silver, gold, jewelry, and cattle. However, for reasons explored below, wealth taxation in the contemporary era has not achieved the prominence of income taxation.

WEALTH TAXATION AND EQUITY

Wealth taxation has been rationalized on the basis of both the benefit and the ability to pay principles of taxation. A traditional view is that the owners of property receive benefits from the state in the form of protection. Thus, it is reasoned, the expenses incurred in the provision of protection services should be paid for by a levy on such property. Similarly, it can be argued that the value of property is enhanced by the provision of sidewalks and streets; hence, it is equitable to collect property taxes equal to this increase in value.

The justification of property taxation strictly on benefit grounds is based on the premise that property owners are the sole beneficiaries of public services. It is more generally accepted now, however, that at least part of the benefits from collective goods and services, such as fire and police protection, are distributed generally among the members of a community. This suggests that non-property owners also benefit from these services, and it follows that such services should be financed by other types of taxes as well.

It would be difficult, of course, to tax property owners only for the proportion of benefits they receive from public services, and actual levies probably diverge widely in many cases from those that could be justified solely on a benefit basis. For example, a significant part of the local property tax is used to finance primary and secondary education. A property owner who has no children in school may have a difficult time accepting the argument that property taxes are payments for the individual benefits received from primary and secondary education.

Wealth taxation can be defended on the ability to pay principle of taxation. A person's wealth is directly related to his/her capacity to pay taxes; if two taxpayers, A and B, earn the same income of $20,000, but A has $10,000 in the form of cash balances while B has no wealth in any form, A is clearly in a better financial position to pay taxes than is B. As the reader will recall from our earlier discussion, however (see Chapter 7), it is difficult to translate this general observation into a rate schedule that can be defended on an objective basis.

WEALTH TAXATION AND EFFICIENCY

Tax levies on wealth generally do not have neutral effects on the operation of the economy. Their principle effect is to reduce the flow of income derived from holding wealth in a taxable form. This reduction adversely affects incentives to save and accumulate wealth, resulting in a less efficient economy. Wealth taxes also force the owners of wealth to be more liquid; that is, to hold wealth in the form of cash balances in order to pay taxes. Thus, wealth taxation can affect the composition as well as the level of wealth in the economy.

Although they may have some of the adverse effects suggested above, there is little evidence to support the view that wealth taxes *seriously* interfere with the efficient operation of the economy. In fact, in comparison to income taxes, one form of wealth levy—estate taxes—may be superior in terms of the principle of neutrality due to the fact that these taxes are not levied on persons who have accumulated wealth during their lifetimes, but are levied instead on the individuals who inherit wealth. Thus, estate taxes may have minimal effects on incentives and current production.

Perhaps the most neutral tax of all is a tax on land. Since the supply of land is perfectly inelastic, the return to land is a pure economic rent, which can be taxed without creating adverse effects on resource supplies. The economic rationale for taxing the economic rent of land is presented later in the chapter, along with some of the objections to taxing land.

WEALTH TAXATION AND INCOME INEQUALITY

Income inequality stems from many sources. Two of the more important are differences in productivity among individuals and differences in individual wealth. Income differences due to variations in productivity appear to be more socially acceptable than those attributable to differences in wealth—especially if this wealth has not been accumulated through efforts of current owners. Wealth taxes—those on inheritances and estates—are often defended as a means of reducing inequality in wealth and, therefore, inequality in income.

Suppose society decides that the main function of death taxes is to reduce inequality in wealth and income. What is the philosophical rationale for this approach? The supporters of this approach first and foremost believe that it is desirable to reduce inequality. Second, they may reason that society is entitled to the wealth of a person; after all, property rights *are* socially defined. Third, they may argue that it is not fair for a person to receive wealth that has not been earned from his/her own efforts.

213

Obviously, there are counterarguments to these views. One is based on the assumed primacy of individual rights. According to this position, a person has the right to transfer wealth before and at death in a manner preferred by that person alone. In addition, critics stress the possible disincentive effects in savings and wealth accumulation mentioned earlier.

What is the social consensus concerning this matter? In most taxing jurisdictions, death tax rate schedules are progressive, suggesting that society favors some redistribution of wealth. On the other hand, a large part of the wealth transferred at death is not taxed because of deductions and credits, suggesting that society does not wish to confiscate wealth at death but only to place limits on the amount that can be transferred.

THE PROPERTY TAX

The property tax is distinctive in many respects. First, it is the only wealth tax that is an important source of revenue. Second, although it has significantly declined in relative importance, especially at the state level, it ranks behind only the individual income tax as a source of tax revenue. Third, it is the major tax source at the local level. Fourth, it is intimately connected with variations in the quality of primary and secondary education. Fifth, it is the most disliked tax.

INSTITUTIONAL BACKGROUND

The property tax has its origin in the colonial period. At that time it was a "classified" tax; that is, a tax on selected pieces of property—primarily land and cattle. During the eighteenth and nineteenth centuries, it was transformed into a more general and uniform tax, and most property became subject to levy at a uniform rate. The move toward a general and comprehensive tax was arrested during this century primarily by the appearance of more intricate and intangible forms of property, such as bonds and stocks. Today, the property tax is essentially a selected tax on real estate and business equipment and inventories.

The property tax currently is the primary source of revenue for local governments, providing over 80% of their total tax collections. At the turn of the century, it accounted for over 50% of state tax revenues as well. Now it is of little importance, providing only 2.3% of total state tax revenue. Thus, while the property tax remains the mainstay of the local tax system, state governments have come to rely increasingly on other tax sources.

CLASSIFICATION OF PROPERTY AND THE PROPERTY TAX BASE

For tax purposes, property can be classified as follows:

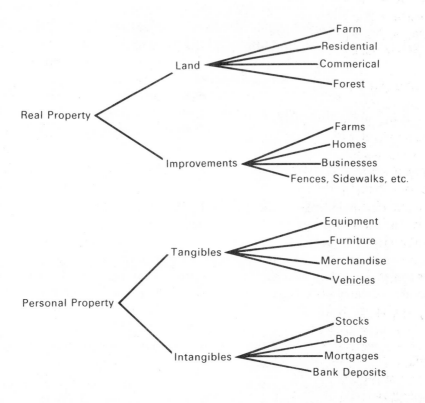

The potential tax base is the value of all of these various forms of property. It has been noted that the trend is moving away from a general property tax. A few states, such as New York, exclude personal property entirely from the tax base. Most states permit the exclusion of certain kinds of tangible personal property, and most completely exclude intangible personal property from the property tax base. The primary reasons for these exclusions are the difficulty in locating personal property, especially intangibles, and the problems involved in estimating its value. Thus, the property tax is essentially a tax on real property, especially improvements. In all, over three-fourths of local property tax revenue is derived from taxes on real property.

PROPERTY TAX ADMINISTRATION

Property tax administration encompasses the processes of assessment, review and equalization, apportionment, and collection. The assessment process entails the determination and the assignment of value to property listed on the tax rolls. Review and equalization involve corrections for assessment inequities. Apportionment is concerned with determining property tax rates and, finally, collection is concerned with the payment of taxes, either voluntarily or involuntarily, through governmental seizure and sale of property.

The Assessment Process

The assessment process is the responsibility of the tax assessor. Although a state agency usually assesses the value of certain kinds of property, such as the operating property of railroads and public utilities, most property is assessed by city and county officials who are either elected or appointed by elected officials. The main tasks of property tax assessors are to discover and list property on the tax rolls and to assign an assessed value or assessment ratio (the ratio of assessed value to market value) to such property. Both tasks require some expertise and experience. This is especially true for the assessment stage of the process, the final result of which is establishment of the property tax base.

The Review Process

The review process is usually conducted by an ex-officio body of the governmental jurisdiction in which the assessment is made. The purpose of this process is to correct for property assessment inequities within a taxing unit and to equalize assessments among units. If the assessment of property was done perfectly, all property would be assessed at full market value and there would be no need for the review process. Of course, the assessment process is far from perfect. Wide variations can be found in assessment practices and in assessments for properties with the same market values. Unfortunately, however, the review process is not perfect either, and inequities remain even after reviews are completed. More will be said about the subject of assessment inequities in a subsequent section of this chapter.

Apportionment

The main task of apportionment is to determine the tax rates to be levied on a particular piece of property. A given piece of property is generally subject to rates levied by several units of government—city, county, state, school districts, and special districts. The property owner can add these several rates to determine the total rate which will be applied to the assessed value of her or his property.

To determine the property tax rate, a unit of government first determines the amount of property tax revenue that is required. This amount is generally the difference between the general expenditures of the unit of government and revenues from other sources. The next step is to divide the amount of revenue needed by the assessed value of property. For example, if a city has an assessed valuation of $20 million and decides it needs to raise $500,000 in property taxes, the city rate will be twenty five mills, or 2.5% ($500,000 ÷ $20,000,000).

Collection

Collection, of course, is the end product of property tax administration. Although the details of collection procedures vary widely, certain basic procedures are usually followed. Most taxing units call for the payment of property taxes in the fall of the year, although many permit payments in installments. Failure to pay at the time or times designated results in taxes being considered delinquent, and penalties and interest can be added to the tax bills of delinquent owners of property. If a delinquent bill remains unpaid, the property eventually may be sold by the government. Voluntary compliance is high, however, and forced sales are usually not necessary. This rule has exceptions, of course; most notably in New York City, where the tax delinquency rate for fiscal 1975 stood at more than 7%, with the City failing to collect some $220 million in property taxes during that year.

LEGAL ASSESSMENT STANDARDS
AND THE ASSESSMENT RATIO

Considerable variation exists in legal assessment standards among the states. Some states require assessments based on full market value; others, on some fraction of market value (Table 10-1). Even in states that have full value (100%) assessment standards, the assessment ratio in practice is less than 100%. As Table 10-1 indicates, the ratio of actual assessment to legal standard in full-value standard states is the same as the ratio of actual assessment to sales price. In fractional value states, however, the ratio of assessed value to sales value is very far below that of actual assessment to legal standard. All states end up with assessment rates that are some fraction of the market value and less than the legal standard.

Although most states require uniform assessment of all kinds of property, assessment ratios vary both within and among taxing units in a state. Such variations reflect property tax inequities. Studies indicate that inverse relationships exist between assessment ratios and market values and between assessment ratios and the age of property. Thus, more valuable property and older property tend to be underassessed. The evidence also reveals that commercial and urban properties have higher assessment ratios than residential and rural properties.

It is easier to achieve horizontal equity if assessment ratios are equalized among taxing units. To illustrate how variation in the assessment ratio results in unequal tax treatment, suppose that two pieces of residential property have the same market value of $20,000, but that property A has an assessment ratio of 50% and property B has a ratio of 25%. With the same tax rate of 5%, the owner of A would pay twice as much in taxes ($500) as the owner of B ($250), even though market values and tax rates are the same.

Finally, alongside and related to the problem of variations in legal assessment standards and assessment ratios is the problem of local underassessment. Local property tax assessors have a general tendency to underassess property in order to minimize conflicts with taxpayers. However, there are further incentives to underassess property. First, in states where state aid to local units is inversely related to the assessed value of property, local assessors often engage in competitive underassessment since lower assessments can result in more state aid and lower local taxes. Second, because other units of government levy taxes on the locally assessed value of property by underassessing property, the local assessor can reduce the total property tax burden on taxpayers residing in his/her district.

TABLE 10–1 LOCAL RESIDENTIAL PROPERTY ASSESSMENT LEVELS AND STATE LEGAL STANDARDS IN SELECTED STATES, 1971

State	Ratio of Legal Standard To Market Value (%)	Ratio of Actual Assessment To Legal Standard (%)	Ratio of Actual Assessment To Sales Price (%)
Full-Value Standard States:			
Oregon	100	87.1	87.1
Kentucky	100	83.8	83.8
New Hampshire	100	65.1	65.1
Florida	100	63.2	63.2
Maine	100	52.9	52.9
Maryland	100	47.8	47.8
Wisconsin	100	46.7	46.7
West Virginia	100	36.2	36.2
Virginia	100	34.8	34.8
New Mexico	100	27.5	27.5
New York	100	25.8	25.8
Missouri	100	23.1	23.1
Texas	100	18.0	18.0
Mississippi	100	14.7	14.7
South Carolina	100	4.0	4.0
Fractional Value Standard States:			
Tennessee	35	93.1	32.6
Georgia	40	89.2	35.7
Iowa	27	86.3	23.3
Michigan	50	83.0	41.5
California	25	80.0	20.0
Nebraska	35	78.6	27.5
Nevada	35	80.0	27.1
Illinois	50	75.6	37.8
Ohio	up to 50	73.8	36.9
Washington	50	72.2	36.1
Kansas	30	71.0	21.3
Indiana	33 1/3	70.6	23.5
Colorado	30	69.0	20.7
Arkansas	20	62.5	12.5
Arizona	18	59.4	10.7
Oklahoma	35	52.0	18.2
Minnesota	30	28.3	8.5

SOURCE: Advisory Commission on Intergovernmental Relations, *Federal-State-Local Finances: Significant Features of Fiscal Federatism* (Washington, D.C.: U.S. Printing Office, 1974), p. 209.

NOMINAL AND EFFECTIVE
PROPERTY TAX RATES

The illustration above shows how differentials in assessment ratios can result in unequal tax payments. Because assessment ratios differ so widely, it is useful to define two indexes of tax rates. The first, the nominal tax rate, is the one applied to the assessed value of property. It is calculated by dividing assessed value into tax collections. For example, if taxes paid equal $1000 and assessed value is $10,000, then the nominal tax rate is 10%. The second type, the effective tax rate, is the one applied to the market value of property. Using the same assessed value, but a market value of $50,000, the effective rate is 2%.

The average effective property tax rate in the United States was 1.98% in 1971 (Table 10-2). This index has risen 48% since 1968. Effective rates tend to be higher in the New England, Mideast, Great Lakes and Plains regions than they are in the Southeast, Southwest, Rocky Mountain, and Far West regions. In 1971, states with effective property tax rates at the top of the list (over 3%) were New Hampshire, Massachusetts, New Jersey, Wisconsin, and Nebraska. In the same year, states at the bottom of the list (under 1%) were West Virginia, South Carolina, Alabama, Mississippi, Louisiana, and Hawaii.

TABLE 10-2   AVERAGE EFFECTIVE PROPERTY TAX RATES, EXISTING SINGLE FAMILY HOMES WITH FHA INSURED MORTGAGES, BY REGION IN 1968 AND 1971

Region	1971	1968
United States	1.98	1.34
New England	2.64	1.72
Mideast	2.20	1.43
Great Lakes	2.12	1.31
Plains	2.37	1.59
Southeast	1.14	.74
Southwest	1.65	1.32
Rocky Mountain	1.85	1.28
Far West	1.74	1.13

SOURCE: Advisory Commission on Intergovernmental Relations, *Federal-State-Local Finances: Significant Features of Fiscal Federatism* (Washington, D.C.: U.S. Printing Office, 1974), p. 174.

WHO PAYS THE PROPERTY TAX?

In the Pechman-Okner study discussed in Chapter 8, it was shown that the incidence of the property tax depends upon the assumptions made concerning the shifting of the tax. Under the assumption that property taxes are paid by the owners of property, property taxes were mildly regressive through the family income class $10,000-$15,000, and then became mildly progressive, reaching 10% on the highest income class of $1 million and over. On the other hand, under the assumption that a part of property taxes are paid in proportion to expenditures on housing and consumption, they were regressive, beginning at 6.5% on the lowest income group and declining to .8% on the highest.

Using different sources of data and a different methodology, statistics collected by the Bureau of the Census (shown in Table 10-3) indicate that real estate taxes are regressive, starting at a very high rate of 16.6% on the lowest family income group and declining to 2.9% on the family income

TABLE 10–3 REAL ESTATE TAXES AS A PERCENTAGE OF FAMILY INCOME, OWNER-OCCUPIED SINGLE-FAMILY HOMES, BY INCOME CLASS AND BY REGION, 1970

Family Income	United States Total	North-east Region	North-central Region	South Region	West Region
Less than $2,000	16.6	30.8	18.0	8.2	22.9
$ 2,000– 2,999	9.7	15.7	9.8	5.2	12.5
3,000– 3,999	7.7	13.1	7.7	4.3	8.7
4,000– 4,999	6.4	9.8	6.7	3.4	8.0
5,000– 5,999	5.5	9.3	5.7	2.9	6.5
6,000– 6,999	4.7	7.1	4.9	2.5	5.9
7,000– 9,000	4.2	6.2	4.2	2.2	5.0
10,000–14,999	3.7	5.3	3.6	2.0	4.0
15,000–24,999	3.3	4.6	3.1	2.0	3.4
25,000 or more	2.9	3.9	2.7	1.7	2.9
All incomes					
Arithmetic mean	4.9	6.9	5.1	2.9	5.4
Median	3.4	5.0	3.5	2.0	3.9

SOURCE: Advisory Commission on Intergovernmental Relations, *Federal-State-Local Finances: Significant Features of Fiscal Federatism* (Washington, D.C.: U.S. Printing Office, 1974), p. 200.

group of $25,000 or more. These two sets of data cannot be completely reconciled because they relate to different years and different collection procedures, but several observations can be made. First, the Census data probably overestimate the burden on very low income groups because of the general tax relief they receive. However, this is offset to some degree by the fact, mentioned above, that assessment ratios tend to decline as market values rise. Second, both sets of data yield similar results for incomes above $5000. In regard to this last observation, the Pechman-Okner study, for the least progressive set of assumptions, shows rates declining from 3.6% to 3.1% between income classes from $5000 to $25,000; whereas the Census data indicate rates declining from 5.5% to 3.3% over the same range.

PROPERTY TAX RELIEF

Exemptions

An old practice of property tax relief is the homestead exemption. Its primary purpose is to encourage home ownership. In states which allow this exemption, it reduces tax payments by reducing the tax base or the assessed value of property. For example, if the assessed value of a home is $5000 and the exemption is $1000, the net assessed value or the property tax base is $4000. To be eligible for the exemption, the homeowner has to reside on the property. Some states also grant property tax relief in the form of exemptions to veterans.

Circuit-Breaker

A recent development in the area of property tax relief for low income families is the state "circuit-breaker" program. In this program, the state government provides tax credits or cash rebates when property taxes are considered to be excessive in relation to family income. The use of the term circuit-breaker to describe this program is based on the similarity between the way in which an electrical circuit-breaker protects against current overload and the way in which the tax relief program protects family income from an "overload" of property taxes.

The circuit-breaker program was pioneered by Wisconsin in 1964. Since then, many additional states have adopted similar programs. In all cases, the tax relief goes into effect when property taxes exceed a certain percentage of family income, although percentages vary among the states. Different types of relief are employed, but usually involve a direct reduction in the property tax bill, a credit against state income taxes, or a cash refund.

Although variations exist among the states, circuit-breaker programs have many common features. Frequently, special provisions are made for elderly property owners with low incomes. Second, many states administer the program through their income tax division, since tax relief is often in the form of a credit against state income taxes. Third, practically all states limit the amount of relief granted, usually to some lump sum amount. Circuit-breaker programs that cover low-income renters, as well as homeowners, state the tax limit as a certain proportion of rent, usually around 20%.

The benefits and costs of circuit-breaker programs vary because of differences among state programs. In the fiscal year 1974, more than three million claimants enjoyed total benefits of almost $450 million, for an average benefit per claimant of nearly $150 (Table 10-4). In some states, the average benefit per claimant was significantly higher. For example, in California, Connecticut, and Vermont, the average exceeded $200. On a per capita basis, Oregon, Michigan, Vermont, and Wisconsin are prominent. In Oregon, per capita tax relief from the circuit-breaker program was $31.78, with over 500,000 families receiving some relief out of a population of 2.2 million. Those states that provide high benefits per capita extend their programs to homeowners and renters of all ages.

PROPERTY TAX REFORM

The Advisory Commission on Intergovernmental Relations (ACIR), a bipartisan body containing representatives from federal, state, and local governments and the private sector, has recommended property tax reform based on four concepts: legitimacy, openness, technical proficiency, and compassion.[1] Legitimacy involves the legalizing of assessment practices by either raising assessment standards or conforming to actual assessment practices. Openness incorporates the basic idea that taxpayers should have

---

1. Advisory Commission on Intergovernmental Relations, *The Property Tax In A Changing Environment* (Washington, D.C.: U.S. Govt. Printing Office, 1974), pp. 1–23.

TABLE 10–4 COSTS (BENEFITS) AND PARTICIPATION RATES OF STATE CIRCUIT-BREAKER PROGRAMS, 1974

States	Total Cost ($1,000)	Number of Claimants	Cost of Claimant $	Cost Per Capita $	Percent of Eligible in Program (%)
Arkansas	166	2,798	59.34	.08	54
California	61,000	302,000	201.98	2.96	80
Colorado	2,355	27,251	86.41	.96	75
Conn.	6,193	19,533	317.05	2.10	60
Idaho	1,871	15,924	117.49	2.42	95
Illinois	21,950	144,647	151.74	1.95	50
Indiana	1,800	44,000	40.90	.33	55
Iowa	2,540	37,000	68.64	1.26	65–70
Kansas	3,149	31,307	100.58	1.38	80
Maine	1,974	13,468	146.56	1.92	N/A
Michigan	129,000	810,000	159.25	14.26	80
Minnesota	10,010	110,000	91.00	2.56	N/A
Missouri	4,709	58,031	81.14	.98	N/A
Nevada	80	1,994	40.12	.14	90
N. Dakota	35	5,052	70.0	.55	50
Ohio	33,000	264,300	124.86	3.20	74
Oregon	70,730	509,000	138.95	31.78	85
Pennsylvania	56,100	410,000	136.82	4.71	N/A
Vermont	4,731	16,400	288.47	10.19	97
West Virginia	166	8,529	19.46	.09	15
Wisconsin	35,411	189,521	186.84	7.75	80
All States	446,970	3,020,755	147.97	4.41	76

SOURCE: Advisory Commission on Intergovernmental Relations, *Property Tax Circuit-Breakers: Current Status and Policy Issues* (Washington, D.C., 1975), p. 5.

a better flow of information with regard to the property tax. Technical proficiency involves the training and ability of the property tax assessor to make accurate estimates of the value of property. Compassion is a concern for relieving low-income families from the burden of property taxes.

Legitimacy

A dominant characteristic of local units is the divergence between the state legal assessment standard and actual assessment practices. Most states have laws requiring property to be assessed at market value or some specific percentage of market value, yet in every state the assessed value is below the legal standard.

The ACIR believes that statewide full market appraisal of property is essential in order for property to be assessed in conformity with legal standards. In states that have full market value legal standards, conformity with the law would mean assessment equal to 100%. In states that have fractional value standards, conformity with the law would necessitate adjusting actual assessment ratios to equal the specific ratio required by law. Whatever legal standard a state follows, conformity to this standard cannot take place without a statewide full market appraisal of property. This is true even for states that permit assessments to vary with types of property.

Openness

Most property owners receive little or no information concerning how their property is assessed, how their property taxes are determined, and the recourse they have if they believe they have been treated unfairly. This may be one reason why taxpayers consider property taxes to be the most unfair of all taxes they pay. In any event, owners should be provided full information, including the full appraised value of their property, the state legal assessment standard, the assessed value of their property, the average assessment ratio in their tax jurisdiction and in the state, the rate applied to the assessed value of their property, the time and place for a review of their assessments and, of course, the amount to be paid and the time and place for payment. Usually, property taxpayers are informed only of their assessments, rates, how much they have to pay, and the time and place of payment. Better and more information to taxpayers may force improvement in the administration of the tax and change its bad image among taxpayers.

Technical Proficiency

Appraising property is not an easy task; it is a job for well-trained professionals. Appropriate tools and techniques must be used in property appraisal. It is a state's responsibility to assure the quality of its assessors and their assessments. Two choices are available to a state in assuming its responsibility: one is the complete centralization of the property assessment system, and the other is a strong system of state and local coordination. In the first instance, the state would have the responsibility of appraising and assessing all property. Uniform statewide treatment of all properties could be approached under this system. Under a strong system of coordination, assessments could remain in the hands of local assessors. The state, however, could set up uniform property appraisal and assessment standards and have the authority to enforce them.

Some states are moving strongly in the direction of improving the quality of assessments. Some require assessors to participate in training programs, some require the certification of assessors based on examinations, and many closely supervise local assessors and provide technical assistance. Yet, much more remains to be done to achieve full technical proficiency.

Compassion

Property tax reform would be incomplete without considering property tax relief to low-income families. Almost all states grant some form of property tax relief, especially to the elderly. An important development has been the provision of the circuit-breaker programs discussed above. Although it is difficult to achieve social agreement on the proper degree of compassion, it seems obvious that we have been moving in the right direction in recent years.

A SITE VALUE TAX ONLY?

There is a vocal group that favors fundamental reform in the current system of property taxation. This group envisages a tax on bare land, called a *site value tax,* as a replacement for property tax levies on improvements and on personal property. Site value taxation is in limited use in the United States. Two cities, Pittsburgh and Scranton, tax land much more heavily then improvements. In addition, the state of Hawaii has developed a property tax system much more dependent upon site value. Site value taxation is extended much further and is found in its purest form in countries other than the United States—principally in some countries of Africa, in Australia, and in New Zealand.[2]

Early support for the taxation of bare land came from the writer and

---

2. John F. Due and Ann F. Friedlaender, *Government Finance,* Fifth Edition (Homewood, Illinois: Richard D. Irwin, Inc., 1973), p. 479.

journalist Henry George. In *Progress and Poverty* (1879), George proposed a tax on the *economic rent* of land as the sole source of tax revenue. George's proposal has been kept alive; however, it has not gained much political support.

The underlying basis of the support for taxing economic rent is the notion that economic rent is *unearned income* that arises due to the fact that the supply of land is fixed or perfectly inelastic. Under this supply condition, increases in demand—for example, from population growth and general economic development—cause land values to rise, resulting in gains to the owners of land who have not made production contributions. It is concluded that since these gains are unearned they should be taxed.

It was mentioned earlier in this chapter that a land tax is considered a neutral tax because it would not reduce the supply of land. It is also true that a tax on the economic rent of land cannot be shifted forward because supply is perfectly inelastic. Thus, the owner of land would bear the burden of the tax in the form of the reduced value of the land. The reduction itself would equal the *capitalized* value of the tax. For example, a tax of $100 discounted at 5% would reduce the value of land $2000 ($100 ÷ .05). It follows that one consequence of the tax-capitalization effect would be to make land cheaper to buy for the purposes of development, including the development of industry and homes.

The theoretical case for site value taxation appears strong. However, there are serious objections to the tax, especially when it is seen as a complete replacement for all other property taxes. Assuming the tax is fully capitalized and land values fall, present owners of land would suffer a significant loss in income. Some owners of land, especially farmers and all owners who have not benefited from past increases in land values, would bear a disproportionately high tax burden. In addition, the benefits of many local government services, such as fire and police services, are directly related to the value of improvements. It can be argued that the taxing of land and not of improvements would destroy this important relationship between benefits and revenues. Finally, critics of site value taxation point out that taxes on the economic rent of land would not provide adequate sums of revenue to warrant its use as the sole type of property tax.

In our view, the critics of a site value tax have not successfully refuted the theoretical support for the tax. However, the supporters of the tax have probably claimed too much for its use as the only source of property tax revenue. It would seem that a case exists, then, for increasing the tax on the bare land, but not for relying on it exclusively.

DEATH AND GIFT TAXES

Death and gift taxes differ in an important respect from property taxes. While property taxes are levied on an annual basis, death and gift taxes are levied only when property is transferred by bequest or gift. Death and gift taxes are not important sources of revenue. However, they fill a necessary philosophical niche in the revenue system.

Death taxes may be levied in two ways—either on the estate of the deceased, or on the property inherited by the heirs of the deceased. The federal government has an estate tax while state levies are in the form of estate and inheritance taxes, primarily the latter.

FEDERAL ESTATE AND GIFT TAX REFORM

The Tax Reform Act of 1976 significantly changed the federal estate and gift tax. Prior to this act, gift tax rates comprised three-fourths of rates imposed on estates. Because of this, lifetime transfers in the form of annual gifts could in effect reduce taxes on transfers at death. With the passage of the 1976 Act, both taxable gifts and estates are subject to a uniform progressive rate schedule (Table 10-5).

Rate Schedule

In addition to establishing a uniform schedule for both estates and gifts, the 1976 Tax Reform Act altered the existing tax rate schedule. Previously, marginal rates ranged from 3% on the first tax bracket to 77% on taxable estates over $10 million. As indicated by Table 10-5, the 1976 Act established rates ranging from 18% on small estates to 70% on estates over $5 million.

Taxable Gifts

Federal estate taxes are computed by applying the appropriate rates to cumulative transfers (lifetime transfers and transfers at death) and subtracting the gift taxes payable. Federal gift taxes are computed by applying the same schedule to lifetime taxable transfers minus gift taxes paid in prior years. Only gifts over $3000 annually per recipient are taxable.

TABLE 10-5   MARGINAL TAX RATES OF FEDERAL ESTATE AND GIFT
TAXES

Taxable Net Estate Or Gift	Marginal Tax Rates (Percent)
0 to 10,000	18
10,000 to 20,000	20
20,000 to 40,000	22
40,000 to 60,000	24
60,000 to 80,000	26
80,000 to 100,000	28
100,000 to 150,000	30
150,000 to 250,000	32
250,000 to 500,000	34
500,000 to 750,000	37
750,000 to 1,000,000	39
1,000,000 to 1,250,000	41
1,250,000 to 1,500,000	43
1,500,000 to 2,000,000	45
2,000,000 to 2,500,000	49
2,500,000 to 3,000,000	53
3,000,000 to 3,500,000	57
3,500,000 to 4,000,000	61
4,000,000 to 4,500,000	65
4,500,000 to 5,000,000	69
Over 5,000,000	70

Unified Tax Credit

Another important change incorporated in the 1976 Act involved the replacement of the $30,000 gift tax exemption and the $60,000 estate tax
exemption with a unified tax credit. The credit increases in $4000 steps
from $30,000 in 1977 to $47,000 in 1981 and thereafter. However, any part
of the credit used to offset gift taxes cannot be also used to offset estate
taxes.

The relationship between the previous allowable exemptions and the
unified tax credit needs to be explained. The new tax credit of $30,000 in
1977 will be worth more than the previous exemption for some estates and
worth less for others. Since estate tax rates are progressive, the exemption
equivalency of the credit will vary inversely with the size of the estate. For

small estates, a $30,000 tax credit can be equivalent to an exemption of $120,666. On the other hand, a taxable estate in excess of $10 million previously could have saved $46,200 with an exemption of $60,000.

Marital Deduction

Prior to the Tax Reform Act of 1976, up to one-half of the estate could be given to the surviving spouse tax-free. Today, the law allows a marital deduction up to $250,000 for estates under $500,000. Larger estates remain subject to the 50% limitation. In regards to gifts, the marital deduction was liberalized by allowing an unlimited deduction for the first $100,000 of gifts between spouses. Before the 1976 Act, only 50% of gifts could be transferred between spouses regardless of the amounts of the gifts.

Gift Tax

The purpose of the federal gift tax is to prevent persons from circumventing the estate tax by giving their wealth away before their death. Prior to the 1976 Tax Reform Act, gifts given above a stipulated dollar amount within three years of death were included in the gross estate of the deceased on the presumption that such gifts were made in the contemplation of death. After December 31, 1976, all gifts made within three years of death, with the exception of the annual exclusion, are automatically included in the donor's estate without regard to the intent of the donor.

In summary, the Tax Reform Act of 1976 made a major stride toward integrating federal estate and gift taxes. Lifetime transfers and transfers at death are subject to the same progressive rate schedule. Lifetime taxable transfers are cumulative for estate tax purpose. A single, unified tax credit replaced the previous gift and estate tax exemptions.

STATE DEATH AND GIFT TAXES

All states except Nevada levy death taxes in some form (Table 10-6). The dominant form is the inheritance tax, which is used in thirty-four states. Two of these states use it in conjunction with an estate tax. The estate tax is used by seventeen states, with six states using only a "pickup" tax designed to pickup the full amount of the federal estate tax credit. The latter is an allowable offset against federal estate tax liability for estate

TABLE 10–6   TYPES OF STATE DEATH TAXES, JULY 1, 1973

Type of Tax	State
"Pick-up" Tax Only	Alabama, Alaska, Arkansas, Florida, Georgia, New Mexico
Estate Tax Only	Mississippi, North Dakota
Estate Tax and "Pick-up" Tax	Arizona, New York, Ohio, Oklahoma, South Carolina, Utah, Vermont
Inheritance Tax Only	South Dakota, West Virginia
Inheritance Tax and "Pick-up" Tax	California, Colorado, Connecticut, Delaware, District of Columbia, Hawaii, Idaho, Illinois, Indiana Iowa, Kansas, Kentucky, Louisiana Maine, Maryland, Massachusetts Michigan, Minnesota, Missoui, Montana, Nebraska, New Hampshire, New Jersey, North Carolina, Pennsylvania, Tennessee, Texas, Virginia, Washington, Wisconsin, Wyoming
Inheritance, Estate, and "Pick-up" Taxes	Oregon, Rhode Island
No Tax	Nevada

SOURCE: Advisory Commission on Intergovernmental Relations, *Federal-State-Local Finances: Significant Features of Fiscal Federatism* (Washington, D.C.: U.S. Printing Office, 1974), p. 296.

taxes paid to the states. This credit has provided an incentive for states to adopt their own estate taxes, and encouraged uniformity among the states.

Most states have both an inheritance tax and a pickup tax. Inheritance taxes are much less uniform among the states than are estate taxes. Inheritance tax exemptions and rates vary among states, and different exemptions and rates apply depending upon the relationship of an heir to the deceased.

Gift taxes are imposed in sixteen states. These taxes, like their federal counterpart, are imposed to avoid the circumvention of death taxes by making gifts before death. Again, similar to death taxes, considerable interstate variations can be found in gift tax exemptions and rates.

THE NET WORTH TAX

A wealth tax which a number of nations use, and which has been considered in this country as a new source of revenue, is the *net worth tax.* This tax is similar to the property tax but differs in two important respects. First, it is a tax on the wealth of a *person* instead of a tax on items of property *per se.* Second, it is levied on *net* wealth rather than on gross wealth. The net wealth of persons indicates their financial worth. It is the difference between the value of personal assets and personal liabilities. For example, a person's net worth in a piece of property valued at $100,000 that has a debt against it of $75,000 is $25,000.

A person's net worth is clearly a better indicator of ability to pay taxes than is the gross value of property owned by a person. Two people, each owning property of the same market value, are not identical in ability to pay taxes unless debt claims against their properties are also identical. Thus, a net worth tax would have to be considered a more equitable tax than one levied on gross wealth, such as the property tax.

ADMINISTRATIVE PROBLEMS

A major problem associated with the net worth tax involves difficulties that could be experienced in tax administration. All assets of individuals would have to be identified, and debt claims would have to be verified. In brief, a balance sheet showing all personal assets, liabilities, and net worth would be required from each taxpayer. It would be a formidable, though not impossible, task to collect the needed information and to check its reliability. Moreover, the always difficult problem would exist of having to determine the value of assets—especially assets that fluctuate in value.

Of course, there is a tendency to overstate the administrative problems connected with a new source of revenue. Voluntary compliance by the taxpayer can be relied upon to some extent. On a more optimistic note, administrative difficulties with a net worth tax may not be much greater than with other taxes, especially levies on income and property. Moreover, a net worth tax integrated with the income tax at the federal level probably could be administered at relatively low cost. In one respect, a net worth tax might even improve the administration of the income tax. Since a net worth tax would require the enumeration of personal assets, it would be easier to administer the taxation of capital gains and income from property.

EVALUATION OF NET WORTH TAXES

Net worth taxes receive strong support on tax equity grounds. Income is generally accepted as the best measure of ability to pay taxes. However, net worth is also a good ability to pay index. Both taxes have their roles in an ideal revenue system. Income taxes favor persons who have little income and a great deal of wealth; net worth taxes favor persons who earn a great deal of income and have little wealth. In combination, the two taxes would distribute the tax burden in a relatively equitable fashion.

Net worth taxes are subject to many of the same criticisms in terms of efficiency as are other wealth taxes and income taxes. Net worth taxes will fall on saving in any form. They differ from income taxes in this respect, as the latter fall only on income yielding assets. Net worth taxes are levied on a broader base then are income taxes; namely, on the entire stock of personal wealth rather than on the wealth acquired during a given year. Thus, for a given amount of tax revenue, net worth tax rates can be much lower than tax rates on income.

Net worth taxes would probably alter individual investment portfolio decisions. They would tend to discourage holding wealth in the form of cash balances, land, and low income yielding assets. Net worth taxes, unlike income taxes, do not penalize persons for acquiring high income yielding (and, probably, high risk) assets. On the other hand, net worth taxes, in comparison to income taxes, would discourage persons from investing in land for speculative purposes; net worth tax liabilities would increase with the acquisition of the land, whereas income tax liabilities would not increase until the land was sold for a capital gain or until the land became an income yielding asset.

SUMMARY

This chapter examines taxes on wealth, that is, taxes levied on the stock of assets. The most important type of wealth tax in terms of tax revenue is the property tax, which is the major tax source of local governments. Inheritance, estate, gift and a new tax source, a net worth tax, are covered also in this chapter.

Properties are classified for tax purposes into real and personal property. Real property is divided into land, such as farm, residential, commercial, and forest land, and improvements, such as farms, homes, businesses, fences, sidewalks, etc. Personal property is divided into tangible (equipment, furniture, merchandise, vehicles, etc.) and intangible (stocks, bonds, mortgages, bank deposits, etc.) personal property. Most property tax revenues are derived from levies on real property.

Most taxpayers consider the property tax the worse tax in existence. In practice, there is some justification for this dislike for property taxes. Local property tax administration leaves much to be desired. There is wide variation in assessment practices. As a result, the assessment ratio, the ratio of the assessed value to the market value of property, varies widely by age, by type, and by location of property. This lack of assessment uniformity creates property tax inequities. Finally, many studies show the property tax to be a regressive tax. However, as noted in the chapter, there is some disagreement about the incidence of property taxes.

There is much interest in property tax reform, stemming from the fact that the local property tax is intricately connected to the financing of primary and secondary education, and from the general recognition that property tax inequities exist. Property tax reforms could include providing the taxpayer with complete information concerning property taxes, establishing a state-wide technically proficient assessment system, and providing property tax relief to low income families.

There is a minority but vocal group that favors rather fundamental changes in the property tax system in the form of replacing the present system with a tax on bare land only, called a site value tax. Site value taxation is only in limited use in the United States but in other countries it is used more extensively. A theoretical case can be made for taxing land. Since land is fixed in supply, property tax levies on land have a neutral effect on the supply of land, and therefore, cannot be shifted forward. Also, it is argued that forces such as population growth that cause land values to rise produce economic rent, that is, unearned income. It is reasoned, then, that taxing land is justifiable since it is a tax on unearned income. There are objections to replacing the current property tax system with only a site value tax. However, the theoretical case for site value taxation is probably strong enough to move in the direction of relying more upon property tax levies on land.

Death and gift taxes differ from property taxes in that they are not levied on an annual basis but only when property is transferred by bequest or gift. Death taxes are in the form of estate taxes levied on the estate of the deceased, or they are in the form of inheritance taxes levied on the property inherited by the heirs of the deceased. The federal government has an estate tax while states levy both forms of death taxes, but primarily reply upon inheritance taxes. Although not important sources of revenue at either the federal or state levels of government, death and gift taxes seem to fill a necessary philosophical niche in the revenue system. The Tax Reform Act of 1976 made great strides toward integrating the federal estate and gift tax system.

Used in other countries, but not in the United States, a net worth tax has certain advantages over wealth taxes such as the property tax. It is a tax on the wealth of persons instead of items of property, and it is levied on *net* wealth rather than gross wealth. The net wealth of persons, the difference between the value of personal assets and personal liabilities, is a better indicator of the ability to pay taxes than gross value of property. However, there are administrative drawbacks to a net worth tax. All assets of individuals would have to be identified, and debt claims would have to be verified. Although not impossible, it might prove difficult to collect the needed information and check the reliability of it. Then, there is always the difficult problem of determining the value of assets—especially assets that fluctuate in value. In general, however, net worth taxes might not be much more difficult to administer than other personal taxes, such as personal income taxes.

In terms of equity, net worth taxes would receive a high ranking, because as previously noted, they are a good indicator of ability to pay. Net worth taxes would tend to alter the kinds of assets held. They would tend to discourage the holding of assets in the form of cash balances, land, and low income assets. In comparison to income taxes, net worth taxes would tend not to penalize persons for seeking high income yielding assets. But like income taxes and other wealth taxes, they would tend to fall on saving and capital accumulation.

SUGGESTIONS FOR FURTHER READING

Musgrave, Richard A. and Musgrave, Peggy B., *Public Finance in Theory and Practice.* Second Edition. New York: McGraw-Hill Book Company, 1973.

Chapter 14 is recommended for further reading. In this chapter, the rationale for wealth taxation is succinctly covered, as well as other topics of interest such as data showing the composition and distribution of wealth.

Advisory Commission on Intergoverment Relations, *The Property Tax In A Changing Environment.* Washington, D.C.: U.S. Govt. Printing Office, 1974.

This reference is referred to in the text. The first covers recent developments in property tax policy and administration, and the second part examines property tax developments on a state-by-state basis.

*

ELEVEN

TAX LEVIES ON CONSUMPTION: ISSUES AND REFORMS

Taxes on consumption are like levies on income in the sense that they are levies on *flows* rather than stocks. They are generally imposed on the seller's side of product transactions, and they are normally not designed to account for differences in income and wealth among individuals. Thus, in regard to the ability to pay principle of taxation, they may be inferior to both income and wealth taxes. Taxes on consumption do have some economic advantages, however, and both their weaknesses and strengths will be evaluated more thoroughly in the discussion which follows.

TABLE 11–1   SALES AND EXCISE TAX COLLECTIONS
AS A PERCENT OF TOTAL TAX COLLECTIONS,
BY LEVEL OF GOVERNMENT IN 1950, 1960, AND 1974

Level of Government	1950	1960	1974
Federal	20.8	12.8	6.7
State	63.7	58.3	56.7
Local	6.0	7.4	8.4

SOURCE: U.S. Bureau of the Census, *Government Finances,* 1950, 1960, and 1973–74.

Consumption taxes on sales play the same role in state tax systems as do income taxes in the federal tax system and property taxes in local tax systems. They are the chief source of revenue of state governments, representing well over 50% of tax collections (Table 11-1). The relative growth in income taxes at the state level in the past two decades has reduced the relative importance of state sales taxes, but no other tax source rivals them as the major source of state revenues, and it is not likely that this dominance will be altered significantly in the future.

TYPES OF SALES TAXES

Sales taxes can assume a variety of forms. First, they may be either *single-stage* or *multiple-stage* levies. A single-stage tax, as the name suggests, is levied at only one level of production; normally, either the retail, wholesale, or manufacturing stage. Multiple-stage sales taxes appear as either *value-added* or *turnover* taxes. As previously noted, value-added taxes are levied on the difference between gross sales and purchases from other firms at each stage of production. In contrast, turnover taxes are levied on gross sales at each stage.

Sales taxes also differ with regard to the tax base. Generally, the base consists of either consumer goods, or consumer and capital goods, or total transactions. In addition, the base itself can be broadly defined (general sales taxes) or narrowly defined (selective sales taxes). Finally, rates can be levied on a per *unit* basis, or as a proportion of the *value* of the commodity.

SINGLE-STAGE VS.
MULTIPLE-STAGE SALES TAXES

Only single-stage sales taxes are used in practice in the United States; multiple-stage taxes are commonly used in some other countries. At one time, the turnover tax was quite popular in Western Europe. It still survives as the chief source of tax revenue in the Soviet Union. Since this tax is levied on gross sales or transactions at each production stage, it can be imposed at a low rate and still bring in a great deal of revenue—an attractive feature from a political point of view. However, it has two significant disadvantages: (1) because the tax is levied on all transactions, taxpayers at later stages actually pay taxes on the tax itself, to the particular disadvantage of products that move through many stages before reaching the consumer; and (2) vertical integration among suppliers is encouraged and competition reduced.

The adverse effects of the turnover tax led many European countries to replace it with a value-added tax on consumption. This tax is normally considered superior to the turnover tax. The first reason for this is that the value-added tax cannot be pyramided because the taxes paid at one stage of production are deducted in determining the tax bill at the next stage. For illustrative purposes, consider a product that goes through four stages of production, subject to a value-added tax at a rate of 1%. In this example, the summation of the value added at each stage

Production Stages	Value Added At Each Stage	Value-Added Tax at Each Stage
One	$ 500	$ 5
Two	1000	10
Three	2000	20
Final	3000	30
Total Retail Value	$6500	Total Taxes $65

equals $6500, or the final value of the product at the retail level. The summation of the value-added taxes at each stage is $65, or 1% of the retail value of the product.

Second, a value-added tax probably will not encourage vertical integration. Suppose, in the previous illustration, that stages two and three are combined. The value added at the second stage would be $3000 and the value-added tax $30. Thus, the retail value of the product would again be $6500 and total taxes $65.

Third, a general value-added tax is equivalent to a single-stage sales tax imposed on retail value (see the above example), and the retail level is generally considered to be the best one for the imposition of broad-based or general sales taxes. Equal rates levied, for instance, at the manufacturing level may not give equal rates at the retail level because price relationships among commodities are not the same at all stages of production. In the case of *selective sales taxes,* however, specific commodities could be taxed at the manufacturing level without encountering this difficulty. Moreover, since the number of sellers is fewer and accounting records are generally better at the manufacturing level, it may be more efficient to levy selective sales taxes at this stage. This advantage may be especially pronounced in under-developed countries where tax enforcement and collection costs are quite high.

BROAD-BASED VS.
NARROW-BASED SALES TAXES

Economists generally favor broad-based taxes, such as the general sales tax, over narrow-based or selective sales taxes. The reason for this is that a more comprehensive tax base yields the same revenue at lower opportunity cost than does a less comprehensive base. The broadest base would include the final sales of both consumer and capital goods. A sales tax levied on these items would be roughly equivalent in efficiency terms to a proportional income tax or a value-added tax on income. However, the general practice of excluding capital goods from the consumption tax base precludes the practical achievement of this result.

Narrow-based sales taxes alter relative commodity prices, thereby changing the pattern of consumer spending and resource allocation. Some selective sales taxes that are imposed, however, are often defended on the grounds that the consumption of certain commodities, such as tobacco and liquor, should be curtailed. Others are defended on the grounds that they represent levies on "luxuries"; that is, consumer items supposedly consumed by wealthier individuals. However, consumption of particular items is not necessarily a good index of ability to pay, and selective sales taxes on so-called luxuries may not always have progressive or even proportional effects.

A final justification of selective sales taxes is that they may be imposed on the users of the services paid for by these taxes, thus scoring well according to the benefit principle. Often, these selective sales taxes are earmarked for the purpose of financing specific goods and services. Gasoline and payroll taxes are good examples of earmarked taxes; the former being generally used to finance highways, and the latter to finance the social security system. Although the impact of earmarked taxes on the distribution of income is not always clear, and the relationship between individual tax payments and benefits is not always very close, the support for this type of levy appears to have some validity.

UNIT VS. AD VALOREM SALES TAXES

Sales taxes can be imposed on either a per unit or value basis. Most selective sales taxes and "excises" are levied on a per unit basis; that is, the amount of tax is the same for each unit produced and sold. Total collections of this type of tax, therefore, are directly related to the volume or quantity sold. Ad valorem or value-based taxes, such as the general retail sales tax, are levied as a percentage of price. Total collections of this tax vary directly, then, with variations in total retail sales.

One result of the difference in tax bases is that ad valorem tax collections will automatically grow during inflationary periods even if the quantity sold does not increase. Per unit tax collections are not nearly as responsive under these conditions. For these reasons, many state and local officials favor the ad valorem tax as a source of revenue for financing expenditures.

GENERAL SALES TAXATION IN PRACTICE

Although the federal government has considered imposing a general sales tax, it has never done so. The general sales tax is currently applied strictly at the state and local levels. The decline in property values induced by the Great Depression began the growth era of general sales taxation at the state level. Mississippi was the first state to adopt a permanent general retail sales tax. Twenty-three other states quickly followed in the 1930s, and twenty-one others have since joined the ranks.

Only two cities, New York City and New Orleans, imposed general sales taxes before 1941. However, many cities have since turned to this levy to assist them in solving their financial plight. Starting in California, the movement has spread to cities in about half the states, and many cities in the remainder are anxiously awaiting the passage of legislation that will enable them to impose a general sales tax. Although not yet a major tax source of local governments in the aggregate, general sales taxes are important to many specific local units.

GENERAL SALES TAX RATES, COLLECTIONS, AND EXEMPTIONS

General Sales Tax Rates

General sales tax rates vary among the states from 2 to 6½% (Table 11-2). The most frequently encountered rates are 3 and 4%, levied by fifteen and seventeen states, respectively. Two states (Pennsylvania and Connecticut) have rates exceeding 5%.

TABLE 11-2   STATE GENERAL SALES TAX RATES AND GENERAL SALES
TAX REVENUE AS A PERCENT OF TOTAL STATE TAX REVENUE IN 1975

State	State General Sales Tax Rates (%) (July 1, 1973)	General Sales Tax Revenue As a Percent of Total State Tax Revenue (%)
Alabama	4	32.0
Arizona	3	42.3
Arkansas	3	32.3
California	4 3/4	35.3
Colorado	3	32.0
Connecticut	6 1/2	40.2
Florida	4	43.0
Georgia	3	36.4
Hawaii	4	49.8
Idaho	3	26.5
Illinois	4	33.9
Indiana	4	45.8
Iowa	3	26.7
Kansas	3	34.3
Kentucky	5	29.0
Louisiana	3	24.0
Maine	5	37.1
Maryland	4	22.9
Massachusetts	3	11.4
Michigan	4	33.8
Minnesota	4	19.0
Mississippi	5	48.6
Missouri	3	37.0
Nebraska	2.5	33.4
Nevada	2	33.7
New Jersey	5	36.6
New Mexico	4	41.9
New York	4	22.4
North Carolina	3	22.3
North Dakota	4	35.6
Ohio	4	30.6
Oklahoma	2	18.4
Pennsylvania	6	26.9
Rhode Island	5	29.4
South Carolina	4	35.3
South Dakota	4	49.7
Tennessee	3.5	41.4

Texas	4	35.0
Utah	4	43.6
Vermont	3	14.4
Virginia	3	21.7
Washington	4 1/2	56.0
West Virginia	3	48.6
Wisconsin	4	23.8
Wyoming	3	47.4

SOURCE: Bureau of the Census, *State Government Finances In 1975* (Washington, D.C.: U.S. Printing Office), p. 20, Advisory Commission on Intergovernmental Relations, *Federal-State-Local Finances: Significant Features of Fiscal Federalism* (Washington,D.C.: U.S. Government Printing Office, 1974) p. 239.

General Sales Tax Collections

In 1975, total state revenues from this source were $25 billion, or 31% of all state tax collections. Just as tax rates vary among the states, so does the relative importance of general sales tax revenue (Table 11-2). Several states are close to the average, but it is clear from casual inspection that there is wide dispersion in the distribution.

Exemptions and Credits

Commodities most frequently exempted from the general sales tax base include food and medicine. Nineteen states exempt food consumed off the premises on which it is sold (Table 11-3). Twenty-nine states exempt medicine in some way. Six states (Colorado, Hawaii, Idaho, Massachusetts, Nebraska, and Vermont) and the District of Columbia allow an income tax credit, or give a cash rebate, for part of sales taxes paid. These exemptions, credits, and rebates are given primarily to offset the presumed regressivity of sales taxes (see Chapter 8).

REGRESSIVITY OF THE GENERAL SALES TAX

A major drawback to the general sales tax is that it is regressive with respect to income. The main reason for this is that the ratio of consumption to income is high among low-income families and tends to fall as income increases. In addition, some of the consumption items that only relatively

243

TABLE 11-3 EXEMPTION OF FOOD AND MEDICINE IN STATE GENERAL
SALES TAXES, JULY 1973

State	Food	Medicine
Alabama	—	X[1]
Arizona	—	X
California	X	X
Colorado	—	X
Connecticut	X	X
District of Columbia	X[2]	X
Florida	X	X
Idaho	—	X
Indiana	X	X
Kentucky	X	X
Louisiana	X[3]	X[3]
Maine	X	X
Maryland	X	X
Massachusetts	X	X
Michigan	—	X[4]
Minnesota	X	X
Nebraska	—	X
Nevada	—	X
New Jersey	X	X
New York	X	X
North Carolina	—	X
North Dakota	X[5]	X
Ohio	X	X
Pennsylvania	X	X
Rhode Island	X	X
Texas	X	X
Vermont	X	X
Virginia	—	X
West Virginia	—	X
Wisconsin	X	X

NOTES:

1. Limited to persons 65 and over.

2. Rate on food is 2%.

3. Rate on food and prescription medicine is 2%.

4. Limited to 50% of the amount charged.

5. Limited to specified items.

REFERENCE: Advisory Commission on Intergovernmental Relations *Federal-State-Local Finances: Significant Features of Fiscal Federalism,* (Washington, D.C.: U.S. Printing Office, 1974) p. 251.

well-to-do persons can afford, such as education and some forms of recreation, are not included in the general sales tax base in most states.

Excluding food from the tax base may reduce the regressivity of the general sales tax. Some studies reveal that when food is so excluded the incidence of the general sales tax is more or less proportional. However, others do not reach this conclusion. For example, one study shows that the Illinois general sales tax is regressive even if food is exempted from the tax base.[1] Perhaps more effective ways of reducing the regressivity of this tax would be to allow an income tax credit or give a cash rebate to low-income families.

INCOME ELASTICITY OF THE GENERAL SALES TAX

Collections from general sales taxes vary with changes in national income. The relationship between tax collections and income is commonly measured as the percentage change in collections *divided by* the percentage change in national income. The value of this ratio is the income elasticity of the tax. In the case of the general sales tax, it is approximately equal to 1. This means that a 10% change in national income will result in about a 10% change in sales tax collections. The income elasticity of state income taxes is higher (1.65), and the income elasticities of some selective sales taxes, such as those on tobacco, are lower than 1.

In general, then, income elasticity measures the sensitivity of a tax to changes in the tax base induced by changes in income. More specifically, for general sales taxes, collections will rise and fall in about the same proportion as does national income. During periods of expansion and inflation in the economy, general sales tax collections will automatically grow and tend to keep up with the rising costs. Of course, during periods of contraction, general sales tax collections will automatically decline. In comparison to state income taxes, general sales tax collections are less sensitive to income change. However, the reverse is true for a comparison with selective sales taxes. General sales taxes, then, represent the middle of the road in terms of revenue stability and sensitivity.

---

1. Due, John F. and Friedlaender, Ann F., *Government Finance,* Sixth Edition (Homewood, Illinois: Richard D. Irwin, Inc., 1977), p. 383.

ISSUES AND REFORMS

Two major issues exist which concern general sales taxation. One concerns the regressivity of the tax, and the other concerns the best way of taxing consumption. General sales taxes are criticized because of their regressive incidence. However, as indicated above, there is some debate among economists as to exactly how regressive general sales taxes are, especially if food is exempted from the tax base.

The regressivity of general sales taxes can be reduced by the use of exemptions, credits, and rebates. Many states exempt food and medicine from the general sales tax base, as has been noted, and a few states give tax credits or cash rebates. Again, the latter two alternatives would seem to be the most effective ways to reduce or eliminate the regressive effects of these taxes.

A new approach to taxing consumption would be to do so more directly by an *expenditure tax.* This alternative will be examined in the final section of this chapter.

EVALUATION OF GENERAL SALES TAXES

General sales taxes have certain advantages and disadvantages. Many of those have already been implied in the previous discussion. The chief advantages are: (1) the tax is a productive revenue source that can be imposed at low, flat rates because it is broadly-based; (2) it provides states with an autonomous tax source that many believe is important in a system of federal, state, and local fiscal relationships; (3) in comparison with selective sales taxes and income taxes with progressive rates, the tax adheres more closely to the principle of efficiency; (4) the administration of the tax is relatively simple and economical; (5) since tax collections vary proportionally with changes in national income, they are relatively dependable sources of revenue; and (6) although general sales taxes tend to be regressive, this effect could be reduced or eliminated by exemptions, credits, and rebates.

The disadvantages of general sales taxes are also numerous. They are: (1) general sales taxes are notably regressive; (2) their indirect and impersonal nature makes it difficult to adjust them in accordance with the personal circumstances of taxpayers; (3) since they constitute such a small percent of sales at a given time, their burden can easily go unnoticed; and (4) since general sales taxes tend to increase the ratio of saving to income, a higher rate of private investment is required to maintain a full employment economy.

Do the many advantages of general sales taxes outweigh the many disadvantages? Should general sales taxes be included in an ideal tax system? There are no clearcut answers to these questions. If they are used, ideally they should be imposed on all consumer goods and services. However, they should be modified wherever possible to fulfill the tax criterion of vertical equity.

SELECTIVE SALES (EXCISE) TAXES

Selective sales or excise taxes are imposed on both per unit and ad valorem bases. All three levels of government levy excise taxes on a wide variety of specific commodities. However, the three most popular commodities are gasoline, tobacco, and liquor.

FEDERAL EXCISE TAXATION

Federal excise taxes have a history as long as that of our nation. External excise taxes (customs duties and tariffs) were the major source of federal revenue until World War I. Internal excise taxes were imposed early in our history; they became important during the Civil War and have generally remained so. However, in more recent times excise taxes have declined rapidly in relative importance at the federal level, primarily because of greater reliance on income taxes. Today, excise taxes rank fourth in terms of revenue generated at the federal level, and represent only 6.7% of federal tax collections (1974).

Although many federal excise taxes were repealed in 1965, they are still imposed on a number of items, such as alcoholic beverages, tobacco products, oil and gasoline, tires, trucks and buses, guns, telephone service, and air transportation. The three most important in regard to revenue generated are those levied on alcohol, gasoline, and tobacco.

STATE SELECTIVE SALES TAXATION

State selective sales tax revenues were $18.6 billion in 1975, providing 23% of total state tax collections (Table 11-4). As was true for the federal

TABLE 11–4   STATE SELECTIVE SALES TAX COLLECTIONS IN 1975

Source	Amount (Thousands of Dollars)	Percent of Total Selective Sales Tax Collections (%)
Motor fuels	8,255,483	44.5
Tobacco products	3,285,851	18.0
Alcoholic beverages	1,963,420	10.6
Insurance	1,750,886	9.4
Public Utilities	1,740,187	9.4
Parimutuels	676,426	3.6
Amusements	98,892	0.5
Other	745,112	4.2
Total	18,566,257	100.0

SOURCES: Bureau of the Census, *State Government Finances In 1975* (Washington, D.C.: U.S. Printing Office, August, 1976), pp. 20–21.

government, the most productive state excise taxes are those imposed on motor fuels, tobacco products, and alcoholic beverages. Other important examples are sales taxes levied on insurance premiums, gross receipts of public utilities, money wagered at race tracks (parimutuels), and amusement admission charges. In a few states, severance taxes are an important source of revenue. These are levied on the removal of natural resources, such as oil, gas, coal and other minerals, and timber.

Motor Fuel Taxes

Motor fuel taxes are state governments' chief source of selective sales tax revenue. With gasoline sales serving primarily as the base, motor fuel tax collections accounted for 44.5% of state selective sales tax collections in 1975. Gasoline tax rates vary among the states, ranging from a high of ten cents to a low of five cents per gallon (Table 11-5). Many states (eighteen) imposed a rate of seven cents per gallon; however, rates of eight and nine cents per gallon were imposed by eleven and ten states, respectively.

Tobacco Taxes

In 1975, all states imposed taxes on tobacco products, with a pack of cigarettes serving as the major tax base. During this year, these taxes produced revenues of about $3 billion, or nearly 18% of state selective sales tax collections (Table 11-4). Cigarette tax rates among the states vary

TABLE 11-5 STATE GASOLINE TAX RATES, JULY 1, 1973
(Per Gallon)

Under 7c	7c	7 1/2c	8 1/2c	9c	10c
Hawaii (5c)	Alabama	Georgia	Arkansas	Kentucky	Connecticut
Nevada (6c)	Arizona	Illinois	Idaho	Maine	
Oklahoma (6.58c)	California	Massachusetts	Nebraska	Maryland	
Texas (5c)	Colorado		West Virginia	Michigan	
	Iowa			Mississippi	
	Kansas			New Hampshire	
	Minnesota			North Carolina	
	Missouri			Vermont	
	Montana			Virginia	
	New Mexico			Washington	
	North Dakota				
	Ohio				
	Oregon				
	South Dakota				
	Tennessee				
	Utah				
	Wisconsin				
	Wyoming				

SOURCE: Bureau of the Census, *State Government Finances in 1975* (Washington, D.C.: U.S. Printing Office, August, 1976), page 310.

widely, ranging from two cents per pack to twenty one cents (Table 11-6). Most states (thirty seven) collect a dime or more per pack of cigarettes, while fourteen states collect fourteen cents or more.

Liquor Taxes and
Other Selective Sales Taxes

The relative importance of sales taxes on alcoholic beverages and other specific sales taxes is shown in Table 11-4. Selective sales taxes on motor fuel, tobacco products, and alcoholic beverages together contribute almost three dollars out of every four dollars of state selective sales tax revenues. Levies on insurance premiums, receipts of public utilities, parimutuels, and amusement admissions contribute most of the revenues unaccounted for by the big three.

EVALUATION OF
SELECTIVE SALES TAXES

Selective sales taxes are far from ideal. For the most part, they are probably regressive, with the bulk of tax payments shifted to consumers in the form of higher prices. Moreover, they alter relative commodity prices, thereby distorting spending and resource allocation patterns.

They are not without some merit, however. As mentioned previously, they provide a large and relatively stable flow of revenues. Moreover, they reduce the degree of reliance on income and wealth taxes, and therefore offset some of the potential adverse effects of these taxes on saving and investment.

The significant decline in federal excise taxes is a trend in the direction of a tax system that is in greater conformity with tax principles. State and local tax systems are becoming more balanced in regard to income, wealth, and consumption taxes. However, the major selective sales taxes will probably remain important sources of revenue.

THE EXPENDITURE TAX: A DIRECT
APPROACH TO TAXING CONSUMPTION

It is clear that sales taxes in practice have several drawbacks. Some of these probably could be reduced if a switch were made from the current indirect method of levying these taxes on production and sales to a method which

TABLE 11-6 STATE CIGARETTE TAX RATES, JULY 1, 1973
(Cents Per Standard Pack of 20)

7c or less	8c	9c	10c	11c	12c	13c	14c or more
District of Columbia (6c)	Alaska	Missouri	Arizona	Kansas	Alabama	Iowa	Arkansas
Indiana (6c)	Hawaii	Oregon	California	Louisiana	Georgia	Nebraska	Connecticut
Kentucky (3c)	Utah	Idaho	Colorado	Michigan	Illinois	Oklahoma	Delaware
Maryland (6c)	Wyoming		Nevada	Mississippi	Montana	Rhode Island	Florida
North Carolina (2c)				New Hampshire	New Mexico	Tennessee	Maine
South Carolina (6c)				North Dakota	South Dakota		Massachusetts
Virginia (2 1/2c)					Vermont		Minnesota
					West Virginia		New Jersey
							New York
							Pennsylvania
							Texas
							Washington
							Wisconsin

SOURCE: Bureau of the Census, *State Government Finances in 1975* (Washington, D.C.: U.S. Printing Office, August, 1976), page 312.

placed the levy directly on consumer spending. Some economists, therefore, favor a direct expenditure or spendings tax.

THE NATURE OF AN EXPENDITURE TAX

Although the expenditure tax is levied on spending rather than income, it would be like the personal income tax in the sense that collections would be based on individual returns. Under most circumstances, the expenditure tax base would be smaller than the income tax base. However, this need not always be the case, for expenditures can be financed out of accumulated wealth or borrowing. Thus, spending can exceed income.

Exclusions, deductions, exemptions, and credits could be incorporated in a personal expenditure tax just as they are in the personal income tax. One advantage of an expenditure tax over a sales tax is that these adjustments could be made to allow for personal differences among taxpayers. However, this may also be a disadvantage if the adjustments fail to improve equity or efficiency. One additional advantage of an expenditure tax over a sales taxes is that the former could be made proportional or progressive, thus weakening the association of consumption taxes with regressive incidence.

ADMINISTRATIVE PROBLEMS

Several difficulties are connected with the administration of an expenditure tax, many of which are encountered in the collection of any personal tax. Taxpayers would be expected to report their consumer spendings just as they are expected to report their incomes, and tax authorities would have to rely on voluntary compliance. However, enforcement still would be required. We cannot be certain whether enforcement of an expenditure tax would be more expensive than enforcement of the personal income tax. Some believe that it would be, but they appear to be matched by a similar number who claim the opposite.

Other problems would certainly be encountered with an expenditure tax. The line between personal spending and business spending cannot always be clearly drawn. As does the income tax, an expenditure tax would provide incentives to shift spending into the business expense category. Spending on consumer durables could also create some problems because these goods are consumed over a period of time. Consumption per year of a consumer durable good would have to be estimated, and consumption over the life of the good would have to be determined. Some items of consumption would undoubtedly escape taxation, such as home-produced foods. Also, if the consumption value of a house is included in the expenditure, tax base, renters are likely to be treated unfairly in comparison to homeowners. It is easy to estimate rent payments as a housing expenditure; however, it would be necessary to impute a rental value to owner-occupied houses in order to assure equal tax treatment.

AN EVALUATION OF THE EXPENDITURE TAX

The nature and some of the administrative difficulties of an expenditure tax have been noted. We are now in a position to evaluate this tax according to the criteria of tax equity and efficiency.

Equity

An expenditure tax is potentially a more equitable tax than a general sales tax because personal differences among taxpayers can be allowed for and because it is probably easier to levy an expenditure tax at proportional or progressive rates.

In comparison to the personal income tax, the case for an expenditure tax is more debatable. Nicholas Kaldor, an economist who has been a leading spokesman for the tax, argues rather convincingly that the rate of personal spending is a better gauge of a person's standard of living than is personal income.[2] He argues further than personal income has some drawbacks as a measure of the *power* to spend; for example, a person can finance spending out of past saving. Kaldor also observes that the problem of determining what is considered income for tax purposes would be resolved automatically if the rate of personal spending was used as the tax base instead of personal income. As a result, equity issues involving capital gains would not arise since an expenditure tax would be indifferent as to the *source* of the power to spend.

---

2. Kaldor, Nicholas, *An Expenditure Tax* (London: George Allen and Univin Ltd., 1955), pp. 46–53.

The defects of personal income as a measure of ability to pay taxes are widely recognized. However, the expenditure tax as an alternative is subject to one major limitation: namely, that the portion of income saved is not subject to taxation. It would not seem fair or equitable to many people to allow taxpayers who save to escape taxes on this part of their income. Thus, the question of whether or not personal income or personal spending is the best measure of ability to pay taxes is debatable on equity grounds alone.

Efficiency

An expenditure tax would not have a neutral effect on the level or composition of economic activity, for it would encourage saving and capital accumulation. However, these effects may be desirable if it is necessary to accelerate the economy's rate of growth. Unfortunately, whether or not there is or will be a lack of saving to finance profitable investments in the country is an unsettled issue. In fact, if planned saving exceeds planned investment at full employment, an expenditure tax may even be judged inferior to taxes which discourage saving, such as the individual and corporate income taxes.

SUMMARY: AN EXPENDITURE TAX

An expenditure tax probably merits more attention than it has received by policy makers. It is a more direct approach to taxing consumption than are sales taxes. It could be levied in a way that would remove the association between consumption taxes and regressive incidence. Also, an expenditure tax avoids some of the difficulties inherent in almost any measure of the power to spend. However, certain problems would be encountered in the administration of the tax.

The opposition to an expenditure tax is strong, especially when it is viewed as a device to replace sales taxes at state and local levels. It is probably easier to administer sales taxes since the seller serves as the collection agent. In addition, sales taxes are collected at each sale, resulting in a small tax payment at a given time. An expenditure tax would necessitate more planning on the part of consumers in order to pay taxes once a year. Of course, this problem could be overcome, in part, by withholding expenditure taxes at the source, similar to withholding income taxes.

SUMMARY

Tax levies on consumption are the chief source of tax revenue of state governments, representing well over 50 percent of state tax collections. Although the rising importance of income taxes at the state level has given a more balanced system, consumption or sales type taxes remain in the dominant position.

Sales taxes can take a variety of forms. In the United States, two types of sales taxes can be distinguished: general sales taxes and selected sales taxes or excises. The general sales tax is levied at the retail level on an ad valorem or value basis. It is a broad-base tax; that is, many commodities are included in the tax base. Selected sales taxes are levied on a specific commodity and usually levied on a per unit basis; for example, the gasoline tax is levied as so many cents per gallon of gasoline.

The chief disadvantage of the general sales tax is that it is a regressive tax, and therefore, violates the ability to pay principle of taxation. The regressivity of the general sales tax could be reduced or even eliminated through the use of exemptions, credits and rebates.

The advantages of the general sales tax are: (1) it is a productive revenue source that can be imposed at low, flat rates; (2) it provides states with an autonomous tax source; (3) since it is a broad base tax, it tends to be more neutral in its effects on the economy than, say, selected sales taxes; (4) the administration of the tax is relatively simple and economical.

Whereas general sales taxes are strictly a state and local government (many cities impose general sales taxes) tax source, all three levels of government impose selected sales taxes. Federal excise taxes have been imposed since the beginning of our nation, and before World War I, in the form of custom duties and tariffs, they were the chief sources of federal tax revenue. However, for many years now federal excise taxes have been replaced by federal income taxes as a chief source of federal revenues.

The three most popular kinds of commodities subject to selective sales taxes are motor fuels, tobacco products and alcoholic beverages. At the state level, approximately three-fourths of state selective sales taxes are derived from levies on these commodities.

Selective sales taxes would not be included in an ideal tax system. Most of them are probably regressive taxes. They alter relative commodity prices and thereby distort spending and resource allocation patterns. The significant decline in selected sales taxes, especially federal excise taxes, is a trend in the direction of an American tax system that is in greater conformity with tax criteria.

Both general sales taxes and selected sales taxes are indirect taxes, that is, they are imposed on production and sales. A more direct approach would be to tax personal expenditures or spending — an approach that is favored by some economists.

An expenditure tax would be like the personal income tax in the sense that collections would be based on individual tax returns. An important advantage of an expenditure tax over current sales taxes is that the former could easily be made proportional or progressive. The chief disadvantage of an expenditure tax is that it would be more difficult to administer.

SUGGESTIONS FOR FURTHER READING

Due, John F. and Friedlaender, Ann F., *Government Finance,* Sixth Edition Homewood, Illinois: Richard D. Irwin, Inc., 1977.

This basic public finance text includes an especially good coverage of sales taxation. Chapters 14 and 15 are suggested for further reading.

Kaldor, Nicholas, *An Expenditure Tax.* London: George Allen and Unwin, Ltd., 1955.

Nicholas Kaldor strongly supports an expenditure tax. His arguments are concisely presented in this reference. For a short review of the case that Kaldor makes for an expenditure tax, read pp. 46–56.

TWELVE

TAXES AND PRICES: RATIONING, REGULATION AND FINANCE

Up to now, the discussion of revenues has been concerned largely with taxes as a means of financing public expenditures and the effect of this process on the goals of equity and efficiency. Little attention has been given to the possibility of deliberately using revenue devices to achieve improved economic welfare. However, taxes or prices can be used to regulate the output of private goods which would be provided in non-optimal amounts. Moreover, in many instances prices can be used to establish the optimal output of publicly-provided goods.

Traditionally, taxes have not been employed widely for regulatory purposes, although levies on certain goods (for example, liquor and tobacco) have been viewed as devices for reducing consumption to socially desired levels. In recent years, however, the discussion of taxes as a regulatory device has focused largely on their usefulness as a tool for reducing pollution. One of the objectives of this chapter is to determine how appropriate they are for this purpose.

Pollution occurs largely because the natural environment is available to some users at a price that fails to reflect its value in alternative uses. The result is an inefficient and/or inequitable use of the environment. A similar phenomenon occurs in the case of outputs financed by public expenditures. Many of these are distributed at prices that are not necessarily consistent with achieving maximum economic welfare. The second objective of this chapter, then, is to determine whether, and how, public outputs can be priced to achieve a more optimal situation.

The discussion is organized as follows. We begin by briefly reviewing the economic dimensions of the pollution problem. This is followed by an evaluation of three means of alleviating the problem: bargaining, regulation, and tax-prices. We then turn to a review of the principles of pricing public outputs, and finally to an evaluation of pricing practices which characterize the public sector.

ENVIRONMENTAL POLLUTION AND PUBLIC ACTIVITY

The essential economic problem is the allocation of resources among users whose total wants exceed the amounts available. For resources that can be exchanged in markets, this problem is resolved by their delivery to users who are willing to pay the largest price for them. The exchange mechanism works fairly well for allocating most resources, especially those to which the purchaser obtains exclusive right of use.

Exchangeable resources are characterized generally by the clear assignment, easy transferability, and inexpensive enforcement of property rights. However, these conditions are not met for the so-called environmental resources: land, water, and air. In many instances, property rights cannot be easily assigned, transferred, or enforced, and the market exchange mechanism cannot be used for their allocation among alternative uses. This has important implications for economic efficiency and equity, and also for the role of government in a predominantly market-directed economy.

THE EFFICIENT LEVEL OF POLLUTION

Environmental resources are useful for a variety of purposes with economic value, even if no market mechanism can register these values accurately. The mantle of air surrounding the earth supports all life systems. However, it can also be used as a receptacle for the waste products of human consumption and production activities. Water resources also provide a variety of goods and services. They can be used for drinking, growing crops, commercial fishing, and recreation. Like air, however, they can also be used as a dump for waste residuals.

To what extent should these resources be used for any particular purpose? If the social objective is economic efficiency, the answer has been provided earlier. The efficient level of any activity is the one which yields the greatest total social net benefits. This principle can be applied easily to the case at hand.

First, it is necessary to recognize that the waste-receptacle capacity of the environment is a source of benefits to both producers and consumers; i.e., they would be willing to pay some sum of money rather than do without this capacity. If wastes can be dumped into the environment, the costs of various production and consumption processes are lower than they would be if this alternative was not available. These cost savings represent the amount individuals would be willing to pay for the use of the environment in this fashion. For a producer, they would be equivalent to the difference such savings make in a firm's profits.

Differences in individual valuations of the environment would occur because of differences in production processes, available pollution technologies, income, and wealth. This implies variation in costs saved at the margin and, therefore, in the marginal benefits of the environment as a waste receptacle. If these marginal benefits were arrayed from high to low, they would trace the familiar downward-sloping marginal social benefit curve.

This situation is depicted in Figure 12-1. In this figure, distances on the vertical axis measure the monetary value of both the marginal social benefits (MSB) and the marginal social costs (MSC—to be discussed) of using the environment as a waste receptacle. The horizontal axis measures the level of waste discharges into a given unit of the natural environment per unit of time.

The MSC of waste disposal are similar to the marginal cost of any economic activity—they depict the highest valued alternative given up for each additional unit of waste. In Figure 12-1, they are depicted as a continuously increasing function of the level of wastes, as a reflection of the assumption that a dirtier environment requires the sacrifice of progressively more valuable alternatives (ultimately, human lives must be sacrificed). This assumption is not necessary to the analysis, however.

It is assumed, moreover, that the environmental unit in question has some natural capacity to absorb wastes. That is, there is a level below which wastes discharged into the environment do not require any sacrifices

FIGURE 12-1
DETERMINATION OF EFFICIENT LEVEL OF WASTE

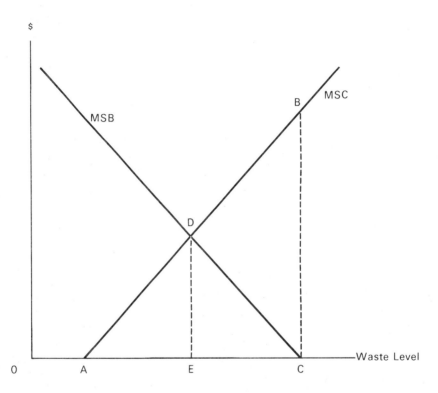

on the part of other users. This level is indicated in Figure 12-1 by the distance OA. Only after the waste level exceeds A is there a pollution problem from an economic point of view.[1]

By now, it should be obvious why the efficient level of waste is OE. As usual, when MSB = MSC, total social net benefits are maximized.

It is easy to see from this presentation that the efficient level of pollution is not zero. There is no guarantee, however, that the efficient level will be achieved. Indeed, it is highly likely that the actual level will exceed OE in the absence of government action.

This result occurs because the absence of property rights in the environ-

---

1. It is entirely possible that OA exceeds the level of waste that an ecologist would perceive as costly. For a good discussion of this issue, see: D. W. Pearce, "Economic and Ecological Approaches to the Optimal Level of Pollution," *International Journal of Social Economics,* Spring, 1974.

ment induces the polluter to view its waste disposal services as a free good; i.e., one with a price of zero. At this price, it is in the polluter's interests to discharge wastes at level OC rather than OE.

Under these circumstances, the environment is used inefficiently as a waste receptacle, resulting in net social losses equal to the area DBC. The environment is used to provide a service that is less valuable at the margin than the other services it is capable of providing.

Waste discharges greater than OA generate a social interest in the pollution problem and eventually lead to a call for government action to solve the problem. Before we review some of the action alternatives available, however, it is necessary to define the socially optimal, as opposed to the socially efficient, level of pollution or waste disposal. Efficiency alone is an insufficient criterion for public policy.

THE OPTIMAL LEVEL OF POLLUTION

The optimal level of pollution (or waste level) is defined as the one which maximizes economic welfare. Because economic welfare depends on considerations of both efficiency and equity, it is essential to determine how our previous results would be modified by equity considerations.

Presumably, in this case (as in others reviewed earlier in this book), the primary concern is that the efficient solution may reflect a socially inequitable distribution of income. Provided that any inequities generated by allocation policy will not otherwise be corrected by deliberate social action, it is appropriate to design solutions to pollution which will correct inequities as well as inefficiencies.

Following our analysis in Chapter 3, this consideration requires a change in the decision criterion from that of maximizing total social net benefits to that of maximizing total *weighted* social net benefits. Ideally, the weights will reflect relative social valuations attached to a dollar received or paid by each individual. Presumably, the size of the weights will be related inversely to an individual's income.

Given this criterion, the optimal level could be equal to, greater than, or less than the efficient level. MSC would be less than marginal *weighted* social costs if costs were paid predominantly by low-income individuals. Correction for this factor would yield an optimum less than OE. A similar result could occur if benefits were distributed mainly to high-income individuals, for in this instance marginal *weighted* social *benefits* could lie below MSB. Of course, an optimum to the right of OE is possible if costs are distributed largely to high-income individuals, or if benefits go mainly to low income individuals.

Beyond these general observations, there is little that can be said in general about the nature of the social optimum. Its exact position must be determined in each individual case. Public policies to control pollution which are not based on this knowledge may reduce rather than increase the level of economic welfare.

SOLUTIONS TO POLLUTION

One of the major objectives of this chapter is to evaluate taxes or prices as a means of achieving the optimal allocation of the environment. However, the use of these instruments presupposes that government activity is necessary to correct non-optimal situations. We begin our analysis, therefore, by examining the view that the private sector can solve the pollution problem by itself.

Bargaining

The notion that the private sector is capable of efficiently allocating environmental resources was first developed by Ronald Coase.[2] If perfect competition is assumed, the essence of his argument can be developed using Figure 12-1. Two cases are possible: one in which the polluter has the right to use the environment as a dump, and one in which property rights are vested in non-polluters.

Consider first the case in which the polluter has property rights to the environment. In the absence of bargaining, the level of wastes is OC, as indicated previously. Non-polluters suffer losses at the margin equal to MSC, while polluters reap gains equal to MSB. For all waste levels from E to C, it is clear that losses exceed gains and that the private solution appears inefficient.

However, there are unexploited opportunities for mutual gain at level C. If the polluter agrees to reduce the level of waste one unit, the non-polluter should be willing to pay any amount up to MSC on that unit as compensation for this reduction. Alternatively, the polluter should be willing to accept any amount equal to or greater than MSB. Clearly, in Figure 12-1, the amount the non-polluter is willing to offer to effect a reduction in

---

2. Ronald H. Coase, "The Problem of Social Cost," *The Journal of Law and Economics,* October, 1960, pp. 1–40.

wastes by one unit from level C exceeds the amount the polluter is willing to accept, and the reduction would occur if compensation could be arranged or a "bargain" could be made. Indeed, since MSC (the maximum potential "bribe") exceeds MSB (the minimum acceptable "bribe") for all units greater than E, bargaining should reduce the waste level to E, the efficient level. Levels less than E would not prevail because the maximum potential bribe is not high enough.

Suppose, alternatively, that property rights are vested in non-polluters. In this case, the "price" of the environment to non-polluters is zero, and they will not supply waste-assimilative capacity that exceeds OA. However, the MSB curve now depicts the maximum amount polluters will pay to achieve this increase. Obviously, for all levels less than E, the compensation that would be offered by polluters would be great enough to compensate non-polluters for an increase in waste. Once again, if bargains could be arranged, the efficient level of waste could be achieved; it makes no difference who has the property rights from the point of view of economic efficiency.

This result has been attractive to many economists, presumably because it appears to vindicate reliance on private exchange. However, it has been subject to several criticisms that severely diminish its value, in our judgment.

First, as E. J. Mishan has argued, the efficient level is not independent of the assignment of property rights.[3] In general, the amount someone will pay to acquire something is less than the amount he/she must be paid to give it up. Thus, the MSB and MSC curves are not unique; their positions depend upon whether polluters or non-polluters can demand compensation.

Second, D. W. Pearce has demonstrated that the bargaining solution is efficient only if perfect competition prevails.[4] This is a very important qualification, inasmuch as imperfect competition would appear to be the rule rather than the exception.

Third, there may be adverse effects on the distribution of income in some bargaining situations. When property rights are vested in polluters, bargaining results in a transfer of income from non-polluters to polluters. If the former group is characterized also by low income, this transfer would probably be considered inequitable. And, although the evidence on this

---

3. E. J. Mishan, "Pareto Optimality and the Law," *Oxford Economic Papers,* 1967.

4. D. W. Pearce, "The Incompatibility of Polluter Pays and Social Efficiency," in *Fiscal Policy and the Environment,* (London: Institute of Fiscal Studies, 1974).

point is skimpy, some evidence does exist which indicates that this is the type of transfer which would occur in many cases. A. M. Freeman, for example, argues that the rich are more capable of moving to areas of higher environmental quality, and finds that concentrations of air pollutants are relatively higher in low-income sections of metropolitan areas.[5] We would hardly be surprised if such results also prevailed for land or water resources, although of course there would be exceptions. In any event, the usefulness of bargaining is not a matter of efficiency alone.

Fourth, in those cases where there are large numbers of polluters and sufferers, it may be very costly to arrange bargains. As the number of involved parties grows, the *transaction costs* of bargaining are sure to grow —perhaps exponentially. In some cases, they appear to be prohibitively high: air pollution in major metropolitan areas, water pollution of major river basins. Indeed, in these instances, transaction costs would probably exceed the net social gains before bargaining.

We seriously doubt that bargaining is the answer to much of the pollution problem. It does not follow, however, the government activity is justified. Nor can government authorities produce efficient or equitable solutions at zero cost. Government activity is justified only if it can be implemented at a lower cost than bargaining, and only if costs of implementation are less than net social losses without such action. To determine whether this is likely, it is necessary to examine the alternative means at the disposal of public authorities.

Taxes

The solution advocated most frequently by economists is the imposition of a tax equal to the marginal social cost imposed by the polluter.[6] Here the government assumes the property rights to the environment and charges the polluter for its use. In terms of Figure 12-1, if a tax per unit of waste equal to MSC or to DE is levied by the government, polluters will choose to dispose of OE units.[7]

---

5. A. M. Freeman III, "The Distribution of Environmental Quality," in A. V. Kneese and B. T. Bower, eds., *Environmental Quality Analysis: Theory and Method in the Social Sciences* (Baltimore: Johns Hopkins Press, 1972).

6. This tax is often referred to as a Pigouvian tax after its initiator, the British economist A. C. Pigou. Pigou first proposed this tax in *The Economics of Welfare,* 4th edition (London: Macmillan and Co., 1932).

7. A tax equivalent to MSC per unit yields less revenue than one equal to DE per unit. Thus,

Another way to examine the tax is to view its effect on the production decisions of polluting firms. This is accomplished with the aid of Figure 12-2, which portrays the situation facing a (typical) perfectly competitive firm which uses the natural environment as a waste receptacle. The firm faces a perfectly elastic (horizontal) demand or marginal revenue (MR) curve for its product. The costs of production it must pay when rights to the environment are not assigned are indicated by the marginal private cost (MPC) curve. The costs it imposes on others by its use of the natural environment as a dump are its marginal external costs (MEC).

In this example, we are viewing pollution as a byproduct, or spillover, of the production of X. It is appropriate, therefore, to distinguish between the costs the producer must pay (MPC) and the costs paid by others (MEC). The sum of the two is the cost to society (the producer plus all other affected parties) of producing X, or the marginal social cost (MSC). The reader must not confuse MSC in this example with MSC in Figure 12-1. The MSC in the latter case refers to the marginal social cost of *pollution,* not the marginal social cost of *production.* If the pollution of Figure 12-1 was a consequence solely of production, then MSC in that figure would be equivalent to the MSC of Figure 12-2.

Before property rights to the environment are assumed by the state, firms maximize profits by producing the level of X where MPC = MR (assumed equal to MSB), or X_p. However, the efficient level is the one where MSC = MR, or X_s. At X_s, total social net benefits from the production of X are maximized.

To achieve X_s, the government can assume environmental property rights and charge firms a tax equal to MEC (or SE) per unit. The firm would consider the tax, then, as a regular cost of production, and base its profit calculation on MPC + MEC, or MSC, rather than on MPC alone. Under these circumstances, it would maximize its profits by producing X_s units.

As appealing as this solution is to many economists, it is subject to several criticisms.

The first criticism can be outlined with the aid of Figure 12-3, which depicts the cost and revenue conditions facing an imperfectly competitive firm that uses the environment as a waste receptacle. This firm faces a downward-sloping demand curve for its product such that demand ex-

---

the former will leave the firm with greater net revenues after the tax is paid. In fact, total payments made for a tax of DE, rather than MSC, per unit may bankrupt some polluters. In such a case, DE would not produce the efficient waste level because it would drive producers out of business and reduce wastes below OE as a result.

FIGURE 12-2
THE EFFICIENT LEVEL OF PRODUCTION WITH
POLLUTION PRESENT–PERFECTLY COMPETITIVE FIRM

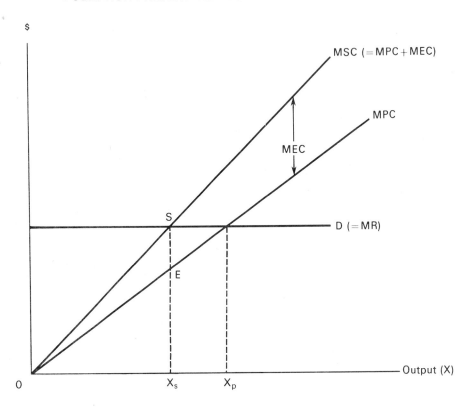

ceeds marginal revenue. In the absense of external benefits, the demand curve measures MSB. The MPC and MSC curves play the same roles as do similar constructs in Figure 12-2.

Before the pollution tax is levied, the firm maximizes profits where MR = MPC, or at output X_p. In this instance, it provides *less* than the socially efficient level of X, or X_s. After a tax equal to MEC is levied, however, it produces an even *smaller* amount (Xp, in this example).

Given the logic of profit maximization and the conditions facing an imperfectly competitive firm, a presumably efficient pollution tax actually induces a change in production in the wrong direction. Here, the effect of one market imperfection offsets the effect of a policy designed to cure another. In an economy full of market imperfections, this can be a serious shortcoming of efficient pollution taxes. (We return to this theme more

FIGURE 12–3
THE EFFECT OF A PIGOUVIAN TAX
UNDER IMPERFECT COMPETITION

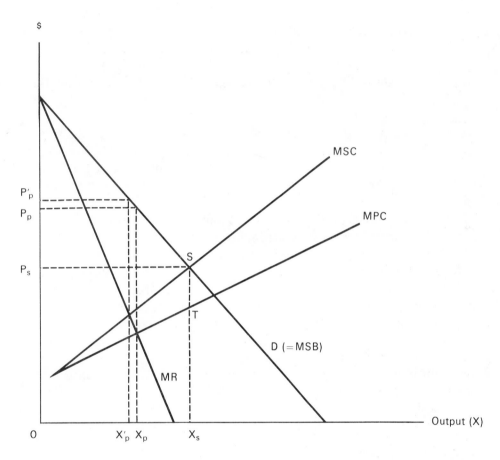

formally in the section on marginal-cost pricing later in this chapter.)

The second objection to the tax solution is that it would require the actual estimation of MEC. It seems sufficient to mention that presently available estimates of MEC are few in number and that additional estimates probably can be made only at relatively high cost. Under these circumstances, one can legitimately raise the issue of whether or not additional information costs would be high enough to offset existing social losses. If they were, efforts to implement the efficient tax would reduce economic efficiency.

The third problem with pollution taxes is that they may be regressive.

In principle, pollution taxes are simply excise taxes levied on particular commodities such as petroleum products, electricity, coal, chemicals, paper, motor vehicles, and minerals. Unfortunately, little data exists at present concerning the incidence of taxes levied on these products. The most important exception seems to be a study by J. M. Schaeffer, which indicates that taxes on all utility expenditures, and on gas and electricity, are regressive.[8] This is a thin basis for criticism of pollution taxes, and much more work needs to be done before a definitive conclusion can be drawn regarding the equity effects of this revenue instrument.

Environmental Standard

In practice, most governments attempt to control pollution by establishing and enforcing standards, expressed either in terms of the receiving environment (e.g., the minimum level of dissolved oxygen in a river) or in terms of the quality of waste. Most of the economics literature argues that standards are an inefficient way of achieving environmental quality. However, their widespread use warrants a careful appraisal.

Most standards are set on the basis of biological criteria, which are used to define pollutant levels that may not be exceeded if undesirable harm to particular life-support systems is to be avoided. Because they are developed in a political environment, however, standards rarely reflect what the biological purists want. Usually, the standards are made less stringent to accommodate the concerns of business and labor.

The primary attraction of standards is that they require less information than pollution taxes. Most proponents of standards would argue that we know very little about the costs or benefits of pollution control. However, it seems obvious that pollutants erode important life-support systems and that it is necessary to take action without first having precise information on economic values.

This argument has some merit in our judgment, but our inability to measure all relevant benefits and costs does not justify just any standard. There is a danger of setting standards so high that the total benefits of control are less than the total costs. Perhaps an even more relevant consideration, however, is that the last few percentage increments in environmental quality are so costly that they seem certain to outweigh the associated incremental benefits.

---

8. J. M. Schaeffer, "Sales Tax Regressivity Under Alternative Tax Bases and Income Concepts," *National Tax Journal* (December, 1969), pp. 516–27.

What little we do know at present about pollution control costs indicate that they probably rise at an increasing rate as the level of control approaches 100%. Thus, it has been estimated that it is as expensive to reduce automobile emission of hydrocarbons, carbon monoxide, and nitrous oxide from a weighted average of 83% to 95% of the 1940 level as it is to reduce emissions from zero to 83%.[9] The 95% level represents that which was specified in the Federal Clean Air Act of 1970 for achievement by 1975. Similarly, in 1972 the Water Pollution Control Act specified these standards: (1) water clean enough for swimming and other recreation uses by 1983; and (2) no discharge of pollutants into the nation's waters by 1985. Considerable savings could certainly be effected by lowering these standards. In Congressional testimony, it was estimated that the move from (1) to (2) would be much more costly than achieving the first standard alone.[10]

The other mistake commonly made with regard to environmental standards is the establishment of uniform standards or uniform means of achieving a standard. Motor vehicles used mainly in rural areas must be equipped with the same emission controls as those operated predominantly in urban communities. Often, all factories in a particular area must reduce pollutants by the same percentage, regardless of how efficient each is in doing so. It would be more efficient to require auto emission controls only on those vehicles most responsible for pollution and to concentrate control efforts on those who can achieve less pollution at lowest costs.

In spite of these problems, the establishment and enforcement of environmental standards will remain the chief focus of pollution control efforts for some time to come. Given this fact, the economists' task is twofold: (1) to develop better estimates of marginal benefits and costs of environmental standards wherever possible; and (2) to aid in choosing least-cost methods of achieving given standards.

Up to now, governments have attempted to achieve given standards by establishing and enforcing legal regulations. Many economists believe, however, that standards can be best achieved by using pollution taxes for this purpose.

Suppose that the same tax per unit is levied on each unit of pollution or waste, regardless of its source. Each source will then determine how

9. As reported in G. L. Bach, *Microeconomics: Analysis and Applications* (Englewood Cliffs, N.J.: Prentice-Hall, Inc., 1977), pp. 207–209.

10. This case is discussed in A. M. Freeman, III and R. H. Haveman, "Clean Rhetoric and Dirty Water," *The Public Interest,* Vol. 28 (Summer, 1972).

much waste it wants to emit into the natural environment by comparing the tax with its marginal cost of waste control (MCC). When the tax exceeds MCC, it will exercise control. When MCC exceeds the tax, it will emit pollutants. Each source is free, of course, to search for the least costly means of achieving control. Indeed, because the tax is a uniform price which must be paid if control is not achieved, the firm can increase its profits by searching for lower-cost technologies.

If under these circumstances a given standard is adopted, the authorities will set an initial uniform tax for each type of pollutant, monitor each source, and collect revenues according to wastes emitted into the environment. Each source will determine how much to emit by comparing the tax and its MCC function. If after some time the total waste level exceeds the standard, the authorities will raise the tax, inducing polluters to reduce their waste emissions. If the level of emission is less than the established standard, taxes will be reduced. By using this method of trial and error, the desired standard can be achieved over time.

Such a method has been used with some degree of success in the Ruhr Valley in Germany and has received increasing attention in the United States, both within academia and the federal government. However, the method is not entirely free of difficulties.

One of the problems with a scheme of this type is that it may induce firms to install pollution abatement equipment in response to the initial tax, which would become unnecessary if the tax was changed in the future in the light of growing evidence that the initial tax was set at too high a level. The probability of a tax change surely exceeds zero unless the authorities have accurate knowledge of MCC for each polluting source.

It is often argued that pollution taxes provide sources with the widest possible choice of ways to reduce pollution. However, the range of choice is no larger for taxes than it is for standards, unless the regulations specify the use of a particular technology. Provisions of the latter type can be eliminated, of course.

There is some belief that a pollution tax would reduce the information costs of achieving a given standard. Polluters need to know their MCC schedules, but the authorities do not need this information. They must monitor the quality of the environment and the effluents of each source, but they would have to do this anyway for the regulation alternative.

The pollution tax appears to have an advantage, then, in terms of required information. But the possibility remains that the trial and error procedures that would be necessary in reality could actually require *more* information on cost functions than economists are wont to believe, if unnecessary investment in pollution control equipment is to be avoided.

Thinking in terms of either regulation or taxation is probably not optimal strategy at the present time. It appears that standard-setting is unavoidable, given the information requirements of an efficient pollution tax scheme and the reservations about their appropriateness in a less than perfect market economy. However, the determination of the best way to achieve given standards would seem to depend on a detailed examination of the particular circumstances of individual cases.

PRICING PUBLIC PRODUCTS

Although most government revenues come from general taxes, a significant proportion is derived from fees or charges for various governmental services and products. Some of these prices are levied merely to raise revenues, with little attention given to the relationships between the prices chosen and the goals of efficiency and equity. However, economists do view prices as allocative and distributive tools, as well as a means of finance. Following a brief review of revenue in the public sector, we will develop the economists' view in some detail.

PUBLIC PRICES AS A
SOURCE OF REVENUE

We use the term "public prices" to identify a particular means of payment for goods provided by or regulated by government agencies. It encompasses what economists have called "beneficiary charges," "user charges," and "fees," as well as prices in the conventional sense. At the federal level, it includes items such as revenues from postal services, the sale of surplus agricultural commodities, the sale of natural resources, grazing fees, license fees, and the sale of recreation permits. At state and local levels, it includes tuition for education, tolls for expressways, charges for public utilities, admission fees for parks, fees for special police services, charges for hospital facilities, revenues from convention centers, garbage collection fees, rents from public housing, revenues from state liquor stores, and fees from a wide variety of licenses. Neither of these lists is exhaustive, of course.

Data which accurately measure the magnitude of revenues collected from public prices are not currently available. Useful measures are provided, however, in data compiled by the Advisory Commission on Intergovernmental Relations (ACIR).[11] At the federal level, the closest measure to what we are seeking is their "charges and miscellaneous revenues," which accounted for $37 billion or 11.3% of total federal revenue in 1976. This was up from $7.4 billion and 9.8% in 1954. At the state and local levels, two accounts are relevant for our purposes: charges and miscellaneous general revenue; and utility, liquor store, and insurance trust revenue. The sum of these sources in 1976 was $81.5 billion, as compared to a 1954 total of $10.4 billion. Given the large growth in total revenues of state and local governments over this period, however, the total accounted for by these sources declined from 29.4% to 27.9%.

It is easy to criticize these data, especially those which pertain to state and local governments where uniform reporting practices are not the rule and the categories may be too broadly defined (insurance trust revenues are a questionable item, for example). However, our purpose here is merely to provide a rough approximation of the relevant totals as a means of counteracting the notion that because the government provides services these services are always provided free of charge.

THE PROPER ROLE OF PUBLIC PRICES

Although public prices are employed widely by governments, especially at the state and local levels, there is a widespread belief among economists that this means of finance is being used neither as fully nor as wisely as it could be.[12] For what publicly-provided goods or services, however, are prices especially appropriate?

The case for the expansion and rationalization of pricing in the public sector is based largely on the contribution this can make to allocative efficiency. Prices can serve as useful signals to government authorities of the services citizens want, of the correct volume of output from public programs, and of the desirability of investing in new physical facilities. Properly used, they may even serve to ration existing capacity more effi-

---

11. Advisory Commission on Intergovernmental Relations, *Significant Features of Fiscal Federalism, 1976 Edition* (Washington, D.C.: Government Printing Office, June, 1976), pp. 30–37.

12. This seems to be the general consensus of the contributors to the most authoritative volume on this subject: S. J. Mushkin, ed., *Public Prices for Public Products* (Washington: The Urban Institute, 1972).

ciently, perhaps thereby eliminating the necessity to add to existing and apparently inadequate facilities.

However, it is not appropriate to price all publicly-provided goods and services. To be eligible for pricing, the output must provide benefits which can be appropriated, in large part at least, by each individual purchaser; that is, the good must have the characteristics which would render it exchangeable in private markets.

Another way to state the preceding condition is that benefits from consumption must not accrue largely in the form of externalities or spillovers. The complete absence of this factor is not necessary, although some goods can be excluded from consideration because of this characteristic. Some examples are national defense, general police protection, and disease control. Many goods and services are currently provided through the public sector, however, that are mainly "private" in nature. This is especially true at the local level.

The other primary reason for not pricing public outputs is that this practice may interfere with the achievement of redistribution or equity objectives. This may be the case either if the policy objective is to redistribute real income in the form of a particular product, or if it is feared that individuals would buy less of some service than the amount considered socially desirable. Indeed, in some cases, equity may require the distribution of services free of charge.

Although a large number of goods and services are eligible for pricing according to the criteria mentioned above, the bulk of the literature is concerned with a relatively small number of cases. A great amount of literature is devoted to the pricing of public utility services, such as water and electricity. The problem of pricing highway services has engaged the efforts of some well-known economists. Recently, much attention has been directed toward the possibilities of pricing education services more fully and to the problem of pricing recreation, airport, and hospital facilities. We will refer to several of these developments in the analysis which follows.

PRICING TO ACHIEVE EFFICIENCY

The appropriate price for a product depends upon the objective the producer wants to achieve. In the public sector, this price will probably vary with each different objective because the government is usually a large enough supplier that it faces a downward-sloping demand curve for its products.

In some instances, in fact, it is the exclusive supplier in the relevant market area.

The effects of different objectives on price can be seen clearly in the classic case of the public utility, a "natural monopoly." Figure 12-4 depicts the situation for a community that receives its water from a single supplier —the local governmental authority. The authority in this case faces the entire demand curve for water, D or MSB (we assume the absence of external benefits). The average total costs of supplying water are indicated by ATC, and the marginal costs by MC. Marginal revenue from sales is indicated by MR.

If the authority desires to maximize profits, it will do so by producing quantity Q_p, where MR = MC, and charging price P_p. Alternatively, the objective may be simply to cover all costs (all variable costs, plus the annual share of fixed costs) of supplying water. In this instance, the appro-

FIGURE 12–4
PRICES AND OUTPUTS FOR A NATURAL MONOPOLY

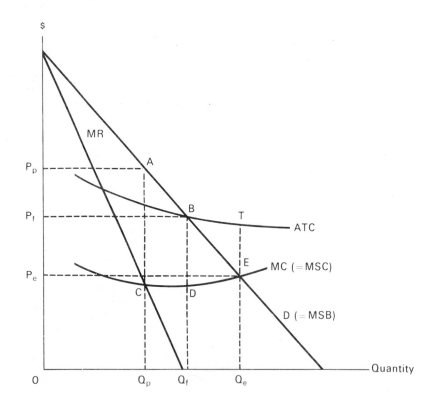

priate quantity is Q_f and the appropriate price is P_f. Finally, the authority may wish to provide the efficient level of output; this requires a quantity and price equal to Q_e and P_e, respectively.

The combination of Q_e and P_e is the one consistent with allocative efficiency because, as outlined previously in this text, it is this combination which maximizes total social net benefits (TSNB). The set Q_f and P_f, on the other hand, reduces TSNB by the area BDE, while the set P_p and Q_p reduces TSNB by this area *plus* the area ABDC. Social efficiency is reduced, then, by a price which just covers all costs, and is reduced even further by a price which maximizes profits.

Such is the standard efficiency case for so-called marginal-cost (MC) pricing. In slightly more sophisticated versions it has been used to develop efficient prices for the rationing of existing transportation and recreation facilities. In other instances, the doctrine has been extended to argue for MC pricing of facilities which experience peak-period congestion, such as highways and airports during rush hours, water supply and electric generating systems during summer months, and telephone systems during business hours.

In reality, very few public products are priced at marginal cost. This practice reflects the concern of public officials for objectives other than efficiency. However, even if efficiency was the actual objective many economists would not advocate the universal adoption of MC pricing.

Problems with MC Pricing

Economists have known for some time that MC pricing is applicable in an unmodified form only in an economy that exhibits the virtual absence of market failure. In real world economies, where this is definitely not the case, the situation can be made even more inefficient if MC pricing is adopted in only a limited segment of the economy. This, at least, is the basic message of the Theory of Second Best, which states that departures from efficiency in some parts of the economy will probably require deviations from efficiency conditions in other parts.[13]

To cope with this problem, economists have developed rules which are general modifications of, or departures from, the theoretically correct rule

---

13. R. Lipsey and K. Lancaster, "The General Theory of Second Best," *Review of Economic Studies,* Vol. 24 (December, 1956).

(in this case, to price at MC). One such modification can be illustrated with a simple example.[14]

Suppose that two modes of transportation are available to commuters. One, an expressway, conveys each passenger at a marginal cost of $1.00 per trip. The other, a rail transit system, can perform the same service at $1.20 per trip. Suppose further that in order to cover average total cost (ATC) it is necessary to charge expressway users $1.50 and rail passengers $1.30.

According to the MC pricing rule, the difference between ATC and MC should be subsidized out of tax revenues and prices of $1 and $1.20 should be charged for each of the modes. Assume, however, that only expressway use is subsidized (operated by a government agency). This means that services priced at MC would be competing with services priced above MC ($1.00 vs. $1.30). The difference in price of $.30 would exceed the difference in real costs of $.20.

From an efficiency point of view, the difference in real cost should guide the choice between modes because this differential is a more accurate index of resources sacrificed by virtue of choosing a particular mode of conveyance. Travelers will be guided by the price differential, however, and tend to choose too much expressway travel and too little rail travel.

A better policy is to price expressway use so that the differential between real costs ($.20) is preserved. This would require a price of $1.10 on the expressway, or a subsidy of only $.40 per passenger per trip. Under these circumstances, commuters would use existing facilities more efficiently.

In reality, the number of substitutes is not restricted to one, as it is in the above example. When larger numbers of related products are involved, the second-best pricing rule becomes more complicated. Roughly, it would call for prices in the controlled product to exceed MC by an amount corresponding to the differential between MC and the price which prevails on the average in the related but uncontrolled commodities. Generally, those commodities which are the closest substitutes for the controlled product should be weighted most heavily in determining the average.[15]

The other problems with MC pricing are of a more practical nature. First, there is the point, obvious to managers and accountants but not widely appreciated by economists, that MC often is extremely difficult (or expensive) to measure accurately. This need not be an absolute barrier to the use

---

14. This example is similar to one developed by Vickrey which appears in S. J. Mushkin, ed., *Public Prices for Public Products*, pp. 56–58.

15. For a good discussion of the practical aspect of the second-best problem, see: W. Baumol and D. F. Bradford, "Optimal Departures from Marginal Cost Pricing," *American Economic Review*, Vol. 60 (June, 1970), pp. 265–283.

of MC pricing, but the marginal cost of determining MC should not be dismissed as trivial.

A similar problem is the possibility of high costs of implementation. Any pricing scheme requires some expenditures for collection. Meters may have to be installed to register the consumption of water and electricity, or toll booths or electronic surveillance equipment may have to be established to monitor transportation facilities. Once again, these costs can be substantial.

Another cost is evident in the case where MC pricing fails to produce enough revenue to cover total costs, as in Figure 12-4. In this example, there is a loss of TE per unit, which must be covered by general tax revenues. Unfortunately, it is difficult to conceive of any practical tax financing plan that will not interfere with efficient resource allocation. One of the costs of MC pricing, then, is the loss in social net benefits occasioned by the marginal increase in taxes. In addition, any administrative and compliance costs of taxation must be added to this account.

Finally, some economists have argued that reliance on MC pricing may result in a failure to undertake needed investment in new facilities.[16] This would be caused presumably by the success of the MC pricing in reducing congestion, thus giving the appearance that existing facilities are adequate. In actuality, however, an expansion of facilities may pass a present-value test rather easily even if the MC pricing scheme makes it appear that expansion is not needed.

Average-Cost Pricing as an Alternative

As mentioned earlier, most prices do not conform to the MC pricing rule. One rule which is widely employed instead is to set price equal to ATC (P_f in Figure 12-4). This rule is especially prominent in public utility rate regulation where the objective is to cover all costs, including capital outlays and a fair rate of return on capital.

The chief disadvantage of this pricing policy has already been outlined: it is probably a source of efficiency losses. Moreover, for some products it may not be any cheaper to implement than MC pricing. This would probably be the case when special devices are necessary to monitor use and levy charges, as in the case of highway systems.

---

16. A good example of this situation appears in: M. Wohl, "Congestion Toll Pricing for Public Transport Facilities," in S. J. Mushkin, ed., *Public Prices for Public Products,* pp. 253–263.

Average-cost pricing has several advantages that cannot be dismissed lightly, however. First, because no losses result, there is no need to use the tax-subsidy mechanism. Thus, the incremental social costs of taxation are avoided.

Second, because authorities are charged under this scheme to avoid losses, the average-cost pricing rule theoretically tends to reduce pressure for premature expansion of facilities, and provides some incentive for managers to lower costs. However, it is doubtful that average-cost pricing has had these effects in practice, primarily because regulatory commissions allow cost increases to be used as the base for determining prices and, ultimately, profits.

Third, average-cost prices may correspond closely to MC prices, thereby diminishing the size of efficiency losses. This would be especially likely when economies of scale are small or when the price-elasticity of demand for the product is quite low. Indeed, in both these cases a second-best price would probably be close to the average-cost price.

For some products, of course, we probably should not employ either MC or average-cost prices but rely instead on the tax system to ration existing capacity. For public roads, governments currently charge user taxes which are levied on certain travel inputs (most notably gasoline) at approximately constant cost per mile. If highway users plan trips on the basis of average variable costs of travel, the addition of taxes results in use being regulated by a price that roughly approximates the average cost price referred to above. The tax then performs a rationing function that promotes more efficient use while at the same time avoiding the high costs of revenue collection.

On theoretical grounds alone it is not clear which pricing alternative is superior or whether some tax policy would be more desirable. Only a well-designed cost-benefits analysis will indicate which of these alternatives is most efficient. Moreover, it seems likely that such an analysis would not have universal application, and that it would have to be repeated for a great many special situations.

Zero or Token Prices

A second type of pricing policy is employed widely in the public sector for goods whose benefits are largely appropriable. This consists of the provision of goods and services at a price of zero, or at prices below marginal costs of provision ("token prices"). These prices represent a subsidy for all but the marginal purchasers, and they are defended most often on equity grounds. However, we want to examine here some of the implications of these prices for achieving economic efficiency.

It follows from our previous discussion that a price of zero is efficient as long as marginal cost equals zero. There are a large number of cases in which this condition is fulfilled in the public sector. A bridge or highway which requires virtually no maintenance or patrol outlays as a function of traffic volume, and which is not congested, fits this mold nicely. However, a policy of zero pricing in this case is subject to the objections to MC pricing mentioned earlier.

If prices are not set high enough to ration public products among users so that there is neither a shortage nor a surplus, some alternative means of rationing must be employed. In many instances, queues can be used, and they are currently employed widely for highways, health, and welfare services. However, other devices are often employed. For example, in public higher education institutions where tuition is probably less than the efficient MC price, test scores and high school class standing serve as rationing criteria. Public park space is often allocated to those who are least sensitive to the invasion of privacy. Although it is possible in these situations for goods to be allocated to those who value them most highly, there is a greater likelihood of this occurring if prices are used as the rationing device.

In many instances, there is little doubt that zero or token prices ration inefficiently. Perhaps the classic case is that of highway facilities (such as bridges or toll roads) for which prices are set initially at a level high enough to pay for the facility but are reduced significantly (often to zero) when the bonds used to finance the facility are retired. Thus, the price for use is high when traffic volumes are low and low when traffic volumes are high. This is precisely the reverse of the pricing policy needed to achieve efficient use of the facility.

Finally, zero or token prices also play a potentially important role in the arena where investment decisions are made. If such prices result in shortages (i.e., excess demand at the government's price), it is likely that considerable pressure will be applied to legislatures to authorize expenditures for additional but not necessarily efficient facilities. R. H. Haveman and M. Mason Gaffney contend that this has been an important phenomenon in the development of federal natural resource policy, especially where irrigation and other water resource projects are concerned.[17] It has undoubtedly

---

17. R. H. Haveman, "Efficiency and Equity in Natural Resource and Environmental Policy"

also contributed to an over-expansion of some transportation facilities at all levels of government. The present authors would also not be surprised to discover that state legislatures have interpreted the excess demand signal incorrectly as an argument for the expansion of educational facilities.

PRICING TO ACHIEVE EQUITY

Economists tend to favor the use of general money transfers for the purpose of achieving greater equity in the distribution of real income.[18] However, transfers of goods and services are widely employed in the public sector. Sometimes they are distributed free of charge; often, prices are set low enough to facilitate the purchase of public products by low-income individuals.

There is nothing wrong with such a practice per se. It can even be efficient if "donors" favor transfers of this type to money transfers. However, it is difficult to establish prices that are definitely redistributive in the right direction. No general guarantee exists that artificially low prices will redistribute income from the rich to the poor.

Whether or not low prices redistribute properly depends both on the nature of the goods and on the redistribution effect of alternative means of finance. Ignoring the latter, artificially low prices will probably redistribute income better for goods which are necessities, or which can be rationed by queues. Assuming equal access to public products, low prices for necessities such as housing, medical care, food, and utilities may provide larger subsidies to low- than to high-income households (especially as a percentage of household income). However, if other goods or services must be purchased in order to enjoy these goods, then low prices may accomplish little because the necessary additional expenditures may effectively price the poor out of the market.

If prices are too low to clear the market, it will be necessary, of course, to ration goods by some means other than price. Here the use of queues may be an efficient way to achieve equity goals. Queues do not increase the money price of goods, but they do increase the price in terms of time. And, because the value of time is probably directly related to income, it

---

American Journal of Agricultural Economics, Vol. 55 (December, 1973); M. Mason Gaffney, "The Water Giveaway: a Critique of Federal Water Policy," in R. Haveman and R. Hamrin, eds., *The Political Economy of Federal Policy* (New York: Harper and Row, 1973).

18. We outlined the rationale for this earlier in Chapters 3 and 6.

is safe to predict that for many public products a relatively high percentage of the individuals in a queue would be the relatively poorer members of society.

However, the poor will not benefit greatly if goods whose purchases are subsidized through low prices require large complementary expenditures. These additional expenditures will often price low-income individuals out of the market. For example, the incidence of visits by this income group to national parks and wilderness areas is usually quite low. The reason, of course, is that expenditures are required for travel and equipment. Similarly, tuition for public higher education is often set quite low as a means of inducing greater number of low-income individuals to acquire college degrees. Unfortunately, tuition accounts for only a small proportion of the total price of this good. The largest proportion is accounted for by earnings forgone—the income a student sacrifices by going to college rather than working. This item is so important in many instances that the provision for low tuition does little to increase college attendance among the poor.

Care must also be exercised when pricing goods whose benefits can be capitalized into property values. The distribution of property ownership is highly progressive. Hence, any good whose subsidized price results in an increase in property values will not have the desired effect on income distribution. A case in point is the sale of Bureau of Reclamation irrigation water at artificially low prices. This tends not only to breed pressure for an excessive amount of investment in this good, but also to redistribute income from the general taxpayer to landowners whose properties increase in value as a result of this pricing policy.

Finally, equity considerations may be important in making the choice between marginal-cost and average-cost pricing. In the declining average cost case of Figure 12-4, marginal cost is less than average cost. If the good is purchased by low income households, *and* the substitution of tax finance for prices does not redistribute income regressively, MC pricing may be better from an equity point of view. Of course, many goods provided publicly do not fit the decreasing-cost model of Figure 12-4. The case where $P = MC$ and $MC > ATC$ is quite feasible. Here, the more equitable price may well turn out to be one equal to average total cost rather then marginal cost.

It is difficult to generalize, then, about the proper price for public goods. In the final analysis, it is necessary to consider each prospect separately and to evaluate the impact of pricing on both efficiency and equity, and then to compare the results with those which would occur should an alternative means of financing be used.

SUMMARY

The existence of environmental pollution in a market economy indicates that resources are not being allocated efficiently. Activities which generate pollution are, in general, inefficiently large. They may be too large from the point of view of equity, as well.

Several alternatives are available to improve the allocation of environmental resources. In the small numbers case, it may be better to leave the parties alone, as it will be in their self-interest to achieve efficient allocation through bargaining. However, most serious pollution problems involve many parties, and significant transactions costs would preclude effective bargains. In addition, a bargaining alternative will produce an efficient solution only if perfect competition prevails. Finally, some bargaining situations would have adverse effects on the distribution of income, thereby reducing welfare, if not efficiency.

The alternative advocated most frequently by economists is the levying of a tax equal to the marginal external cost imposed by the polluter. Under competitive conditions, such a scheme induces polluters to reduce production to the socially efficient level. However, this alternative actually increases inefficiency in imperfectly competitive markets. Moreover, it would be difficult to implement without considerable effort (and expense) to measure marginal external cost, and without designing essentially regressive tax programs.

In practice, most governments rely on the establishment and enforcement of standards to achieve a cleaner environment. One apparent attraction of this approach is that it requires less information than the imposition of correct pollution taxes. However, *existing* standards often produce very high costs at the margin.

Many economists are hopeful that taxes can be used more effectively to achieve existing standards than the establishment and enforcement of legal regulations. Such a method has theoretical appeal. It has also been used successfully in the Ruhr Valley of Germany. Under certain circumstances, however, this kind of tax plan could produce excessive investment in pollution abatement equipment.

Governments do not raise all of their revenues by levying taxes. A significant proportion, especially for state and local governments, comes from goods and services sold at a price. A primary issue, then, is the proper role of prices for government goods. Not all publicly-provided goods can be sold at a price. This is especially true for those goods whose benefits cannot be enjoyed solely by their owner. In many cases, however, prices can be established to promote greater efficiency.

In an economy free of market failures, it is appropriate for public authorities to set prices equal to marginal cost. In the real world, efficient prices are likely to be different from marginal cost, with the exact differences depending on the nature and extent of existing market failures.

An additional problem with marginal cost pricing is that it would be extremely costly to estimate marginal cost in many instances. In some cases it may even be necessary to spend large sums of money just to collect revenues, while in others a marginal cost price may not produce enough revenues to finance the expenditure in question. In addition, there may be circumstances in which marginal cost pricing will be so successful in rationing existing facilities that efficient expansion plans are not considered as an alternative.

Governments do not typically charge marginal cost prices, but rely instead upon average cost, token, or zero prices. Average cost prices can be relatively efficient, although they do not tend to promote efficiency in practice. Zero or token prices often result in inefficient use of existing facilities, and increase pressure to undertake new, but relatively inefficient, investment projects.

The chief rationale for zero or token prices is that they do not preclude the poor from consuming the goods and services provided by public projects. Such prices do not always have this effect, however, especially where complementary expenditures are required, or benefits of low prices can be readily capitalized into property values.

SUGGESTIONS FOR FURTHER READING

Dorfman, Robert, and Dorfman, Nancy, eds., *Economics of the Environment,* 2d. Ed., New York: W. W. Norton, 1977.

This is an excellent collection of readings on the economics of the environment. Readers of this chapter would find Chapters 1, 6, 9, and 10 in the Dorfmans' to be extremely useful for achieving greater mastery of this subject area.

Vickrey, William, "Current Issues in Transportation," In Neil W. Chamberlain, ed., *Contemporary Economic Issues,* Rev. Ed., Homewood, Ill.: Richard D. Irwin, 1973, pp. 219–300.

This essay contains several sections on the problems of pricing transportation services, written at a relatively elementary level. Most of the pricing issues raised in the chapter in the text are examined by Vickrey in his essay.

PART 4

STABILIZATION AND DEBT POLICY

THIRTEEN

AN ANALYSIS
OF NATIONAL INCOME

The purpose of this chapter is to develop a theoretical framework for analyzing and understanding the forces operating in the economy which determine the levels of production, income, and employment. This chapter develops a model of the private economy; the next chapter adds the government sector to the model and examines the impact of government. Together, these two chapters form the theoretical basis for the development of fiscal theory and the evaluation of fiscal policy and debt management policy, which are treated in subsequent chapters.

In this chapter, two markets are visualized—the commodity or product market and the money market. The focal point in the commodity market is on the determination of national income; in the money market, economic forces that determine the rate of interest are stressed. The interrelationship between the two markets is naturally of major concern.

The method used throughout this chapter and the next is equilibrium analysis. Economic forces are thought of as moving always in the direction of an equilibrium; for example, the level of national income where no further changes would result without a change in a dependent relationship among two variables or a change in an independent variable or variables. When it is said that national income is determined or the rate of interest is determined, this means that an equilibrium has been reached. Once the conditions of equilibrium are understood, then, a disturbance such as a change in a variable can be analyzed as to its impact on the economy. In an equilibrium approach, the beginning point and the ending point are equilibria. The analysis encompasses tracing in a logical sequence the forces operating in the economy that move the economy from one equilibrium to another.

The development of a model of the private economy is done with the assistance of numerical and graphical illustrations. Other methods could have been used, but they would have added little to the foundation necessary for evaluating the major issues of stabilization policy.

THE COMMODITY MARKET

AGGREGATE DEMAND

Consumer Demand

Aggregate demand (D) is composed of consumer demand (C) and investment demand (I), hence, $D = C + I$. Suppose at first that we assume that investment demand is given or that it is an exogenous factor. This means that the forces determining investment demand are not to be explained. We will now concentrate on the forces influencing consumer demand and later do the same for investment demand.

Many forces shape and direct consumer demand. Some of these forces are tastes and preferences, money income, monetary wealth (money balances, securities, and real assets), and prices. Money income and wealth obviously are important factors determining consumption since the ability to spend is governed by these factors. Prices are similarly important, for the real ability to buy changes as prices change. National income analysis is usually developed around the proposition that consumption is a stable function of income. Figure 13-1 (based on data in Table 13-1) shows consumer demand and the relation between consumption and national income.[1] The other factors determining consumption are assumed to be given and may be introduced into the analysis by causing a shift in consumer demand. For example, a decrease in prices may be treated as

---

1. The relation between consumption and income shown is based on the linear equation, $C = a + bY = 25 + .8Y$ where a is a constant showing consumption when income is zero and b the slope of the line. By substituting different values for Y, C is derived, as shown in Table 13-1.

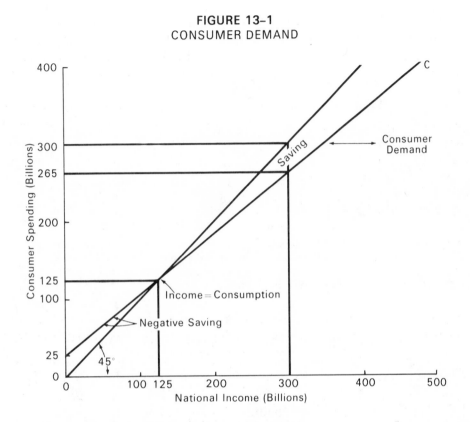

FIGURE 13-1
CONSUMER DEMAND

causing consumer demand to shift to the left, indicating a greater amount consumed at every income level, since the purchasing power of money is greater. However, in most instances, factors other than income which determine consumption are assumed to be unchanged unless specified.

Figure 13-1 and Table 13-1 show consumer demand in graphic and tabular form. Consumer demand is a schedule showing planned consumption at different levels of income. Since income which is not consumed is saved, a schedule of planned saving at different levels of income is shown in Table 13-1 and could be shown, of course, in a graph. As income rises, consumption rises, but not as much as income; hence, the difference between income and consumption—saving—grows as income grows. (This proposition is a stability condition of the model.) The implication of this proposition about consumer demand should become clear later. Consumer demand, or the propensity to consume schedule, shows two important things: (1) the amount consumers plan to spend at a level of income, or the

TABLE 13-1   CONSUMER DEMAND
(in Billions)

National Income	Planned Consumption	Planned Saving	Marginal Propensity to Consume	Marginal Propensity to Save
0	25	−25	—	—
100	105	− 5	.8	.2
125	125	0	.8	.2
200	185	15	.8	.2
300	265	35	.8	.2
400	345	55	.8	.2
500	425	75	.8	.2

NOTE: The data for the table above and the graph based on these data were derived from the equation, $C = a + bY$ where $a = 25$ (a constant which shows consumption when Y is zero) $b = .8$ (the marginal propensity to consume or the slope of the consumer demand schedule).

average propensity to consume (consumption divided by income); and (2) the change in consumption due to a change in income or the marginal propensity to consume (change in consumption divided by change in income). The marginal propensity to consume is an important concept, and for the consumer demand schedule shown in Figure 13-1 the marginal propensity to consume is four-fifths, or 80%, which means that consumption changes are 80% of any change in income.[2] The marginal propensity to consume (*MPC*) plus the marginal propensity to save (*MPS*) always must be equal to one, since a change in income which does not change consumption an equal amount must change saving by the difference.[3] The marginal propensity to save for the consumer demand schedule derived in Figure 13-1 is one-fifth, or 20%.

Assuming no investment, the equilibrium or maintainable level of national income in Figure 13-1 is $125 billion. Consumer demand intersects the 45° line in Figure 13-1 at this level of income. The 45° line in Figure 13-1 is used to show possible points of equilibrium in that it represents points where total spending in the economy is equal to the costs of producing the

---

2. The marginal propensity to consume is the slope of consumer demand schedule and is constant an the linear or straight line equation used.

3. MPC + MPS = 1; hence, 1 − MPC = MPS.

national output; that is, where aggregate demand might be equal to aggregate supply. Any level of income above or below $125 billion would set in motion economic forces causing income to move in the direction of a new equilibrium. For example, suppose the level of income was $300 billion (Figure 13-1). Aggregate spending (C = $265 billion) would be far less than the costs incurred ($300 billion) to produce the national output. Therefore, production and employment in the economy would tend to fall until the equilibrium level of income ($125 billion in the example) is reached.

Investment Demand

Investment spending is the purchase of capital goods such as buildings, equipment, and inventories. Net new investment means that society is adding to its stock of capital goods. It was assumed that net new investment was zero, and under this assumption equilibrium in the commodity market[4] occurred where consumption equaled national income. Let us suppose that investment spending is $35 billion; what, then, is the equilibrium level of national income?

The added investment spending of $35 billion means that at the previous equilibrium level of income ($125 billion) aggregate demand (C + I = $160 billion) is greater than aggregate supply, or that investment is greater than saving, which is an alternative explanation. Under these conditions, national output and employment tend to rise, causing national income to rise. As national income rises, consumption and saving rise until a new equilibrium is reached. What is the new equilibrium level of income?

Figure 13-2 shows investment spending of $35 billion added to the consumer demand schedule, and Figure 13-3 shows the investment and propensity to save schedule. Investment is assumed to be independent of income; hence, in Figure 13-2, the C + I line is exactly parallel with the consumer demand schedule, and in Figure 13-3 the investment line shows that investment is $35 billion at every level of national income. The relation between investment and changes in income is discussed later in this chapter.

The new equilibrium level of income is $300 billion (Figures 13-2 and 13-3). This is the only level of income where the condition of equilibrium

---

4. There is investment when the stock of capital goods remains the same. This investment is replacement investment; that is, investment necessary to replace the "using up" of capital goods. Gross investment is the term used to include replacement investment.

FIGURE 13–2
CONSUMER AND INVESTMENT DEMAND

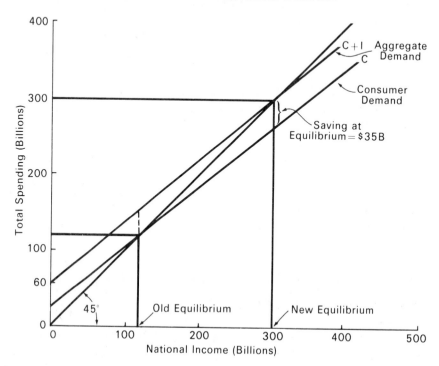

FIGURE 13–3
SAVING AND INVESTMENT

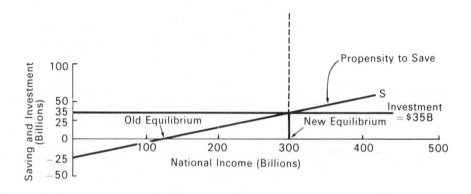

is fulfilled; that is, the level of income where income equals consumption plus investment, or when saving equals investment. This may be clarified in equation form and by substituting data:

$$Y = C + I \; ; S = I$$
$$300 = 265 + 35 \; ; 35 = 35.$$

A rise in investment of $35 billion increases the level of national income from $125 billion to $300 billion, or a rise in national income of $175 billion. How is this possible?

The Multiplier Principle

The relation between a given change in investment (ΔI) and a resulting change in income (ΔY) is explained by the investment multiplier principle. The multiplier (k) itself is a number which may be defined as the ratio of a change in income to a change in investment, or $k = \frac{\Delta Y}{\Delta I}$. In the example above, $k = \frac{175}{35}$ or 5. The importance of the multiplier is that it shows how much national income changes for a given change in investment. But why will income change more than the given change in investment? What does the multiplier depend on?

The size of the multiplier depends on the marginal propensity to consume. The size of the multiplier increases as the *MPC* increases (approaches one), and the size of the multiplier decreases as the *MPC* decreases (approaches 0). The *MPC* is the slope of the consumer demand schedule, and is four-fifths in the example given. The multiplier is derived from the *MPC;* it is the reciprocal of one minus the *MPC*.[5] For example, assuming the *MPC* is four-fifths, the multiplier, *k*, is equal to $\frac{1}{1 - 4/5}$ or 5. The multiplier may be derived from the marginal propensity to save:

$$k = \frac{1}{MPS} = \frac{1}{1/5} = 5$$

---

5. The derivation of the multiplier from the *MPC* may be shown as follows: $k = \frac{\Delta Y}{\Delta I},$ but $\Delta Y = \Delta C + \Delta I$, and $\Delta I = \Delta Y - \Delta C$; therefore, $k = \frac{\Delta Y}{\Delta Y - \Delta C},$ or $\frac{\Delta Y}{\Delta I} = \frac{\Delta Y}{\Delta Y - \Delta C}$

Dividing both sides of the equation by ΔY, we have $k = \frac{\Delta Y / \Delta Y}{\frac{\Delta Y}{\Delta Y} - \frac{\Delta C}{\Delta Y}} = \frac{1}{1 - MPC}.$

TABLE 13–2   MULTIPLIER PRINCIPLE
(One period lag between a change in income
and a change in planned consumption)
(MCP = 4/5)

Period	Planned Investment (billions)	Planned Consumption (billions)	Planned Saving (billions)	National Income (billions)
1	0	125	0	125
2	0	125	0	125
3	35	125	0	160
4	35	153	7	188
5	35	175.4	12.6	210.4
6	35	193.3	17.1	228.3
7	35	207.6	20.7	242.6
.	.	.	.	.
.	.	.	.	.
.	.	.	.	.
N	35	265	35	300

The commonsense notion of the multiplier principle is that one person's spending is another person's income. A change in investment changes income, which in turn induces a series of new consumption flows. A multiplier example worked step-by-step will clarify the multiplier process. Table 13-2 shows how income rises from a rise in investment assuming a marginal propensity to consume of four-fifths and a one period lag between a change in income and a change in planned consumption and planned saving. Periods 1 and 2 show consumption, saving, and income under the previous assumption that new investment is zero. Now, investment rises to $35 billion in period 3, causing income to rise to $160 billion $(C + I)$ in period 3—a rise in income of $35 billion. Since the MPC is four fifths, in period 4 planned consumption rises by four fifths and planned savings rises by one fifth of this rise in income. Therefore, in period 4 planned consumption rises to $153 billion, which is a rise of $28 billion (4/5 $\times$ $35 billion), and planned saving to $7 billion, which is a rise of $7 billion (1/5 $\times$ $35 billion). National income in period 4 is $188 billion $(C + I)$, which is a rise in income of $28 billion between periods 3 and 4. In period 5, then, planned consumption rises by four fifths of the rise in income of $28 billion, and planned saving rises by one fifth, and so on. In every subsequent period, planned consumption and planned saving rise until national income reaches $300 billion. Income ceases to rise further at this level of national income, for planned savings equal planned investment at $300 billion, or aggregate demand equals aggregate supply.

In the example just given, the total rise in national income is $175 billion; this rise is divided between a rise in planned consumption of $140 billion, which is four fifths of the rise in income, and a rise in planned saving of $35 billion, which is one fifth of the rise in income. If the marginal propensity to consume had been three fourths, the rise in income would have been $140 billion $\left(\dfrac{1}{1 - \text{MPC}}\right) \times \Delta I$, and the division of this rise in income between planned consumption and planned saving would have been $105 billion and $35 billion, respectively.

The Marginal Propensity to Invest

The economic model developed thus far is based on one economic relation and one exogenous variable. The economic relation is the relation between consumption and income, and the exogenous variable is investment. Given the propensity to consume schedule and investment, it has been shown that the level of income is determined. Now, suppose that the rate of

TABLE 13–3 PROPENSITY TO INVEST
(in Billions)

National Income	Planned Investment	Marginal Propensity to Invest
0	5	.1
100	15	.1
200	25	.1
300	35	.1
400	45	.1
500	55	.1

NOTE: Data for Table 6–3 was derived from the equation $I = c + dY$, where c equals 5 (a constant showing investment when Y is zero); $d = .1$ (the marginal propensity to invest or the slope of investment schedule).

investment depends on income. Figure 13-4, based on data in Table 13-3, shows the propensity to invest schedule, or investment at different levels of assumed income. The slope of the investment schedule is the marginal propensity to invest (*MPI*), and in the investment schedule shown is one tenth, which means that a change in investment resulting from a change in income is one tenth of the change in income. For example, a change in income of $10 billion induces a $1 billion change in investment.

It should be fairly obvious that if both consumption and investment change as income changes, an *autonomous* change in investment will have a larger multiplying effect on income than is the case when only consumption is considered to be a stable relation to income. An autonomous change in investment which changes income not only induces a change in consumption, but also induces a change in investment, depending on the marginal propensity to investment. The multiplier which previously was equal to $\dfrac{1}{1 - MPC}$ now becomes equal to $\dfrac{1}{1 - MPC - MPI}$. If the *MPC* and *MPI* are .8 and .1, respectively, as is assumed, the super multiplier is $10 \left(\dfrac{1}{1 - .8 - .1} \right)$.

Investment spending is a much more unstable factor than is implied by the propensity to invest schedule. The wide variations in investment which are observed are explained by other economic factors. We will now discuss

FIGURE 13-4
PROPENSITY TO INVEST

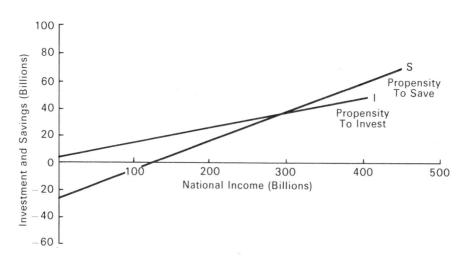

some of the economic factors determining autonomous investment; that is, investment not directly related to income.

Determinants of Autonomous Investment

Autonomous investment depends on all the economic forces influencing and determining profit expectations, which include all economic forces influencing and determining current and expected costs and revenues. Important forces operating on costs are the productivity of labor and capital and resource prices, especially expected resource prices. Important forces operating on revenue are the forces determining prices, both current and future.

It is convenient and accurate to discuss these forces influencing investment activity in terms of the rate of interest and the rate of profits expected from investment. The rate of interest is the rate of return on loans; that is, the ratio of the interest income received from lending money to the dollar amount loaned. For example, a $100,000 loan which pays $10,000 per year is returning $10\% \left(\frac{\$10,000}{\$100,000} \right)$. The subsequent discussion has reference to the economic rate of interest; this is the rate of interest excluding administrative costs associated with loans and risks. The rate of profits expected from new investment, often referred to as the marginal efficiency of capital, is the ratio of the expected *net* revenue from the investment asset to the cost of the asset in question.[6] If the expected net revenue from purchasing a capital asset of $100,000 is $10,000, then the expected profit rate from the new investment is $10\% \left(\frac{\$10,000}{\$100,000} \right)$. The marginal efficiency of capital is the rate of return over cost.

Under what conditions will it be profitable to increase investment? Assume that a prospective investor has $100,000 presently earning 5% from lending, and that this loan will be paid off shortly. The prospective investor will soon, then, have four alternatives. He may spend this money for

---

6. The marginal efficiency of capital is the rate of discount which equates the prospective net income (difference between gross income and expenses) from the investment asset to the purchase price or cost of the investment, or

$$C = \frac{y_1}{1 + r} + \frac{y_2}{(1 + r)^2} + \frac{y_3}{(1 + r)^3} + \ldots + \frac{y_n}{(1 + r)^n}$$

consumption, perhaps gracious living abroad for a year. He may hold this money in checking accounts.[7] He may wish to make another loan at 5%, or higher if the market rate of interest has risen, or he may invest it; perhaps he may wish to build new apartment houses and receive rental income. We will rule out the first two alternatives, consuming and hoarding, and concentrate attention on his last two alternatives. Suppose he finds that the *current* average rate of return from renting apartments similar to the ones he contemplates building is 20%. Assuming that he can earn only 5% on a new loan, would he have a strong tendency to invest? Not necessarily, for the current rate of return on existing investment is not the same as the expected rate of return on additional investment. However, if he calculated that the expected rate of return was above the rate of interest, his inducement would be strong.

The example above is somewhat simplified, for people who invest may not be the same people who have funds to invest. However, the example may serve to explain the relation between the rate of interest, the marginal efficiency of capital, and investment. From this discussion, it may be stated that investment depends on the expected profit rate and its relation to the rate of interest. Given the rate of interest, a schedule may be derived showing the rate of investment in the economy at different expected profit rates. This is the investment demand schedule, and it is a negative sloping schedule reflecting the principle of diminishing marginal productivity of capital. The investment demand schedule is assumed to be stable unless otherwise stated; however, sudden shifts in investment demand may occur from changes in the state of expectations, from technological changes, from population trends, and so on.

Figure 13-5 shows that, given a rate of interest of 6%, aggregate investment spending would be equal to $40 billion. Any investment over $40 billion is not undertaken, for additional investment is expected to return less than 6%. On the other hand, aggregate investment of less than $40 billion will not exist for long, since additional investment would be expected to return more than 6%. Therefore, it is reasoned that investment is determined in this instance at a rate of $40 billion. This is the equilibrium rate of investment under these assumptions, and this investment is altered only if there is a change in the rate of interest or, more important, a change in the investment demand schedule.

---

7. Money deposited at a bank gives rise to excess bank reserves and may, of course, be loaned by the bank and, hence, may not be held idle.

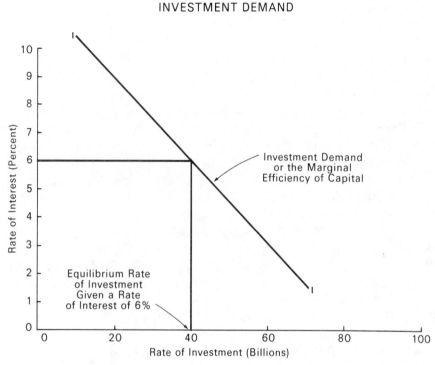

FIGURE 13–5
INVESTMENT DEMAND

THE MONEY MARKET

The commodity market has now been developed. We will extend the model to include the forces operating in the money market; that is, the forces underlying the demand for and supply of money. After this is done, the economic model will be completed and examples will be given to illustrate the operation of the economic model constructed.

THE DEMAND FOR MONEY

Money primarily serves two functions, and the demand for money may be derived from these two functions.[8] Money serves as a medium of exchange

---

8. There are other functions of money; however, it is assumed that the other functions are not important for our purposes, or that they may be included under one of the functions given.

and as a store of value. The medium of exchange function of money gives rise to the demand for money for current transactions, and may be called the transaction demand for money. The store of value function gives rise to the demand for money in order to be liquid, and may be called the liquidity demand for money. The demand for money is the desire for cash balances and is some fraction of national income.

Given the institutional arrangements of the economy concerning the pattern of money payments for goods and services, the desire for money for current transactions depends largely on the level of economic activity or the level of national income. Generally speaking, the need for money for transactions rises when the level of national income rises, and falls when the level of national income falls; hence, the transaction demand schedule for money shows a direct relationship between the level of income and the amount of money demanded for transactions (Figure 13-6).

The liquidity demand for money is the desire to hold wealth in the form of money. The cost of holding wealth in the form of money is the interest income which could have been earned if wealth was held in another form (debts and/or real assets); hence, the alternative cost of holding wealth in the form of money rises or falls according to the rise or fall in the rate of interest. The alternative advantage which holding money affords is liquidity; namely, the ability to buy something without having to sell an asset at a capital loss. One has complete liquidity when he/she holds money; he/she gives up some liquidity when wealth is held in other forms. The interest rate may be thought of alternatively as the cost of liquidity and as the price paid to overcome liquidity. The desire for liquidity depends on the rate of interest and is inversely related to it (Figure 13-6).

There would be little need to desire money for liquidity purposes if the future rate of interest were certain, but it is this very uncertainty about the future rate of interest (and future security prices) that is important in determining money balances held today. A market rate of interest which is considered below normal (the future market rate is expected to rise) will increase the desire for liquidity, for the cost of liquidity is considered to be low relative to the future, and it will be advantageous to sell securities today since future security prices are, it is believed, going to be lower.[9] A

---

9. Note that the rate of interest on fixed-income-yielding securities and security prices are inversely related. For example, a $100 income from a security that has a market price of $1000 is 10%. But a decrease in market price to under $1000 means a rise in the rate of interest to above 10%, and a rise in the price of the security means a fall in the interest rate.

FIGURE 13-6
THE DEMAND AND SUPPLY OF MONEY

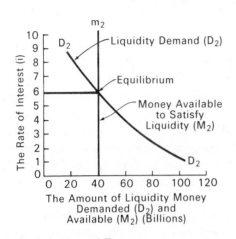 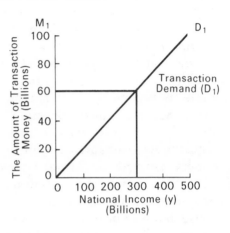

Explanation of Terms

D_1 = Transaction Demand for Money ($D_1 = T_{(y)}$)
M_1 = Transaction Money
D_2 = Liquidity Demand for Money ($D_2 = L_{(i)}$)
M_2 = Money Available to Satisfy Liquidity
M = Total Stock of Money Assumed to be $100 Billion ($M = M_1 + M_2$)

market rate of interest considered to be above normal (future rate expected to fall) will decrease the desire for liquidity, since the cost of liquidity now is presumed to be high relative to the future, and security prices are expected to rise.

SUPPLY OF MONEY

The supply of money in the economy is controlled largely by Federal Reserve monetary policy. The Federal Reserve is charged with the responsibility of determining the availability and cost of money and credit. An important way in which the supply of money is controlled is through the activities of the Open Market Committee of the Federal Reserve, which influences the supply of money by buying and selling government securities. Open market purchases by this committee have the effect of increasing cash reserves of commercial banks which, in turn, tend to increase commercial bank lending and therefore the supply of money. Open market sales by this committee decrease the ability of commercial banks to lend and therefore discourage them from lending, and this tends to decrease the supply of money.

The Federal Reserve may influence the availability and cost of money and credit by discouraging or encouraging commercial banks to borrow from the Federal Reserve. This may be done indirectly by the rediscount rate—that is, the discount rate charged a commercial bank for borrowing from the Federal Reserve—or directly by encouraging or discouraging the banks to use the rediscount procedure. Commercial banks may take commercial paper (promissory notes, etc.) and borrow from the Federal Reserve, using the paper as collateral. However, the Federal Reserve may not always have the welcome sign out for such a practice. Furthermore, commercial banks have shown a traditional reluctance to be in debt to the Federal Reserve. It is sometimes said that the importance of Federal Reserve discount rate policy is more in terms of the "tone" it sets in the market rather than in terms of any direct influence it may or may not have on the supply of money.

The Federal Reserve also may change, within certain legal limits, the legal reserve requirements which govern the ratio of demand deposits to cash reserves that commercial banks may have. Increasing the legal reserve requirement reduces excess cash reserves of commercial banks, thereby discouraging bank lending and tending to reduce the availability of money and credit. On the other hand, decreasing the legal reserve requirement tends to have the opposite effect of increasing excess cash reserves, encouraging bank lending, and increasing the availability of money and credit.

The total supply of money is assumed to be given, and therefore in our model the supply of money is constant unless otherwise specified. With a constant supply of money, the amount of money available to satisfy the desire for liquidity is the difference between the total supply of money and the amount of money demanded to satisfy transaction needs. For example, referring to Figure 13-6, if the level of national income is $300 billion, the desire for money to satisfy transaction needs is $60 billion. Given the supply of money of $100 billion, $40 billion is available to satisfy the desire for liquidity. The money available to satisfy liquidity and the liquidity demand schedule determine the rate of interest, which is at 6% in Figure 13-6.

EQUILIBRIUM ANALYSIS

The economic model which has been constructed shows that the determinants of national income and the rate of interest are aggregate demand, aggregate supply, demand for money, and supply of money. For the model to be in equilibrium, aggregate demand must equal aggregate supply, or planned investment must equal planned saving, and the amount of money demanded must equal the amount of money supplied. We will now illustrate the working of the model with specific examples. The method of approach is to begin at equilibrium. The variable to be analyzed disturbs equilibrium. The analysis then proceeds to trace the economic forces operating until equilibrium is restored.

EXAMPLE ONE: AN AUTONOMOUS
RISE IN INVESTMENT DEMAND

The equilibrium level of income is $300 billion (Figure 13-7), and the equilibrium rate of interest is 6%. A rise in investment demand (a shift to the right in the investment demand schedule) means that the expected profit rate on new capital assets is in excess of the market rate of interest at the current rate of investment. Hence, there is a profit incentive for new investment. As a consequence, the rate of investment rises, for example, to $55 billion, a rise of $20 billion as shown in Figure 13-7, and via the multiplier principle the level of national income moves in the upward direction to a new equilibrium. Assuming a marginal propensity to consume of four fifths, will the new equilibrium of income be at $400 billion, as is shown by the intersection of the saving schedule with the new investment? This depends on what is happening in the money market. For one thing, we know that as the level of income starts to rise, the need for transaction money rises. If there are no changes in the total supply of money and liquidity demand, less money is available to satisfy liquidity demand and upward pressures on the rate of interest are exerted. These upward pressures on the rate of interest would tend to discourage investment and dampen or offset the original impact of new investment on income. Therefore, if the full effect of the multiplier is to be felt in the commodity market, an important assumption has to be made about the money market; namely, the supply of money is rising, or liquidity demand and/or transaction demand are falling.

FIGURE 13–7
A RISE IN INVESTMENT DEMAND

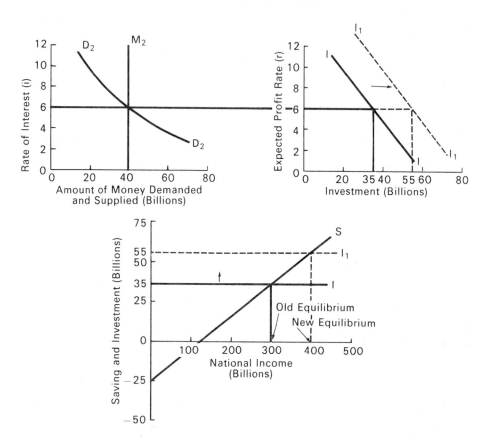

The important thing to remember about a rise in investment demand, which so often happens in the economy due to the dynamic variables which determine investment demand, is that it provides a vital stimulant to the growth in national income. This growth in national income may, however, be completely or partly repressed by repercussions in the money market.

EXAMPLE TWO:
AN INCREASE IN LIQUIDITY DEMAND

An increase in liquidity demand (a shift in the liquidity demand schedule to the right) means that at every rate of interest the desire for liquidity is greater. This increased demand for money may occur when there is a crisis in the economy. Assuming no change in the availability of money to satisfy liquidity, the rate of interest tends to rise under these conditions (Figure 13-8). The effect of a higher rate of interest is to discourage investment and, therefore, cause a fall in national income and a new equilibrium at a lower level of income.

Two things may occur to mitigate this downward movement in national income due to the rise in liquidity demand. First, the decline in national income reduces the need for transaction money and releases additional money to satisfy the desire to hold wealth in the form of cash. Second, the general fall in prices usually accompanying a fall in national income may

FIGURE 13-8
AN INCREASE IN LIQUIDITY DEMAND

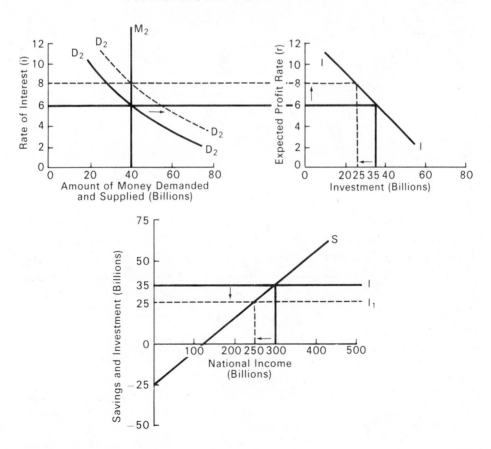

tend to increase consumption since real cash balances rise as prices fall. This additional transaction money available to satisfy liquidity and this strengthening of consumer demand take place as a consequence of decline in national output and prices and, hence, do not alter the above conclusion that a rise in liquidity demand tends to lower the equilibrium level of national income.

EXAMPLE THREE: AN INCREASE IN THE SUPPLY OF MONEY

An increase in the supply of money, given the economic relations established in the model, tends to decrease the rate of interest which, in turn, increases the rate of investment, causing national income to rise in the

FIGURE 13-9
A RISE IN THE STOCK OF MONEY

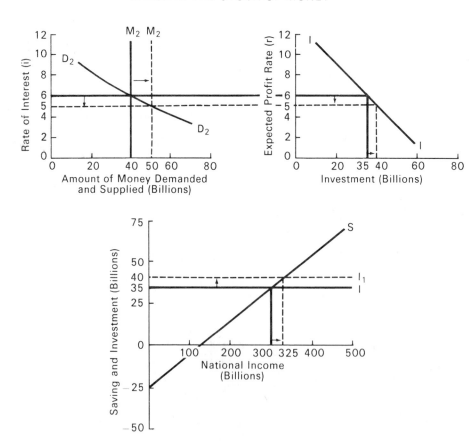

familiar manner already discussed. An increase in the supply of money means that at the current rate of interest there is an excess of actual cash balances over desired cash balances. This "excess" money, which it might be called, may flow into the securities market, or it may flow into the commodity market. If it flows into the securities market, security prices will rise or, alternatively, the interest rate will fall until the excess money is absorbed. On the other hand, if this excess money flows directly into the commodity market, the rise in transaction needs eventually will absorb it. In any event, a rise in the supply of money tends to increase national output and employment.

SUMMARY

An economic model based on modern national income theory has been constructed. An economic model provides a frame of reference for a better understanding of the real economy and attempts to relate certain economic behavior, which may be observed and empirically tested, in a meaningful way. The model developed does not include all the growing body of knowledge known as aggregate economic theory. An attempt has been made to develop a theoretical economy based largely on the principles of supply and demand which may accurately serve as a guide to economic thinking concerning the direction of movement of the economy in which we live. The next chapter will extend the model to include the economic activities of government in order to provide the basis for an understanding of the economic impact of government.

SUGGESTIONS FOR FURTHER READING

Dernburg, Thomas F. and McDougall, Duncan M., *Macroeconomics,* Fifth Edition, New York: McGraw-Hill Book Company, 1976.
This is a good intermediate level text on macroeconomics. Chapters 4–8 are suggested for further study.

FOURTEEN

THE ECONOMIC IMPACT OF GOVERNMENT

The economic model constructed in the last chapter will now be extended to include government. One economic activity of government is added to the model each time in order that the effect of this one government operation may be seen. Later in the chapter, the economic impact of the combined economic activities of government is discussed. Spending is the first economic activity of government to be introduced. What happens to the model when the government makes a $20 billion purchase?

THE IMPACT OF GOVERNMENT
SPENDING AND TAXING

GOVERNMENT SPENDING (G)

We will start at the equilibrium level of national income of $300 billion with consumption at $265 billion and investment at $35 billion (Chapter 13, Figure 13-2 or 13-3). Suppose there is government spending of $20 billion, which means that total spending or aggregate demand is $320 billion (C + I + G). At the current level of national income, aggregate demand is in excess of aggregate supply, or investment and government spending are greater than planned saving. The addition of $20 billion in government spending disturbs equilibrium in the commodity market and starts an upward movement in national income similar to the one started by an addition of investment to the model. How much will national income rise as a result of adding government spending of $20 billion?

Again assuming the marginal propensity to consume is four fifths, as we did in the previous chapter, the multiplier is five and, ignoring the money market for a moment, the new equilibrium is $400 billion (Figure 14-1). Only at this level of income are the equilibrium conditions fulfilled.

$$Y = C + I + G \; ; \; 400 = 345 + 35 + 20$$
$$Y - C = I + G \; ; \;\; 55 = 55$$
$$S = I + G \; ; \;\; 55 = 35 + 20.$$

It can be seen that government purchases of final output of goods and services stimulates national output and employment in the economy similar to the stimulation provided by private investment. In the example above, the rise in government spending increases income via the multiplier process until planned savings rise enough to equal the rise in government spending. When this occurs, saving equals investment plus government spending, which is the new condition of equilibrium in the commodity market.

Assuming no change in the total supply of money, the rise in national income caused by the government spending will increase the rate of interest. This rise in the rate of interest is caused by a decrease in the money available to satisfy liquidity, since a rising level of national income necessitates larger money balances for transaction purposes (Chapter 13, Figure 13-8). The rise in the rate of interest tends to decrease investment and, therefore, tends to alleviate the expansion in national income. Thus, when the interactions between the commodity and money markets are considered, the new equilibrium level of income may not reach the $400 billion mark which the multiplier process might lead one to expect. For the full impact of the multiplier principle to take place from a rise in government spending, the supply of money has to rise, or it must be assumed that the investment demand schedule is completely interest inelastic; that is, the rate of investment is completely unresponsive to a change in the rate of interest. It is believed that investment demand is interest inelastic and that a rise in the rate of interest will bring about a less than proportional decrease in investment. Hence, the effect of the rise in the rate of interest is likely to be only a dampening influence on the expansion of the national income. We will clarify the case by assuming that the rise in government

FIGURE 14–1
INCOME DETERMINATION WITH GOVERNMENT SPENDING

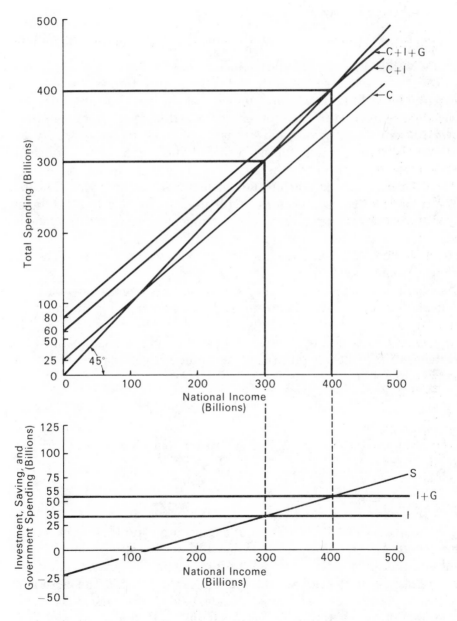

spending is accompanied by a rise in the supply of money and, hence, no change in the rate of interest.

GOVERNMENT TAXES (Tx)

The economic model has been extended to include government spending, and now will be extended further to include government taxes. The introduction of tax revenues (Tx) necessitates the clarification of a few terms. The term national income is a measurement of the net value of final goods and services produced in the economy based on factor or resource prices. However, when final goods and services produced in the economy are measured in market prices, the net value of these goods and services is greater than national income because indirect government taxes are included in market prices and are not included in factor prices. The net national product or income is the term used to include indirect taxes. Therefore, with the introduction of government taxes to our model, the term net national product or income will be used, rather than national income. The symbol Y will denote net national income, rather than just national income.

Another thing that must be made clear is that consumption now becomes dependent on income after taxes; that is, private disposable income (Y_D). Private disposable income Y_D equals consumption plus saving and may be written as $Y_D = C + S$. Saving includes business and personal saving. Since private disposable income plus taxes equals the net national income, then:

$$Y = Y_D + Tx$$
$$Y = C + S + Tx.$$

Substituting $C + I + G$ for Y, we get a new condition of equilibrium:

$$C + I + G = C + S + Tx$$
$$I + G = S + Tx.$$

We will discuss this new condition of equilibrium, and then examine the impact that adding $25 billion in taxes to our model will have on the equilibrium level of income. Before the introduction of government taxes, the only leakage in the flow of income was saving; that is, the difference between national income and consumption. Saving, of course, may return to the flow of income through investment and, with the addition of government spending to the model, saving may return to the flow of income through investment and government spending. Therefore, excluding government taxes, aggregate supply and aggregate demand are equal to one another when the part of national output which is not consumed (saving) equals investment plus government spending. Only in this case will consumption plus investment plus government spending equal the costs of producing the national output. Saving may be greater than investment, but government spending must equal this excess of saving over investment for an equilibrium. Now, with the addition of government taxes there are two leakages in the flow of income—saving and government taxes. Hence, aggregate supply equals aggregate demand when the two leakages—saving and taxes—are matched by investment and government spending. Saving may not equal investment, and government spending may not equal government taxes, but saving plus taxes must equal investment plus government spending at equilibrium.

Suppose government taxes of $25 billion are added to the economic model, which was in equilibrium at a level of national income of $400 billion (Figure 14-1). What is the new level of income and why? What is the impact of taxes on consumer demand? We will answer the latter question first. It is assumed at first that government tax revenue is independent of changes in income. Hence, our economic model in the commodity market is now composed of three autonomous variables—investment, government spending, and government taxes—and one economic relation—consumption depends on disposable income. Looking closely at Table 14-1, we will compare consumption at each level of net national product, before and after taxes. After taxes, and assuming the same marginal propensity to consume four fifths (as we have in the last chapter and this one), consumer spending is less by $20 billion at every level of income and saving is less by $5 billion at every level of income. This means a decrease in the consumer demand schedule (a shift to the right) and a decrease in the saving schedule (a shift to the right)—the expected influence from a rise in taxes. Taxes are paid out of consumption and saving. Another way of saying this is that a rise in taxes decreases private disposable income and, hence, decreases consumption and saving. A fall in taxes would have just the opposite effects—a rise in disposable income, and a rise in consumption and saving.

Figure 14-2 illustrates the impact of adding $25 billion in taxes to the model. The level of net national income decreased $100 billion. The new equilibrium level is $300 billion. Only at this level of income is saving plus taxes equal to investment plus government spending. First, notice that the

TABLE 14–1 CONSUMPTION BEFORE AND AFTER TAXES
(in Billions)

	Before Taxes					After Taxes			
Y	Y_D	C	S	Tx	Y	Y_D	C	S	Tx
0	0	25	−25	0	0	−25	5	−30	25
100	100	105	− 5	0	100	75	85	−10	25
200	200	185	15	0	200	175	165	10	25
300	300	265	35	0	300	275	245	30	25
400	400	345	55	0	400	375	325	50	25
500	500	425	75	0	500	475	405	70	25

Y = net national income.
Y_D = private disposable income.
C = consumption ($C = a + bY_D = 25 + 4/5 Y_D$)
S = saving ($S = -a + (1-b)Y_D = -25 + 1/5 Y_D$).
Tx = taxes = $25 billion.

primary impact of a rise in taxes is to decrease the saving schedule; if the consumer demand schedule were illustrated, a decrease in consumer demand would beevident. Since the *MPS* and *MPC* are one fifth and four fifths respectively, and the rise in taxes is $25 billion, the saving schedule shows a $5 billion decrease in saving at every level of income, and the consumer demand schedule would show, if illustrated, a $20 billion decrease in consumption at every level of income. At the previous equilibrium level of income of $400 billion, saving ($50 billion) plus taxes ($25 billion) is greater than investment ($35 billion) plus government spending ($20 billion); hence, the previous equilibrium level of income is now not maintainable, for at this level aggregate supply is greater than aggregate demand. Second, notice that the fall in income is much greater than the rise in taxes. In this case, the fall in income is exactly four times the rise in taxes. Taxes have a multiplier effect on income. This is true because the impact of the rise in taxes is to decrease consumption which, in turn, decreases income, which decreases consumption, and so on.

The tax multiplier (k_{Tx}) is the regular multiplier minus one and is negative, since taxes have an impact on income opposite that of investment or government spending. For example, the regular multiplier is five, since the marginal propensity to consume is four fifths. Thus,

$$k_{Tx} = -(k - 1) = -(5 - 1) = -4$$

hence,

$$\Delta Y = k_{Tx} \cdot \Delta Tx = -4 \cdot \$25 = -\$100$$

or,

$$k_{Tx} = -\frac{\Delta Y}{\Delta Tx} = -\frac{\$100}{\$25} = -4.$$

The tax multiplier is one less the regular multiplier because the initial impact of taxes is on disposable income, whereas the initial impact of investment on government spending is on national income. In the case of taxes, the chain of causation runs from taxes, to disposable income, to consumption, to national income, to consumption, and so on; whereas in the cases of investment and government spending the chain of causation runs from spending directly to national income and then to consumption. Another way of looking at this is that spending on final goods and services produced in the economy is directly part of the flow of income. A rise in government taxes does not decrease the flow of income directly; only when consumption decreases is the flow of income smaller.

Table 14-2 shows the tax multiplier at work and demonstrates what has been said. Notice that the rise in taxes in period 2 does not decrease income, but in period 3 (a one period lag assumed) the rise in taxes of $25 billion reduces consumption by $20 billion, which reduces national income $20 billion (MPC = 4/5). This drop in national income of $20 billion reduces consumption in period 4 by $16 billion (4/5 × $20 billion). The rest of the table shows the familiar multiplier route toward the new equilibrium level of income.

Again, it is necessary to note what may be happening in the money market as a result of this impact of government taxes. Under the strict assumptions of the model developed, the effect on the money market of the fall in income in the commodity market would be to cause a slowing of the downward forces operating on national income. Perhaps the new level of national income would settle somewhere between $300 billion and $400 billion. A fall in national income tends to release additional money for liquidity demand and, as explained, tends to reduce the rate of interest, so the final income level will depend on the responsiveness of new investment to this change in the rate of interest. If it is assumed that the rate of investment does not respond to a change in the rate of interest, the level of national income will be determined at $300 billion, as the tax multiplier

FIGURE 14–2
THE IMPACT OF A $25 BILLION RISE IN TAXES

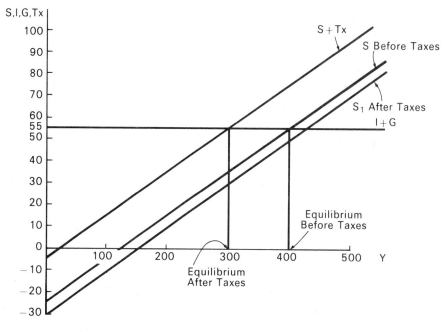

Y = Net National Product
I = Investment = $35 Billion
S_1 = Saving Schedule After Taxes
G = Government Spending = $20 Billion
S = Saving Schedule Before Taxes (S = −25 + (1−4/5) Y_D
S+Tx = Saving Plus Taxes When Taxes are Equal to $25 Billion

analysis explains. The important thing here is to be able to explain why the new equilibrium income level may be less than that indicated by multiplier analysis.

THE MARGINAL PROPENSITY TO
TAX (MPTx)

It was assumed in the last section that tax revenues were constant at $25 billion and that changes in income did not alter this assumed level of taxes. The level would remain fixed only if all taxes were "lump sum" taxes—that is, completely independent of income—or if taxes were related to

TABLE 14–2 THE TAX MULTIPLIER EFFECT
(One Period Lag)
MPC = 4/5
(in Billions)

Period	C	I	G	Tx	Y_D	Y
1	345	35	20	0	400	400
2	345	35	20	25	375	400
3	325	35	20	25	355	380
4	309	35	20	25	339	364
5	296.2	35	20	25	326.2	351.2
.	.	.	.	.	.	.
.	.	.	.	.	.	.
.	.	.	.	.	.	.
N	245	35	20	25	275	300

C= consumer spending. I= investment spending.
G= government spending. Tx= government taxes.
Y_D = private disposable income. Y= net national income.

income, in which case tax rates would have to change just in the direction and at the rate necessary to keep tax revenues constant. In any event, it is unrealistic to suppose that tax revenues remain constant as income changes, for most taxes are related directly or indirectly to income. The relation between a given change in income and the resulting change in tax revenues is the marginal propensity to tax or

$$MPTx = \frac{\Delta Tx.}{\Delta Y}$$

Suppose that the MPTx is 10%. This means that for every $100 change in income in the economy tax revenues change by $10 (.10 × 100). Thus, a fall in net national income would cause tax revenues to fall and tend to reduce the multiplier effect. Before going further, we will assume that the MPTx is constant and that the relation between tax revenues and income is defined in equation form as

$$Tx = c + dY,$$

where c is a constant, showing tax revenues when income is zero, and d is the MPT_x. The equation is linear, which means that the slope of the scheduled derived is constant. Assuming c is $20 billion and d is one tenth,

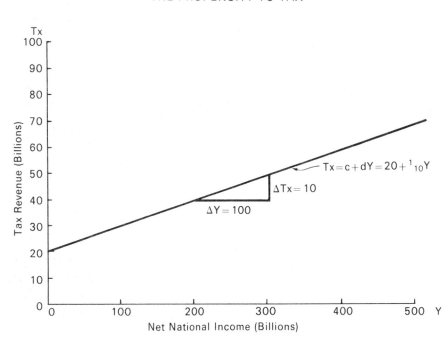

FIGURE 14-3
THE PROPENSITY TO TAX

tax collections at various levels of national income can be derived (Figure 14-3).

The tax structure shown in Figure 14-3 can be viewed as consisting of two taxes—a lump sum tax of $20 billion and a proportional income tax levied at a rate of 10%. In combination, these two would make the tax rate structure regressive because of the lump sum tax. If there was no lump sum tax ($c=0$), the tax structure would be proportionate with everyone paying 10% of his/her income in taxes.

Built-in stability or automatic stability is added to our model when taxes are a function of income. The reason for this is that in such a case tax collections automatically increase and decrease with each rise and fall in national income, and therefore mitigate such fluctuations. More technically, when taxes are a function of income the size of the multiplier is reduced. Thus, any given change—for example, in investment or government purchases—will not have as large a multiplier effect on national income.

For the MPT_x to reduce the size of the multiplier, the MPT_x has to reduce the effective MPC since the multiplier is derived from it. The effective

MPC is always the change in consumption due to a change in disposable income. Now, since a part of any change in national income is going to be diverted to taxes, disposable income will not change as much as national income. For example, if the MPT_x is 10% the *marginal rate of retention* is equal to one minus 10%. Thus, for every \$1 change in national income, disposable income will change 90¢ $(= 1 - .1)$.

To verify further the impact of the MPT_x on the effective MPC and the multiplier, examine the following problem. Assume the MPC is four-fifths and the MPT_x is one-tenth. The effective MPC would be:

$$
\begin{aligned}
MPC_e &= MPC(1-MPT_x) \\
&= 4/5 \ (1 - .1) \\
&= 36/50 \\
&= .72.
\end{aligned}
$$

The multiplier would, then, be calculated in the usual manner as follows:

$$
\begin{aligned}
k &= \frac{1}{1-MPC_e} \\[2ex]
&= \frac{1}{1-.72} \\[2ex]
&= \frac{1}{.28} \\[2ex]
&= 3.57.
\end{aligned}
$$

TRANSFER PAYMENTS (TR)

It has already been noted in an earlier chapter that the government makes two general types of expenditures. One is the type of government spending discussed thus far in the chapter—government spending (G) for final goods and services produced. This spending is a part of aggregate demand for goods and services, and is sometimes referred to as resource using or productive spending, since resources are used directly in the production of these final goods and services purchased by the government. Another way in which the government spends money does not represent a payment to resources for current contributions to production and, hence, does not *directly* add to national income. This type of government expenditure is a transfer of purchasing power from the government to some individual and is called a government transfer payment. This will be designated as Tr in order to distinguish it from government spending on final goods and services. Examples of government transfer payments are welfare payments, relief, unemployment compensation, and subsidies to farmers and other groups. The crucial distinction of a transfer payment is that it is a payment to a resource which has not contributed to current production.

Government transfer payments are similar to taxes in that both transfers and taxes affect private disposable income directly, rather than affecting national income. They are different in that they have exactly opposite effects on the level of national income. A rise in taxes decreases disposable income which, in turn, decreases consumption through the tax multiplier process. A rise in government transfer payments increases disposable income and, hence, increases consumption through what now may be called the government transfer multiplier, k_{Tr}. The transfer multiplier is the regular multiplier minus one. Therefore, if the marginal propensity to consume is four fifths, the regular multiplier is five and the transfer multiplier is four. Suppose we add government transfer payments of $25 billion to the economic model. This would cause the level of income to rise by $100 billion, restoring the equilibrium level of net national income ($400 billion) prior to the introduction of a $25 billion rise in government taxes.

A $25 billion rise in government transfer payments shifts the consumer demand schedule to the left (and shifts the saving function to the left), indicating that at every level of national income more will be consumed (and more saved). Referring to Figure 14-2, which shows the impact of the $25 billion rise in taxes, the addition of $25 billion in transfers would mean that saving plus taxes minus transfers would equal investment plus government spending at a $400 billion equilibrium level. Government taxes and transfers exactly offset each other; hence, the equilibrium level before taxes is restored.

EQUILIBRIUM CONDITIONS IN THE EXPANDED MODEL

The economic model now is extended to include government spending (G), government taxes (Tx), and government transfer payments (Tr). Equilibrium conditions exist in the commodity market when aggregate demand equals aggregate supply as before the introduction of government, but now this equality of aggregate demand and aggregate supply exists when:

$$Y = C + I + G + Tr - Tx$$
$$Y - C = I + G + Tr - Tx$$
$$S = I + G + Tr - Tx$$
$$S + Tx - Tr = I + G$$

Substituting data used in developing the model, we have:

$$400(Y) = 345(C) + 35(I) + 20(G) + 25(Tr) - 25(Tx)$$
$$55(Y - C) = 35(I) + 20(G) + 25(Tr) - 25(Tx)$$
$$55(S) = 35(I) + 20(G) + 25(Tr) - 25(Tx)$$
$$55(S) + 25(Tx) - 25(Tr) = 35(I) + 20(G)$$

THE NET EFFECTS OF
A GIVEN FISCAL OPERATION

The discussion thus far has entailed an examination of the economic impact on the level of income of a single government activity; namely, a rise in government spending, a rise in taxes, and a rise in government transfer payment. This was done so that the economic model could be developed step by step, and so that the economic effect of a single government activity might be observed. The rest of this chapter will involve a further elaboration of the impact of government by considering the net effects of the entire fiscal operation; that is, the net effects of combined government expenditure and revenue operations. This discussion is a preview to subsequent chapters involving government fiscal policy and fiscal theory.

A RISE IN GOVERNMENT
SPENDING FINANCED BY TAXES

It generally was believed that a rise in government spending financed by an equal rise in government taxes would tend to have a neutral effect on the economy. A knowledge of the government spending multiplier and the tax multiplier shows that balancing the budget at a higher level of government spending and taxing tends to have an expansionary influence on the economy. For example, a rise in government spending of, for example, $5 billion will tend to stimulate a $25 billion rise in income, assuming a marginal propensity to consume of four fifths; whereas an equal rise in government taxes tends to reduce income only $20 billion. Hence, the net effect of financing a $5 billion rise in government spending from a rise in taxes of $5 billion is to increase net national income by $5 billion—the rise in government spending. This is called the balanced budget multiplier. The balanced budget multiplier is one, as may be observed.

The balanced budget multiplier hypothesis rests on several assumptions. First, it must be assumed that government spending is of the income-creating or resource-using variety; if the money spent by the government is a transfer payment, the rise in net national income caused by the rise in government transfer payments would be exactly offset by the fall in income caused from taxes. Second, it must be assumed that the rate of interest remains unchanged, for instance, because of a rise in the supply of money. Third, a rise in government spending occurs without an opposing change in private spending. Government spending is sometimes said to frighten away private spending. Fourth, the marginal propensity to consume has to be the same for the recipients of government spending and for the taxpayers. Otherwise, it would be possible for the tax multiplier to be the same or larger or smaller than the expenditure multiplier. These qualifications must be made concerning the balanced budget multiplier hypothesis. It is generally concluded that a rise in government spending financed from a current tax surplus tends to be expansionary.

A RISE IN GOVERNMENT SPENDING FINANCED FROM GOVERNMENT BORROWING

Financing government spending from government borrowing usually is referred to as government deficit financing, since the government has incurred debt in order to pay for government spending. The net effect of government deficit financing depends on the contractionary influence of government borrowing, which depends on the type of government debt incurred. Government borrowing may be in the form of selling government securities to nonbanks (individuals, businesses other than commercial banks, etc.), commercial banks, and Federal Reserve Banks. Suppose first that the government finances $5 billion of government spending by selling government securities to nonbanks. What are the likely net effects of this fiscal operation?

We will for a moment concentrate attention on the possible economic effects of government borrowing from nonbanks, since the effects of government spending are clearly expansionary via the multiplier principle. The effects of individuals' buying government securities (lending to the government) depends on what individuals would have done with the money used to buy these securities if the government had not incurred debt. One alternative would be for individuals to have used this money to pay for consumer goods. In this event, the effect of government borrowing is to reduce consumption. Another alternative is for individuals to have saved and to have used this saving directly to finance private investment or indirectly to finance private investment by buying new issues of private securities. In either case, private investment has been reduced. Another way in which private investment may be reduced as a result of government borrowing is through a higher rate of interest; when the government sells government securities, it is competing with private borrowers for loanable funds, and this competition may tend to depress security prices and increase the rate of interest. A final alternative open to individuals is to have held in idle form the money used to buy government securities; that is, cash balances. Assuming individuals would have selected this final alternative, the net effect of the deficit-financed government expenditure is clearly expansionary, and more expansionary than if any of the other alternatives had been selected. Even in this case, a reduction in cash balances may have some discouraging influences on consumption. In conclusion and in comparison to financing a rise in government spending from taxes, the net effect of government spending financed by borrowing from nonbanks is likely to be much more expansionary. The contractionary influences of government borrowing from individuals and businesses would never be expected to offset the expansionary influences of government spending financed in this manner.

The overall effect of a rise in government spending financed by government borrowing from commercial banks and Federal Reserve Banks is the most expansionary way of paying for government spending. The reason for this is that government borrowing from commercial banks and Federal Reserve Banks is analogous to the government's printing money to pay for something, since money is usually created when this kind of government deficit spending is involved. Some qualifications, however, are in order, especially concerning government borrowing from commercial banks.

Suppose the government sells $5 billion in securities to commercial banks in order to cover checks written by the government to pay for goods and services. Commercial banks, then, are exchanging part of their excess cash reserves for government loans. In this example, cash reserves of banks are decreased by $5 billion, and government loans outstanding held by banks are increased by $5 billion. At the same time, the recipients of the government checks deposit $5 billion in commercial banks, increasing demand deposits and cash reserves of banks by $5 billion. The primary impact on commercial banks of the entire fiscal operation is an expansion in government loans offset by an increase in demand deposits; that is, the money supply. Government debt has been monetized in the sense that money is created (the rise in demand deposits) as a result of government borrowing from commercial banks.

Certain qualifications must be made to the above conclusion that government borrowing from commercial banks creates money. First, it must be assumed that banks have "excess" cash reserves. Otherwise, banks could not add to their government loans outstanding without contracting private loans, which would result in no change in bank loans outstanding and, hence, no change in demand deposits. Second, it must be assumed that banks are not reducing their demand for private loans. This amounts to the same thing stated in the first qualification. However, the point to be made here is that banks may have excess cash reserves and still reduce their demand for private loans as a consequence of buying government securities.

Government borrowing from Federal Reserve Banks to finance government spending results in money creation and, hence, the net effect is completely expansionary in accordance with the multiplier principle. Government borrowing from the Federal Reserve generally has no contractionary effects, since the Federal Reserve increases government balances in exchange for the government securities purchased. Then the government can pay for goods and services by writing checks on these new treasury balances at the Federal Reserve, and when these checks are cleared through the banking system, government debt is monetized because of the rise in demand deposits which takes place.

A CURRENT TAX SURPLUS USED TO RETIRE GOVERNMENT DEBT

The net effect of a government balanced budget and the net effect of a government budget deficit have been discussed. We will now consider a government budget surplus and examine the net effect of a budget surplus used to retire government debt. A government budget surplus means, of course, that current tax revenues are in excess of government spending. A budget surplus may be held in treasury cash balances at the Federal Reserve and, if it is, the impact of a budget surplus is completely contractionary, similar to a rise in government taxes already discussed. However, a budget surplus may be used to retire government debt and, if it is, some of the contractionary effects of the budget surplus may be offset.

Suppose a current tax surplus is used to retire government debt held by individuals, businesses, etc. The liquidity position (a rise in cash balances) of individuals and businesses will be enhanced in such an event, which may encourage private spending directly, or encourage it indirectly via a lower rate of interest. However, the net effect of using a tax surplus to retire nonbank-held government debt is still expected to be contractionary; the tax surplus directly reduces spending and saving in the economy, whereas it is much less likely that retiring government debt will increase spending and saving as much.

The net effect of disposing of a government budget surplus by retiring commercial-bank-held debt is similar to the net effect of retiring nonbank-held government debt. Sometimes it is concluded that the overall contractionary effect of using a budget surplus to retire bank-held government debt is less than retiring nonbank-held government debt, since retiring government debt held by commercial banks directly increases cash reserves only, while retiring government debt held by non-banks directly increases demand deposits and cash reserves of commercial banks. However, this differential effect of retiring government debt is removed if the primary and secondary effects are considered. Therefore, it may be better to return to the original conclusion that using a tax surplus to retire government debt has an overall contractionary effect on the economy

SUMMARY

The first part of this chapter extended the economic model to include the government sector of the economy. Government spending on final goods and services produced, government taxes, and government transfer payments were added one at a time to the model in order to view the economic impact of each on the level of net national income. The last part of the chapter examined the net effect of entire fiscal operations, such as financing government spending by taxes, financing government spending by government borrowing, and using a budget surplus to retire government debt. Some basic points to keep in mind are:

1. Government purchases of goods and services directly stimulate aggregate demand and supply in the economy, and multiple effects may be expected via the multiplier process.

2. Government transfer payments indirectly stimulate aggregate demand and supply by increasing the purchasing power in the hands of certain groups, and the transfer multiplier is one less the regular multiplier.

3. Government taxes are paid out of income and wealth. Current consumption, saving, or liquid assets may be reduced by taxes. Taxes have a multiple contractionary influence on prices and national output.

4. Government borrowing reduces the liquidity of the public, tends to increase the rate of interest, and therefore exerts a downward influence on private spending in the economy.

5. The exception to the effects ascribed to government borrowing above is government borrowing from commercial banks and Federal Reserve Banks. In this case, government borrowing is similar in effect to that of "green-backing"; that is, creating money.

6. The net effects of a balanced budget involving government purchases of goods and services tend to be expansionary subject to the qualification of no change in private spending. The net effects of a balanced budget involving transfers are neutral subject to the same qualification stated above.

7. The net effect of a budget deficit tends to be expansionary, with the degree of expansion depending on how the deficit is met. Government borrowing from commercial banks and Federal Reserve Banks tends to have the greatest expansionary effect, since demand deposits of commercial banks generally rise when government spending is financed in this manner.

8. The net effects of a budget surplus are contractionary, the degree depending on how the surplus is disposed of. The greatest contractionary effect of the budget surplus is exerted on the economy if the surplus is simply held in idle balances or used to retire Federal Reserve Bank-held debt. If the surplus is used to retire bank-held and nonbank-held debt, the net effects of the surplus are less contractionary.

SUGGESTIONS FOR FURTHER READING

Dernburg, Thomas F. and McDougall, Duncan M., *Macroeconomics*, Fifth Edition, New York: McGraw-Hill Book Company, 1976.
Chapters 4–8 are suggested for further reading.

FIFTEEN

FISCAL POLICY AND EXPERIENCES

Fiscal policy evolved out of the Great Depression of the 1930s and the theoretical writings of many economists, especially the works of John M. Keynes, a British economist, and his American counterpart, Alvin H. Hansen. Keynes' celebrated book, *The General Theory of Employment, Interest and Money,* was published in 1936 and laid the theoretical foundation for the development of fiscal policy. Hansen and others developed and refined fiscal theory, and the process of refinement continues to this day.

Fiscal policy and theory have not been free of criticism. Professor Milton Friedman, a Nobel Prize winner, and others hold that there are important theoretical weaknesses and practical problems which seriously reduce the efficacy of fiscal policy. It has been popular to place economists into two schools of thought—the classicists and the Keynesians. This division is not precise because nearly all economists have been influenced by both classical and Keynesian economics. Under the strict assumptions of classical economics, there would be little or no disagreement among economists in regard to fiscal policy, primarily because there would be little or no need for it. In this world, the economy would experience steady growth, with market forces automatically assuring full employment without inflation. Under the strict assumptions of the Keynesian system, automatic forces would not work as well because of institutional rigidities, and an unemployment equilibrium could ensue.

Although it is tempting to do so, this chapter does not examine per se the classical-Keynesian controversy. Instead, the objectives are: (1) to explain the meaning and goals of fiscal policy; (2) to explain its limitations; (3) to discuss alternative fiscal programs; and (4) to examine fiscal policy experiences in the 1960s and 1970s.

FISCAL POLICY AND ITS GOALS

Government fiscal policy is a conscious attempt to direct the economic activities of the government toward the accomplishment of two of society's goals—economic stability and economic growth. Neither stability without growth nor growth without stability is desirable. What is needed is economic stability with economic growth, and these are the dual goals of fiscal policy.

The tools of fiscal policy are government spending, taxing, borrowing, lending, buying, and selling. Fiscal policy operates through the market mechanism. It attempts to direct the movement of forces in the market, but does not attempt to replace the problem-solving mechanism of the market. This distinction is important. During World War II, the government inaugurated a price control and rationing system. Prices no longer moved in response to supply and demand, but reflected the ceilings placed on them by government decree. Fiscal policy as defined here does not function in this way. Relative prices are free to fluctuate in accordance with market forces, but an important force operating in the market is the activity of the government. Fiscal policy attempts to maintain a given level of aggregate demand in the economy rather than coping with problems in individual markets.

Fiscal policy is an alternative to an all-out planning policy. Such all-out planning usually necessitates government ownership of key industries— iron, steel, coal, and others—as in England, or the complete government ownership of all resources as in Russia. It would be possible, however, to control a few key sectors of the economy and to rely on fiscal policy without going as far as either England or Russia. For example, in this country the farming sector of the economy is under government control but the industry is not socialized.

It is possible that the proper use of fiscal policy can give us the best of both worlds. If fiscal policy is successful in directing total spending in the economy so that both a high degree of stability and growth are achieved, the private economy may still have ample room to operate and solve most of its other problems. The cyclical variations which have characterized the private economy should not make one lose sight of the vitality, strength, and capacity of the private economy to allocate scarce resources.

ECONOMIC STABILITY

Stable Prices

The objectives of economic stability are stable prices and full employment.[1] Within an environment of stable prices, sharp up-and-down movements in the average price level are absent. However, the prices of individual commodities will be left free to fluctuate according to individual demand and supply conditions. It is important to realize and to understand that both price level stability and flexibility of relative prices must be achieved if economic stability is to be accomplished within the institutional framework of a relatively free economy.

Full Employment

A full employment economy does not mean that everyone is employed.[2] It does not mean that part-time workers (students, housewives, and others) are under strong pressures to take full employment jobs, nor does it mean that full-time workers are under pressure to work overtime and that the retired are asked to come out of retirement. Full employment means that no significant involuntary unemployment exists. It means that people who are qualified and willing to work, and who are willing to accept the going wage rate, can find employment without considerable delay. Unemployment of a temporary nature, such as seasonal and frictional unemployment (people changing jobs, lags in adjustments processes), and the voluntary decision to withdraw services from the market for whatever reason are not considered unemployment problems from the economic point of view.

A full employment economy is one in which production is at such a high level that any further increase in aggregate demand results in marked

---

1. Emile Despres, Milton Friedman, Albert G. Hart, Paul A. Samuelson, and Donald H. Wallace, "The Problem of Economic Instability," *AEA Readings in Fiscal Policy,* eds. Arthur Smithies and J. Keith Butters (Homewood, Illinois: Richard D. Irwin, Inc., 1955), p. 406.

2. *Ibid.,* p. 406

upward movements in the price level rather than in increases in physical production. This policy target may produce an unemployment rate that is rather high in order to avoid the threat of serious inflation.

Fiscal policy hopes to accomplish both stable prices and maximum production. A stable price level associated with low production levels is undesirable, as are maximum production levels associated with rapidly rising prices. Indeed, neither price level stability nor maximum production may be desirable goals in and of themselves. Only where both stable prices and full employment exist are the goals of economic stability fully realized.

FULL EMPLOYMENT AND INFLATION

In economic life, where phenomena are complex and interrelated, it is too much to expect that the twin goals of economic stability will be completely realized. As has been previously pointed out, resources will not be fully employed in every line of economic activity at the same time; therefore, shortages in materials, machines, and personnel appear in certain sectors of the economy before they appear in others. Once near-maximum production and employment levels are reached, it may be economically undesirable to attempt to reach the magic goal of full employment because of the inflation which may ensue.

Pure inflation—that is, rising prices not associated with rising output—has adverse economic effects. This kind of inflation results in an arbitrary redistribution of income in favor of certain income groups and causes overexpansion in some sectors of the economy and underexpansion in others. Of course, the concept "pure inflation" is like the concept "full employment." It is not easy to draw the line between increases in aggregate demand which increase prices only (pure inflation), and increases in aggregate demand which increase output only. These are theoretically important concepts, but we may be confronted with a slightly different situation in the real world. Increases in physical output may be very difficult to separate from increases in money output.

The possibility of obtaining full employment without inflation is small. Indeed, social welfare may be maximized not by trying to accomplish each goal completely, but by trying to accomplish both approximately. A reasonable amount of inflation—price rises of 4 to 5% a year—may be the price society is willing to pay for near-full employment levels. Or a reasonable amount of unemployment—5 to 6% of the labor force—may be the price society is willing to pay for a relative degree of price stability.

FIGURE 15-1
INFLATION AND UNEMPLOYMENT RATES

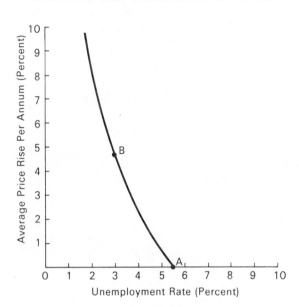

A large amount of empirical evidence supports the proposition that a choice has to be made between price stability and full employment. Paul A. Samuelson and Robert M. Solow, for example, estimated the relationship between the average rise in the price level and unemployment rates, based on twenty-five years of data.[3] This estimated relationship is shown in Figure 15-1. Price stability, point A, corresponds to a 5.5% unemployment rate. An unemployment rate of 3%, point B, corresponds to an inflation rate of 4.5% per year. The range of choice is indicated by points on the line between points A and B. The period of the 1960s, which was not covered in the Samuelson and Solow investigation, shows a similar relationship between changes in the price level and changes in the unemployment rate. However, according to a study by George Perry, the range of choice, or the trade-off between the rate of inflation and the rate

3. Paul A. Samuelson and Robert M. Solow, "Our Menu of Policy Choices," in the *Battle Against Unemployment,* ed. Arthur M. Okun (New York: W. W. Norton and Company, Inc., 1965), pp. 71–76.

of unemployment, worsened in the 1960s.[4] This means that to maintain a given rate of unemployment the inflation rate is higher or, alternatively, to maintain a given rate of inflation the unemployment rate is higher. Perry's estimate was that at a 4% unemployment rate the annual rate of inflation was 1.7% higher in the late 1960s than it was in the mid-1950s.

CONFLICTS WITH ECONOMIC GROWTH

Government fiscal policy does not only have the role of promoting economic stability, but also the role of fostering economic expansion. Economic stability may be looked upon as the cyclical or short-run goal of fiscal policy, and economic growth (increase in real per capita income) as the long-run goal. Even though economic expansion has been a dominant characteristic of our society, economic growth cannot be taken for granted.

The role fiscal policy is to play in the expansion of our economy is less certain than its role in economic stability. One view is that fiscal policy only needs to create a social climate favorable to growth so that the growth potential inherent in the capitalist engine will be allowed to run its natural course. Alternatively, government fiscal activities must not *stifle* growth in the economy. Taxes should be selected which will not discourage incentives to make risky investments.

The essential problem is a conflict between stability and growth. Growth means change, and change means reallocation in the economy. Growth entails directing resources into a rearrangement of existing facilities, the use of new techniques of production, new products, a new consumer want, and so on. In all cases, growth threatens existing economic activities and may rock the boat rather severely. But the economic instability inherent in economic growth is only one side of the picture.

Economic growth which generates instability also needs stability in order to flourish. New investment is more responsive to a stable environment than to an unstable environment characterized by uncertainty, mass unemployment, or serious inflation. What is needed, of course, is the degree of economic stability which will foster economic growth rather than stifle it, and the degree of growth which will permit economic stability rather than create serious problems of instability.

---

4. George L. Perry, "Changing Labor Markets and Inflation," *Brookings Papers on Economic Activity,* Vol. 3 (1970), p. 433.

LIMITATIONS OF FISCAL POLICY

The limitations of fiscal policy may be divided into two general classes. First, fiscal policy is not appropriate for problems which call for structural adjustments. Second, fiscal policy is limited operationally, since its success depends on such things as accurate forecasting and appropriate timing.

STRUCTURAL ADJUSTMENTS

One concern about fiscal policy is that it may not bring about the adjustments needed to restore stability and may even impede these adjustments.[5] Suppose that a recession starts because of a maladjustment in the production process; that is, the production of some goods is not maintainable for the existing *distribution* of private demand. Government fiscal policy may maintain the *level* of demand but may do little if anything to adjust the distribution of money flows to the distribution of goods and services. Price and/or output adjustments are required for individual commodities.

This basic limitation to fiscal policy may be exemplified in what is called the "uneasy triangle"—referring to the intricate relationship of wages, prices, and employment.[6] In Figure 15-2, full employment output is at OQ_1 and a stable price level at OP_1. Suppose that money wage rates are increased through union bargaining. The effect of higher wage costs is to decrease aggregate supply to S_1S_1. If the government attempts to maintain full employment through increasing demand to D_1D_1, inflation results (OP_2). If the government attempts to maintain prices through decreasing demand (D_2D_2), unemployment results (OQ_0). Increases in wages unaccompanied by increases in productivity cause inflation and/or unemployment. Government fiscal policy may reach one of its objectives only by moving further from the other.

---

5. Summer H. Slichter, "The Economics of Public Works," *A.E.A. Readings In Fiscal Policy,* eds. Arthur Smithies and J. Keith Butters (Homewood, Illinois: Richard D. Irwin, Inc., 1955), pp. 38–50.

6. Joseph P. McKenna, *Aggregate Economic Analysis* (New York: Dryden Press Inc., 1955), p. 231. See also Milton Friedman, "A Monetary and Fiscal Framework for Economic Stability," *A.E.A. Readings in Monetary Policy,* eds. Friedrich A. Lutz and Lloyd W. Mintz (Homewood, Illinois: Richard D. Irwin, Inc., 1951), p. 380.

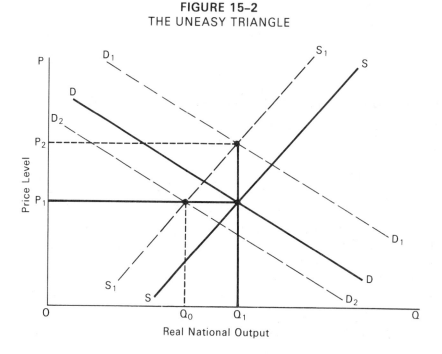

FIGURE 15-2
THE UNEASY TRIANGLE

OPERATIONAL LIMITATIONS

Operational problems associated with fiscal policy—such as those of timing and magnitudes—limit its effectiveness. The problem of timing arises because the phases of a cycle cannot be predicted accurately. Lags will occur between the time at which appropriate action is called for and the time at which this action can be initiated and its effects felt in the economy. Methods and techniques of forecasting economic trends have been much improved in recent years. Yet, very accurate predictions should not always be expected. Economic activity is recorded fairly well by economic indicators. We know where we have been better than we ever have before, but data on future rates of consumer and investment spending cannot be collected today.

Once economic indicators reveal the probable fiscal action which should be taken, there is a period before it can be initiated and another before the economic effects of such action are felt in the economy.[7] Any fundamental

---

7. Friedman, *ibid.,* pp. 382–85.

change in government spending and taxing would necessitate Congressional action. Such action takes time. Strong cumulative upward movements in economic forces leading to serious inflation, or strong cumulative downward movements leading to mass unemployment, may take place during the interval. The likelihood of cumulative swings taking place is further enhanced because the effects of the fiscal action will take time to work themselves out.

Even if the direction of movement of economic activity could be anticipated, and even if the appropriate fiscal action would be forthcoming at the right time, there is still the problem of how much fiscal action is needed. Economists may agree that during periods of inflation government spending should be reduced relative to taxes, and that during periods of deflation government spending should be increased relative to taxes. However, there may be substantial disagreement over the size of government spending and taxes. What *size* deficit or surplus to run is the vital question. A large deficit spending program during periods of recessions may plunge the economy into inflationary troubles, and a budget surplus necessary to control inflation may cause unemployment.

ALTERNATIVE FISCAL THEORIES

Since the writing of *The General Theory* in 1936, three alternative fiscal theories and policies have emerged. The true significance of that book may be manifested in the development of these alternatives. Prior to *The General Theory,* no consistent body of economic knowledge existed which justified directing government spending and taxing toward the goal of economic stability. The policy goal was to balance the budget.[8] If this goal was not achieved, the results were believed to be wasteful government expenditures, currency devaluation, and a reduction in real income. The only exception to this rule of annually balancing the budget was government loan financing to pay for long-term nonrecurring government expenditures.

Assuming no problems of economic instability, the rule demanding an annual balanced budget may have been the appropriate guide to fiscal policy. However, since the goals of fiscal policy are economic stability and growth, the appropriateness of a given budget policy depends on prevailing

8. Jesse Burkhead, "The Balanced Budget," *A.E.A. Readings in Fiscal Policy,* eds. Arthur Smithies and J. Keith Butters (Homewood, Illinois: Richard D. Irwin, Inc., 1955), p. 3–17.

economic conditions. The fiscal policies to be discussed are substitutes for the annual balanced budget policy under a wide variety of real circumstances.

A MANAGED COMPENSATORY
FISCAL POLICY

A managed compensatory fiscal policy is championed by many writers in this country and has been promoted vigorously by Alvin H. Hansen.[9] The prime objective of this policy is to smooth out extreme economic fluctuations which occur because of volatile private spending. The role of fiscal policy is to stabilize total spending or demand in the economy. This can be done by spending to compensate or offset changes in private spending. When private demand falls, resulting in an economic contraction and unemployment, government spending should rise; when private demand rises, resulting in inflation, government spending should fall. The appropriate budget policy is dictated by existing conditions in the economy. A budget deficit in deflationary years and a budget surplus in inflationary years would be called for and would replace the rule of a balanced budget in every year.

The large fluctuations in national income observed in Figure 15-3 represent fluctuations in the economy which are due to changes in private demand without any offsetting changes in government spending. The smaller fluctuations represent movements in aggregate demand after compensatory fiscal action. Budget deficits during periods of falling output and prices will tend to check or offset the downward trends. Budget surpluses will tend to offset upward trends.

The proponents of managed compensatory fiscal policy also argue that budget surpluses accumulated in the good years may be used to retire government debt incurred in the bad years in order to enable the budget to be balanced over the business cycle. However, if the deficits exceed the surpluses, the public debt will grow. But, if national income is growing faster than the public debt, the size of the debt relative to national income is falling. The relative size of the public debt is more important than its absolute size because society's ability to service the debt is taken into

9. Alvin H. Hansen, *Monetary Theory and Fiscal Policy* (New York: McGraw-Hill Book Co., Inc., 1949), chaps. 12–23.

FIGURE 15–3
A MANAGED COMPENSATORY FISCAL POLICY

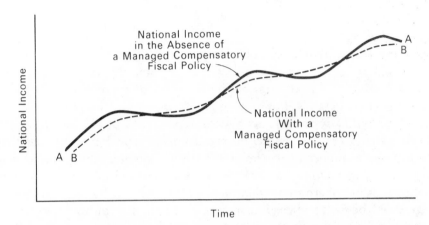

Explanation: The cyclical fluctuations in national income indicated by AA are the fluctuations assumed to exist in the economy in the absence of alternative budget deficits and surpluses. The smaller fluctuations in national income indicated by BB have resulted because of the offsetting effects of budget deficits during periods of economic contraction and unemployment, and the offsetting effects of budget surpluses during periods of economic expansion and inflation.

consideration. The proponents of a managed compensatory fiscal policy reason that if the choice is between unemployment or a rising public debt, a larger debt is the preferable alternative.

AUTOMATIC FISCAL POLICY

An alternative which has gained many adherents is an automatic fiscal policy of built-in stability. Can automatic changes in tax revenue and government spending occur so as to stabilize production and employment at high levels, thereby eliminating the need for a managed compensatory policy? The most outspoken group to answer this question in the affirmative is the Committee for Economic Development (CED).[10]

10. Research and Policy Committee of the Committee for Economic Development, *Taxes and the Budget: A Program for Prosperity in a Free Society* (New York, November, 1947).

We will explore how such a program for economic stability might work. Government expenditures would be determined on the basis of relative merit (ideally, by the allocation branch of the budget). Once the level of government expenditures was determined, it would remain fixed over the business cycle except for those expenditures which would vary automatically, such as unemployment compensation payments, welfare payments, and subsidies to farmers. Tax rates also would be held constant over the cycle and would be set so that tax revenue would equal government spending at a predetermined level of employment; for example, 93%. Assuming full employment is defined as a situation where 96% of the labor force is employed, at full employment a moderate budget surplus would result.[11]

Suppose the economy is at a level of national income where the federal budget is in balance when a contraction in economic activity begins. Given constant levels of government spending and tax rates, cash payments to the public would begin to exceed cash receipts from the public due to the automatic decline in receipts. The resulting deficit of the government would rise as the recession worsened and would act as an offsetting force in the economy. Conversely, starting at a balanced budget again, an expansion would increase receipts from the public relative to payments, resulting in a budget surplus. This surplus would rise automatically as the economy moved further below the 93% level of employment. A budget deficit (surplus) automatically appearing when contractionary (expansionary) forces set in would tend to stabilize economic activity around the 95% level of employment.

The automatic rise in receipts when the economy moves toward full employment, and the automatic decline in receipts when the economy is moving away from high employment levels, is due to the built-in stability of the tax system—especially the federal income tax component. Taxes levied on income vary directly with changes in income assuming fixed tax rates; therefore, when national income rises and falls, income tax collections behave similarly. This means that as national income rises diposable income (income after taxes) does not rise as much, and when national income falls disposable income does not fall as much. The feature of the federal personal income tax which makes the best example of a built-in stabilizer is its progressive rate structure. A given percent change in per-

---

11. Committee for Economic Development, *Fiscal and Monetary Policy for High Employment* (New York, December, 1961), p. 26.

sonal income will result in a greater percent change in personal income tax collections, since federal personal income tax rates rise faster than personal income rises.

There are built-in stabilizers on the expenditure side as well. Certain transfer payments automatically vary with employment conditions. The outstanding example is government unemployment compensation payments. These expenditures automatically rise when unemployment rises and automatically fall when unemployment falls. Government subsidies to farmers and people on public assistance tend to vary countercyclically. Therefore, the automatic fall in payments when the economy is expanding and the level of employment is rising, and the automatic rise in payments when the economy is contracting, tend to be stabilizing.

FISCAL POLICY FOR FULL EMPLOYMENT AND MAXIMUM GROWTH

There is little disagreement as to the need for countercyclical fiscal action in an economy characterized by frictions and inflexibilities. There is basic disagreement, however, as to *how much* fiscal action is needed to keep the economy prosperous and growing. Managed compensatory fiscal policy was developed as a reaction to the depression of the 1930s, and has the purpose of attempting to stabilize economic activity during the business cycle. There is the implication that market forces, except for short-run cyclical disturbances, are directing the economy toward optimum growth. A policy of automatic stabilization, which has gained supporters since World War II when the economy has been at high levels of production, implies also that market forces may not produce optimum growth in the long run. Concern about the short-run problem of economic instability is matched by concern over the long-run problem of economic growth. The fear is that without appropriate fiscal actions maximum long-run growth may not be achieved.

Figure 15-4 shows what is involved in a fiscal policy for full employment *and* maximum growth. The upward trend line (BB) represents maximum production and utilization of all resources. The cyclical fluctuations in the economy are indicated by line AA. As shown, national income is below the maximum production level except in one period, indicating excess capacity, unemployment, and failure of the economy to reach its full growth potential during most of the time period. Whereas a managed compensatory

FIGURE 15-4
FISCAL POLICY FOR STABILITY AND GROWTH

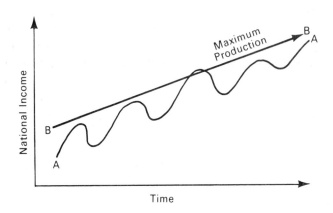

Explanation: Line AA shows the cyclical variations in the economy. Line BB shows the maximum production and growth potential in the economy. A budget deficit is called for any time line AA fails to reach line BB, or maximum production and income. A budget surplus is called for when line AA goes above line BB, since inflation exists.

fiscal policy may call for a budget surplus during relatively prosperous years and a budget deficit during relatively lean years, a fiscal policy for full employment and growth would call for a budget deficit in every year that maximum production is not realized. During the time period illustrated, this means a budget deficit in every period except the one when increases in aggregate demand result in increases in prices only. Thus, a period of pure inflation would be the only time in which a budget surplus would be appropriate.

DISCRETIONARY FISCAL ACTION VERSUS AUTOMATIC FISCAL ACTION

A managed compensatory fiscal policy and a policy for full employment and maximum growth are alike in that they are both discretionary; that is, the action undertaken depends on the discretion of fiscal authorities—namely, officials in the executive and legislative branches of our government. A "let's wait and see" policy of a President and a prolonged period of time before new legislative action is taken may seriously hamper discretionary fiscal action.

Time lag problems were mentioned earlier in this chapter. These problems may be partially overcome by establishing a Board of Fiscal Authorities which would have certain powers delegated by Congress. For example, the Board of Fiscal Authorities may have the power to vary the minimum income tax rate, for example, from 10 to 20%. Power to vary this rate would mean that countercyclical fiscal action could be taken without waiting for new tax legislation. Congress may also grant power to the Authorities to change public construction expenditures by stipulated amounts, for instance, plus or minus $5 billion.

Even with a discretionary fiscal policy, the problems of forecasting, timing, and magnitudes would still remain. The success of countercyclical fiscal policy depends to some extent on how accurately the timing of cyclical movements in the economy can be forecast and how accurately the severity of the cyclical movements may be predicted. Forecasting methods and techniques have been improved in recent years; however, they still leave much to be desired. From the significant work of the National Bureau of Economic Research, it has been discovered that certain economic series lead both an upturn and a downturn. These sensitive indicators provide "tips" as to what may be expected. However, fiscal policy is still very much an art.

Usually, it is agreed that a policy of built-in stability overcomes the problem of forecasting, since it automatically comes into play with changes in economic activity. This may be partially granted, but if the success of a policy of economic stability is measured by preventive action prior to the advent of the problem of instability the weight of this argument is diminished. In addition, even with built-in stability, some discretionary fiscal action may be necessary. Automatic budget surpluses and budget deficits may not *prevent* upward and downward cumulative movements in economic activity.

THE FULL EMPLOYMENT
BUDGET SURPLUS OR DEFICIT

Budget surpluses and deficits may occur automatically due to changes in income, or they may occur due to discretionary fiscal action. The President's Council of Economic Advisors uses the concept of a full employment budget surplus or deficit to separate the two causes and to compare the relative effects of various fiscal programs. The full employment budget surplus for a given level of expenditures and tax rate structure is the budget surplus that would occur if the economy were at full employment. In Figure 15-5, CD and CE measure the full employment budget surpluses under fiscal programs AA and BB, respectively. The difference between the actual budget surplus or deficit and the full employment budget surplus indicates the budget surplus or deficit that occurs because the economy is not at full employment. For example, assume the fiscal program is indicated by AA and that the economy is at a 94% employment rate. The actual budget is balanced. The full employment budget surplus is $5 billion. The difference in this case ($5 billion) results from the automatic decline in revenues generated by the economy operating at less than full employment.

The full employment budget surplus may also be used to indicate the relative expansionary effects of different fiscal programs. The fiscal program that would give the smallest budget surplus or the largest budget deficit at full employment is the most expansionary fiscal program. For example, program AA is more expansionary than BB.

FIGURE 15-5
AUTOMATIC AND DISCRETIONARY BUDGET SURPLUSES AND DEFICITS

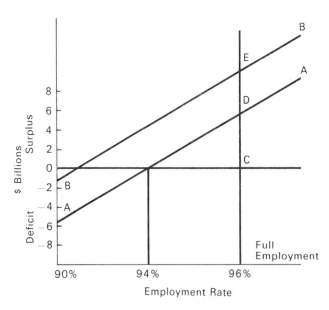

EVALUATION OF ALTERNATIVE
FISCAL POLICIES

While a managed compensatory fiscal policy differs from the fiscal policy of full employment and economic growth by degree, this degree of difference is important. A managed compensatory fiscal policy gives the private economy considerable room to operate, assumes that market forces will drive the economy in the right direction if aided by a stabilized aggregate demand, and is sensitive to inflation and possibly to the growth in public debt. This policy tolerates some unemployment as a price that must be paid to enhance the degree of flexibility in the economy.

In comparison, a fiscal policy for full employment and economic growth would tackle the unemployment problem more vigorously and attempt to maintain aggregate demand at full employment and maximum growth levels at all times. Without direct intervention in the market, such a fiscal policy will have difficulties in overcoming pockets of unemployment in the economy which may exist because of individual changes in demand, increases in wages without increases in productivity, the downward rigidity of administered prices, and so on. Aggregate demand may be kept at high levels by and through appropriate fiscal action, and needed adjustments of production to individual changes in demand may take place if aggregate demand is relatively high. However, full employment may require a great deal of market intervention.

The fiscal policy of automatic stabilization is appealing since it comes into play without new legislation or the actions of a discretionary fiscal authority. Proposals to modify the federal tax and expenditure structure to enhance built-in flexibility are steps in the right direction. It is doubtful whether complete reliance can be or should be placed on only such fiscal action. The defense against economic instability should not be limited to one line of fiscal action but should include several alternatives. A fiscal policy of automatic stabilization should be our first line of defense against economic instability, but not the only defense. Discretionary fiscal action should be employed under many circumstances.

COORDINATING MONETARY
AND FISCAL POLICY

Even though there is a certain amount of disbelief that a flexible monetary policy alone can accomplish the task of full employment, it can be effective if combined with fiscal policy. The policy pursued by the Board of Governors of the Federal Reserve System largely controls the availability and cost of money and credit. Given a high level of total private spending in the economy, supported by a high level of government spending, it may be that a flexible monetary policy is quite important and that monetary policy is strategic in keeping economic fluctuations to a minimum. Decreasing the availability of money and increasing its cost may be effective in checking upward price movements. Increasing the availability of money and decreasing its cost may be effective in encouraging economic expansion if cumulative forces are reduced by the maintenance of aggregate demand through government purchases, transfer payments, and tax reductions.

It has been argued that monetary policy should concern itself primarily with the task of making sure that the supply of money is rising to meet the needs of an expanding economy, and with being certain that the cost of money (rate of interest) is kept at a level conducive to economic stability and economic expansion. In this case, problems of inflation and unemployment would be handled by the appropriate fiscal action. This implies much more flexibility in fiscal policy than now exists or may exist in the future. The best approach may be for monetary and fiscal policy to be more closely coordinated and for both to be made as flexible as possible in order to meet the challenges of economic stability and growth.

FISCAL POLICY EXPERIENCES

The record of discretionary fiscal action is not impressive. Why not? Is the theory on which it is based a weak one? Discretionary fiscal action has not been systematically tried over any extended period of time. Thus, the effectiveness of the theory behind fiscal policy has yet to be ascertained. The disappointing record of policy can probably be traced largely to fundamental operational limitations, and also to the fact that policy is developed in a political environment. Fiscal policy did work quite well in the first half of the 1960s, however, thus offering hope that it could work with some effectiveness in the future.

ISSUES OF THE 1960s

The major issues in the first half of the 1960s were the slow pace of economic growth and unemployment. The major issue in the second half was inflation. The economy moved into the 1960s with a large GNP gap—the difference between GNP at full employment and actual GNP. The aim of fiscal action was to eliminate this gap along lines described in the previous section under the heading of "Fiscal Policy for Full Employment and Maximum Growth." Several measures were undertaken to accomplish these objectives. First, private investment was encouraged by permitting faster depreciation of capital goods and allowing a 7% investment tax credit (1962). Second, consumer and investment spending were stimulated by personal and corporate income tax cuts in 1964 and 1965. Third, a wage-price guideline program was established to keep wage and price increases in major industries within limits compatible with a stable growing economy.

The economy responded well to these fiscal actions. By the end of 1965, full employment had been achieved (Table 15-1). This mission was accomplished with little inflation. The price index which economists prefer—the GNP implicit price deflator—increased only 7.4% between 1960 and 1965 or at an average annual rate of less than 2%.

The issues of growth and unemployment were quickly forgotten in 1966; defense spending was rapidly accelerated without reducing other federal spending or increasing taxes, and the issues of the Vietnam war and inflation surfaced. The cries of economists for an increase in taxes to slow down inflation in 1966 and 1967 were not heeded soon enough by politicians. By the time Congress enacted a 10% surtax on personal and corporate income in 1968, inflationary forces were strong and difficult to combat. Also, the tax increase in 1968 was temporary. This reduced its effectiveness because consumers viewed its impact as a transitory loss in disposable income and maintained their previous spending.[12] However, the main lesson to learn from the inflationary period of the 1960s was that fiscal actions were not taken soon enough to control inflation.

ISSUES OF THE 1970s

Many important concerns have emerged in the 1970s: the coexistence of inflation and unemployment; the Nixon experiment with wage-price con-

---

12. Charles E. McLure, Jr., "Fiscal Failure: Lessons of the Sixties," in *Economic Policy and Inflation In the Sixties* (Washington, D.C.: American Enterprise Institute for Public Policy Research, 1972), pp. 81–82.

TABLE 15-1 GROSS NATIONAL PRODUCT IN CONSTANT DOLLARS, GNP IMPLICIT PRICE DEFLATOR, AND UNEMPLOYMENT RATE, 1960–1976

Year	Gross National Product (Constant 1958 dollars) ($ Billions)	Implicit Price Deflator (1958 = 100)	Unemployment Rate (%)
1960	487.8	103.3	5.5
1961	497.3	104.6	6.7
1962	530.0	105.7	5.5
1963	550.0	107.1	5.7
1964	577.6	108.9	5.2
1965	617.8	110.9	4.5
1966	658.1	113.9	3.8
1967	674.6	117.6	3.8
1968	707.6	122.3	3.6
1969	725.6	128.2	3.5
1970	722.5	135.2	4.9
1971	745.4	141.6	5.9
1972	790.7	146.0	5.6
1973	839.2	154.3	4.9
1974	821.2	170.2	5.6
1975	816.1	185.8	8.5
1976	866.6 (prelim.)	195.3	7.9 Dec. preliminary)

SOURCE: U.S. Department of Commerce, *Survey of Current Business* (U.S. Printing Office: Washington, D.C.)

trols; food and fuel shortages; the two-digit inflation of 1974; the worst recession (in 1973–75) since the 1930s; and the slow recovery of 1975–76.

Inflation and Unemployment

The decade got off to a bad start with both rising prices and rising unemployment in 1970 and 1971. This situation was not a completely new experience, but the extent of the problem was unprecedented. Although fiscal and monetary policies appeared to have been working reasonably well under the circumstances, wage-price controls were initiated in 1971, evidently because it was believed that these policies could not continue to cope with the inflation-unemployment dilemma.

Wage-Price Controls

Our experiences with wage-price controls from 1971 and 1974 left much to be desired. Distortions, misallocations, inequities, and scarcities were common. Unfortunately, the money supply increased rapidly during this period, and the impact of fiscal policy as measured by the full employment budget surplus ratio (the ratio of the full employment budget surplus to potential GNP) was expansionary in both 1971 and 1972 (Figure 15-6). The adverse effects of wage-price controls would have been less if these events had not occurred.

To make the problem even greater, these expansionary policies were in full swing when food and fuel shortages became apparent in 1973. This combination of events set off a recession in the last part of 1973 which was accompanied by a two-digit inflation; that is, a rate of inflation over 10%.

The 1973–1975 Recession

The 1973–1975 recession started with strong inflationary forces operating in the economy and with a relatively high rate of unemployment (5%). By the time the period was over, the unemployment rate reached 8.5% and the rate of inflation, although high by historical standards, was reduced to a more respectable rate of 5 to 6%. What brought on this recession? Was fiscal policy a contributing factor? There were many causes, among them the tripling of oil prices,[13] shortages of basic materials, the erosion of real consumer income by inflation, slumps in the housing and auto markets, and fiscal policy in the form of a growing full employment budget surplus ratio in 1973 and 1974.

The Recovery in 1975 and 1976

The leading economic indicators revealed that the economy was beginning to turn around in the spring of 1975. By the fall of 1975 it was more evident that the economy was expanding again. Thus far, the expansion into early 1977 has not been spectacular. Excess production capacity and high unem-

---

13. Gardner Ackley attributes the basic cause of the decrease in consumer spending to a $20 billion annual tax levied on consumers by the unilateral rise in the price of imported oil. See Gardner Ackley, "Two Stage Recession and Inflation, 1973–1975," *Economic Outlook USA,* Vol. 2, No. 1 (Ann Arbor: University of Michigan Survey Research Center, 1975), p. 6.

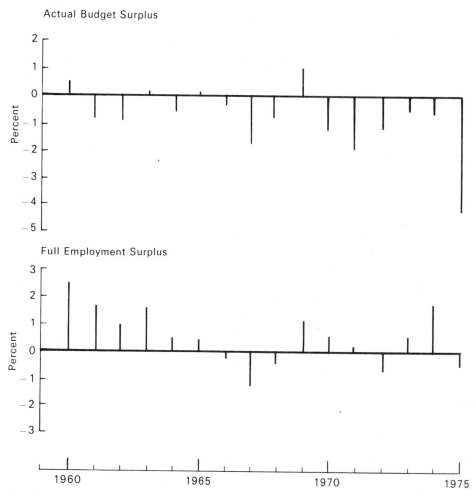

FIGURE 15-6
ACTUAL BUDGET SURPLUS AND FULL EMPLOYMENT BUDGET SURPLUS
AS A PERCENT OF POTENTIAL GNP, FISCAL YEARS 1960-1975

Actual Budget Surplus

Full Employment Surplus

Source: Henry Owen and Charles L. Schultze (Editors), *Setting National Priorities: The Next Ten Years* (Washington, D.C.: the Brookings Institute, 1976), p. 275.

ployment rates continued to dominate the scene in 1976 and at the beginning of 1977. Fiscal policy has been one of gradualism. Tax cuts were passed by Congress to boost the economy in 1975 and 1976, and newly elected President Carter asked Congress for a package of individual and business tax cuts and expenditure increases which, if granted, will stimulate the economy over the next two years. Even assuming that Congress enacts most of the Carter fiscal program, the growth rate in the economy is not expected to move the economy to near full employment production levels in 1977.

If this is the economic situation in 1977, stronger fiscal actions may be necessary. The tax cut program thus far proposed will not have the same relative impact as the 1964 tax cut did, even though the dollar amounts are about the same. The economy is much larger today. A larger cut is required in order to have the same relative effects on the economy.

SUMMARY: FISCAL POLICY EXPERIENCES

Fiscal policy was effective in the first part of 1960s when it was systematically pursued. Stabilization efforts gave way to political considerations in the last half of the 1960s, and we failed to control inflation. Fiscal policy was placed aside in 1971 in favor of wage-price controls because of scepticism concerning the effectiveness of fiscal and monetary policy. Fiscal actions probably contributed to the 1973–1975 recession. In general, fiscal policy has lost some of the prestige that evolved out of its effectiveness in the early 1960s. However, fiscal policy primarily in the form of tax cuts will probably be counted on in 1977 to move the economy toward full employment with an acceptable rate of inflation.

SUMMARY

The goals of fiscal policy are economic stability and economic growth. Economic stability requires a stable price level and full employment. Economic growth means a rise in per capita real income. Fiscal policy is a conscious attempt to direct government spending, taxing, borrowing, and other economic activities of the government toward the accomplishment of the goals of fiscal policy.

Fiscal policy operates through the market mechanism and does not attempt to replace the problem-solving mechanism of the market. For example, wage and price control policies of the government which prevent the market from solving problems should not be identified and confused with fiscal policies. Fiscal policy is aimed at directing the market economy rather than supplanting it. In addition, fiscal policy is concerned with the stability and growth in aggregate demand instead of demand for products in individual markets.

Fiscal policy is limited in two basic ways. First, it is not designed to and cannot cope with problems that call for fundamental or structural adjustments in the economy such as real scarcities in food and energy. Second, there are operational limitations to fiscal policy resulting from the problem of predicting the future course of economic events and the influence of the political environment in which policy is determined. Three operational problems can be identified: the problem of *timing* (the appropriate time to take action), the problem of *magnitudes* (how much action to take), and the problem of *lags* (the time that lapses before a problem is recognized, before actions are taken, and before actions have their effects).

Three alternative fiscal theories have been developed over time. They are: (1) a managed compensatory fiscal policy, (2) an automatic fiscal policy, (3) a fiscal policy for full employment and maximum growth. A managed compensatory fiscal policy was championed by Alvin R. Hansen in the late 1940's. Hansen argued for the replacement of the rule of a balanced budget in every year with the rule of possibly balancing the budget over the business cycle. The thinking behind Hansen's argument was that cyclical fluctuations would be smoothed out by the government pursuing a budget surplus policy when the economy was expanding too fast, and pursuing a budget deficit policy when the economy was contracting. The effect of a surplus is to slow down the expansion; the impact of a deficit is to slow down the contraction. Thus, budget surpluses in good years and deficits in bad years would tend to stabilize aggregate demand and the economy over time.

An alternative to the above program is an automatic fiscal policy program. This would operate as follows. The rate of federal spending would be determined, first, based upon social priorities and society's demand for government goods and services. Second, tax rates would be set so that tax collections would be equal to government spending at a predetermined level of employment, say, 93 percent. After the rates of spending and taxing are determined, they would not be altered except over a long period of timedue to changes in society's demands. Under conditions of constant tax and spending rates, the federal budget would automatically show a surplus when the economy expanded above the predetermined level of 93 percent. Also, when the economy contracted below the 93 percent level of employment, budget deficits would automatically occur. These budget surpluses and deficits automatically arising out of cyclical fluctuations in the economy would tend to dampen the cycle and stabilize the economy.

A managed compensatory fiscal program and an automatic fiscal program are alike in an important way, and they differ in an important way. They are alike in that they both suggest replacing the traditional rule of balancing the budget in every year. They are different in that a managed compensatory fiscal program provides for discretionary decision making by the fiscal authorities in regard to the timing and magnitudes of the changes in rates of taxing and spending; while an automatic fiscal program relies completely on automatic changes in tax collections and expenditures.

The growth of the economy in the 1950's was below historical trends. As a result, a new fiscal policy evolved in the early 1960's, called by its supporters a fiscal policy for full employment and maximum growth. This policy was like the managed compensatory fiscal policy in that it was a discretionary policy; however, it placed much more emphasis on growth. The argument was that deficit federal spending is called for any time the economy is not operating at its full growth potential. Thus, budget deficit policies would be pursued even in years when the economy was expanding as long as the economy was still operating below full employment or its potential.

Our fiscal policy experiences are not impressive. This could be in part due to the fact that fiscal policy in practice has never been systematically pursued over any long-run period of time. Also the disappointing record could be merely reflecting the fundamental and operational limitations of fiscal policy.

Fiscal policy has to be given some credit for promoting growth in the economy during the first part of the 1960's. Several discretionary fiscal measures were taken to increase the pace of growth. First, private investment was encouraged by allowing a 7 percent investment tax credit (1962). Second, both consumer and investment spending were stimulated by tax cuts in 1964 and 1965. Third, guidelines were established that probably had some influence on keeping wage and price increases in major industries within the limits compatible with a stable growing economy. Underlying the 1961–1965 expansion, of course, was a strong private sector. The end result was a full employment economy by the beginning of 1966. This expansion was accomplished with little or no inflation—a fact which has become even more memorable in view of the high rates of inflation ever since. In the latter part of the 1960's, the primary problem was inflation. The appropriate fiscal policy was to increase tax rates and cut government spending. Instead, Congress paid little attention to the arguments in favor of increases in taxes, and government spending was increased, primarily due to the acceleration of the war in Viet Nam. Finally, by the time

Congress did enact a 10 percent surtax on personal and corporate income in 1968, inflationary forces were strong and difficult to combat. The failure of fiscal policy during the period was a failure to use it appropriately.

The economy experienced both rising prices and unemployment in 1970 and 1971. Confidence in monetary and fiscal policies to cope with these problems apparently was at a low point. In any event, wage and price controls were established in 1971. As a result, inflation was suppressed for awhile, but scarcities were not. Finally, wage and price controls broke down and were completely phased out in 1974. In the same year, the economy went into a serious recession and the rate of inflation exceeded 10 percent. Policy mistakes of the past, the energy crises, shortages of basic materials, erosion of the real consumer income by inflation, and slumps in the housing and auto markets were all contributing factors to the dismal state of the economy in 1974.

The recession ended in spring, 1975, and the economy began expanding in the fall. This expansion has continued to the present time (September, 1977). Fiscal policy has been one of gradualism. Tax cuts were passed by Congress to boost the economy in 1975 and 1976, and the Carter Administration proposed further tax cuts and expenditure increases in 1977. Although the predicted range of inflation (5–6 percent) and the predicted range of unemployment (6–7 percent) for 1977 are short of the goals of economic stabilization, they reflect a move in the right direction.

SUGGESTIONS FOR FURTHER READING

Blinder, A. S., and Solow, R. M., "Analytical Foundations of Fiscal Policy," in *The Economics of Public Finance,* eds., Blinder and others. Washington, D.C.: The Brookings Institution, 1974.

This is an excellent treatment of the major theoretical issues concerning fiscal theory and policy.

American Economic Association. Arthur Smithies and J. Keith Butters (eds.), *Readings in Fiscal Policy.* Homewood, Illinois: Richard D. Irwin, Inc., 1955.

This reference contains papers and articles that provide a background to comtemporary thinking on fiscal theory. Pages 405–450 are recommended for learning the thinking of most economists concerning fiscal policy in the early 1950s.

Charles E. McLure, Jr., "Fiscal Failure: Lessons of the Sixties," in *Economic Policy and Inflation In the Sixties,* Washington, D.C.: American Enterprise Institute for Public Policy Research, 1972.

Fiscal policy during the 1960s is critically examined.

*

SIXTEEN

THE FEDERAL DEBT AND ITS ECONOMIC IMPACT

The debt of the U.S. government arouses much interest and causes much discussion. Yet very few people know what is meant by the federal debt—what it consists of, who owes it, the reasons for its existing size, and what its consequences may be. This chapter is organized to first examine the historical absolute and relative growth in the federal debt. The second major topic deals with structural characteristics; namely, the types of federal securities outstanding and the ownership pattern. From this background of the debt's history and its features, we move into the subject area of debt management policy. The final part of the chapter analyzes the primary and secondary effects of the debt.

HISTORICAL PERSPECTIVE

In this historical overview, the growth pattern in the absolute size of the debt is first described. This is followed by relating the growth in the federal debt to growth in the nation's output, GNP, and to the growth in state and local debt.

PATTERNS OF GROWTH
IN THE FEDERAL DEBT

The federal debt outstanding was $644 billion at the end of fiscal year 1976 and could top $700 billion in fiscal year 1977. However, these facts have little meaning by themselves. They take on meaning if viewed within a historical framework of change and growth. By tracing the historical changes in the federal debt, two things can be accomplished: the evolutionary process of the debt can be clarified, and at the same time the debt can be analyzed from the perspective of specific dates.

Two behavior patterns of the federal debt have been outstanding since 1790. Until the 1930s, the federal debt displayed a series of significant rises followed by subsequent falls. Since the 1930s, the federal debt has shown an upward trend. As might be expected, the largest increases in the federal debt are typically associated with an emergency—a war or depression. During the Civil War, the federal debt exceeded $1 billion for the first time, reaching $2.75 billion by 1866. During World War I, the federal debt rose far above the Civil War high, reaching $25.5 billion in 1919. During the next decade, the federal debt was reduced to $16.9 billion, its size at the outbreak of the economic crisis in 1929. This date marks the end of the cyclical pattern.

The decade of the 1930s witnessed a new behavior pattern. During this decade and since, the total federal debt has shown mainly an upward trend rather than the fluctuations displayed in the past. There are important reasons for this new behavior. The economic depression of the 1930s necessitated deficit government spending, spurring growth in the debt of approximately $27 billion between June 20, 1929, and June 30, 1940. Then the debt grew tremendously during World War II as a result of the decision to finance over one half of World War II government expenditures by debt financing. By the end of June, 1946, the total federal debt was $269 billion.

There was talk of debt retirement at the end of World War II, and even some success, for the national debt was reduced to $252 billion in 1948. Reductions occurred again in 1951, 1956, and 1957. However, these reductions did not arrest the upward trend, and in the 1960s and 1970s the federal debt continued to grow.

Among the various reasons which exist for the historical growth in the federal debt, the two most important ones are wars and recessionary conditions in the economy. As mentioned above, World Wars I and II and the Great Depression accounted for a major share of the increases in the federal debt. This tendency was repeated in the 1950s and 1960s due to the Korean

War and two recessions in the 1950s, the Viet Nam War in the 1960s, and the fact that the economy was recovering from a recession in the first part of the latter decade. More recently, large increases in the federal debt have been associated with the 1973–75 recession and its aftermath.

FEDERAL, STATE, AND LOCAL GOVERNMENT DEBT

Total government debt was approximately $881.4 billion at the end of fiscal year 1976 (Table 16-1). State and local government debt represented 28.1%, while federal government debt represented the remaining 71.9%. Since 1949, the size of state and local debt has displayed growth similar to that of the federal debt. However, the growth in state and local debt is associated more closely with the long-term capital expansion needs of these governments than with wars and cyclical fluctuations in the economy.

It is more meaningful, however, to relate the growth in federal, state, and local debt to the growth in the economy. As a percent of the GNP, total government debt declined rapidly during the decade of the 1950s and continued to decline until 1974 (Figure 16-1). During the decade of the 1950s, the decline was due to federal debt falling relative to the GNP. State and local debt grew relative to the GNP during this period. In the 1960s, the decline in total government debt as a percent of GNP was again due to the relative decline of federal debt, as the ratio of state debt to GNP crept upward while local debt remained a stable percent of GNP. The debt of all three levels of government has remained a fairly constant percent of GNP in the 1970s. Federal debt was 39.8% of GNP in 1970, declined to 35.8% in 1974, and returned to 39.8% in 1976. As a percent of GNP, state and local debt has been extremely stable in the 1970s, with state debt fluctuating between 4.4 and 5%, and local debt fluctuating between 10.4 and 10.9%.

STRUCTURAL FEATURES OF THE FEDERAL DEBT

The federal debt discussed thus far is also called the gross public debt. It includes all federal securities outstanding: interest-bearing and non-interest securities held by governmental agencies and trust funds, the non-banking public, the Federal Reserve Banks, and commercial banks. The

FIGURE 16–1
IN RELATION TO GROSS NATIONAL PRODUCT, TOTAL GOVERNMENT
DEBT HAS REMAINED FAIRLY CONSTANT IN RECENT YEARS

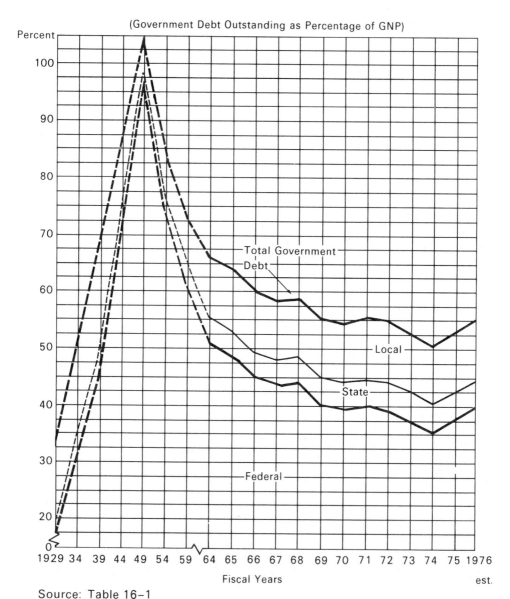

(Government Debt Outstanding as Percentage of GNP)

Source: Table 16–1

TABLE 16-1   GROSS FEDERAL DEBT, STATE DEBT, AND LOCAL DEBT,
1929–1976
(Government Debt Outstanding at End of Year)

Fiscal Year	Gross Federal Debt	Total State Debt	Total Local Debt	Gross Federal Debt	Total State Debt	Total Local Debt
	Amount (in Billions)			As a Percent of GNP		
1929	$ 16.9	$ 2.3	$ 14.2	16.9	2.3	14.2
1939	40.4	3.5	16.6	46.1	4.0	18.9
1949	252.8	4.0	16.9	96.6	1.5	6.5
1954	270.8	9.6	29.3	74.5	2.6	8.1
1959	284.7	16.9	47.2	60.4	3.6	10.0
1964	316.8	25.0	67.2	51.4	4.1	10.9
1969	367.1[1]	39.6	94.0	40.6	4.4	10.4
1970	382.6[2]	42.0	101.6	39.8	4.4	10.6
1971	409.5	47.8	111.0	40.2	4.7	10.9
1972	437.3	54.5	120.7	39.3	4.9	10.9
1973	468.4[3]	59.4	129.1	37.8	4.8	10.4
1974	486.2	65.3	141.3	35.8	4.8	10.4
1975	544.1	72.0 est.	155.5 est.	37.8	5.0	10.8
1976	633.9	78.5	169.0	39.8	4.9	10.6

SOURCE: Advisory Commission on Intergovernmental Relations, *Significant Features of Fiscal Federalism* (Washington, D.C., June 1976), p. 63.

NOTES:

[1]During 1969, three government-sponsored enterprises became completely privately owned, and their debt removed from the totals for the Federal government. At the dates of their conversion, gross Federal debt was reduced $10.7 billion.

[2]Gross Federal debt was increased $1.6 billion due to a reclassification of the Commodity Credit Corporation certificates of interest from asset sales to debt.

[3]A procedural change in the recording of trust fund holdings of Treasury debt at the end of the month increased gross Federal debt by about $4.5 billion.

major types of issues are marketable, non-marketable, and special issues (Table 16-2). Marketable issues are bought and sold in the market by investors. The prices of marketable securities are determined by forces operating on the demand for and supply of securities. Non-marketable securities are non-negotiable debt instruments and cannot be exchanged in the market. They may, however, be redeemed in cash or converted into another issue. Special issues are federal securities sold only to the various government trust funds and agencies.

TABLE 16–2   GROSS FEDERAL DEBT BY TYPE OF SECURITY
(November, 1976)

Type of Security	$ Billions		Percent of Gross Federal Debt
Gross Federal Debt		644.6	100.0
Marketable Debt		415.4	64.4
Bills	161.7		25.1
Notes	213.0		33.0
Bonds	40.7		6.3
Nonmarketable Debt		99.3	15.4
Foreign Issues	22.5		3.5
Savings Bonds & Notes	71.9		11.1
Other[1]	4.9		0.8
Special Issues		126.7	19.7
Other[2]		3.2	.5

SOURCE: *Federal Reserve Bulletin* (Washington, D.C., Board of Governors of the Federal Reserve System, December 1976), p. A34.

NOTES:

[1] Includes depository bonds, retirement plan bonds, Rural Electrification Administration bonds, state and local government bonds, and Treasury deposit funds.

[2] Includes convertible bonds and non-interest-bearing debt.

MARKETABLE FEDERAL ISSUES

Three decades ago, the federal debt consisted almost completely of marketable debt. Since the 1930s, however, marketable federal debt as a percent of the total federal debt has decreased in relative importance (to 64% in November, 1976). This decrease has been due to the growth of non-marketable debt and special issues to meet the needs of government trust funds.

The three major types of marketable issues now outstanding are: treasury bills that are regularly offered with 3-month and 6-month maturity dates but cannot exceed 1 year to maturity; treasury notes that mature between 1 to 10 years; and treasury bonds that mature in more than 7 years. Treasury bills are normally classified as short-term securities, treasury notes as immediate-term securities, and treasury bonds as long-term securities.

Though treasury bills, notes, and bonds differ essentially in the length of the borrowing period, they may differ in other ways as well.[1] First, certain issues may be sold at a discount rather than at fixed interest rates. Second, interest rates vary on issues with different maturity dates. Third, statutory interest rate limitations are imposed on some issues. Fourth, some government securities may be redeemed before maturity. Fifth, certain issues can be used to make tax payments. Sixth, some securities may be reserved for particular buyers. Seventh, there are differences in how ownership of marketable government securities may be transferred; and finally, interest payment dates may also vary.

Method of Sale

The main method of selling marketable securities today is the *auction*. Treasury bills are auctioned off on a discount basis with the face or par amount payable at maturity. The interest on bills is in the form of the difference between the price paid and the par value. The way the auction works is as follows. Bidders in the auction state the quantity of bills they desire and the price they are willing to pay. Prices are stated on the bases of 100, with no more than three decimals, such as 98.039. The annual rate of return associated with the price can be calculated in the following manner:

$$\frac{Par - Price}{Par} \text{ X } \frac{360}{\text{Number of days to maturity.}}$$

For example, a 180-day bill priced at 98.039 would provide an annual rate of return of 3.9%:

$$\frac{100 - 98.039}{100} \text{ X } \frac{360}{180} = .03922 \text{ or } 3.9\%.$$

Two auction methods have been used in recent years to sell treasury notes and bonds—the *price* auction and the *yield* auction. Beginning in

---

1. Helen J. Cooke, "Marketable Issues of the United States Treasury," *The Treasury and the Money Market* (Federal Reserve Bank of New York, May, 1954), p. 25; Margaret E. Bedford, "Recent Developments In Treasury Financing Techniques," *Monthly Review* (Federal Reserve Bonds of Kansas City, July–August 1977), p. 12. This section heavily relies on these references.

1970, notes and bonds were sold on a price auction basis, at a fixed coupon rate—the rate associated with the price at par. Since competitive bids reflect the relative attractiveness of the coupon rate, bids are offered above par, at par and below par. Thus, bids above par indicate an effective rate above the coupon rate; bids at par indicate an effective rate equal to the coupon rate; and bids below par indicate an effective rate below the coupon rate.

Since its introduction in 1974, the yield auction has become the main method used to sell notes and bonds. Instead of setting the coupon rate, as in the case of the price auction, the coupon rate is determined in the market. After the Treasury announces the amount to be sold, competitive bids are made to two decimal places, for example, 6.45%. After the auction closes, the Treasury accepts bids starting with the bids with the lowest yields.

Interest Rates

Interest rates on marketable issues basically depend on the forces operating behind the demand for and supply of securities. The government cannot raise $100 for 3% interest when the market rate is 4% for bonds of similar risk. The actual market rate on comparable securities determines what the government must pay to borrow money.

Actually, there is no such thing as *an* interest rate for government securities. Rather, there is a structure or pattern of rates, determined by differences in certain security characteristics. Usually, short-term securities can be offered at lower rates than long-term securities since the chance of significant fluctuation in market price diminishes as the loan period shortens. The spread between short and long issues may be quite narrow, however, as a reflection of supply and demand conditions for short- and long-term money. Conditions may even exist in which short-term rates are above long-term rates.

The government enters the money and capital markets just as any private borrower does. The government is confronted with a market demand and competing borrowers. If the government is to sell its securities, it must offer better terms, including lower prices. Usually, the Treasury has to compete for loanable funds through competitive bids. Government authorities may lower the cost of borrowing by decreasing the market rate of interest through increases in the supply of money, or it may require by law that specified institutions hold additional reserves in the form of government securities, thereby coercing an increase in demand. However, if the authorities do not resort to coercion and/or inflationary practices, they must pay the market-determined price.

NONMARKETABLE FEDERAL ISSUES

Non-marketable or non-negotiable federal issues were offered for the first time in 1935, grew to significance during World War II, and have remained so since. However, since the early 1950s, non-marketable federal issues have declined in relative importance. These issues comprised 15% of the federal debt outstanding in 1976 as compared to 33% in 1951. The primary types of non-marketable government securities are savings bonds, investment bonds, and foreign issues.

Savings Bonds

The most important type of non-marketable government security is the U.S. savings bond. Savings bonds generally have been issued in order to attract the current saving of the public, and they have been fairly successful. These issues are offered at slightly higher yields than comparable maturing marketable bonds, are redeemable in cash after specified short periods, and are protected against losses from security price declines because the redemption price is based on a fixed schedule.[2]

Savings bonds are designated by series; for example, series E, H, J, and K. These series may differ in a number of ways, such as the way interest is paid, the size of the interest rate, restrictions on purchase, date of maturity, and length of time the bond must be held before redemption. The familiar series E savings bonds, purchased on a large scale during World War II, may serve as an example. This bond was offered at a discount ($18.75), and at maturity (ten years) would pay the owner $25.00. While series E bonds could be redeemed at any time before maturity, the redemption value of the bond was based on a rising interest schedule in order to discourage early redemption. The interest paid was approximately 3% if held to maturity, although it was possible to extend the period of maturity for another ten years and earn a higher interest rate.

---

2. Helen J. Cooke, "Cash Borrowing of the United States Treasury: Non-marketable Issues," *The Treasury and The Money Market* (Federal Reserve Bank of New York, May, 1954), p. 16.

The redeemable feature of savings bonds makes them nearly as liquid as money. Series E bonds are redeemable two months after the issue date, whereas other savings bonds may be converted into cash after only six months. This high-liquidity feature of savings bonds posed some difficulty after World War II when individuals redeemed them in order to pay for consumption that had been postponed during the war.

Investment Bonds

Two series of investment bonds, A and B, have been sold. Series A bonds sold at 2.5% when offered in 1947. They were attractive to institutional investors because they were redeemable. Generally, they were offered to mitigate upward pressures on long-term government security prices. Series B investment bonds were offered for 2.75% in April, 1951. They were not redeemable into cash, as were series A bonds, but they were convertible into five-year marketable treasury notes. Investment bonds outstanding have declined steadily, and they now comprise less than 1% of the outstanding debt.

Foreign Issues

Foreign issues are non-marketable certificates of indebtedness, notes, and bonds in the Treasury foreign series and foreign currency series issues. These issues have increased in the 1970s. In December of 1969, foreign issues represented 1% of the gross federal debt. Today (November, 1976) they represent 3.5%. Although a small percent of the total federal debt, federal issues comprise 22.6% of the non-marketable debt.

SPECIAL GOVERNMENT ISSUES

The Treasury offers securities called "special issues" directly to the so-called U.S. government investment accounts, which are trust funds operated by the federal government. There are twelve trust funds, the more important of which are the federal old age and survivors insurance trust fund, the federal employees' retirement fund, the national service life insurance fund, the unemployment compensation fund, the railroad retirement fund, and the federal disability insurance fund. The reserves of these funds consist largely of U.S. government securities.

Special government issues represented approximately 19.7% of the gross federal debt outstanding in November, 1976. Changes in special issues reflect mainly the receipts and expenditures of the trust funds. An excess of trust funds receipts over expenditures is used to acquire government securities; an excess of expenditures over receipts is financed by selling government securities. The economic impact of these funds depends on what the government does with the money received when it runs a surplus and where the government gets the money when it incurs a deficit. For example, the effect of a trust fund surplus is contractionary by itself, but if the government exchanges special issues for this surplus and spends the proceeds so obtained the overall effect may not be contractionary. The effect of a trust fund deficit is normally expansionary, but if the government decreases spending in other directions, increases taxes, or creates new debt in order to cover this deficit the overall effect may not be expansionary.

THE OWNERSHIP PATTERN OF THE FEDERAL DEBT

The gross federal debt is held by U.S. Government agencies, trust funds, and Federal Reserve Banks, and by private institutions and individuals. In September, 1976, the government-held component accounted for $242.5 billion, or 38.2% of the gross federal debt (Table 16-3). The remainder of the debt was held by private investors ($392.2 billion, or 61.8%).

Some economists believe that the debt held by government agencies is "fictitious debt" and should be excluded from the total. As mentioned above, government securities held by government agencies and trust funds are special issues distributed directly to these accounts—usually when tax surpluses arise. Federal securities held by Federal Reserve Banks are the result of open market operations designed to control the availability of money and credit in the economy. Generally, changes in federal securities held by Federal Reserve Banks will be reflected in opposite changes in federal securities held by the private sector.

"Private" investors include commercial banks, mutual savings banks, insurance companies, other corporations, state and local governments, individuals, foreign investors, and other investors. These investors acquire and hold federal securities for a variety of reasons, not the least of which is that these securities are a low-risk, income-yielding asset.

TABLE 16-3   GROSS FEDERAL DEBT BY OWNERSHIP
(September, 1976)

	$ Billions	Percent of Gross Federal Debt
Gross Federal Debt	634.7	100.0
Held by Government:	242.5	38.2
U.S. Govt. Agencies and Trusts	146.1	23.0
Federal Reserve Bonds	96.4	15.2
Held by Private Investors	392.2	61.8
Commercial Banks	93.3	14.7
Mutual Savings Banks	5.3	0.8
Insurance Companies	11.6	1.8
Other Corporations	25.7	4.0
State & Local Governments	39.1	6.2
Individuals	99.7	15.7
Foreign and International	74.6	11.8
Other[1]	42.9	6.8

SOURCE: *Federal Reserve Bulletin* (Washington, D.C.: Board of Governors of the Federal Reserve System, December 1976), p. A34.

[1]Consists of savings and loan associations, nonprofit institutions, corporate pensions trust funds, and dealers and brokers.

THE MATURITY DISTRIBUTION OF MARKETABLE SECURITIES

Most of the federal debt is concentrated at the short end of the market; that is, most of the debt is in the form of treasury bills and notes. Approximately one-half of the marketable federal debt matures within one year (Table 16-4). Another 31.3% matures in one to five years. Only 17.6% of the marketable debt is in the form of long-term debt that matures in five or more years.

This concentration of the federal debt at the short end of the market means that the U.S. Treasury frequently enters the market to refund or refinance the debt. A debt of a given size with a longer maturity distribution would probably result in better planning and allow for smoother debt management operations. Also, a debt consisting largely of short-term securities may make it more difficult for the Federal Reserve to control inflation because of its high liquidity. However, the official Treasury ob-

TABLE 16-4   PERCENT DISTRIBUTION OF MARKETABLE SECURITIES BY
MATURITY AND BY TYPE OF HOLDER, OCTOBER 31, 1976

Type of Holder	Within 1 Year	1–5 Years	5–10 Years	10–20 Years	Over 20 Years
	(Percent of Total Held)				
All Holders	50.8	31.3	11.4	3.2	3.2
Held by Government	46.7	32.2	11.2	4.7	5.2
Held by Private Investors	52.4	31.0	11.5	2.7	2.5

SOURCE: *Federal Reserve Bulletin* (Washington, D.C.: Board of Governors of the Federal Reserve System, December, 1976), p. 435.

jective to lengthen the maturity structure of the federal debt has fallen well short of the mark.

THE FEDERAL DEBT MANAGEMENT POLICY

Federal debt management policy is not in the limelight as much as are fiscal and monetary policies, yet it is closely related to both. This section of the chapter examines the meaning, significance, and principles of this type of policy.

DEBT MANAGEMENT DEFINED

Federal debt management should be clearly distinguished from fiscal and monetary policy. Fiscal policy involves government spending, taxing, and borrowing to achieve the goals of economic stability. Monetary policy is exercised by regulating the flow and cost of money and credit. Debt management operates within the environment established by fiscal and monetary policy but is not strictly a part of either. Debt management takes as "given" the size of the debt and the general conditions prevailing in the money market.[3] The purpose of debt management is to establish the terms on which new federal issues are sold and maturing issues are refinanced. Federal debt management refers, then, to the decisions concerning the types of issues offered, the proportionate amounts of each, the pattern of

---

3. Henry C. Murphy, "Debt Management," *Fiscal Policies and the American Economy,* Ed., Kenyon E. Poole (New York: Prentice-Hall, Inc. 1951), p. 159.

maturities, the pattern of ownership, and the determination of all the other general characteristics of the federal debt, such as the conditions on which certain issues are redeemable, callable, or usable for tax purposes, and other special provisions between the government and lender.

THE SIGNIFICANCE OF DEBT MANAGEMENT

The significance of federal debt management stems from two sources: the economic impact which the federal debt has on the economy, and the interrelatedness of debt management policy with fiscal and monetary policies. Economic repercussions take place when changes in the size of the debt or in its basic characteristics occur, such as changes in the maturity distribution and pattern of ownership of the debt.

Because debt management policy does not *directly* produce changes in the size and relative flow of government spending and taxes, or changes in the money supply, the argument has been advanced that debt management policy is not as important as are fiscal and monetary policies. This may be true. However, debt policy may have repercussions on fiscal and monetary policies. Changes in the pattern of maturities and ownership which affect the rate of interest offered on both new and maturing federal issues may have economic effects which either offset or strengthen the policy pursued by fiscal and monetary authorities.

PRINCIPLES OF DEBT POLICY

Economic Stability and Growth

The first and perhaps foremost task of debt management is to further the attainment of economic stability and growth. This means that federal debt policy should be effectively coordinated with fiscal and monetary policy. Policy goals of the U.S. Treasury, such as that of minimizing interest payments on the debt, should be abandoned if they create a conflict between debt policy and monetary policy. Such a conflict arose after World War II, when monetary policy was subservient to a low-interest federal debt policy. The result was a serious inflation which might have been avoided.

Two prevailing views concern the role of debt policy in the national program of economic stability and growth. The first view ascribes a positive role to federal debt policy, along with fiscal and monetary policy, in directing the economy. The terms of new issues, refinancing, and retirement, as well as other management variables, would be guided by the objectives of growth and stability.

The second view gives federal debt policy a neutral role. Federal debt policy per se would attempt to neither directly encourage nor discourage stability and growth. This achievement is to be left up to competitive forces, supplemented by the orderly direction of fiscal and monetary policy. The task of debt policy is to carry out the managing of the debt with as little influence on the economy as possible, and without interfering with the objectives of fiscal and monetary policy.

It is unlikely that federal debt operations will ever be neutral in their economic effects. It is possible, however, for the Treasury to borrow the necessary funds in such a way that debt operations are largely consistent with the general aims of fiscal and monetary policy. During periods of full employment, government borrowing from non-bank sources is preferable to borrowing from bank sources, since the latter type of borrowing is likely to increase the money supply. Shortening the federal debt maturity structure tends to increase the liquidity of the federal debt, which may be advantageous during periods of recession and unemployment. Under some circumstances, a largely neutral federal debt policy may call for no basic changes in the structural characteristics of the federal debt.

Needs of Investors

A second principle of federal debt management involves the selection of the type of government security and the arrangement of the terms of exchange between government and lender so that the needs of investors are best satisfied. If this objective was achieved, the degree of investor satisfaction from a given size federal debt would be maximized. By bargaining with each class of investor, the government may secure certain advantages in exchange for supplying securities which are demanded.

In any voluntary exchange transaction, both parties in the exchange mutually benefit; otherwise, the exchange does not take place. Short of coercion, the government will experience difficulties in managing the federal debt unless attention is paid to the needs of investors. Suppose that an equilibrium exists with the present federal debt structure (the degree of investor satisfaction is maximized) and the government wishes to lengthen the average maturity of the debt. This could be done only if terms on long-term securities are made more attractive. Further assume that to carry out the selling operation the government pays higher interest while all other terms remain the same. This means, then, that the same size federal debt can be serviced only with higher costs (taxes). If the interest rate is kept the same, the funding operation may be possible only if the government improves other terms of the exchange. The Treasury has to recognize to some extent the needs of the market in framing debt policy. If the pattern of debt ownership, the type of federal issues, and the pattern of federal debt maturities do not conform fairly closely to what is needed, fluctuations will occur in the securities market until equilibrium is reached.

Minimizing Interest Cost

Another principle of federal debt policy often advocated is that of keeping the total interest on the debt as low as possible. Interest payments on the debt are financed from tax revenue, and keeping these payments as low as possible minimizes tax collections. Assuming that this principle may be followed without jeopardizing the other principles of debt management, minimizing the costs of servicing the debt is desirable.

In many instances, a policy of minimizing interest payments conflicts with the objectives of fiscal and monetary policy. To minimize interest costs, long-term securities should be issued during periods of low interest rates, and short-term securities issued during period of high interest rates. This policy is likely to have a destabilizing effect on the economy. Low interest rates usually prevail during periods of low production levels and high unemployment. The issue of a substantial quantity of long-term securities when the economy is already depressed tends to increase long-term rates and discourage private investment at a time when fiscal and monetary actions are designed to promote expansion. Conversely, the issue of short-term securities when the economy is expanding reduces the demand for long-term funds, thereby reducing the long-term rate at a time when a high rate may be required to stabilize the economy. A minimum-cost federal debt policy cannot be defended if by pursuing such a policy inflation is promoted when the economy is in an inflation, and recessionary forces are strengthened when the economy is in a recession.

Reducing the Liquidity of the Federal Debt

It has been official policy for some time to reduce the concentration of the federal debt at the short end of the market by converting or funding the short-term debt into long-term debt. Obviously, this goal of funding has not actually guided federal debt policy, for the average maturity of the debt has decreased. It appears that this principle of debt management is not considered to be as important as others.

Many economists favor reducing the liquidity of the federal debt. An outstanding spokesman for this viewpoint was Henry C. Simons, who suggested converting into very long-term securities or consols (government securities which have no maturity dates) as much of the short-term debt, when it comes due, as is consistent with the objectives of economic stability.[4] Such a policy, if successful, would certainly relieve many problems now associated with managing the federal debt. However, the economic impact of such an operation would tend to exert strong upward pressures on long-term rates of interest and downward pressures on short-term rates, since the demand for long-term funds will increase and the demand for short-term funds will decrease.

Three limitations may be placed on the amount of short-term debt that can be funded. The first two concern the responses of private investors to an increase in the long-term rate of interest and the possible effects that changes in the short- and long-term rates of interest may have on the U.S. international balance of payments. Funding would have to stop before increases in the long-term rate of interest significantly discouraged the rate of private investment. Otherwise, unemployment would rise. In addition, a fall in short-term money rates in the U.S. that encouraged a movement of short-term funds and gold away from the U.S. to other financial centers should be avoided.

The third limitation to the lengthening of the maturity structure of the federal debt is the disequilibrium which may occur if recognition is not given to the needs of investors. The argument already has been advanced that if maximum investor satisfaction is desirable, government debt forms and terms will correspond to the needs of investors. Given the right terms of sale even normally short-term investors may hold long-term debt, but the government may not be willing to meet these terms. Certain investors are looking for an interest-yielding, highly liquid debt, and the marginal preference may be for holding money before holding long-term debt.

---

4. Henry C. Simons, "On Debt Policy," *AEA Readings in Fiscal Policy,* eds. Arthur Smithies and J. Keith Butters (Homewood, Illinois: Richard E. Irwin, Inc., 1955), pp. 223–32.

THE ECONOMIC IMPACT
OF THE FEDERAL DEBT

The subsequent discussion is divided into two parts. The first part examines the *primary impact or burden* of the federal debt. In dealing with the primary impact, two time periods are considered—the present when the debt is incurred, and the future when the debt is serviced. Also, in the discussion of the primary impact, an internally-held debt is distinguished from an externally-held debt. The second part of the discussion is concerned with the *secondary effects* of debt; that is, its impact on production, distribution, and prices.

PRIMARY IMPACT

The primary impact or burden of the federal debt has provoked much discussion among economists. The beginning point of much of this discussion is the difference between federal debt that is internally or externally held.

An External Federal Debt

External debt is that which is held by foreign institutions and individuals. When such debt is created, the debtor country has foreign currency claims against goods and services produced in the creditor country. Thus, foreign goods and services can be purchased without giving up domestically produced goods and services. Because the primary burden is normally defined as the value of goods and services sacrificed because of the debt, there is no burden in the present on the debtor country. In the future, however, the debtor nation has to divert some of its domestic production to service the debt; that is, to meet interest and principle payments. Thus, there is a future primary burden of an external federal debt in the form of a sacrifice in domestic production.

External Federal Debt vs. Private Debt

An external federal debt is similar to private debt in regard to the primary burden. When private institutions and individuals incur debt, they receive money claims over goods and services without a current sacrifice; that is, without giving up presently available goods and services. However, in the future, private debtors will have to give up real income in order to service their debts. The primary burden of private debt, then, is shifted to the future, just like an external federal debt.

An Internal Federal Debt

The major part of the federal debt is held internally; that is, by institutions and individuals in the U.S. Under these circumstances, the analogy between federal and private debt does not hold. The reason for this is that an internal federal debt can be serviced without an aggregate sacrifice in production or real income. It is true that taxes must be raised in the future to meet the interest changes on the debt. But since the debt is held internally, it is serviced through an internal tax-interest payment process. This process does not directly affect the *level* of total production in the economy. Of course, there is a transfer of purchasing power from taxpayers to bondholders, and this transfer may alter the *distribution* of income. However, the effect of debt servicing on the distribution of income is not usually considered a primary burden but a secondary effect. After dealing with two questions often raised by the public concerning the federal debt, these secondary effects will be examined.

Can Debt Financing Lead to Bankruptcy?

This question is often raised in public discussion and debate, and many people apparently believe that federal debt financing *can* lead to bankruptcy. Their reasoning is based primarily—and erroneously—on an analogy between private debt and federal debt. Individuals and businesses can go bankrupt if they cannot meet the claims of their creditors. The federal government, on the other hand, can for all practical purposes always meet the claims of internal creditors by raising taxes or by creating money to pay them. The important difference between the federal government and private debtors is this: the federal government has the power to tax and to create money while private debtors do not. Although it could be imagined that the federal government could use its powers to create debt, to tax, and to create money in such a way that could result in serious adverse effects on the economy, the possibility of the federal government going bankrupt in any legal sense is so remote that it is not a major concern among economists.

Can Real Costs Be Shifted to the Future?

The possibility of shifting the primary burden or real costs of federal debt financing to the future has been discussed already. However, the issue is raised again because the view held by the public and supported by some economists is that federal debt financing results in the present generation passing the primary burden of the debt to future generations. James M. Buchanan is the primary proponent of the view that the primary burden of debt financing is shifted to the future. Buchanan's reasoning is along the following lines.[5] If a burden exists when federal debt is created, it must be on the private lender who has parted with funds in order to purchase government debt. However, the private lender has not suffered a burden in an economic sense, but has only looked at alternative costs and come to the rational decision of preferring, at the margin, government securities. Hence, resources—or claims on resources—are transferred to the government without a burden or sacrifice.

Buchanan further argues that in the future when the debt is serviced, a burden exists in the form of a claim on the taxpayer's income, and that this claim cannot be offset by the interest income of government bondholders. The interest income of private lenders would be the same in the absence of government debt, since private lenders would have bought private debt instead of government debt. It is assumed here that the interest rate is unaffected by the government debt and that the economy is at full employment.

Buchanan takes an individualistic approach to the primary burden question, which has the advantage of not obscuring the alternatives of bondholders and not permitting a net offsetting of individual costs and benefits when the debt is serviced. As Buchanan points out, there are individual costs and benefits in the future which should not be completely ignored and which should, perhaps, be treated as a byproduct or a secondary effect of the debt.

Buchanan's arguments have not in general altered the thinking of most economists concerning the real costs or the primary burden of debt financing. The real costs of increasing federal spending are still viewed by most economists as sacrifices or decreases in private production. During periods of full employment, these costs are equal to the value of private goods and services that could have been produced by the resources used in the federal

---

5. James M. Buchanan, *Principles of Public Debt* (Homewood, Illinois: Richard D. Irwin, Inc., 1958), pp. 48–63.

sector. In periods of war, the real costs of tax and debt financing occur in the present in the form of losses in human lives, as well as losses in civilian goods and services. During periods of unemployment, the real costs of tax and debt financing are again in the present; however, these costs may be low depending upon the level of unemployment and the sacrifice in private production that takes place. In summary, aggregate real costs of increased federal activity cannot generally be shifted to the future. They are borne at the time during which the increase in federal spending takes place. The method used to finance the increase does not alter this conclusion.

SECONDARY EFFECTS

The economic significance of the federal debt lies in its secondary effects; that is, its impact on real output, the distribution of income, and prices.

Reduction in Real Output

Financing and servicing the debt may possibly reduce private investment. When federal debt is incurred, private investment may be reduced due to the higher rate of interest caused by government borrowing. If debt financing results in a decline in private investment, the capacity of the economy to produce goods and services will be less in the future and, as a result, production and income may decline. In addition, the mere presence of a large debt coupled with high interest costs may adversely affect private investment through its psychological effect on the business community. Finally, taxes raised to service the debt may shift the investment schedule downward, resulting in decreases in income and employment.

Redistribution of Income

The redistribution-of-income effects of servicing the federal debt depend on the nature of the tax system and the distribution of bond ownership. Assume that both the tax system and the distribution of bond ownership are progressive; i.e., the amount of taxes (bonds) as a proportion of income rises as income rises. If the degree of progression is the same for taxes and bond ownership, then servicing the debt will not change the distribution of income. However, the federal tax system is probably not as progressive as is the distribution of ownership of government securities. Considering the legal tax exemption opportunities on fairly high income, it seems probable that the net effect of servicing the federal debt is to redistribute income from high-consumption groups to high-saving groups. If this is true, a lower proportion of income is spent on consumption and a higher proportion is saved. This means that a higher rate of investment is necessary to maintain the equilibrium level of income. If the larger flow of saving is not directed into new real capital formation, the redistribution effects of servicing the public debt are deflationary.

Inflationary Effects

Inflationary effects may result from the debt if the supply of money was increased when it was created. Indeed, some inflationary potential resides in government securities by virtue of their high liquidity. Government borrowing from the banking system is typically accompanied by an increase in the supply of money. Under some circumstances, the increase in money will exceed the increase in goods and services available. The outcome is a fall in the value of money relative to the value of goods and services, or a rise in the value of goods and services relative to that of money. The commodity in excess supply falls in value relative to the value of other things, whether money or goods. Hence, when a rise in the money supply parallels a rise in government debt, inflationary pressures rise.

The mere existence of federal debt may foster inflationary pressures by increasing the propensity to spend of those bond-holders to whom debt is a highly liquid asset. This occurs because the debt serves as a substitute for savings out of current income. Commercial banks may also have a greater tendency to lend, since government securities are an important part of a bank's secondary reserves.

The Efficacy of Monetary Policy

The ability of monetary policy to control inflation may be lessened by the ownership of the government debt. This is especially true because the debt is predominately short-term, and serves therefore as a source of funds on the basis of which bank loans and deposits can be expanded. The public may also add to the spending stream by selling bonds to the Treasury, as can be done with series E savings bonds, or by selling securities in the marketplace, in order to acquire money for expenditures on goods and services. If monetary policy becomes subservient to debt policy, as occurred after World War II, and monetary authorities support government bonds prices at par, then government debt is the same as money to the owners and control over spending in the economy is significantly reduced.

SUMMARY

The historical growth in the gross federal debt is closely connected with wars and recessions. Since World War II, the federal debt has not grown as fast as state and local debt or the GNP. The 1973–75 recession arrested the decline in the federal debt as a percent of the GNP. However, the ratio of the federal debt to GNP was the same in 1976 (39.8 percent) as it was in 1970.

Federal debt management is concerned with the structural features of the debt outstanding, such as the kinds of federal issues, the ownership pattern, and the maturity distribution of the debt. Although probably not as important as fiscal and monetary policies, federal debt management policy has to be coordinated with fiscal and monetary policies; for, the foremost task of all three types of policy is to further the attainment of economic stability and growth.

The discussion of the economic impact of the federal debt was divided into two parts: the primary impact or burden of the debt, and the secondary effects. In the discussion of the primary burden of the federal debt, an internally held debt was distinguished from an external debt. The primary burden of the former is in the present in the form of a sacrifice in private goods and services. The primary burden of an externally held debt occurs in the future; for the sacrifice in domestic production takes place in the future when the debtor nation has to export more than it imports in order to service the external debt. Although many people apparently believe that the primary burden of an internally held debt can be shifted to future generations, the real costs of debt financing cannot be shifted.

The secondary effects of the federal debt are concerned with the impact of the debt on the operation of the economy. Financing and servicing the debt may reduce real private output. Government borrowing may increase the rate of interest and discourage private investment. The distribution of income may be altered by the federal debt. Which way the distribution of income will be altered when the debt is serviced depends upon the incidence of the tax system and the distribution of bond ownership. Finally, a large debt outstanding tends to be inflationary; that is, the tendency to spend may be greater as a result of people holding highly liquid federal securities. The ability of monetary policy to control inflation may also be reduced due to large holdings of federal securities.

SUGGESTIONS FOR FURTHER READING

Laird, W. P., "The Changing Views on Debt Management," *Quarterly Review of Economics and Business,* (Autumn, 1963), p. 7.

This article contains a thorough treatment of the various views of economists concerning debt management policy.

Buchanan, James M., *Principles of Public Debt,* Homewood, Illinois: Richard D. Irwin, Inc., 1958.

Buchanan challenges the conclusions of most economists in regard to the primary burden of federal debt financing. He argues that the primary burden of an internally held debt is shifted to further generations.

Mishan, E. J., "How to Make a Burden of the Public Debt," *The Journal of Political Economy* (December, 1963), p. 529.

Mishan critically examines the arguments of James M. Buchanan and others who argue that debt financing shifts the burden to future generations.

PART 5

FISCAL
FEDERALISM

*

SEVENTEEN

PRINCIPLES OF FISCAL FEDERALISM

Much of this book has been concerned with how public sector economic activities can be arranged to enable the nation to more closely achieve its economic goals. In this chapter, we explore an additional dimension of this problem: the assignment of particular functions or tasks to the government unit or units that can best perform them.

Governmental services in the United States are not provided by a single, central government. Rather, they are provided by thousands of governmental units, ranging from the multi-purpose central government to the single-purpose special district, all of which are loosely tied together in a fiscal, as well as a political, federation. Our primary objective is to develop the principles by which the fiscal aspects of this structure should be organized.

To achieve this objective, it is necessary to determine the governmental structure that is best suited for performing the stabilization, distribution, and allocation functions. We will show that the stabilization and distribution functions can best be performed by the central government. However, lower level governments must play a critical role if we wish to achieve efficiency in the provision and financing of public goods and services.

THE STABILIZATION FUNCTION

The problem of aggregate stability has been analyzed in Chapters 13–16, which demonstrated that when a purely private economy failed to achieve full employment and a stable price level, fiscal and monetary tools could be employed to move us closer to these goals. It was implicitly assumed, but never rationalized, that the stabilization function should be performed by agencies related to the central government; chiefly, by those that control the money supply and the size and composition of the Federal budget. The reasons for this choice will now be explained.

MONETARY POLICY

Two primary types of money are used in the American economy: checking account balances (demand deposits) and currency outstanding (Federal Reserve Notes). The amount of the former can be closely controlled by the actions of the central banking (Federal Reserve System) authorities. The latter is a liability of the Federal Reserve Banks, although the central banking authorities have only a small amount of control over this type of money. However, inasmuch as demand deposits finance nearly 95% of all transactions, the money supply can be closely regulated by agencies related to the central government.

It was not always so. During many periods in our history, there was no central bank and private banks issued currency. Unfortunately, these periods were characterized by considerable instability in prices and employment. It is now widely acknowledged that the lack of a strong central bank contributed materially to this instability.

Without such an institution, the nation's currency was largely created through the various activities by which private banks acquired income-earning assets: chiefly, making loans and buying securities. Since private banks are in business to make a profit, there was an inducement to expand their portfolio of these assets by printing new currency. The inevitable result was frequent over-issue and rapid deterioration in the value of currency outstanding.

The banking system had a significant capacity, then, for generating inflation. Unfortunately, its operations also tended to intensify instability in employment. This was largely a consequence of the widespread use of correspondent banking.

This practice resulted in the deposit of large sums of money by outlying banks in the banks of the nation's financial centers, chiefly New York City and Chicago. During downturns in the economy, when withdrawals at outlying banks were increasing, the nation's largest banks would lose deposits rapidly because of the cumulative effort of the outlying banks to meet the demands of their customers. The all too frequent result was financial panic, rapidly declining investment, and a subsequent decline in total spending.

The lessons of history were relatively clear by 1913 when Congress instituted the Federal Reserve System. The nation needed a central bank to ensure better aggregate economic performance.

FISCAL POLICY

Although monetary policy is important, it is our position that it is not a sufficient means for achieving stability and that we must rely in many instances on the proper conduct of fiscal policy. There are, moreover, good reasons to believe that fiscal policy can be more efficient if conducted by the central government rather than by lower governmental units.

As indicated earlier, the government may be required to run a deficit as a means of achieving full employment. Often, this deficit must be financed by the sale of government bonds. As argued previously, there are no practical limitations on the debt that the central government creates in this fashion. However, state and local governments are severely constrained in issuing debt because a large portion of the debt of each unit is likely to be held by citizens who reside in other units.[1] Thus, when payments are made to these individuals, there is a transfer of real wealth out of the issuing jurisdiction (rather than the predominantly financial transfer within the jurisdiction that characterizes the sale of debt of the central government). State and local debt is likely to be a "burden," as we have previously defined it.

Deficit spending could not be relied upon to any appreciable extent at the state and local levels because these economies are too "open"; i.e., there are large flows of real and financial assets between areas. This feature of state and local economies would also reduce the impact of any fiscal policy conducted by the governments of these units. The chief reason for this is

---

1. In addition, state and local governments are often limited by law to a small amount of deficit spending financed by borrowing. Indeed, many lower governments must balance their budgets annually.

that each unit imports a large proportion of the goods and services consumed by its citizenry. Under these circumstances, much of the spending initiated, for example, by expansionary fiscal policy would be for imports. Therefore, the change in income (in the unit) resulting from a change in government expenditures—the state or local fiscal multiplier, as it were—would be relatively small.

This does not mean, of course, that state and local fiscal policy would have *no* effect on national economic stability. Indeed, it can and has. During the depression of the 1930s, for example, almost half of the federal budget deficits were offset by reduced expenditures of lower governments. State and local fiscal policy, then, can affect the national economy, but there is no assurance that it will be correct from a national point of view.

Alternatively, suppose that the rate of unemployment in a particular state is too high and that the government authorities reduce state taxes as a means of correcting this problem. This will increase the level of spending within the state, and state income and employment will rise. At the same time, however, much of the spending increase will be on goods imported from other states. If the exporting states are also suffering from too much unemployment, the fiscal policy of the importing state creates external benefits in exporting states. If the exporting states are suffering from inflation, external costs are created.

Other possible variations on this theme exist. The point, however, is that the importing state will not consider these externalities in making a decision in the interests of its citizenry. Thus, from a national point of view, each state is likely to produce too much or too little fiscal policy. Strictly speaking, this is not an efficiency-relevant externality, but rather is a stabilization-relevant externality. The two are not as far apart as one might suppose, however, since full employment is a necessary condition for perfect efficiency.

The spatial externalities that are likely to occur indicate a need for central coordination of fiscal policy even if state and local budgets are to be used as policy instruments. Without such coordination, we would have little assurance of the correct amount of restraint or expansion even if all units were pursuing the same goals.

Finally, there is no guarantee that each unit *would be* pursuing the same goals; i.e., that they would choose the same terms of trade between unemployment and inflation. Thus, some units could be conducting expansionary policy while others would be restraining their economies, merely because the several units were attempting to achieve different mixes of employment and price stability.

Our conclusion is that the goals of full employment and/or a stable aggregate price level can be achieved more efficiently by manipulating the budget of the central government. There is also a greater probability in this case that these ends could be achieved more equitably, since a central decision could be designed in accordance with the spatial distribution of the benefits and burdens of stabilization policy.

THE DISTRIBUTION FUNCTION

Suppose, however, that one goal is a more equitable distribution of personal, or family, income. Are we not better off relying exclusively on each government unit to conduct its own policy in this regard? Here again, the consensus answer of economists appears to be "No."

TAX AND TRANSFER PAYMENT PROGRAMS

If greater equity requires the redistribution of income from individuals (families) with high incomes to those with low incomes, there are many tax or transfer payment programs that could be used to achieve the necessary degree of redistribution. It is likely, however, that such programs conducted extensively by state and local governments would generate their own inequities and, in addition, create greater inefficiency in the allocation of resources.

Regions of the nation exhibit wide disparities in income and wealth per capita. Those which enjoy relatively high income and wealth can support a transfer payment program of a given size by collecting lower tax revenues per capita than it would be necessary for a poorer region to collect from its citizens. Such an arrangement would violate the principle of horizontal equity; namely, that individuals in equal circumstances be treated equally.

However, if the citizens of each unit were to make the same tax effort (for example, by paying the same average percentage of their wealth and income in taxes), there would be significant disparities among regions in expenditures on redistribution programs. Consequently, individuals would migrate from regions in which such expenditures are small to those in which they are large. Such migration would probably be a source of inefficiency, inasmuch as it would not be induced by differences among regions in competitively-determined resource prices. Indeed, this *has* been the experience of New York City, where abnormally high welfare payments have attracted large numbers of unskilled individuals.

One way to minimize these effects is to establish national norms for the distribution of personal income and to finance such a program by using taxes that are not location-specific; i.e., that individuals or firms cannot avoid by locating in another jurisdiction.

MERIT GOODS

The achievement of a more equitable distribution of personal income is not necessarily the only income distribution objective. One social goal may be to ensure the provision of some minimum quantity of merit goods. What are the implications of this objective for the design of a governmental fiscal structure?

Merit goods, it will be recalled, are those that society deems so important that some minimum quantity is regarded as a fundamental right (and, in some cases, a fundamental obligation). Education is a good example. Because the acquisition of education is such an important element of equal opportunity, we regard some minimum quantity as both a right and a duty.

The chief characteristic of merit goods is that they are distributed directly in the form of services rather than income. In the absence of government assistance, the quantity that would be acquired would depend on the distribution of personal income and the nature of individual preferences. This combination of factors would not always provide the socially desired minimum level of merit goods. However, general transfers of income would not necessarily solve this problem because recipients would be free to buy *any* goods or services rather than merely those deemed socially meritorious. Thus, governments often transfer some goods directly in order to ensure a closer correspondence between individual and social choice.

State and local governments vary widely in their abilities to provide merit goods, just as they do in their abilities to redistribute personal income. Therefore, some activity by the central government is required to assure minimum provision at approximately the same levels across jurisdictions. This would undoubtedly involve federal financing of goods and services. However, federal *administration* of the distribution programs may be neither necessary nor desirable.

THE ALLOCATION FUNCTION

So far in this chapter, we have presented arguments which imply a primary role for the central government in achieving aggregate stability and a more equal distribution of income. The situation is much diffferent if the objective is efficiency through the governmental provision of goods and services. In this instance, decentralized units play a critical role. It is not possible to describe this role in great detail here. However, the following discussion clearly indicates that it is important.

PERFECT CORRESPONDENCE

Let us begin by imagining a situation in which no expenditure programs have been assigned to any governmental unit. Assume, moreover, that no jurisdictional boundaries exist. Under these circumstances, the problem is one of determining the optimal program jurisdiction, defined in this instance as the one which provides an efficient output of the program in question. If we assume further that the existing population is distributed uniformly in a spatial sense, the optimal jurisdiction can be defined in terms of the population size which supports an efficient level of program output.

To facilitate the analysis and discussion, assume that it is possible both to define the program and to measure its output. It is easier to accomplish the former than the latter. We can distinguish, for example, between education, health, welfare, defense, transportation, and police programs in both very broad or narrow terms; however, it is difficult to measure the output of these programs. This is an important problem, but its solution is not critical for the points to be made. Thus, we assume simply that output can be specified in terms of some service unit of a given quality.

All programs would seem to share certain characteristics. First, as service units are provided to additional individuals, the marginal benefit of these units will eventually decline. This is true whether the program provides significant external benefits, such as national defense, or virtually no external benefits, such as a sewer system in a rural community. Second, the cost of supplying an additional unit to an additional individual will eventually rise. This would be true even for programs which may initially enjoy economies of scale.

Neither of these propositions is novel. The first is a restatement of the law of demand, while the second merely recognizes the applicability of the law of increasing opportunity cost to the provision of public goods and services. However, these principles do facilitate the development of the notion of an efficient program size.

A program is of efficient size when the cost of supplying a service unit to an additional individual (the marginal cost) is just equal to the value placed on an additional service unit (the marginal benefit). This level corresponds to a population size of E individuals in Figure 17-1.

The efficient jurisdiction for a government providing only program A can now be determined. It is simply one which has political-fiscal authority over E individuals. If we knew the location of the source of program supply and the spatial distribution of the E individuals, we could also specify the area over which the government should have jurisdiction. Whether the efficient program jurisdiction is defined in terms of individuals or area, one feature of the solution stands out: namely, all benefits and costs are contained within the jurisdiction. Economists say in a situation like this that all benefits and costs are *internalized.* Some economists define

FIGURE 17–1
MARGINAL COSTS AND BENEFITS OF PROGRAM A

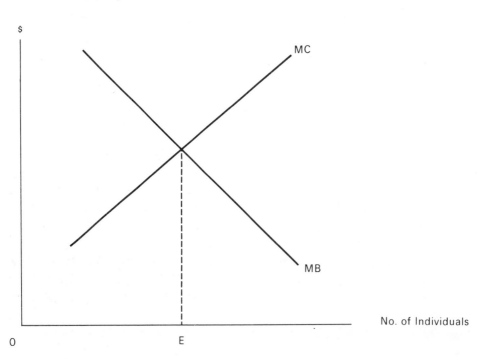

this situation as one in which there is a *perfect correspondence* between program effects and program jurisdiction.

We should expect to encounter great variety in program jurisdiction; let us see why by examining some of the more important determinants of efficient size.

As a first approximation, there are two determinants of the efficient jurisdiction (measured, as above, in terms of individuals served): the program type, and the quality of program output.

Program Type

Differences in programs of a given quality are important because each program will have different demand and cost conditions associated with it. Insofar as these differences are reflected in the MB and MC curves, there will be differences in efficient program jurisdictions.

We would expect to encounter a wide variety of MB curves, just as we encounter a wide variety of demand curves for private goods. The demand for public goods would vary according to the number of direct and indirect beneficiaries, their preferences among all goods, their incomes, the prices of privately and publicly-provided substitutes and complements, and so on. At one extreme would be goods and services from which few people benefit, either directly or indirectly, and on which these people place a relatively low valuation. Such goods would require a relatively small size jurisdiction in terms of population and/or area for perfect correspondence. Examples in this category are local streets and sewer systems, streetlights, and small neighborhood parks.

At one other extreme are programs which benefit a large group, directly or indirectly, and on which beneficiaries place a relatively high value per unit. Such programs require a relatively large jurisdiction for perfect correspondence, as in the extreme case of national defense.

Program Cost

Programs also vary according to costs of provision. Program costs (for a service unit of given quality) themselves can vary for a wide variety of reasons: differences in rate and volume of output; location of consuming population relative to supply source; state of technology, and productivity of inputs. As long as variations among programs result in variations among marginal costs, cost factors alone will prescribe a wide range of jurisdictions for achieving perfect correspondence.

Contracting

It bears repeating that the relevant cost from the point of view of determining an efficient program jurisdiction is the cost of *providing* a service unit to an additional individual. The unit may or may not be *produced* by the authorities of the jurisdiction. Ideally, it should be produced by each jurisdiction only if all economics of scale in production can be so achieved. If they cannot, then it will be more efficient for a jurisdiction which is too small to achieve these economies to buy the service from another jurisdiction or from a private producer and merely distribute the service to its customers. Such a practice has been employed widely in the nation's larger metropolitan areas, where one jurisdiction contracts with a larger, more efficient producing jurisdiction for the purchase of services it cannot produce as cheaply itself.

The outstanding example of this practice is the Lakewood Plan, developed in Los Angeles County, California. The city of Lakewood was incorporated in 1954 as the first complete "contract city" in the United States. Although it had a population approaching 80,000 at that time, it was organized without any municipal departments and only ten full-time employees. All services were provided through preexisting special districts or by contracts with county agencies.

Within the next decade, twenty-five new cities modeled after Lakewood were incorporated in the county. This number included some cities that were predominantly residential, some that were predominantly industrial, and some that were largely agricultural. Within the group, average community income and wealth varied widely. In general, however, the Lakewood Plan afforded each community the opportunity to exercise its own preferences for municipal goods and services at relatively low cost by contracting with relatively more efficient producing agencies.

Program Quality

In addition to the above factors, the efficient jurisdiction can vary as a result of variations in program quality. In many instances, variations in program quality will affect both the MB and the MC. Presumably, the relationship would be a direct one in both cases; i.e., an increase (decrease) in quality would increase (decrease) both the MB and MC curves. Whether there would be a change in the size of jurisdiction necessary for perfect correspondence would depend on the separate effect on each curve in each particular case. This would depend, in turn, on the characteristics comprising the quality of a service unit and their associated costs and benefits.

Conclusions

Such are the major ingredients for determining efficient program jurisdictions. Undoubtedly, they could be combined in numerous ways, making the determination of *the* optimal jurisdictional structure an extremely complex affair. Nevertheless, an exercise such as this does yield some useful insights.

First, it reinforces the point that an efficient solution, as always, requires a comparison of the factors underlying both supply and demand. Much of the early discussion of this topic in economics literature suffers from neglect of this basic truth. Indeed, in some of the early literature the optimal jurisdiction is defined almost exclusively in terms of economics of scale in production. That this is much too narrow a criterion should be obvious by now.

Second, although we cannot specify *the* optimal structure, the analysis suggests the need for a wide variety of efficient single-purpose (or program) jurisdictions. Surely, it suggests a large amount of decentralization in the provision of government goods and services.

Third, although the jurisdictions are single-purpose, the possibility is raised of interaction among them as a means of achieving greater efficiency —in this instance, by contracting for services.

The structure implied so far bears little resemblance to the one encountered in reality. This raises the obvious question: Is there any basis in economic theory for the more familiar pattern of multi-program, multi-level jurisdictions? The answer appears to be "Yes" if we consider more fully a variety of complications we have ignored to this point.

ECONOMIES FROM COMBINING FUNCTIONS AND DECISIONS

With the exception of the single-purpose special district, employed widely for the provision of elementary and secondary education and utilities, government units typically administer a wide variety of programs. Although this structure has probably evolved more as a response to political than to economic factors, at least some common administration of different programs would be consistent with achieving economic efficiency. The purest situation would be one in which several programs were of the same or similar efficient size, as defined previously, but the programs could share fixed inputs, such as land, capital facilities, or administrative talent. Common administration of these programs could result in real cost-savings from arrangements which reduced input costs per service unit.

A bigger impetus toward multi-purpose government units is provided, however, by the savings they facilitate in *political decision-making costs.* If every type of public good or service were provided by a separate jurisdiction and political authorities were responsible to the citizenry, the processes of disseminating information and administering elections, and of citizens acquiring and weighing information and voting, would be extremely costly (in real or opportunity-cost terms). It is not hard to appreciate that the alternative where the citizen is required to vote infrequently for representatives who will help direct the provision of a wide variety of goods and services can be a relatively more efficient way of acquiring citizen input.

Such an arrangement would be less efficient, of course, if public goods and services could be sold at market-clearing prices. Political decision-making costs would be replaced, in this instance, by private decision-making costs. Presumably, self-interested individuals would find ways of minimizing this overtime. As the reader is no doubt aware by now, however, there are economical, political, and ethical limits on the free use of the pricing mechanism as a means of financing and distributing goods and services provided through the public sector.

POLITICAL DECISION-MAKING
COSTS AND JURISDICTIONAL SIZE

Political decision-making costs have another important dimension. We have noted how the costs of obtaining agreement may be reduced through election of representatives to a multi-program government unit. The costs of obtaining agreement can probably also be reduced by reducing the number of people from among whom agreement must be obtained.

Thus, political decision-making costs would be expected to rise as the number of people in a jurisdiction rises. It follows that the efficient-sized jurisdiction will be smaller than determined previously.

Political decision-making costs have two effects, then: (1) they make it more economical to have multi-program jurisdictions; and (2) they make it more economical to have relatively smaller jurisdictions.

EFFICIENCY FROM
OVERLAPPING JURISDICTIONS

Arguments have been presented so far which indicate that some range of multi-purpose independent jurisdictions is consistent with achieving efficiency. Presumably, this structure means that each citizen will be served by more than one government unit, but that no more than one unit will provide the same service for a given individual. Each government, then, is assumed to have a monopoly in the provision of its services.

From their study of the economic effects of monopoly in the private sector, economists have generally concluded that, for a given state of technology and costs, monopoly produces inefficiency in resource allocation. The evidence also indicates that cost-saving innovations are developed and adopted at a slower rate in highly concentrated industries. Moreover, the barriers to entry in these industries protect relatively high-cost producers and facilitate the practice of various forms of discrimination.

There is little reason to believe that the same tendencies would not be present in public jurisdictional monopolies. We would expect greater efficiency to be achieved, therefore, if citizens had some choice of the unit from which they could "purchase" government goods and services. Thus, there is an efficiency basis for overlapping jurisdictions in the provision of some goods and services.

Most of the multi-unit provision in the public sector is complementary rather than competitive; the prime examples being the programs of central government grants to state governments and of state government grants to local governments. However, some competition does prevail, especially in the provision of legal services where legislatures and courts representing broader units of government have frequently served to lessen discrimination sanctioned by lower level governments, and in those metropolitan areas where a system similar to the Lakewood Plan is operative.

EFFICIENCY AND POLITICAL
EXTERNALITY COSTS

Even if all of the preceding conditions were achieved, the structure of governments which emerged would still not necessarily be the one which achieved maximum efficiency. It is likely that the average jurisdiction would be too large because *political externality costs* have been ignored.

This particular cost arises because we do not sell government goods and services, but rather we typically use some voting procedure to determine indirectly the amounts that will be provided and the taxes that will be paid to ensure their provision. Usually, we vote for representatives, using a majority rule. Those who lose the vote have indicated that they choose not to *buy* the proposed package of programs. Of course, they must do so anyway. Presumably, because they voted against the package, the marginal benefit they perceive from its provision is less than the tax-price they perceive they will be required to pay. The difference between marginal benefit and tax-price represents an efficiency loss or net cost to these individuals. The sum of these costs aggregated across all individuals in the community represents the loss in consumer/taxpayer welfare occasioned by the method of collective decision-making. They are costs attributable to the politcal process; hence, political costs. They are, moreover, costs of majority rule for which the minority is not compensated; hence, political *externality* costs.

It seems reasonable to assume that these costs are less for relatively homogeneous communities; i.e., those that contain voters with similar tastes and preferences for publicly provided goods and services. Because people differ so widely in this regard, political externality costs are minimized with a governmental structure that offers a wide variety of goods and tax-prices. The units in this structure are likely to be small because this enhances the possibility for achieving homogeneity in tastes and preferences. Here again the Lakewood Plan cities provide an example of this principle in operation.

The preferences of consumers/taxpayers are best served, then, by a government structure composed of relatively small, hetergeneous units. Alternatively, the efficient size of any single program unit will be smaller than indicated in Figure 17-1 due to the aforementioned political externality costs.

INEFFICIENCIES IN GOVERNMENTAL STRUCTURE

It is easy to see from the preceding analysis that the task of specifying the efficient governmental structure is extremely complex. Indeed, given the large number of relevant variables involved, a detailed design seems out of the question.[2] However, exercises such as this do provide benchmarks against which various arguments can be evaluated.

Once we know the ingredients of an efficient solution, it becomes easier to evaluate proposed changes in organizational structure. For example, the analysis indicates that there are efficiencies attributable to relatively small governmental units, primarily in the form of lower political decision-making and political externality costs. Given these, there appears to be a need for caution in adopting policies designed to consolidate governmental functions or units, such as has been proposed for many metropolitan areas.

Perhaps just as important, however, is the fact that once we know the ingredients of an efficient solution it is easier to identify jurisdictional arrangements that are not efficient. It should not be surprising to encounter such situations frequently, inasmuch as most jurisdictional boundaries and public program assignments are made on the basis of non-economic considerations.

Jurisdictional Externalities

We encounter inefficiency in governmental structure when imperfect correspondence exists between efficient jurisdictions and actual jurisdictions. One of the primary reasons for this kind of inefficiency is the existence of jurisdictional externalities (spillovers).

A jurisdictional external benefit is present when some of the benefits attributable to the provision of a government good or service are enjoyed by residents of some other jurisdiction. A jurisdictional external cost occurs when some of the costs of provision spill over to residents of another jurisdiction.

Jurisdictional externalities are similar to the efficiency-relevant externalities discussed in chapters 2 and 12, although they differ in two respects. First, they are produced by the actions of government authorities and not by private individuals or firms. Second, they reflect inadequacies in governmental organization rather then the inability of private markets to handle transactions where private property rights are not clearly established.

---

2. It should also be remembered, that the efficient governmental structure is not equivalent to the best structure. There are more ingredients of the good life than the efficient provision of public services. Moreover, even an efficient economic area must be defined in terms of private economic activity as well.

However, their effect is similar to that of private sector externalities in that they create inefficiency in resource allocation.

In the case of jurisdictional external benefits, the producing jurisdiction would ideally provide additional service units up to the point where marginal costs to the jurisdiction are equal to marginal jurisdictional benefits. However, in this case marginal benefits are less than marginal social benefits, and too little of the good or service in question will be provided. Perhaps the classic example of this is education, a case in which many individuals educated in a particular jurisdiction migrate to another jurisdiction. The migrating individual transmits benefits to the area to which he or she migrates. However, from the point of view of the producing jurisdiction, these external benefits are irrelevant and their value will not be considered in deciding how much education to provide.

The irony of this particular case is that much of our education is provided publicly, ostensibly because an inadequate amount would be provided privately. However, merely providing the service publicly is not a guarantee that the correct amount will be provided. We cannot assume a priori that the existing structure of public institutions is efficient in itself.

In the case of jurisdictional external costs, too much will be provided of the good or service whose provision generates the cost. Unfortunately, as in the private sector, no mechanism operates to ensure that public authorities will incorporate these costs in their decision-making. Indeed, we can safely assume that authorities in the producing jurisdiction are concerned only with the costs visited upon the residents of their community. Thus, we should not be surprised, for example, to encounter air and water pollution generated by public production or sewage disposal.

A closely related concern is that the prevailing governmental structure will not facilitate the design of public policy to reduce or offset the effects of pollution generated by private activities. In the Los Angeles basin, for example, much of the air pollution generated in the central city is transported by prevailing breezes to inland suburbs. If the governments of the central communities are concerned only about the welfare of their citizens, they will have little incentive to reduce air pollution to a socially efficient level.

Based on concerns such as these, some economists have argued that jurisdictional externalities require the establishment of larger jurisdictions than would be required to achieve efficiency in their absence. Using this device, the externalities can be "internalized" in the jurisdiction. The evolution of wide-area air pollution control districts (as in Southern California) is consistent with this principle; so, too, are wide-area emergency facilities, mosquito abatement programs, and health services.

Of course, separate governmental units need not be established to monitor the production of goods and services with jurisdictional externalities. Governments with broader jurisdictions could simply impose certain regulations upon other governments, or upon citizens and firms residing in overlapping jurisdictions. Alternately, intergovernmental grants could be designed to encourage the expansion or contraction of programs with jurisdictional externalities. The last of these options is one of the topics in the next chapter.

Taxes

Up to now in this chapter, we have ignored the revenue side of the budget. Jurisdictional efficiency will be affected, however, by the nature of the tax system used to finance governmental expenditures.

Ideally, the types of taxes used and the rate structure for each should be designed to facilitate the efficient assignment of goods and services among political-fiscal jurisdictions. Two principles are important in this regard: (1) those who benefit from the provision of the goods and services should pay; and (2) tax rates should be equal to the value each individual places on the last unit consumed. If the tax system reflects these two principles, there should be a minimum of jurisdictional spillovers and a natural matching of taxpayer preferences with taxes paid. The greater the degree to which these principles are violated, the greater the likelihood of jurisdictional spillovers and taxpayer discontent. In the latter case, it will eventually reach a level which induces individuals to move to a jurisdiction where the taxes for public services and the marginal benefits perceived by them from their provision are more closely matched.

Although it is relatively easy to specify the principles for designing an efficient tax system, it would be much more difficult to do so in practice. In many instances, the benefit principle could not be implemented because the benefits of certain public goods are inherently unmeasurable (national defense) or simply too expensive to measure. In many other cases, existing institutions and practices would constitute an effective barrier to the design of an efficient tax system.

In reality, the tax system falls short of perfect efficiency in several ways. First, none of the major taxes are designed as pure benefit taxes. This creates a situation in which benefits perceived from public services are often different from taxes, thus creating an incentive for the mobility of households and productive resources.

Second, the tax system is often poorly designed to regulate flows of individuals and resources across existing jurisdictional boundaries. This problem is most acute in metropolitan areas where services financed by the residents of one part of the region (for example, by property taxpayers in the central city) are often consumed by residents of another part (suburban commuters). This fiscal mismatch also involves citizens residing in more than one state as well, so that taxpayers of one state may be subsidizing citizens of another. Perhaps the classic example of this is that of individuals who move from the states in which they are educated to other states.

Third, the tax system cannot be easily employed to offset jurisdictional spillovers. Central city residents can attempt to charge suburban dwellers for services provided by levying parking fees or city sales taxes, but these are blunt and often ineffective instruments for this purpose. For some resource flows among jurisdictions (educated individuals, for example), it is almost impossible to arrange for compensation among states and cities.

Fourth, the tax system can provide incentives for the perpetuation of inefficient producing units. This can work in two directions. On the one hand, state tax laws have often encouraged the proliferation of local school districts, many of which were inefficiently small. On the other hand, tax laws have encouraged the development of governmental units that are inefficiently large for the provision of public services by providing an incentive to cities to annex surrounding residential, commercial, and agricultural areas.

These are only a few of the items in a full-scale evaluation of the effect of the tax system on jurisdictional efficiency. We will not pursue this theme further because the bulk of public policy to achieve greater jurisdictional efficiency is concerned with intergovernmental grants—the topic of Chapter 18. However, changes in the tax system to achieve this goal may be a promising area for additional research.

SUMMARY

In this chapter we have examined the problem of assigning fiscal tasks to federal, state and local units of government. As a first approximation, tax and expenditure programs should be assigned so that the government sector maximizes its contribution to the goals of efficiency, equity and stability.

The achievement of aggregate stability requires the exercise of monetary and fiscal policy by the federal government. Our history provides good evidence that effective monetary control requires a federally-supervised central bank. Fiscal policy is the proper province of the federal government because it can engage in effective deficit finance, achieve the full impact of changes in expenditures, avoid the creation of stabilization—relevant externalities, and pursue a consistent course toward the goal of aggregate stability.

The achievement of greater equity in the distribution of income also appears to require a large dose of federal government fiscal activity. Federal expenditures can be designed particularly to offset those disparities in wealth and income among the states that create differences in the spatial distribution of government redistribution expenditures. Such an arrangement can probably even be justified in terms of its effect on economic efficiency.

When we turned to the allocation function, we defined a much larger role for lower-level government units. To achieve efficiency in the assignment of expenditure programs it is necessary to achieve perfect correspondence, and to expand programs to the level where $MSB = MSC$. MSB and MSC differ greatly as a consequence of differences in program type and quality, producing a wide range of optimal size programs. Such a dispersion requires single purpose governmental jurisdictions which vary accordingly in terms of geographical scope.

Governments typically perform many functions. It is efficient for them to do so in order to reap economies from combining administrative functions, and to effect savings in political decision-making costs. The latter are also instrumental in making it more economical to have smaller jurisdictions.

Although much of our analysis to this point implies that citizens would be served most efficiently by a single governmental unit, this will not be the case if government monopolies created in accordance with such a plan are themselves inefficient and insufficiently progressive. Some competition among units serving the same citizenry may be highly desirable.

One final factor appears to indicate a tendency toward small units if efficiency is to be achieved. Because government decisions are made through a complex political process, significant political externality costs are created. It seems reasonable to assume that these costs are less for relatively homogeneous and/or smaller communities.

Our criteria cannot be used to specify an accurate assignment of functions among governments. However, they indicate clearly the need for multi-level, multi-functional jurisdictions, ranging in size from very small special districts to the national government. Moreover, our criteria can be used to identify situations that are inefficient.

Some of the outstanding examples of inefficiency are created by jurisdictional externalities. A classic case on the benefit side is education, which often produces significant positive spillovers. On the cost side, most metropolitan areas abound with instances of negative spillovers in the formof air and water pollution. One way to reduce these externalities is to expand the size of the governmental unit in order to internalize them.

It is necessary, finally, to design the tax system so that it promotes an efficient governmental structure. To do so, it is necessary to rely on benefit taxes, and to set tax rates equal to the marginal social benefits from government goods and services. In reality, the system differs greatly in content and structure from this ideal.

SUGGESTIONS FOR FURTHER READING

Oates, Wallace B., *Fiscal Federalism,* New York: Harcourt, Brace, Jovanovich, Inc., 1972.

Chapters 1, 2, and 4 develop the principles by which a fiscal federation should be organized.

Bish, Robert L., *The Public Economy of Metropolitan Areas,* Chicago: Markham, 1971.

In this book, Bish uses some basic assumptions of non-market decision making to rationalize the fiscal structure of metropolitan areas. This is a topic that is closely related to the one treated in the present chapter.

EIGHTEEN

THE SHARING OF FEDERAL
REVENUES WITH STATE
AND LOCAL GOVERNMENTS

The revenues of state and local governments are derived largely from taxes, user charges, and grants from higher-level governments. Some of the economic effects of the major state and local tax instruments were examined in chapters 8–11, and user charges were analyzed in Chapter 12. In this chapter we will examine the economics of grants-in-aid from the federal government to state and local governments.

Available data indicate clearly that federal grants are an important source of revenue to lower-level governments. In 1975, this type of aid totaled nearly $52 billion, accounting for almost one-fourth of all state and local expenditures and 17% of all expenditures of the federal government.[1] The manner in which these funds are allocated is an important determinant of the effectiveness of our system of fiscally interdependent governments.

We begin our inquiry by examining the rationale for intergovernmental grants in terms of the normative framework of the public sector established earlier. Next, we develop a few criteria for designing an efficient system of categorical grants. Following that, we examine existing grants of this type and evaluate them in terms of these criteria. The chapter closes with

---

1. For informative data on the size and composition of the federal grant program see: U.S. Government, *The Budget for Fiscal Year 1975,* Special Analysis N. Washington: USGPO.

a brief appraisal of unconditional grants, with special reference to the program of general revenue sharing.

THE OPTIMAL EMPLOYMENT OF FEDERAL GRANTS

We have argued previously that it is useful to view the budget as an instrument for achieving three distinct though interrelated objectives: efficiency in resource allocation, equity in the distribution of income and merit goods, and aggregate stability. We begin our analysis of intergovernmental grants by determining whether and how they may be employed as a means of achieving each of these objectives.

ALLOCATIVE EFFICIENCY

To achieve the first objective it is necessary to correct various "efficiency failures" that would be produced by the normal operation of the economy. Within the public sector, some inefficiency results from imperfections in the institutional structure of political and fiscal federalism. These imperfections are the proper target of intergovernmental grants.

There are four types of imperfections: (1) jurisdictional externalities (spillovers); (2) unequal government budget constraints; (3) social imbalance; and (4) unequal tax-prices. We will examine each of these briefly.

Jurisdictional Externalities

Inefficiency in governmental structure occurs when there is imperfect correspondence between efficient and actual jurisdictions. As indicated in Chapter 17, one of the primary reasons for imperfect correspondence is the existence of jurisdictional externalities. A jurisdictional external benefit is present when some of the benefits attributable to the provision of a government good or service are enjoyed by non-residents. A jurisdictional external cost occurs when some of the costs of provision are paid by non-residents.

To achieve efficiency, each jurisdiction should provide service at the level where marginal *social* costs (MSC) are equal to marginal *social* benefits (MSB). However, they will provide the amount at which marginal *jurisdictional* benefits (MJB) equal marginal *jurisdictional* costs (MJC) if they act rationally in their own interest. In the case of benefit spillovers,

MJB < MSB and too little of the service in question will be provided. The classic example of this is education, a case in which individuals educated in one jurisdiction migrate to other jurisdictions, thereby transmitting various benefits across governmental boundaries. Benefit spillovers are also attributable to highway systems and to a host of services provided by governments in metropolitan areas.

The irony of these cases is that such services are provided through the public sector partially because an inadequate amount would be provided privately. However, *there is no guarantee that the correct amount will be provided publicly.* It depends upon whether the existing structure of public institutions facilitates such a result.

In the case of jurisdictional external costs, too much will be provided of the service in question because MJC < MSC. Unfortunately, as in the private sector, there is no mechanism which induces public authorities to consider these costs when making allocation decisions. Indeed, we can probably safely assume that authorities in the producing jurisdiction are concerned only with the costs perceived by the residents of their community. Thus, the numerous instances of air and water pollution generated by public power production or waste disposal activities is hardly a surprising phenomenon.

Intergovernmental grants can be employed to induce smaller governmental units to produce larger amounts of services that provide jurisdictional external benefits. Ideally, the federal government can transfer just enough money to state and local governments to induce them to provide socially efficient quantities. To achieve this result at lowest opportunity cost, the grant must be earmarked for this particular purpose; that is, it must be a *categorical grant.* If the funds are not restricted in this fashion, receiving units will probably use some of them to expand other services or substitute them for a general reduction in tax revenues.

Choosing the right type of grant is only the first step, however. Additional features must be incorporated in the grant formula to accomplish the desired result at minimum cost. These features will be described in some detail later in this chapter.

Unequal Government Budget Constraints

To achieve efficiency, resources should be allocated to the private sector or to the particular government where they would yield the greatest net benefits. However, governments make budget decision without explicit evaluation of precluded alternatives. Moreover, they vary in their ability to raise revenues. Consequently, some may expend all of their funds but still have more efficient projects unfunded than the projects actually funded by other units or various segments of the private sector. In such instances, differences in budget constraints produce an inefficient allocation of resources.

State and local governments have relied traditionally upon revenue sources that grow more slowly than the sources tapped by the federal government. In the last three decades, however, they have faced rapidly growing demands for social services. This trend has been most apparent for local governments in metropolitan areas where population growth has been highly concentrated. For these areas, especially, there is a possibility that budget constraints preclude the funding of efficient projects.

If the projects so precluded are more efficient than those actually funded in the federal sector, the federal government should transfer funds from their less efficient projects to local governments in the form of grants. The proper grants in these instances would be categorical ones, with expenditures confined solely to the relatively more efficient local alternatives.

Social Imbalance

To some observers, the problem just outlined is symptomatic of a more *general undersupply* of services by state and local governments. Whether these observers are correct or incorrect is a matter of continuing debate, the elements of which we will review later in this chapter. However, if they are correct, intergovernmental grants can be used to modify the situation.

If there is an undersupply of state and local government goods relative to private goods, then there is a "social imbalance" between the private and public sectors. This imbalance can be corrected directly by increasing state and local tax collections. However, if this is not feasible (for example, for political reasons, or because each government fears that others will not go along and raise their taxes also), then revenues may be raised by the federal government and transferred to other governments in the form of an *unconditional* grant; i.e., one that can be spent for any purpose.

The unconditional grant is appropriate only if the program in which there is an undersupply of public goods cannot be precisely determined. If this can be done, even if the number of programs is large, categorical grants are appropriate. Presumably, then, unconditional grants are appropriate only if uncertainty exists as to the extent of the alleged social imbalance but not as to its direction. In practice, of course, there is a great deal of controversy over whether or not a social imbalance exists and, if so, in which direction—too many private or too many public goods.

Unconditional grants may also be appropriate, of course, if there is a general undersupply of state and local services relative to federally-provided services. In this case, additional revenues do not have to be raised by the federal government before the grant can be made; existing revenues can be transferred directly.

Unequal Tax Prices

The final course of inefficiency concerns the differences among jurisdictions in the amount of taxes that residents pay for equal service units of publicly-provided goods. In general, such differences reflect existing variation in taxable wealth among jurisdictions, with the citizens in wealthier jurisdictions paying a smaller "tax-price" per unit than citizens in poorer jurisdictions.

These differentials in tax-price are not evidence per se of inefficiency. However, they may produce inefficiency by inducing taxpayers to migrate from poor to wealthy jurisdictions. This would be true whenever the migration occurs solely to acquire lower-cost public goods and not because of differentials in real costs or rewards.

If migration occurs because tax-prices are lower only on certain services, then categorical grants for these services are appropriate—provided that larger amounts per capita are awarded to poorer governmental units. It is more likely, however, that tax-prices will be lower on all government goods and that unconditional grants based on some measure of ability-to-pay will be the appropriate instrument.

DISTRIBUTIVE EQUITY

The second objective of government budget policy is to secure a more equitable distribution of both income and merit goods. As outlined in Chapter 2, the former goal is a necessary condition for increasing economic welfare, while the latter is a condition imposed by the political process. In both cases, however, the relevant beneficiary of redistribution activity was presumed to be the individual economic unit.

We have argued earlier (in chapters 6 and 17) that redistribution to individuals ought to be performed by the federal government, in order to avoid inefficiencies created by state and local finance of this function. Federal grants can be employed for this purpose; however, there is a debate over whether these grants ought to be in the form of goods and services (categorical) or money (unconditional) grants made directly to individuals. In Chapter 6 we argued that the individual unconditional grant is the preferred alternative.

Although the individual is the proper focus of policy designed to enhance economic welfare, there is a great deal of concern about equity in the provision of government services among jurisdictions. This concern is based on solid evidence: there is considerable variation among government units in terms of expenditures per capita for particular public goods and services and presumably, therefore, in *real* public goods and services provided per capita. Intergovernmental grants in either money or in-kind can be designed, then, to equalize real government services among jurisdictions. Indeed, many of the existing intergovernmental grant programs were adopted because of the desire to reduce perceived inequalities among jurisdictions, although emphasis has been placed on assisting lower governments to achieve minimum rather than equal levels of services.

AGGREGATE STABILITY

The third objective of government budget policy is to achieve aggregate stability, including low rates of unemployment and inflation and a desirable rate of economic growth. It is entirely possible to use intergovernmental grants as a tool for achieving these goals. The important question, however, is whether they are better than the alternatives.

The goal of aggregate stability can be achieved more fully in many circumstances by a planned full employment surplus or deficit in the federal budget. If a surplus is planned, it can be realized by raising tax rates or by reducing purchases or transfer payments. Similarly, a deficit can be accomplished by lowering tax rates or by increasing purchases and transfers. Since intergovernmental grants are a type of transfer payment, it follows that they could be used as a stabilization device.

However, if transfer programs are designed to achieve an efficient or equitable allocation of resources, as we have argued they should be, then increasing or decreasing them to achieve stabilization would be inappropriate. The reason is simple: changes required for stabilization may be inordinately large or small from the point of view of economic efficiency and equity. Stabilization should be achieved instead through changes in tax rates that are as neutral as possible with respect to efficiency and equity. Adherence to this principle of rational budgeting would help to insure that expenditure programs are adopted or deleted on their merits alone and not as temporary measures to put people to work or to reduce inflation.

THE OPTIMAL DESIGN OF CATEGORICAL GRANTS

The arguments above can be summarized briefly. The achievement of a welfare optimum requires full employment, efficiency in the allocation of resources, and an equitable distribution of personal income and merit goods. To attain full employment it is desirable to vary tax rates but not to vary intergovernmental grants. Similarly, it is desirable to vary transfers and taxes to attain greater equity in the distribution of personal income, but intergovernmental grants are too blunt an instrument for this purpose. Both categorical and unconditional grants can be used, however, to achieve greater efficiency and greater equality in government services. To be truly effective for these purposes they must be designed carefully. In this section we review some of the major problems in their design.

CORRECTING FOR EXTERNAL BENEFITS

Suppose the task is that of designing a grant that will induce local government authorities to expand the interstate highway system, on the grounds that this system provides benefits for many non-residents. In Figure 18-1 we have depicted the relevant economic concepts. The MSC curve shows the marginal social costs of expanding highway facilities. To simplify the analysis, it is assumed that MSC is constant and equal to MJC. The MJB curve depicts the value of the benefits perceived by the local authorities from increments to the system. The vertical distance at each level reflects the value to local user of savings in reduced travel time and other transport costs. MJB declines because successfully larger facilities provide trips of diminishing value to users.

Figure 18-1 also shows the value of the highway system to non-residents, as the vertical distance between MSB (marginal social benefit) and MJB. This distance, the marginal external benefit (MEB) of the system, is assumed to be the same for each increment to facilities.

It is in the interests of local decision-makers to provide level F_3. How-

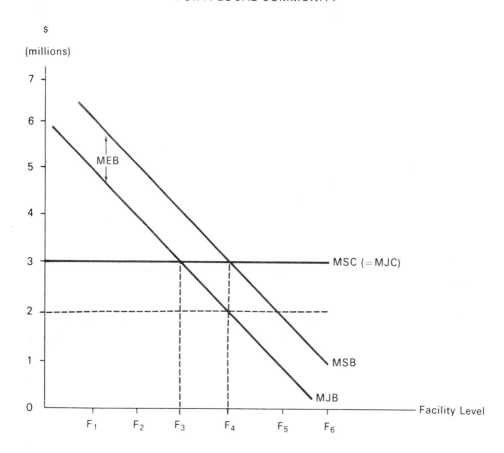

FIGURE 18–1
BENEFITS AND COSTS OF HIGHWAY FACILITIES
FOR A LOCAL COMMUNITY

ever, the efficient level is F_4, where MSC = MSB. Thus, this component of the interstate highway system will be too small if it is built solely in accordance with local preferences. Local decision-makers can be induced to provide F_4, however, by a subsidy equal to $1 million per unit. This would lower the effective local cost to $2 million per unit, and at this cost F_4 units would be desired.

This subsidy is equivalent to a categorical, matching, open-ended grant. It is categorical because the funds may be spent only for expansion of interstate highway facilities. It is equivalent to a matching grant which requires the local community to spend $2 for every $1 of federal funds. The matching *ratio* is one-half, and the federal government pays one-third of the per unit cost. Finally, it is an open-ended grant because the upper limit is determined solely by the local demand for and supply of highway services.

Although the model employed to develop these points is quite simple, it can be used to illustrate some of the difficulties encountered in designing a grant that will induce efficiency in resource allocation.

Measuring Benefits

The problems encountered in measuring benefits are similar to those discussed for public expenditures in general in chapters 4–6. The measurement problem is compounded, however, by the need to identify the *spatial incidence* of externalities. It is necessary to know both "how much," and "where" the impact lies. So far, little research has been devoted to this problem, with the notable exception of some studies of benefit and cost spillovers of higher education.[2]

Setting Matching Ratios

The above analysis indicates that the matching ratio must be set at a particular value to achieve the desired result. A corollary of this principle is that matching ratios must vary if there are variations among the recipients in the parameters of the model depicted in Figure 18-1.

The first source of variable matching ratios is variations in the size of MEB among jurisdictions. To show why, we have constructed Figure 18-2. This figure depicts the cost and benefits conditions for two communities, A and B. MJB and MJC are assumed equal for both. Community B generates larger MEB per unit of X, however, and requires a larger per unit grant (P_b − Pb) to move to the efficient level (X_e) than does A (a grant of P_a − Pa). Since $P_a = P_b$, the efficient matching ratio is larger for B than for A. Obviously, a uniform ratio would not induce the required pattern of adjustment.

Matching ratios must also vary if variations exist in the level of MJC. This case is depicted in Figure 18-3, where communities C and D are alike except that C has higher MJC than does D. Because MEB is the same for both, the required grant is the same size per unit of X. However, since D

2. See: Burton A. Weisbrod, *External Benefits of Public Education: An Economic Analysis,* Princeton U., 1964; Werner Z. Hirsch, Elbert W. Segelhorst, and Morton J. Marcus, *Spillover of Public Education Costs and Benefits,* University of California, 1964.

FIGURE 18–2
BENEFITS AND COSTS OF PUBLIC SERVICE X
FOR TWO COMMUNITIES WITH VARIABLE MEB

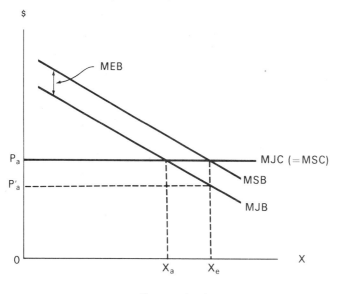

Community A

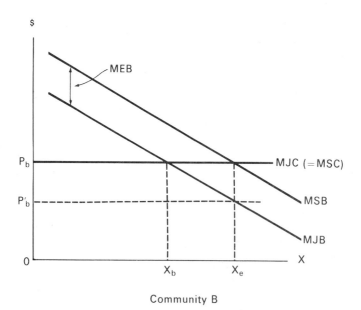

Community B

experiences lower MJC, its *matching ratio* is larger: $(P_d - Pd)/Pd > (P_c - Pc)/Pc$.

Finally, matching ratios must vary if recipients differ in their ability to "export" part of the local tax bill. Part of the taxes of all lower-level governments are paid by nonresidents. Those communities for which non-residents pay a larger proportion of taxes will have relatively lower MJC curves. The effect of tax exporting is to create a difference between MSC and MJC, as shown in Figure 18-4. If, as in that figure, the amount exported equals MEB, no grant is necessary. Surely, in the more general case, variations in grants to achieve the socially efficient level X_e will be required.

No Matching Ratio

Although categorical grants in general require some level and pattern of matching ratios, there are some cases in which they can be dispensed with for all practical purposes. The classic cases are those in which basic research is to be conducted in the public sector, or new programs and approaches are the subjects of public experiments. Here the benefits are so uncertain but potentially so widespread that the bulk of benefits will be external in a spatial sense, and the best practical alternative is complete federal funding.

Determining the Total Subsidy

A final problem is the determination of the total subsidy for each eligible jurisdiction. This amount varies directly with differences in both MEB and the tax-price elasticity of demand for the program in question. If there are no effective constraints on the federal grant budget, this problem is solved simply by using an open-ended grant. If there are effective limits on the size of the grant program, the budget must be allocated so that marginal social net benefits per dollar are equal among jurisdictions.

INDUCING THE EFFICIENT PROVISION OF MERIT GOODS

Categorical grants often have to be designed to further the attainment of "minimum national standards" in the provision of particular goods and services. Generally, these standards reflect perceived social need in the areas of health, education, welfare, housing, transportation, and community development.

FIGURE 18–3
BENEFITS AND COSTS OF PUBLIC SERVICE X
FOR TWO COMMUNITIES WITH VARIABLE MJC

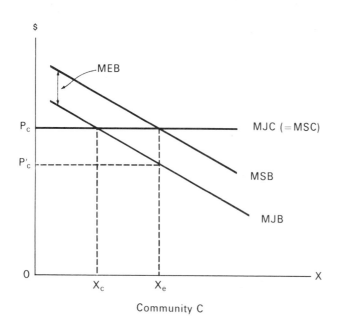

Community C

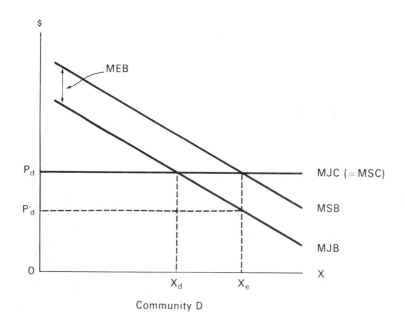

Community D

FIGURE 18–4
BENEFITS AND COSTS OF PUBLIC SERVICE X
WITH TAX-EXPORTING

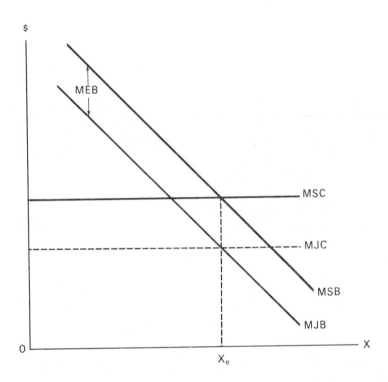

The first step in the design of these "merit grants" should be the development of an accurate, unambiguous measure of the extent of the problem. This involves the determination both of what we should be achieving (the "standard") and of what we are achieving among the various governmental units. The gap between these is a measure of social "needs." Once these "needs" have been determined, funds can be disbursed among state and local governments to fulfill them.

This much is probably obvious. What appears to be a relatively simple problem, however, turns out to be one that is not easy to solve in practice. It is difficult to define desired standards of achievement that will receive widespread support, especially among economists, for they recognize that sacrifices are necessary to fulfill perceived needs. However, economists should insist that social standards be set only after careful consideration of the opportunity costs occasioned by their achievement. Alternatively, grants should provide support for the programs which show promise of attaining the desired standards at minimum opportunity cost.

Thus, efficiency requires the allocation of funds according to how effectively they can be used to reduce unmet social needs, not according to which governments have the greatest needs. To achieve maximum effectiveness, funds should be allocated according to: (1) how close a government is to achieving the desired standard before the grant is made; (2) the tax-price elasticity of the demand for the service in question; and (3) the marginal cost of providing relevant services. Each of these criteria can be translated readily into the elements of grant design examined previously: the size of the total subsidy, and the level and pattern of matching ratios.

The total subsidy required increases with increases in marginal cost; it diminishes the closer the unit is to achieving the standard before the subsidy, and the greater the price elasticity of demand. Similar relationships were relevant for grants to correct benefit spillovers. Moreover, both types of grants require variations in matching ratios for variations in marginal cost. However, unlike spillover grants, merit grants require variations in matching ratios because of variations in price elasticity.

This last design principle can be illustrated simply with the aid of Figure 18-5, which depicts cost and benefit conditions for two communities, A and B. Both provide units of M, the merit good, at the same marginal cost. However, the price elasticity of demand for community A is less than for B over the relevant range. Given the same initial level, M_1, for both communities, it is evident that B requires a smaller grant per unit (ef), and hence a smaller matching ratio, to achieve the desired level M_s, than does A (which requires eg per unit).

CATEGORICAL GRANTS IN PRACTICE

The principles developed above can be used to evaluate existing categorical grants. However, these programs must also be evaluated in terms of their operating efficiency and how well they are achieving certain equalization objectives of the grant system. The former of these is a necessary component of the efficiency test, while the latter is required to reflect the growing importance of this objective in the design of existing grants. Both criteria will be introduced at the appropriate point in the discussion which follows.

It is helpful to begin with an overview of the components of the federal grant system. Table 18-1 lists the major programs for fiscal year 1975 and the approximate expenditure for each. All but three of those listed are relatively narrow categorical grant programs. The exceptions are general

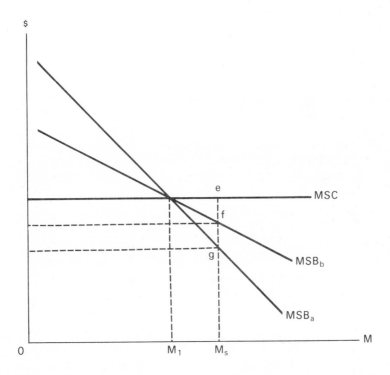

FIGURE 18–5
GRANTS FOR A MERIT GOOD

revenue sharing, consolidated education grants, and grants for comprehensive personnel training. The first of these is, for the most part, a truly unconditional grant; the latter two can be used to support a wide variety of education and personnel training programs. Approximately 81% of the total, then, is for categorical grants, with the programs listed accounting for over two-thirds of the grants of this type.

This system of categorical grants appears to be designed to serve four major purposes: (1) to correct jurisdictional spillovers; (2) to provide merit goods; (3) to alleviate poverty; and (4) to equalize either service levels or tax effort among jurisidictions. Although it is possible to identify the major objectives of the system, it is not generally possible to categorize individual grants according to the objective served. With the exception of the program of water pollution control, designed to reduce spillover costs (purpose 1), the typical grant serves several purposes. Thus, education grants are provided partly because education is a merit good and partly because it produces benefit spillovers. Similarly, the Medicaid program reduces the incidence of poverty while also providing a highly desired

TABLE 18–1   MAJOR INTERGOVERNMENTAL GRANTS
FISCAL YEAR 1975

General Revenue Sharing	$ 6.5 billion
Medicaid	6.5
Federal-Aid Highways	4.6
Income Maintenance	4.3
Food Stamp	3.9
EPA (Water Pollution Control)	3.5
Social Services	2.0
Consolidated Education Grant	1.9
Comprehensive Manpower Training	1.6
Child Nutrition	1.4
Low-Rent Housing	1.4
Urban Renewal	1.1
Major Programs	$38.4 billion
Miscellaneous	13.3
Total	$51.7 billion

SOURCE: U.S. Government, *The Budget for Fiscal Year 1975,* Special Analysis N.

merit good. Low-rent public housing both reduces poverty and satisfies a collective demand for better quality shelter.

SPILLOVER GRANTS

Congress has invoked spillover correction as a major rationale in establishing the federal aid programs for both highways and water pollution control. The former program supports both the U.S. and interstate highway systems, ostensibly providing general benefts from enhanced defense capabilities and improved interstate commerce. The latter program supports the construction of municipal sewage treatment facilities, hopefully reducing the spillover costs of water pollution.

In spite of the fact that both programs are intended to correct certain jurisdictional failures, it is doubtful that they do so in an efficient manner. The highway aid programs dispense funds on the basis of population and road mileage, with uniform matching funds by the state required for each program (for U.S. highways, 50%; for interstate highways, 10%). Although a rough correspondence may exist between spillover benefits and the population and mileage parameters, uniform matching ratios are bound to produce an inefficient pattern of response.

The water pollution grant program probably serves no better according to this criterion. It also incorporates a uniform matching ratio for municipalities (they must provide $25 for every $75 granted). However, it has two other weaknesses that are probably of greater importance: (1) it reflects a standard that, if achieved, would occasion extremely large opportunity costs; and (2) it is not the most efficient way to achieve higher water quality. In the first instance, the goal is to eliminate the discharge of *any* pollution into *any* navigable waterway by 1985. Surely the efficient level of discharge is not zero, as our analysis in Chapter 12 clearly indicates. In the second instance, narrow categorical grants are likely to be inefficient instruments of pollution control because the costs of control are not passed along to polluters (households and industries) and the search for lower cost alternatives is not encouraged.

MERIT GRANTS

The majority of categorical grants are intended to induce the greater provision of merit goods such as medical care, food, housing, and social services. For many of these, funds are allocated among the states on the basis of number of individuals in some "target population"; i.e., the one which "needs" assistance. Some programs still disburse funds on the basis of total population, however, and target populations often encompass individuals who do not need assistance. Because of these practices, funds are sometimes disbursed to the wrong individuals, thereby reducing the operational efficiency of the program (reducing benefits per dollar spent). Perhaps the best examples of this failure occur in the poverty grant programs, as indicated in Chapter 6.

Nearly all of the major categorical grants require some matching by recipients. Most of these have uniform matching ratios. As usual, this is a potential source of inefficiency in the allocation of federal revenues. There are some notable examples of variables matching grants, however; the federal share of Medicaid costs ranges from 50 to 83%, and a similar allocation formula may be used for various public assistance and social service grants.

Variable ratios for these programs have *not* been established, however, as a means of achieving a more efficient allocation of federal funds. Rather, they are tied to per capita income, with a higher federal share accorded the

417

lower income states. Thus, they represent an attempt to achieve greater equalization among the states in the provision of merit goods by offsetting differences in ability to pay. Such a feature is also efficient if the "need" for medical care, public assistance, and social services is greater in lower income states and if these states also exhibit greater price elasticity of demand and lower marginal supply costs for these services. If they do not, there is a conflict between efficiency and equalization.

Actual experience with particular programs indicates that per capita income equalization formulas are not a very effective means of achieving greater equalization. Studies of the impact of Medicaid and nonmedical welfare payments show that federal grants have actually widened the gap in assistance levels between rich and poor states.[3] These results imply that the wealthier states may have a greater price elasticity of demand for welfare assistance and may be less likely to substitute federal for state finance because of this. Alternatively, poorer states may not be able to take advantage of the more generous federal sharing arrangement afforded them because they are already making an unusually large tax effort to support their existing public services. However, studies of the relationship between tax collections and tax capacities among the states fail to show a significant relationship between lower per capita income and indexes of tax effort.[4]

In fact, if equalization in the provision of merit goods requires larger per capita grants to lower income states, then the existing grant system must be judged a failure. Studies by Roy W. Bahl and Jeremy J. Warford and by Richard A. Musgrave and Peggy B. Musgrave indicate that no significant negative relationship exists between total categorical grants per capita and income per capita.[5] However, this result is not very surprising, given the belated and relatively small overt commitment to equalization in the federal grant program.

Like many social institutions, the system of categorical grants fails to achieve all of the objective prescribed by economists. That this is not fatal

---

3. See: Bruce C. Stuart, "Equity and Medicaid," *Journal of Human Resources,* Vol. VII, no. 2. (Spring, 1972), pp. 162–178.

4. For a brief review of the evidence see: Richard A. and Peggy B. Musgrave, *Public Finance in Theory and Practice,* Second Edition, New York: McGraw-Hill, 1976, pp. 645–646.

5. Roy W. Bahl and Jeremy J. Warford, "Real and Monetary Dimensions of Federal Aid to States," in K. Boulding and M. Pfaff, eds. *Redistribution to the Rich and the Poor,* Belmont, Cal.: Wadsworth Publishing Company, 1972, pp. 116–130; Musgrave and Musgrave, *Public Finance in Theory and Practice,* pp. 657–660.

to its public acceptance is clearly implied by its rapid growth in the last three decades. This indicates both that the economists' criteria are not a sufficient basis for achieving a political consensus, and that the program has been at least somewhat effective in increasing the provision of state and local services desired by the public. Still, the program does have its critics in the political arena as well. There are those who are opposed to federal aid in any form because of the fear that federal control will accompany federal financing, while others believe that a change in form will improve the system. The latter group has been successful in recent years in promoting the adoption of grants with broader purposes as supplements or replacements for narrow categorical grants. One of these, the general revenue sharing grant, is the subject of the next section.

GENERAL REVENUE SHARING

In spite of the fact that unconditional intergovernmental grants have a role to play in the optimal budget, the United States had virtually no grants of this type until the State and Local Fiscal Assistance Act of 1972 ushered in the program of general revenue sharing. Today, this grant accounts for almost 12% of all funds disbursed to state and local governments. It appears to be a relatively permanent feature of the federal aid scene, having just recently (October, 1976) received a five-year extension from Congress. Given the large amount of money involved and the significant departure from the tradit!onal view that categorical grants are the appropriate tool of fiscal federalism, general revenue sharing deserves a closer look.

General revenue sharing (GRS) is an old idea, having been suggested initially as a cure for state and local government financial problems by Alvin A. Hansen and Harvey S. Perloff in the 1940s.[6] The idea was championed next in the 1950s, first by Walter Heller and then by a Presidential Task Force headed by Joseph Pechman.[7] The group ultimately developed the details of a proposal now referred to as the Heller-Pechman plan, probably the most direct source of ideas for today's program.

In spite of the venerability of the ideas, the political support necessary to ensure its congressional acceptance developed slowly. A major reason is

---

6. Alvin A. Hansen and Harvey S. Perloff, *State and Local Finance in the National Economy,* New York: W. W. Norton, 1944.

7. A good elementary review of the Heller-Pechman proposal appears in: Walter W. Heller, "Should the Government Share its Tax Take?" in *Saturday Review,* March 22, 1969.

that GRS was a relatively controversial alternative. Indeed, it still is, although proponents are now much more numerous in Congress than they used to be.

ADVANTAGES

GRS is attractive to its proponents for a wide variety of reasons, some political and some economic, In a political sense, it is viewed as a means of widening the field of fiscal choice for state and local authorities. Advocates of "states' rights" and "local autonomy" emphasize this particular consequence of the unconditional nature of this type of grant. This aspect of the program was viewed as a means of implementing the "New Federalism" of the Nixon-Ford administrations; a program which advocated more planning and management of public services by state and local governments and less of the same by the federal government.

Greater involvement by the former in planning their own fiscal affairs also has an economic rationale. Ideally, it is argued, state and local authorities should be able to plan a more efficient set of programs because they have superior knowledge of demand and of the unmet "needs" of their constituents. This position is supported by the notion, developed in Chapter 17, that smaller governmental units facilitate the choice of a more efficient set of programs from the point of view of taxpayers.

According to proponents, efficiency gains will also be realized if funds are transferred from existing categorical grants. First, there will be savings in administrative and information costs, both of which are alleged to be excessively high under the categorical system. In addition, there will be gains attributable to a lessened degree of budget distortion at the state and local levels; i.e., these governmental units will be less likely to transfer funds from higher value uses, as they have allegedly been induced to do by categorical grants.[8]

The biggest efficiency gains, however, are presumed to result from the correction for a general undersupply of state and local public services. This

---

8. Categorical grants have the effect of reducing the cost or relative price to the grantee of providing particular public goods or services. This reduction should increase the amount of these services that government officials wish to purchase. However, because of the grant, the price that the grantee government must pay is less than the marginal jurisdictional benefit of the program. It is possible, therefore, that the subsidy provided by the grant will induce the transfer of government expenditures from programs which yield inherently greater benefits.

situation is alleged to be a result of an excessive degree of taxpayer opposition and a fear of tax competition among state and local authorities, both of which produce a slow rate of growth in tax revenues. This tendency toward ineffciently small budgets is supposedly reinforced on the expenditure side by benefit spillovers, especially in metropolitan areas.

Finally, proponents stress the possibilities for equalization afforded by GRS. In the Heller-Pechman plan, which proposes an allocation of funds solely on the basis of population, this would be accomplished automatically because a greater proportion of revenues would be collected from relatively richer jurisdictions. Also, GRS would tend to keep the tax system from becoming more regressive to the extent that it promoted a postponement of both federal tax decreases and state-local tax increases.

Proponents believe, then, that GRS will be an effective means of restoring political choice to lower levels of government, and that significant gains in efficiency and equity will result from program adoption and implementation.

DISADVANTAGES

Opponents dispute most of the arguments outlined above, however. First, they question the wisdom of promoting greater state and local political autonomy by pointing to instances in which choices by these governments have not always produced socially desired results. Prime examples are afforded by the long struggle for civil rights at the state and local levels. Second, they dispute promises of greater equity, noting that what really counts is the extent of redistribution among individuals and not among governmental units.

Critics of GRS also challenge claims of greater efficiency. Basically, they do not believe that state and local authorities are particularly adept at planning programs to fit the preferences of the local citizenry simply because they are closer to the problem. Similarly, critics emphasize the fact that GRS breaks the link between tax and expenditure decisions, thereby weakening the incentive to use funds according to taxpayer preferences.

Opponents have also argued that GRS may simply introduce new technical inefficiences. For one, it may lead to the support of political units that are really too small to achieve economies in the provision of public services. For another, GRS may simply induce the growth of a state and local bureaucracy that, in the judgment of some observers, is even less efficient than the federal bureaucracy.

Finally, opponents argue that the evidence of a general undersupply of state and local goods and services is not compelling. They grant the evidence of increased taxpayer resistance but believe this to be a reflection of a low value attached to the corresponding programs. They question the wisdom of a fear of "tax competition" by pointing out that this is not necessarily a very important determinant of location decisions. The importance of benefit spillovers is generally acknowledged, of course. However, critics do raise the possibility that this is offset to some degree by "tax-exporting," which induces governments to over-spend because it lowers real costs to their citizens.

FEATURES

These criticisms of general revenue sharing were not persuasive enough to prevent GRS from being enacted. As designed in the 1972 legislation, Congress has provided for the allocation of approximately $30 billion ($5–7 billion per year) over a five-year period (1972–1976) to some 38,000 governmental units. Renewal legislation adopted in 1976 extended the program for three and three-fourth years (through 1980) at $6.65 billion per year.

Each state's share is determined by using the more favorable of two different formulas. The Senate formula favors rural states, while the House formula favors urban states. Both formulas prescribe an increase in the state's share when its population is relatively larger than other states, its relative tax effort is higher, and its relative per capita income is lower. The House formula adds an increase to the share for a relatively larger percentage urban population and relatively higher state income tax collections. One-third of the state's share is given to the state government and two-thirds of the share is distributed to local governments. The distribution of the local share among the county areas is based on the relative size of population, per capita income, net non-school taxes for general purposes, and aggregate personal income. The distribution within a county area among the county government and municipalities is based on the relative amount of non-school taxes collected by each.

States have been free to use their portion as they choose; the grant has been truly unconditional. Local governments were initially allowed to spend their funds only for "priority programs." The list of programs was so long, however, that virtually all important governmental functions were included. The only significant exceptions were operating expenses for education and welfare functions supported heavily by previously-enacted categorical grant programs. The renewal legislation enacted in 1976 eliminated these priority programs. The grant also became unconditional for local governments.

To some degree, of course, the House and Senate formulas are a result of necessary political compromises. However, they also reflect some of the traditional priorities of the federal categorical grant system. Both the relative per capita income and urban population factors, for example, result from a judgment that state and local "needs" are higher in low income and urban governmental units. The relative income factor is included as a means of redistributing income among jurisdictions. The tax effort and income tax provisions can be viewed as additional inducement for state and local governments to alleviate their alleged undersupply of goods and services to a greater degree than would a lump sum grant unrelated to their own revenue raising efforts.

It is still too early for a definitive report on the effect of general revenue sharing on efficiency and equity. As the evidence and analytical studies accumulate, however, it will be interesting to see which of the two positions reviewed above turns out to be more nearly correct.

SUMMARY

Federal grants to lower-level governments can be designed to move us closer to our social goals. They are useful first as a corrective for various efficiency failures encountered in the public sector. These failures are of four types: (1) jurisdictional externalities, (2) unequal government budget constraints, (3) social imbalances, and (4) unequal tax-prices.

Government categorical grants can be used to induce lower-level governments to provide more of those goods or services which yield significant external benefits. Categorical grants can also be used to increase resources of governments that are precluded from implementing efficient programs by budget constraints. *Un*conditional grants may be used to increase revenues to governments providing *generally* deficient levels of goods and services. Finally, this type of grant can be employed to correct disparities in tax-prices among jurisdiction which induce inefficient migration.

Government grants are also appropriate instruments for achieving greater equity among jurisdictions in the provision of real goods and services. Indeed, many of the existing grant programs were adopted for precisely this purpose.

It is possible even to use intergovernmental grants to achieve aggregate stability. However, rational budgeting requires that they not be employed as temporary means of reaching this goal.

It is far easier to justify grants in general terms than it is to design them to achieve desired goals most efficiently. However, some general design principles can be readily developed using relatively simple economic theory. To correct for external jurisdictional benefits, it is necessary to provide a categorical grant to a lower-level government with a matching requirement that just induces the recipient to provide the socially efficient level of services. The only exceptions to this are the cases in which basic research is conducted in the public sector or new programs are the subjects of public experiments.

Categorical grants can also be designed to further the attainment of "minimum national standards". To achieve maximum effectiveness in this regard, funds should be allocated according to: (1) how close a government is to achieving the desired standard, (2) the tax-price elasticity of demand for the service in question, and (3) the marginal cost of providing relevant services.

In reality, the system of categorical grants is designed to serve four major purposes: (1) to correct jurisdictional spillovers, (2) to provide merit goods, (3) to alleviate poverty, and (4) to equalize service levels or tax efforts among jurisdictions. However, most grants serve more than one of these purposes simultaneously.

A few categorical grants are designed to correct spillovers. It is doubtful if they do an efficient job in this regard. The majority of categorical grants are intended to provide merit goods. Here, too, actual design differs widely from the theoretical ideal. Some programs allocate funds to the wrong reference groups; some fail to use correct matching requirements; and many fail to promote greater equalization, even when this is one of their allowed purposes.

In recent years there has been a movement toward greater reliance on unconditional grants. The primary example of this is the general revenue-sharing program adopted in 1972 and renewed in 1976. Proponents view general revenue sharing as a means of establishing greater local autonomy, of ensuring better representation of local preferences, of saving administrative costs, and of effecting jurisdictional equalization. Opponents question the wisdom of relying on state and local officials, and they dispute the claims that general revenue sharing will promote greater efficiency.

SUGGESTIONS FOR FURTHER READING

Break, G. F., *Intergovernmental Fiscal Relations in the United States,* Washington, D.C.: Brookings Institution, 1967.

Although a bit dated, this book still provides a good general review of the program of intergovernmental grants.

Oates, Wallace, B., *Fiscal Federalism,* New York: Harcourt, Brace, Jovanovich, Inc., 1972.

Chapter 3 is a good theoretical review of the intergovernmental grant program.

Nathan, Richard P. and Adams, Charles F., Jr., *Revenue Sharing: The Second Round,* Washington, D.C.: Brookings Institution, 1976.

This is the second Brookings study of federal revenue sharing, based on a review of experiences over the first five years.

*

INDEX

427

†